SUDAN ARCHAEOLOGICAL RESEARCH SOCIETY
PUBLICATION NUMBER 5

Meinarti I

The Late Meroitic, Ballaña and Transitional Occupation

William Y. Adams

BAR International Series 895
2000

Published in 2016 by
BAR Publishing, Oxford

BAR International Series 895

Sudan Archaeological Research Society Publication 5
Meinarti I

ISBN 9781841710945 paperback
ISBN 9781407352374 e-format
DOI https://doi.org/10.30861/9781841710945
A catalogue record for this book is available from the British Library

BAR Publishing is the trading name of British Archaeological Reports (Oxford) Ltd.
British Archaeological Reports was first incorporated in 1974 to publish the BAR
Series, International and British. In 1992 Hadrian Books Ltd became part of the BAR
group. This volume was originally published by Archaeopress in conjunction with
British Archaeological Reports (Oxford) Ltd / Hadrian Books Ltd, the Series principal
publisher, in 2000. This present volume is published by BAR Publishing, 2016.

BAR
PUBLISHING

BAR titles are available from:

BAR Publishing
122 Banbury Rd, Oxford, OX2 7BP, UK
EMAIL   info@barpublishing.com
PHONE   +44 (0)1865 310431
FAX   +44 (0)1865 316916
www.barpublishing.com

Dedicated to

THABIT HASSAN THABIT

Sometime Commissioner for Archaeology in the Sudan

Who ordered me to begin the Meinarti dig, and whose
unstinting support enabled me to finish it

CONTENTS

Please note that additional material is available to download from www.barpublishing.com/additional-downloads.html

LIST OF TABLES

LIST OF FIGURES

Please note that the Figures marked * are available to download from www.barpublishing.com/additional-downloads.html

LIST OF PLATES

PREFACE

Between 1960 and 1970, the Sudan Antiquities Service[1] carried out extensive surveys and excavations throughout the entire region of Sudanese Nubia that was to be flooded by Lake Nubia, from Faras in the north to Dal in the south. The work of the surveys extended over an area more than 150 kilometers long, including the west bank of the Nile and all of the island sites from Faras to Gemai, and both banks, as well as the islands, from Gemai to Dal. Altogether, during the ten years of its operation, the survey recorded 590 sites, and carried out some excavation in a large number of them.[2] Although this work was sponsored and largely financed by the Antiquities Service, supervisory and technical personnel as well as certain items of equipment were provided through the generosity of the United Nations Educational, Scientific, and Cultural Organization (UNESCO). Consequently, the operation has come to be known as the Unesco Archaeological Survey of Sudanese Nubia.

Interim reports were published after each field season in the journal *Kush*.[3] However, the Sudan Government for many years had neither funds nor facilities to pay for the publication of final reports, and these volumes have, as a result, been very long delayed. A single volume, *Ceramic Industries of Medieval Nubia* (Adams 1986), was published in 1986 with the aid of one-time grants from the University of Kentucky and from Unesco. However it is only now, through the generosity of the Sudan Archaeological Research Society, that funds and facilities have been provided for the publication of remaining volumes in the series, *Memoirs of the Unesco Archaeological Survey of Sudanese Nubia*. The present work is Volume 3 in that series; it will be followed by at least four additional volumes.

Of the various projects undertaken in the course of the Unesco Archaeological Survey, by far the largest was the excavation of the deeply stratified *kom* (mound) site of Meinarti, situated on an island about 10 km to the south of Wadi Halfa. Excavations, conducted over a period of 12 months in 1963 and 1964, revealed that the site had been occupied for more than twelve centuries, from Meroitic times until the end of the Middle Ages. Eighteen different stratigraphic layers were uncovered, embracing more than 50 buildings, and yielding more than 1500 registered artifacts.

The present work is the first of a projected four volumes that will describe the excavations and the finds at Meinarti; it deals specifically with the pre-Christian periods, from about A.D. 200 to 600. However, the volume also includes a lengthy initial chapter which will introduce readers to the site and the circumstances of its excavation; it is meant as an introduction to all of the Meinarti volumes. *Meinarti II* will deal with the remains from the earlier part of the Christian period, between about A.D. 600 and 1200, *Meinarti III* with the later Christian and post-Christian periods, from about 1200 to 1600, and *Meinarti IV* will be devoted entirely to the church and cemetery at Meinarti, whose history spanned the whole of the Christian period. A final volume, *Meinarti V*, will be a retrospective overview of the social and cultural history of the community, and its place in Nubian history more generally. Additional volumes in the *Memoirs* series will report on surveys and excavations along the west bank of the Nile between Faras and Gemai, and along both banks between Gemai and Dal.

Authorship and responsibility

The excavation of Meinarti was not originally foreseen as part of the Unesco and Antiquities Service program of operations. The site for many years had been included within the Buhen concession granted to the Egypt Exploration Society. It was not until the early spring of 1963 that the late Professor Emery announced that the E.E.S. would be unable to undertake the dig, and relinquished the concession. At that point in time, impounded lake waters were expected to begin covering the site in less than eighteen months. Since there was, at so late a date, no possibility to recruit another foreign expedition to take over the dig, the operation became by default a responsibility of the Unesco-Antiquities Service survey. Excavations were begun immediately, and continued virtually until the last possible moment, being suspended only for the hottest midsummer months. The field operations will be much more fully detailed in Chapter 1.

At the time when Meinarti was "dropped in our laps," the Unesco supervisory team consisted only of Hans-Åke Nordström and myself. Mr. Nordström however was in the process of winding up his term of service in the Sudan, and was busy completing the documentation on sites that had already been dug. Consequently the day-to-day supervision of the Meinarti operation was left in my hands alone. Anthony Mills joined the Unesco team, as a replacement for Mr. Nordström, in the fall of 1963, but it was immediately necessary for him to assume direction of the survey operations as they proceeded southward from Gemai to Dal. Only on the rarest of occasions was he able to spell me off for a day or two at Meinarti.

In consequence, the Meinarti dig from first to last was very much a one-man operation, so far as supervision and

[1] Now known as the Corporation for Antiquities and National Museums.

[2] For enumerations see Adams 1961a, 10; Adams 1962a, 12; Adams and Nordström 1963,12-15; Adams 1964c, 216; Mills 1965, 3-12; Mills and Nordström 1966, 4.

[3] Adams 1961b; Verwers 1961; Adams 1962a; Verwers 1962; Adams and Nordström 1963; Adams 1964c; Adams 1965c; Mills 1965; Mills and Nordström 1966; Mills 1968.

documentation were concerned. It was I who wrote all the field notes, drew all the plans and cross-sections, took, developed, and printed all the photos, registered nearly all the artifactual finds, and counted every potsherd. Because the University of Kentucky is no better provided with facilities than was the Sudan Antiquities Service, it is also I who have drawn all of the illustrations in the present volume. It is evident therefore that whatever shortcomings may be encountered in the documentation and in the reporting on Meinarti are purely my responsibility. Some of those shortcomings, imposed by our limited resources and by the extreme urgency under which the dig was carried out, will be further considered in the Introduction.

With regard to the line drawings of artifacts, a word of caution is in order. With a few exceptions, they have not been drawn "directly from life," because the objects themselves are in Khartoum and are not accessible to me. The line drawings appearing in this and subsequent volumes are mostly enlarged from small drawings entered on the object registration cards, and these may not be totally accurate as to detail.

In the circumstances, it seems rather contrived, or at least formalistic, to employ the pronoun "we," or to use impersonal constructions, in describing the Meinarti operations. Throughout this work I will deliberately use the first-person singular pronoun in discussing what was and was not done.

About the text

It is one of the unique peculiarities of our archaeological discipline that we feel compelled to report everything we find, whether or not it has any specifiable significance, and whether or not it is relevant to our original reason for digging. This self-imposed obligation stands in contrast to the prevailing standard of reporting in all the other social and behavioral sciences. The ethnologist, the sociologist, and the psychologist will normally publish summaries of their findings, and perhaps selected case materials, but will omit all findings that are not relevant to the purpose of the study.

A proper site report, on the other hand, is a vast and non-selective catalogue of everything found; in effect a data bank. It has been stated that, ideally, the reader of such a report should be able fully to reassemble the original site, from the information provided. The inevitable result however is that site reports are tedious reading, and they are in fact very seldom "read," in the conventional sense. Rather, they are "used." No one except a few long-suffering reviewers is ever likely to read them through from cover to cover. Others will delve into them selectively, just as one would an encyclopedia, in serch of information on particular topics such as pottery or architecture or burial remains. Those seeking a more general overview will perhaps skim through, look at the pictures, and then read the conclusions. Consequently, I think that a site report, like any other archive, should above all be user-friendly.

With that in mind, I have striven to make each section of this report as nearly self-contained as possible. Hopefully, the reader interested in pottery will find everything he or she needs within the section on pottery, without having to refer backward or forward to any other section of the manuscript. The inevitable result however is that a certain amount of basic background information is repeated from section to section of the text. This may perhaps elicit comment from reviewers, but it is unlikely to be noticed by most others.

Acknowledgments

The Sudan Antiquities Service

I certainly would not like to suggest that the Meinarti dig was, or could have been, carried out without professional or technical assistance; nor would it have been possible without the continued and complete financial and logistic support of the Sudan Antiquities Service. The contribution of the Antiquities Service personnel to the success of the Meinarti operation cannot be overstressed, for they relieved me of nearly all of the financial and logistic burdens that normally plague an excavation director, allowing me to be a full-time archaeologist. Collectively, we had by this time become a smoothly functioning Antiquities Service team, achieving a level of efficiency that I have never been able to approach in subsequent excavations.

I must begin my long list of acknowledgments with the name of the late Sayyed Thabit Hassan Thabit, to whom this volume is dedicated. He was the Sudan Commissioner for Archaeology, and in some sense my boss, throughout the time of the Meinarti excavations. In earlier seasons Thabit and I had had some differences (see Adams 1992, 12-13) but by 1963 they had been fully ironed out, and no one could have been more fully supportive of every aspect of the work at Meinarti than was the Commissioner. Relationships and judgments in that part of the world tend to be strongly personal, and once Thabit decided that I was all right, it followed *a priori* that whatever I wanted to do was also all right. As a consequence, whatever I wanted in the way of laborers or equipment or other facilities, I generally got without question. It was Thabit who successfully defended the continuation of my work at Meinarti in the spring of 1964, when because of a financial crisis the Minister of Education has asked that it be shut down.

Equally essential was the support and assistance of the late Negm el-Din Mohammed Sherif, and the late Gamal Ahmed Hassan, who at the time of the dig were respectively the Inspector of Antiquities, and the Clerk of the Antiquities Service, in Wadi Halfa. While the Commissioner was generally far away in Khartoum, they were the Antiquities Service officials on the scene, with whom I dealt on a day-to-day basis. They were both, in many different ways, as helpful and supportive as was Sayyed Thabit, in seeing that the Meinarti work went forward as smoothly and as rapidly as circumstances would allow. Among many other things, it was they who undertook to recruit, transport, house, and pay the laborers, relieving me of what are normally very irksome jobs. Both men were to become lifelong friends, to whom previous reports of mine have been dedicated.[4]

Another important obligation is to Arbab Hassan Hafiz, then a Technical Assistant in the Antiquities Service Wadi Halfa office. Arbab was present on the Meinarti dig throughout every day, and looked after practical arrangements connected with the housing, transport, and payment of the laborers. In addition, he frequently assisted me in mapping and in recording cross-sections.

The list of acknowledgments must surely include also the name of Reis Youssef Mohammed Youssef, my foreman at Meinarti and several other digs. Youssef was in a class by himself, among all of the Egyptian foremen that I have employed over the years. He was not a stern taskmaster, by comparison to some of the others, for he was quiet and introspective by nature. He was however a profoundly analytical thinker—the only foreman I have ever encountered who understood not only archaeological tactics but archaeological strategy, in the same terms that I do. He was trying at all times to think ahead, and anticipate the next excavation objectives, much as I was. More than once when I suggested a particular area to be excavated next, he would propose what was in fact a superior alternative, in terms of my own excavation strategy. Very occasionally I made it a point to visit the site on a Friday, our day off, in order to have time to look at things and mull over possibilities without the encumbrance of supervising the laborers. And several times I found Youssef already there, doing the same thing.

I cannot fail to mention, finally, the loyal and dedicated assistance of the late Abdou Fereiq, the Antiquities Service driver who brought me daily to and from the digs, but who also was willing to take me anywhere else at any time, and sometimes on a moment's notice.

UNESCO

Throughout my time in the Sudan, including the Meinarti dig, I was nominally an employee of the United Nations Educational, Scientific, and Cultural Organization, which paid my salary as well as furnishing various items of technical equipment. My official title was Liaison Officer, and my official duty was to maintain liaison between the various agencies contributing to the Nubian Monuments Campaign in the Sudan: UNESCO itself, the Sudan Antiquities Service (as it was then called), the various foreign archaeological missions that came to assist in the salvage campaign, and the foreign governments that contributed funds toward the dismantling and re-siting of temples. In the terms of my appointment nothing was said about actual excavation, and in my annual reports to Paris I never mentioned it. My employers were nevertheless fully aware that at least 80% of my time was spent in excavations, and I have to thank them for their willingness year after year to connive at the fiction that I was mainly doing desk work.[5] I am happy to thank UNESCO also for the gift of a great deal of invaluable photographic and surveying equipment, which among other things allowed us to set up a darkroom in Wadi Halfa.

During the time of the Meinarti dig I had also two field assistants provided through the generosity of UNESCO: Hans-Åke Nordström during the initial (spring 1963) season, and Anthony Mills during the second (1963-1964) season. They were officially designated as Liaison Assistants, and were supposed to be helping me in some unspecified way in my diplomatic activities. In fact they too were almost wholly involved in excavations for the Sudan Antiquities Service. While I was digging at Meinarti they were simultaneously working at other sites and surveys, but they were able from time to time to spell me off at Meinarti if other duties called me away.

Professional favors

The cameraderie and the sense of common mission that existed among the different archaeological teams working in Sudanese Nubia was one of the truly extraordinary features of the Nubian Monuments Campaign, remembered fondly by all of us. Among other things it made possible a wide sharing of expertise between specialists attached to different missions. This was of crucial importance in the recording and analysis of material from Meinarti, much of which lay beyond the limits of my own professional competence. The late Mr. Jozef Gazy, loaned by the Polish Expedition at Faras, spent a month in reconsolidating and then removing the mural paintings from the Meinarti Church[6] and the Eparchal complex of late medieval times.[7] The artist Abdel Rahman eff. Hag el Amin, employed temporarily by the Antiquities Service, made life-size tempera reproductions as well as miniatures of all the murals on the site. Hand-copies of various mural inscriptions and graffiti were made at different times by Dr. Richard Pierce of the Chicago Oriental Institute Expedition, Mr. A. F. Shore of the British Museum, and my assistant Mr. Anthony Mills. A latex squeeze of an important incised graffito was made by Prof. Dr. Fritz Hintze of the Humboldt University expedition. Antiquities Inspector Negm el-Din Sherif provided translations of three Arabic tombstones found on the site (Sherif 1964). The Physical Anthropologists George Armelagos, David Greene, and George Ewing, of the University of Colorado Expedition, undertook

---

[4] Adams 1994b is dedicated to Gamal Ahmed Hassan; Adams and Adams 1998 is dedicated to Negm el-Din Sherif.
[5] For more detail on how my role and activities in the Sudan developed over time see Adams 1992, 3-27.
[6] To be reported in *Meinarti IV*.
[7] To be reported in *Meinarti III*.

the complete job of analyzing the skeletal remains unearthed in the Meinarti cemetery.[8] Members of various other foreign missions visisted the dig from time to time on their days off, and sometimes made valuable suggestions or asked searching questions. My thanks go to all of them not only for professional assistance but for personal friendship that has persisted, in nearly every case, down to the present day.

Several individuals volunteered their assistance in the analysis of material finds after the conclusion of the dig. In Khartoum, Professor David Whiteman of the Department of Geology, University of Khartoum, kindly furnished petrographic identifications for most of our stone artifacts, and Miss Christine Wilson rendered valuable assistance in the registration and sometimes the drawing of artifacts. Later, identification of four Ptolemaic and Roman coins was provided by staff members in the Department of Coins and Medals in the British Museum. Mr. Ray Winfield Smith, then Director of the American Research Center in Cairo, examined all of the extensive glass sherd collections from Meinarti, and wrote a summary report that is quoted in this volume. Dr. George Scanlon, also of the American Research Center in Cairo, provided tentative identification of a coin weight.

The family

The part played by my wife Nettie in every aspect of my life, professional as well as personal, is too well known to all Nubiologists to require elaboration here. Because at the time of the Meinarti dig our two sons were very young, she was not able often to visit the site, but she did much of the preliminary registration of the objects brought in from the field, and much of the labelling of photographs. In addition of course she managed our Wadi Halfa household — no mean chore, as anyone familiar with the circumstances of field life in the Sudan will attest. Our sons Ernest and Ned, then aged four and two, were obviously not in a position to help very much, but sometimes they did a little preliminary sorting of sherds (such as picking out glazes from the others), and sometimes they helped me in the darkroom by moving prints from bath to bath.

The editor

It goes without saying that I owe an incalculable debt to my long-suffering editor, Derek Welsby, who undertook the complex and onerous job of preparing this work for publication. Even more importantly, his meticulous attention to every detail of the text and the illustrations has saved me from innumerable errors of commission and omission. If any remain, the fault is assuredly mine alone.

---

[8] To be reported in *Meinarti IV.*

INTRODUCTION:
THE SITE AND ITS EXCAVATION

Before its inundation in 1965, the island of Meinarti was situated just at the foot of the Second Nile Cataract, 10 km south of the town of Wadi Halfa (Fig. 1). It was a relatively small, boat-shaped island, with maximum dimensions of about one kilometer from north to south, and three hundred meters from east to west. The island was situated almost exactly at the middle of the Nile channel, equidistant from the east and west banks. At the north, however, only a rather small channel, dry at the lowest Nile season, separated Meinarti from the neighboring and larger island of Majarab. It is possible that this channel did not exist in medieval and earlier times; in any event it was always easy to cross. Almost certainly, the farmland of Majarab formed the main agricultural resource base for dwellers at Meinarti. In modern times there was almost no cultivation at Meinarti itself, apart from *seluka* land along the margins of the river, while the whole surface of Majarab was intensely cultivated (see Pl. 1a).

Unlike the high, rocky islands within the Second Cataract, Meinarti was formed almost entirely of low-lying alluvium, except for a small granite outcrop at the upstream end. It was this outcrop, together with higher islands just to the south, that split the current of the Nile into two streams, allowing the downstream buildup of alluvium that formed the islands of Meinarti and Majarab. Because of its low ground, Meinarti was always subject to periodic flooding, a circumstance that played a major role in the history of settlement on the island.

In terms of its strategic location, Meinarti occupied exactly the same position in relation to the Second Cataract as did the island of Elephantine to the First Cataract. That is, it was the last place that could be reached, at all times of the year, by large watercraft traveling upriver. Any cargoes destined for places further to the south would have to be transferred to smaller vessels, and possibly also to wait for the season of the high Niles, before passing through the cataracts. This circumstance was clearly important in shaping the histories of settlement both at Elephantine and at Meinarti.

The site of Meinarti (6-K-3)

The archaeological site of Meinarti, which forms the subject of this and subsequent monographs, was situated at the southern or upstream end of the island. It was designated in our survey archives as Site 6-K-3, and is so identified in most of the excavation records.[1] Before excavation it was a stratified mound (*kom*) measuring 175 meters from north to south, with a maximum width of 95 meters from east to west. The highest point, near the southern end, was twelve and one-half meters above the level of the alluvial floodplain (Pl. 1b). The site before excavation gave the appearance of a rather steep-sided heap of sand, crowned at the top by the ruins of a massive, mud brick building which the Anglo-Egyptian garrison in the late 19th century had used as a gun emplacement (Pl. 1c). Further down the sides of the mound, remnants of brick construction could be seen projecting at many points. The surface, as always in Nubian habitation sites, was thickly strewn with potsherds as well as scattered and fragmentary brick rubble. Figure 2 shows the contours of the southerly portion of the mound, before excavation.

Between February, 1963 and June, 1964, one-half of the Meinarti mound was excavated in its entirety, under circumstances that will be described more fully below. The site was found to contain a stratified sequence of 18 occupation levels,[2] most of which extended throughout the whole surface area of the site. They represented an occupation beginning in the late Meroitic and ending in the early post-Christian period; that is to say, from the 2nd or 3rd century to the 17th century A.D. Each level was identified by well-defined, compacted occupation surfaces, by a set of architectural remains associated with those surface, and by fill deposits overlying the surfaces. (The question of how levels were differentiated in practice will be considered in detail in later pages.) The successive development of the community, from Meroitic to post-Christian times, is shown in summary form in the series of schematic plans in Figures 3 and 4.

Chronology and nomenclature

At the time of excavation, *levels* were simply assigned numbers, from 1 to 18, in stratigraphic order; that is, in the order of discovery. Subsequent to the excavations, and after careful analysis of all the recovered evidence, the occupation history of the community was divided into *phases*, each represented by one of the 18 numbered levels. It should not be supposed however that a "phase" is just another name for a "level," for the preserved archaeological remains designated as a level are a kind of "snapshot" only, while a phase designates a complete episode of occupation, encompassing all the things that happened during that period of time. To put the matter in the simplest terms, a level is an archaeological construct, designating a complex of associated physical remains (floors, walls, and associated artifacts and refuse). A phase however is a historical construct, designating an episode of occupation. Levels are quintessentially a method of stratigraphic recording, and are necessarily numbered in order from the top down. Phases, as a method of historical reconstruction, are numbered from the bottom up, or in other words in actual historical order. The relationship between levels and phases will be much more fully

---

[1] For the system of site numbering see Adams 1961a, 8.

[2] Exclusive of the 19th century Anglo-Egyptian military occupation, which was designated as Level 1.

1

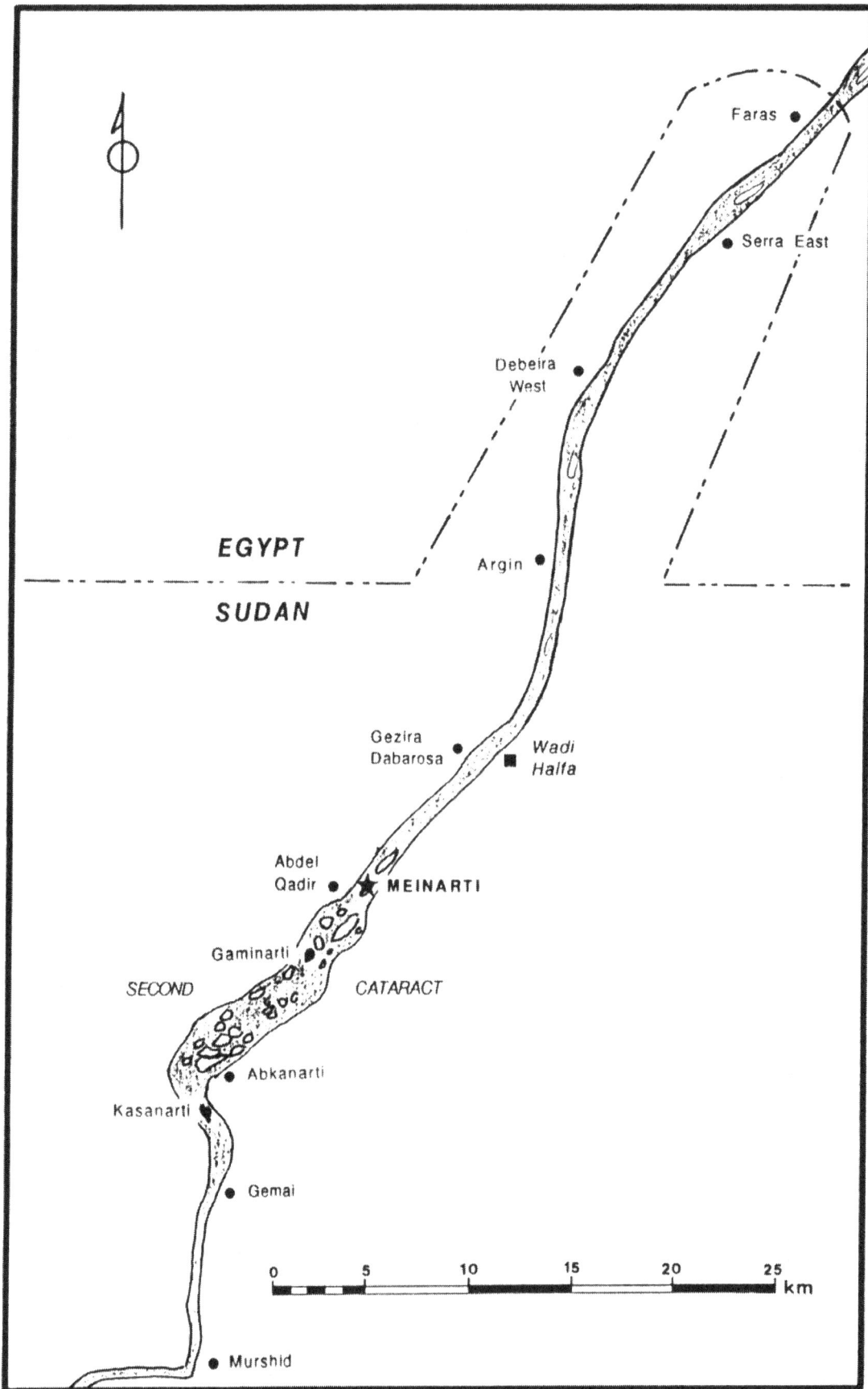

Figure 1. Map of a portion of Nubia showing location of Meinarti.

considered in later pages, for both are important to any critical understanding of the Meinarti archaeological record.

It was clear from the stratigraphic evidence that the occupation at Meinarti had not been continuous; there had been periodic abandonments caused by flooding, by enemy action, or for reasons unknown. Episodes of continuous occupation between such hiatuses were designated

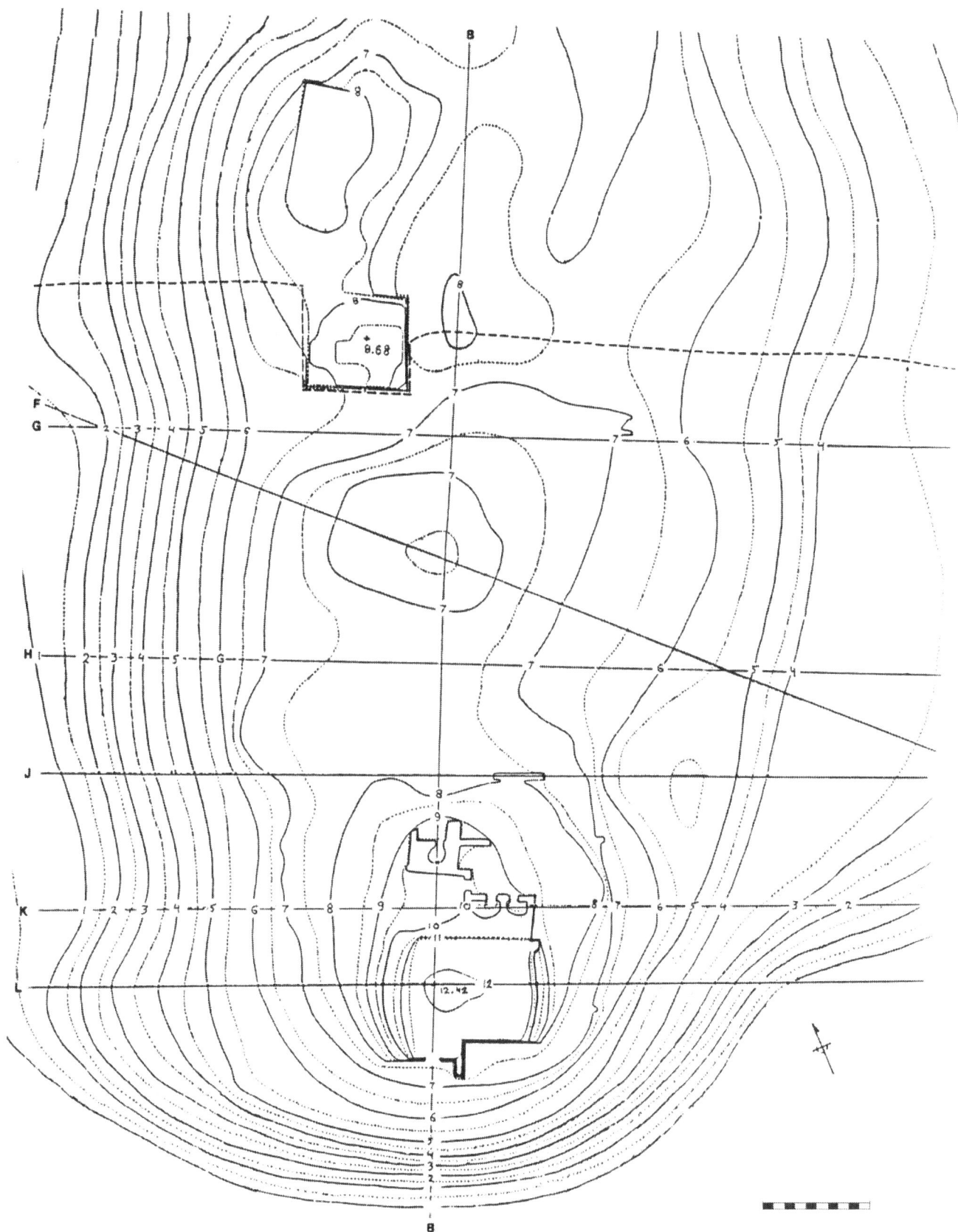

Figure 2. Contour map of the southern (excavated) portion of the Meinarti mound, before excavation. Figures are elevations above the Nile floodplain, in meters. Straight, solid lines are cross-section lines; see Figures 4 and 5. The dotted line is the limit of excavation.

as major phases, and were numbered in historical order, from 1 (earliest) to 7 (latest).[3] Each had begun with a wholesale rebuilding, and had ended with an episode of

[3] Including the Anglo-Egyptian military occupation of the late 19th century.

major destruction, and/or an interval of abandonment.

Within each major phase, from two to four subphases could be recognized. Each was differentiated from its predecessor by a set of major or minor architectural modifications, and usually also by the buildup of occupation surfaces to increasingly higher levels. The different

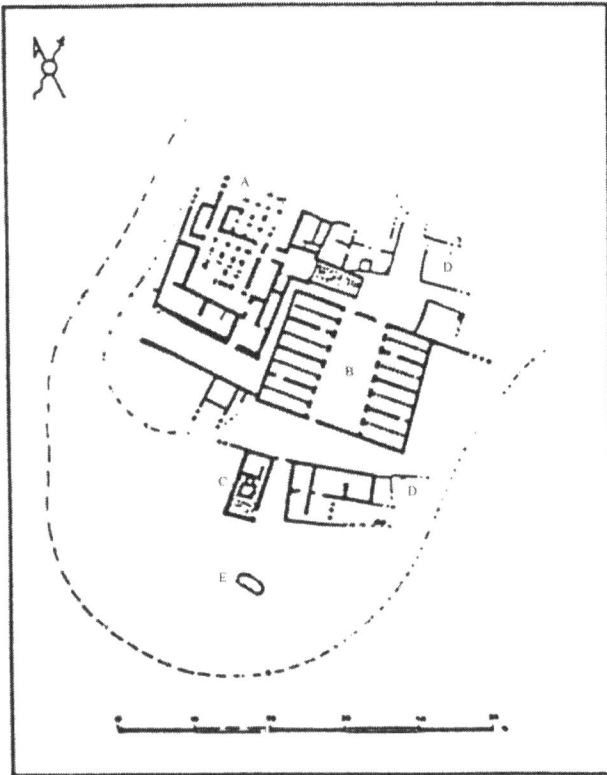

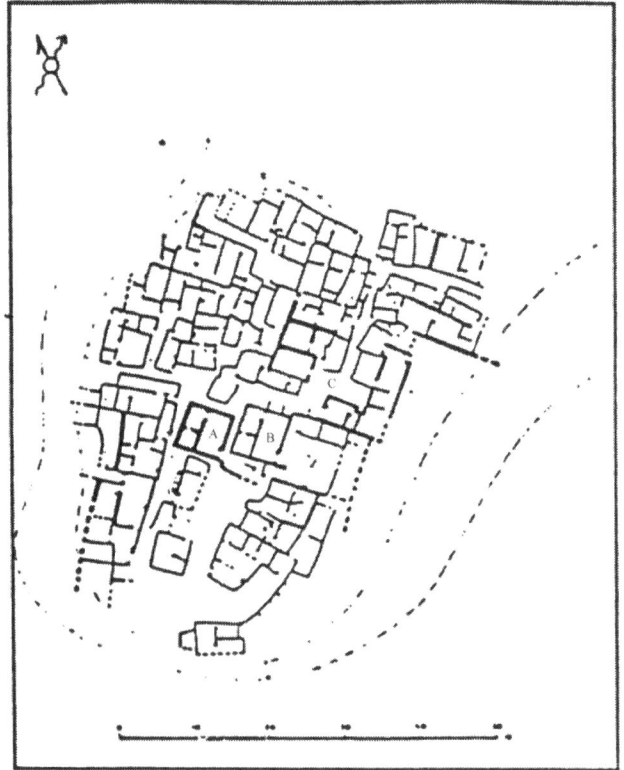

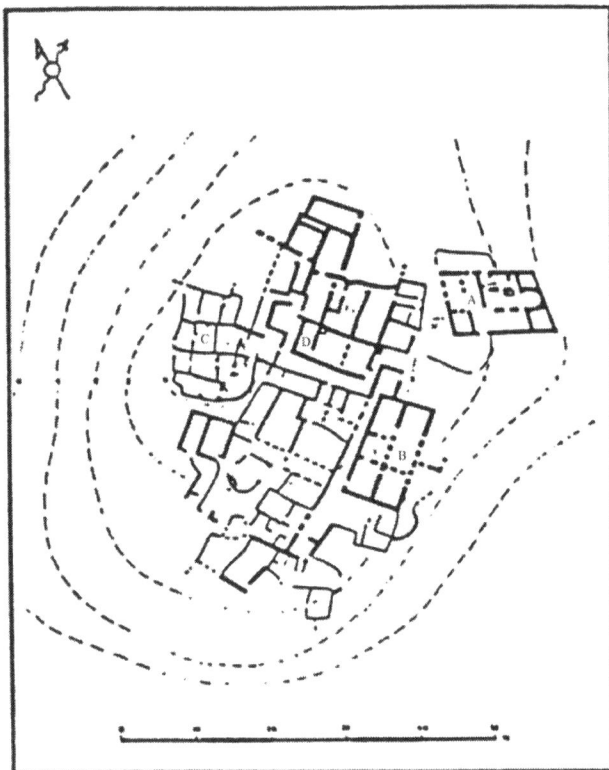

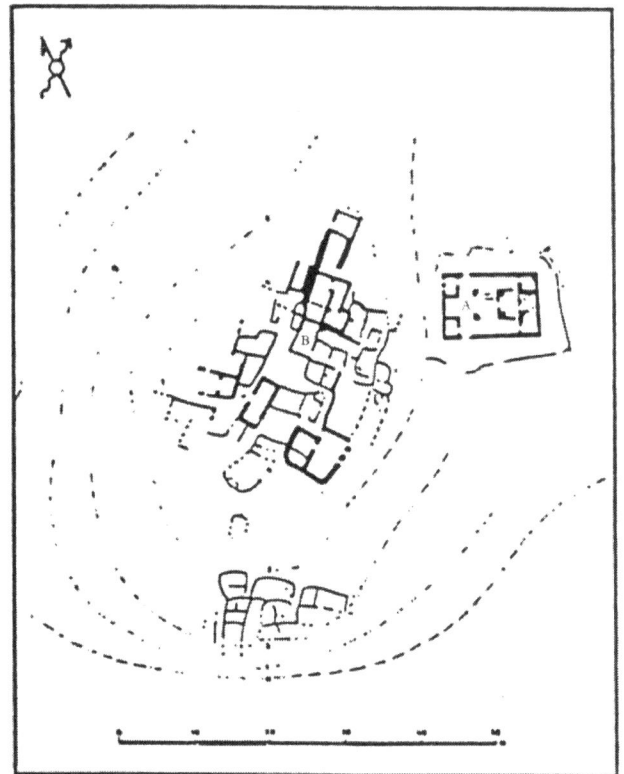

Figure 3. Sketch plans of Levels 18 (Subphase 1a), 15b (Subphase 2a), 13 (Subphase 3a) and 11a (Subphase 3d).

subphases within any major phase were designated by the letters a, b, c, and d, following the phase number. For

example, Phase 1 comprises the late Meroitic Subphase 1a (represented by Level 18), late Meroitic Subphase 1b

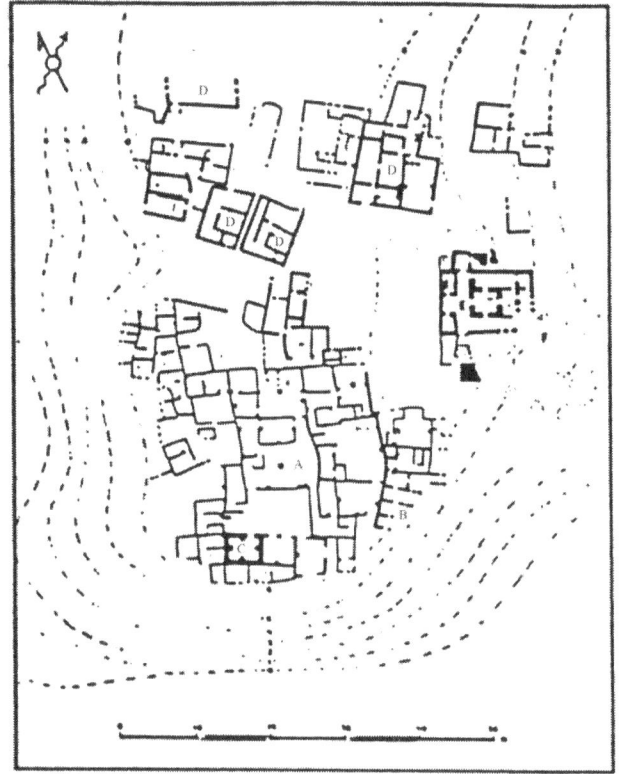

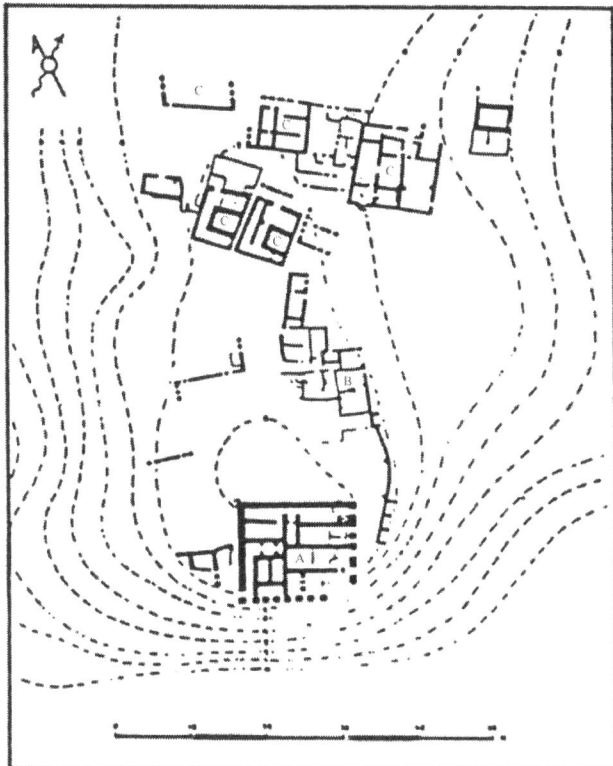

Figure 4. Sketch plans of Levels 9 (Subphase 4a),
5 (Subphase 5a) and 3 (Subphase 6a).

(represented by Level 17), and early Ballaña Subphase 1c (represented by Level 16), after which there was a hiatus of unknown length before the beginning of Phase 2 (beginning at Level 15b). In the text that follows both level and phase designations will be used, depending on whether the site is being described in archaeological (i.e. physical) or in historical terms.

Table 1 gives a conspectus of the 18 levels and the 18

TABLE 1. CHRONOLOGY OF MEINARTI PHASES AND LEVELS

Phase	Strat. level	Historic period[1]	Est. dates, A.D.[2]
7	1	Modern	1886-1890
Abandonment of the medieval community			*1600*
6b	2	Post-Christian	1500-1600
6a	3	Terminal Christian	1400-1500
Occupation by Beni Kanz and Beni Ikrima, + hiatus 1365-1400			
5c	4	Late Christian 2	1300-1365
5b	5	Late Christian 1	1265-1300
5a	6	Late Christian 1	1200-1265
Invasion and destruction by Shams ed-Dawla			*1172-1174*
4c	7	Late Christian 1	1100-1172
4b	8	Classic Christian 2	1050-1100
4a	9	Classic Christian 2	1020-1050
Hiatus followed by total rebuilding			*1000-1020*
3d	11a*	Classic Christian 1b	960-1000
3c	11b	Classic Christian 1a	850-960
3b	12	Early Christian 2	750-850
3a	13	Early Christian 1	660-750
Arab invasion; major flood damage and rebuilding			*650-660*
2c	14	Transitional	575-650
2b	15a	Late Ballaña	500-575
2a	15b	Late Ballaña	475-500
Major hiatus followed by rebuilding			*425-475*
1c	16	Early Ballaña	400-425
1b	17	Late Meroitic	350-400
1a	18	Late Meroitic	200-350

[1] According to the system of Christian Nubian phase designations first designated in Adams 1964c, 243-6.

[2] Dating based mainly on pottery finds. For the system see Adams 1986, 601-33. The dates given here have been revised more than once, and do not always correspond those appearing in the preliminary excavation reports.

* There is no Level 10, as this number was not assigned.

phases and subphases that make up the architectural and the historical record at Meinarti. They are listed here in stratigraphic (i.e. reverse chronological) order.

The present volume deals with Phases 1 and 2, comprising remains of the Meroitic and Ballaña periods. *Meinarti II* will cover Phases 3 and 4, the Early and Classic Christian remains, *Meinarti III* will cover Phases 5 and 6, the Late and Terminal Christian remains, and *Meinarti IV* will describe the island church and cemetery. A final volume, *Meinarti V* will review the general processes of growth and decay, continuity and change, that affected the community during the fourteen centuries of its history, and will consider how these bear on our understanding of Nubian cultural history more generally. The present chapter however is intended as an introduction to all the volumes.

Taphonomic processes
Throughout the occupation at Meinarti, as well as in the centuries after its abandonment, the site was subject to processes both of aggradation and of destruction. The two were going on more or less simultaneously, with the result that the mound was growing continually higher in the middle, through the accumulation of sand and debris, while the edges were regularly eaten away by floods. It was this combination of factors that sculptured the mound into the steep-sided shape that it exhibited at the time of excavation (Pl. 1b). The following were major or minor

taphonomic processes that could be recognized:

Sand accumulation. Archaeologists working on the west bank of the Nile are accustomed to find their sites buried under great heaps of overburden—the coarse golden sand of the Western Desert. The grains of this sand however are so heavy that they are not carried on the wind; they travel only as moving dunes. As a result, not only the east bank but all of the islands in the river are free from this overburden. The fine white sand of the Nile riverbed is however another matter, for it is very readily carried on the wind.

During most of every year, except at the season of the High Niles, the island of Meinarti was bordered on the north (the windward side) by a broad sandbar, as can readily be seen in the aerial photo (Pl. 1a). Blowing sand from this source was the principal contributor to the buildup of the mound, and accounted for at least 90% of all the fill encountered in the excavations. A recent ethnographic description from West-Central Africa (Aebi 1997) provides a perfect model for understanding the growth of the Meinarti mound:

"The people of Araouane continue to live in *banco* (a kind of adobe without the straw) houses around which the winds pile up even higher mounds of sand that eventually "flood" the dwellings. When this happens, the villagers simply remove the roof beams, build higher walls on top of the older ones, set the door higher, and install a new roof. After centuries of topping off the walls,

6

Araouane now sits on a giant dune, its original rooms many stories down in the sand. According to local legend, great treasures were once hoarded under the sandy floors of these subterranean spaces as insurance against times of war and famine. The ... inhabitants still bury anything they consider valuable in the sandy floors of their houses" (Aebi 1997, 84).

The rate of sand accumulation at Meinarti is most dramatically illustrated in the case of the Meinarti Church. When first constructed, at Subphase 3a (*c*. 660 AD) the building stood on a slightly elevated platform, whose eastern end was approximately one meter higher than the adjoining ground surface. By the time of Subphase 3c (*c*. A.D. 900) sand had accumulated sufficiently so that the eastern end was at ground level, while near the western end it was necessary to build a retaining wall opposite the north doorway, to keep sand from drifting into the building. By Subphase 4a (*c*. A.D. 1100) it was necessary to build steps outside each of the two church doors, descending from the outside ground surface which was now considerably higher than the thresholds. Those stairways were extended upward at each succeeding phase, as the drifted sand continued to accumulate. By the time of the building's final abandonment, at the end of Subphase 5c (*c*. A.D. 1365) the stairway leading down to the south door comprised no fewer 11 steps, descending from a level over 150cm higher that of the church floor (Pl. 1d). The north door by this time had been blocked up altogether and abandoned, as had the windows high in the north and west walls of the building.

Refuse deposition. The dumping of domestic refuse did not play a large role in the buildup of the Meinarti mound, as it did for example at Qasr Ibrim (see Adams 1996, 8-10). Very little deposit was encountered in the excavations that could be identified as midden. This was due partly to the fact that organic refuse of all kinds was dissolved away by the action of moisture—either by flooding, at the lower levels, or by capillary moisture at the higher ones. As always in habitation sites, potsherds were the main refuse that endured, but even these were not as thickly scattered over the floors, and in the fill between floors, as might have been expected. It seems probable that the Meinarti residents threw much of their rubbish down the slopes of the mound, where it was carried away by subsequent floods. The main places where unmistakable midden deposits—including enormous numbers of potsherds—were encountered were in latrines, which were regular features of Classic and Late Christian houses.

Building demolition and renewal. In many *tell* sites of the Near East, building rubble forms a very considerable part of the fill material, as old walls were periodically pulled down, and their debris served as a foundation upon which new ones were built (see Lloyd 1963, 13-21). Surprisingly, there was little evidence of this at Meinarti, despite the wholesale rebuildings that had taken place at the start of each major phase. So far as the lower levels (essentially Levels 11-18) were concerned, this could be explained by the fact that, during periods of abandonment, standing walls were carried away by flood action. Consequently, the only parts of the walls that survived were those

lower portions that had already been buried in sand before the floods arrived. But it was also true, even in the upper levels, that new walls were commonly built up directly on the stumps of old ones, making use of whatever masonry was still standing. Even where there was obvious evidence of demolition, however, it appears that the dismantled bricks were mostly hauled away, or perhaps in some cases reused. Brick rubble was abundant only in the uppermost fill, dating from after the final abandonment of the site.

Intrusion of graves. During the Classic and Late Christian periods, a substantial area at the east side of the Meinarti community was occupied by a cemetery. Many and perhaps most of the graves had rectangular brick superstructures, typically about 60cm high, and these like everything else in the community became sanded over in time. Once they had disappeared from view, they were very often cut through by grave shafts dug at a later period. There is no indication that this was ever deliberate; the grave diggers simply had no idea what was under the ground when they began digging. Graves however were always confined to the cemetery area adjoining the Meinarti church. In only one place was there evidence that graves had been intruded into what had formerly been a building.

Flood damage. The earliest structures at Meinarti, those of Level 18, were built on a shallow accumulation of sand, whose surface was generally no more than one meter above the level of the Nile floodplain (see Figures 5 and 6). As a result of this low-lying situation, the structures at this and all the other earliest levels were subject to repeated destruction by floods, at the season of the High Niles. By the time of Level 13 (= Subphase 3a), however, the top of the mound had reached a height of four meters, and the uppermost structures were probably affected only by rare, exceptionally high floods. By the time of Level 9 (= Subphase 4a) the height had reached over five meters, and it was clear from their excellent preservation that the structures from this and later periods had never been reached by floodwaters. On the other hand, the swirling waters at all periods continued to eat at the lower edges of the mound, often causing the deposits above to slump and slide down, carrying with them the outermost walls of buildings. As a result of these processes, the original, outermost limits of the settlement were not preserved at any level.

Violent destruction. Evidence of violent destruction, either by enemy action or by the inhabitants themselves, was rare at Meinarti. During most of the Christian period, from at least 650 to 1250, peace reigned throughout Nubia, and in any case Meinarti in those years was not a place important enough to constitute a major military target. The historically attested raid of Shams ed-Dawla in 1172-73, which wrought enormous damage at Qasr Ibrim (Adams 1996, 6), is reported by some chroniclers to have carried upriver as far as the Second Cataract (Monneret de Villard 1938, 197), and indeed it may have caused the temporary abandonment of the site at the end of Phase 4. However, there was no evidence of actual destruction at Meinarti that could be attributed to these invaders.

Other Arab sources tell that, around the year 1365,

Meinarti (called in Arabic records the Island of Michael—see below) had been occupied by semi-nomadic bands of the Beni Ikrima (see Vantini 1975, 539). There was definite evidence of destruction that could be attributed to those intruders, whose incursion terminated the occupation at Phase 5 (Level 4). The marauders defaced the murals in the Meinarti Church and in another public building, and it looks also as if they used the houses at the northern end of the village as animal pens. They did not however actually pull down any walls. The evidence of their action will be much more fully discussed in a subsequent volume (*Meinarti III*).

Apart from the episodes just mentioned, the only other evidence of violent destruction at Meinarti was in the very large Administration Building built during the initial Meroitic occupation (Subphase 1a, = Level 18). This structure had almost certainly been burned at the end of Phase 1a; whether by hostile marauders or by the action of the Meinarti inhabitants themselves, or by accident, could not be determined.

Post-abandonment decay. As nearly as can be calculated, Meinarti was finally abandoned around 1600 AD. At that time the principal feature of the site was House I, a massive, two-storey "castle-house" at the southern end of the mound.[4] After the time of abandonment, the most southerly rooms of this structure had fallen away when the mound directly below them was eaten into by floods. The remaining lower rooms survived largely intact until the end of the 19th century, when they were deliberately filled with rubble in order to provide the foundation for a gun emplacement built by the Anglo-Egyptian garrison during the time of the *Mahdiya*. Apart from House 1, there were also scraps of surviving masonry at several places on the mound surface, suggesting the presence of other buildings in the Terminal Christian and early Post-Christian periods. In the centuries after abandonment, these had almost entirely disappeared through a combination of natural decay, brick-robbing, and the use of the mound surface as an animal pen.

Human disturbance, Although the Meinarti mound was always subject to natural destructive forces, it seems to have been entirely spared from two kinds of man-made disturbance that caused considerable damage at other Nubian sites. Nowhere in the excavated area was any evidence that brick walls had been mined away to provide *maroq* (or *sebbakh*, as it is called in Egypt) to fertilize the fields. This may be due to the fact that, after the abandonment of the village, there was little or no cultivation practiced on the island of Meinarti. There was also no evidence of the intrusion of storage pits, a practice that has caused extensive damage at Qasr Ibrim and other Nubian sites (Adams 1996, 11-12). The explanation in this case seems quite clear. The very soft sand deposit at Meinarti, when wet, would not have provided effective storage for grain and other perishable goods, and when dry it would not hold any kind of a vertical profile, allowing for the digging of pits.

The nature, extent, and condition of the remains
At the beginning of excavation, the excavated area at

[4] For a general discussion of castle-houses see Adams 1994a.

Meinarti measured approximately 80 meters north-south by 70 meters east-west, encompassing just under one-half of the total surface area of the mound. As the work progressed downward, the extent of the excavated area from north to south diminished slightly but continuously, because it was not possible to maintain a vertical face at the northern edge of the excavations (cf. Fig. 5). By the time Level 18 was reached, the excavated area measured about 60 meters from north to south, and comprised about one-third of the total mound area.

Architectural remains did not cover the total of the excavated area, at any level. It was presumed that they had originally done so, but the outer edges of the settlement at the south, east, and west sides had repeatedly been destroyed by a combination of flooding and slumpage, and none of the surviving buildings could be presumed with certainly to represent the original outer limit of the settlement. In addition, the settlement at most and perhaps all periods extended northward beyond the limit of the excavation; that is, it was partly buried within the unexcavated northern half of the mound.

The horizontal extent of the preserved remains varied enormously from level to level, depending on how much destructive activity had taken place during and subsequent to the time of occupation. The smallest area covered by preserved remains[5] was about 900m², at Levels 3 and 11a; the largest area was about 5600m² at Level 8. Table 2 shows the maximum north-south and east-west extent of the preserved remains, and the area covered by them, for each level. Table 3 shows, in percentage terms, the approximate extent and the nature of change that took

TABLE 2. EXTENT OF PRESERVED
ARCHITECTURAL REMAINS AT EACH LEVEL

Level	Maximum north-south[*] extent in m.	Maximum east-west extent in m.	Area in m²
1	25	20	500
2	(Not separately measured)		
3	43	30	900
4	70	65	3500
5	70	65	3800
6	70	80	4300
7	80	75	4800
8	80	85	5600
9	80	80	5200
11a	50	50	900
11b	50	60	1050
12	50	55	2300
13	60	50	2100
14	60	50	2000
15a	60	50	2300
15b	60	50	2500
16	40	30	1100
17	30	40	1100
18	45	45	1600

[*] North-south and east-west dimensions are measured in conformity with the orientation of the buildings (i.e. Nile north), not in relation to magnetic north.

[5] Exclusive of those of the Anglo-Egyptian occupation at Level 1.

TABLE 3. PERCENTAGE OF ARCHITECTURAL CHANGE BETWEEN SUCCESSIVE LEVELS
(All figures are percentages)

Levels	Surviving		Added		Lost		Area change	Total change*
	Unchanged	Modified	Over previous	On new ground	Built over	Abandoned		
2>1		85	15				-45	100
3>2			(Not separately calculated)					
4>3	5		10		75	10	-75	95
5>4	40	35			20	5	-10	35
6>5	10	25	30	20	10	5	-10	75
7>6	10	15	30	5	30	10	-10	80
8>7	50	20	5		25		-15	35
9>8	80	10	10				+10	10
11a>9		5	95				+475	95
11b>11a	50	35				15	-15	30
12>11b	5	65		10		20	-55	50
13>12	10	70		5		15	+10	45
14>13	10	15	30	20	20	5	+5	80
15a>14	25	40	15		20		-15	50
15b>15a	85	15					-10	10
16>15b	15	15	40	40			+125	75
17>16	5	15	25	30	20	5		85
18>17	10	35	5	15	10	25	-30	65

* Calculated as 100%, minus the figure for structures surviving unchanged, minus 2/3 of the figure for structures surviving with modifications.

place between each pair of successive levels.

The extent of vertical preservation (i.e. the height of standing walls) varied as much as did horizontal preservation, and for the same reasons. The highest standing walls were usually found, of course, in the center of the site, where sand accumulation was greatest, while preserved heights became lower and lower toward the outer margins—a condition that can be perceived clearly in Plate 16a in the present volume. The highest standing walls found in any building were those of the "castle-house" (House I) of Phase 6 (Levels 3 and 2), which still stood to a height of over 4 m, even after the demolition of the upper storey in the 19th century (Pl. 1c). In the earlier levels, the walls at Phase 4 (Levels 7-9), were exceptionally well preserved, standing in a few places to their original height of just about 2 m. In one house, some of the original roof timbers remained *in situ*. Preservation was also good in Phase 5 (Levels 4-6) and Phase 2 (Levels 14-15b); in each case some walls in the center of the site were standing to a height of 180cm. Preservation was mediocre at best in Phase 1 (Levels 16-18), where there had been extensive flood damage, and it was extremely bad in Phase 3 (Levels 11a-13), for reasons that are not fully clear. At Level 11a, no wall stood as much as one meter high.

Architectural remains. With only the rarest exceptions, construction at Meinarti was in mud brick throughout the whole history of the community. Brick sizes were typically 33 x 16 x 9 m in the Meroitic and Ballaña levels, increasing to 36 x 18 x 8cm in the Early and Classic Christian levels, and to 40 x 20 x 8cm in the Late and Terminal Christian levels. No building was constructed originally of stone, but coarse stone masonry was used occasionally to rebuild damaged walls, and a few buildings rested on stone foundations. However, the majority of walls had either *rollag* foundations (i.e. a course of bricks laid on edge), or no foundations.

Architectural standards and conventions varied enormously from phase to phase. The original Meroitic buildings of Phase 1 were very large structures with stout, straight walls, mostly from 60 to 100cm thick; almost certainly they were the work of professional builders. After damage by floods (and in one case by a fire), they were repaired in increasingly haphazard fashion at Subphases 1b and 1c. After a hiatus of perhaps a century, the whole village was rebuilt in the late Ballaña period (Subphase 2a) as a densely nucleated cluster of ordinary houses, mostly rather irregular in shape and having walls no more than 20cm thick. These structures underwent relatively minor modifications at Subphases 2b and 2c, and then at the beginning of the Christian period, at Subphase 3a, the whole village was rebuilt once again, and a church was added at the east side. The somewhat enigmatic evidence suggests that the new buildings were originally stout, straight-walled affairs, but almost immediately they began to be attacked by destructive forces which can only have been exceptionally high floods. They were then rebuilt several times, in Subphases 3b, 3c, and 3d, in increasingly haphazard fashion, until by Subphase 3d what little survived of the village was a chaotic cluster of highly irregular-shaped, mostly small rooms with walls of many different thicknesses.

After another hiatus, the whole village was again rebuilt at Subphase 4a, in the latter part of the Classic Christian period. It was once again a nucleated cluster of houses, separated by narrow streets and small plazas, but the houses were both considerably larger and more regular in outline than those at Phase 2, and nearly all walls were straight. Without exception however the walls were only 20cm thick, comprised of stretcher bricks only. There were very minor modifications at Subphases 4b and 4c, involving some rearrangement of interior partitions and some addition of new houses, and then another abandonment during which some of the houses were sanded up virtually to the level of their timbered roofs. The reasons for this abandonment are not entirely clear; they will be more fully considered in a later volume.

The village was again rebuilt at Subphase 5a, at the beginning of the Late Christian period. The earliest, somewhat enigmatic remains from this phase include three very large, open courtyards at the south; a large, irregular cluster of thin-walled rooms to the north of them; and then three free-standing, stout-walled houses at the north. At Subphase 5b however the courtyards were subdivided into a cluster of large and small rooms which appear to have been some sort of integrated complex. The walls within the complex were still almost entirely thin (20cm) and were somewhat irregular, but to the north there were now at least seven of the stout-walled, free-standing houses. These structures, which were clearly family residences, were regular in plan and had vaulted ceilings; they were again probably the work of professional builders.[6] The changes at Subphase 5c were relatively minor, and involved mostly the rearrangement of partitions within the monastic complex. A significant addition however was the building of a massively walled watchtower at the southwest corner of the complex.

Phase 5 was almost certainly terminated by the invasion and temporary occupation by Beni Ikrima nomads, mentioned earlier. They seem to have used the stout-walled houses as animal pens, but made no use of the integrated complex other than to deface the paintings in its refectory. After they had left there seems to have been a considerable hiatus, during which all of the buildings were deeply filled with wind-blown sand. When the Christian inhabitants returned, they restored a few of the better preserved rooms of the complex for use as workshops, but none of the stout-walled houses at the north were reoccupied. Directly on top of the sanded up remains of the complex, however, the returnees built a massive, two-storey "castle-house" of a type which made its appearance all over Lower Nubia in the last centuries of the Christian period (see Adams 1994a). There were apparently several other new buildings as well, but only the scantiest traces of them survived. The castle-house on the other hand remained in good shape, and continued to be occupied until perhaps a century after the end of Nubian Christianity, or around A.D. 1600. In its latter years the interior of the building was subjected to a number of modifications, designated as Subphase 6b. But after about 1600 the whole site was abandoned for nearly three centuries, until a gun emplacement was built on top of the sanded-up castle-house in the time of the *Mahdiya* (Phase 7).

Interior features such as mastabas, corner bins, fireplaces, and grain silos (*qusebas*) were present to some extent at all phases. They were exceptionally numerous, and also exceptionally well preserved, at Phase 4.

Floors. Floor surfaces at Meinarti, both within and surrounding the houses, could usually be easily recognized by their compacted surfaces and by quantities of sherds,

charcoal, ash, and occasionally artifacts scattered over them. Within the houses, identification was often made doubly secure by the presence of mastabas, storage bins, and other features built directly on the floors. The only houses on the site within which no floors could be clearly identified were those that had apparently been used by the Beni Kanz and Beni Ikrima as animal pens, at the end of Phase 5.

The Meinarti Church when originally built (as Church XXXVIII) had a floor of small river cobblestones, though it was soon overlaid with mud. No other building had a complete flooring of stone or brick, but a few individual rooms, at several levels, had either flagstones or brick flooring. However, the vast majority of floors, at all levels and phases, were of hard-packed mud. The original (i.e. lowest) floor in any room was likely to be a smooth, hard, wet-laid affair which was probably installed at the same time when the interior walls were plastered. Re-floorings at a later date however varied considerably in hardness and in evenness. Some were wet-laid, and probably were associated with re-plastering, but a good many were not.

It was evident within most houses that the floor levels had not built up gradually, as an incidental consequence of occupation. There was not, therefore, a succession of micro-levels in most rooms. Rather, room floors seem to have been kept clear of refuse and sand for considerable periods, until a decision was made to re-floor. At that time a certain amount of sand (typically from 10 to 25cm) was likely to be laid down over the old floor, before a new one was laid. In some houses at Phase 4, the buildup of floors had required a simultaneous heightening of the walls, as the original ceilings had become too low for comfort. This probably happened at other phases as well, but it was only in the Phase 4 levels that the walls were preserved to a sufficient height so that the additions to their tops could actually be identified.

The situation was different in the narrow streets and plazas that adjoined the buildings, for here occupation surfaces did for the most part build up gradually and continually. Moreover, the open spaces were rarely given a deliberate surface covering of mud, although there were exceptions. As a result, the exterior deposits commonly exhibited a succession of micro-levels, and the choice of which ones to choose as numbered levels for mapping purposes was sometimes rather arbitrary. Those surfaces that were given level numbers, and mapped on the cross-sections (Figures 5 and 6), generally had three distinguishing features. First, they were exceptionally hard and compacted, indicating a considerable period of stable usage. Second, they exhibited a scatter of charcoal, ash, and sherds. Third, they could be directly connected with floor levels within the houses. This was possible at Meinarti because most house doorways did not have raised thresholds, making it possible to follow occupation surfaces from the outside to the inside of houses.[7] For the same reason, floor surfaces could be followed from one room to another within the houses.

---

[6] They conform to a type elsewhere called "unit houses," which became common all over Nubia in the Late Christian period. See Adams 1977, 492-3.

[7] In contrast to the situation at Qasr Ibrim, where nearly all doorways had raised thresholds. See Adams 1996, 39.

Fill. The nature of the fill material within and around the Meinarti buildings has already been suggested in earlier paragraphs. By volume it certainly consisted at least 90% of fine, white, wind-blown sand. The amount of other material mixed with the sand varied according to the circumstances of occupation and of deposition. Sand which accumulated during periods of actual occupation was likely to contain substantial quantities of potsherds, ash, and charcoal. Sand which accumulated during periods of abandonment was largely free of occupation debris, but might contain brick rubble from decaying buildings. As already noted, however, brick rubble was a much smaller component of the fill than might have been expected, considering the number of rebuildings that took place.

Apart from latrine deposits, the densest fill at Meinarti was that encountered in the houses of Phase 2 and Phase 3. The Ballaña period, represented by Phase 2, seems to have been an exceptionally "trashy" one, not only at Meinarti but a many other sites (cf. Plumley and Adams 1974, 217 and 225). Phase 2 house floors were covered by extraordinary quantities of broken pottery, ash, brick rubble, and even quite a few complete vessels (as shown in Plates 16e-f). By contrast the fill at Phase 3 was relatively poor in potsherds and artifacts, but the sand fill was mixed with unusually large amounts of dissolved mud. The possibility that the site was subjected to some exceptional and heavy rainstorms at this period is one that will be considered in a later volume (Meinarti II).

Indoor toilets, situated always in a small room at the back of the house, were a regular feature of the Meinarti houses at Phases 4 and 5. The ceramic toilet fixture itself was set into a raised platform, and the deposit beneath the platform was in most cases a very dense mixture of sand, dissolved mud, dissolved fecal matter, and large quantities of potsherds, many of exceptional size. However, no such deposits were found in the pre-Christian and Early Christian levels.

The cemetery. At Phases 4 and 5, and possibly Phase 6, the east side of the Meinarti community was occupied by an extensive cemetery. Altogether, 323 graves were excavated, of which 119 were covered by brick superstructures. Like all other components of the site, the cemetery remains were stratified, mainly as a result of sand accumulation. Earlier graves and their superstructures were gradually sanded over and disappeared from view, and then later graves were sometimes unintentionally intruded upon them. The later and higher-level graves, dating from Phase 5, were almost entirely lacking in superstructures, possibly because they had been destroyed by surface deflation following the abandonment of the site. On the other hand the superstructures dating from Phase 4 were extraordinarily well preserved, except where they had been dug through by later graves. The structures were of several types; they will be the subject of extensive discussion in the volume Meinarti IV. [8]

No soft tissue material was preserved on the bodies, as the cemetery like the rest of the site had been subject to flooding and capillary moisture. The bones however were generally well preserved, except in the lowermost graves where they were often very brittle. The excavation of the cemetery was overseen by the Physical Anthropologists George Armelagos, George Ewing, and David Greene of the University of Colorado, who collected all of the bones and sent them to Colorado for study. They have subsequently provided the basis for a number of published reports.[9]

Artifactual material. As in all habitation sites, the overwhelming majority of artifactual remains consisted of pottery vessels and their fragments. Sherds were scattered abundantly through all of the levels, but a rather surprising number of complete vessels were also found. They occurred very largely in two loci: at Phase 2 (all levels) and at Phase 5b (specifically Level 5). During the Ballaña period (Phase 2), small wine goblets and cups seem to have been so cheap and plentiful that they were treated much as we treat paper cups today. They were abandoned in substantial numbers on the house floors, and were simply floored over when new floors were installed.[10] At Subphase 5b, vessels were found in a few large caches, where they had been deliberately buried under house floors prior to a temporary abandonment of the region ordered by the Nubian king.[11] In addition to these finds, a great many hand-made cooking pots (shown in Plate 19a) had been buried up the rims under house floors, especially at Phases 2 and 3. These were of course recovered intact when we dismantled the floors.[12]

In addition to ceramics, there were also numerous small items of iron, copper, copper-alloy, glass, and mud, and a few items of bone and ivory. These were almost certainly things that had been lost, forgotten, or occasionally buried in flood-borne deposits. Altogether, 1507 portable artifacts were registered in the course of the excavations; they are summarized numerically in Tables 5 and 6. The nature of the artifactual finds will be described in more specific terms in a later section.

There had been enough wetting of the Meinarti deposits, either directly by flooding or indirectly by capillary action, so that almost no organic materials were preserved. The main exceptions were found in the artifact caches of Subphase 5b, which in addition to their very numerous pots contained a few examples of textile, and artifacts of wood and leather. Preservation in these cases could be attributed to the fact that the caches were both underlain and overlain by densely compacted floors. Because of wetting also, objects of iron and copper were nearly always heavily corroded. On the other hand preservation of pottery was generally excellent, except for those objects recovered from latrine deposits. These latter had usually been heavily permeated with salt, which often caused the outer surfaces and decoration to flake off.

[8] For the preliminary report see Adams 1965c, 169-71.

[9] See, among other sources, Greene 1966; Greene 1967; Greene 1972; Greene 1982; and Greene 1984.

[10] This was conspicuous also at Qasr Ibrim; see Plumley and Adams 1974, 217 and 225.

[11] For the historical documentation see Vantini 1975, 479 and 684.

[12] The same feature is sometimes still found in Nubian houses today.

The excavations

Although, prior to 1963, a good many Christian Nubian sites had been excavated by me and by others, few of them had been occupied long enough to exhibit much stratigraphy.[13] The different sites did not, in toto, provide a complete and connected record of cultural development during the medieval period. It was therefore evident, from the start, that the most significant results to be obtained at Meinarti would come through a careful, level-by-level stripping of the site, which would furnish a connected history at least for this one community. It was also evident however that a complete excavation of the entire mound was out of the question, in the period of about 18 months that remained before its inundation. I estimated that, with a labor force of maximum size, I might be able to excavate about half of the total mound area, down to its lowermost levels. Accordingly I selected the southern and higher half of the mound for investigation, and the work from beginning to end was confined within that area.

Excavations began on 10 February, 1963, with a force of 150 Nubian laborers. This was a considerably larger crew than I had employed on any previous dig, but I considered it the minimum necessary if any significant results were to be achieved at Meinarti. After one month, when regular working routines had been developed, and when the nature of the deposits became apparent, the workforce was increased to 200. Excavations then continued until 2 May, by which time daytime temperatures were approaching 40° Celsius.

At the time when work was suspended for the summer, the excavations had penetrated down only to Level 6 (Subphase 5a), with the tops of the Level 7 (Subphase 4c) walls just beginning to appear. There was of course no way of estimating how many levels might still underlie, but the highest point on the mound, as it then survived, was still about 6 m above the surface of the floodplain. It was clear therefore that only a massive effort, larger than anything heretofore, would succeed in reaching the lowest levels before the impounded Nile waters began to rise in the fall of 1964. Excavations were therefore resumed on 10 September, 1963—by far the earliest date on which we had ever begun work—with a force increased to 250 men.

Work continued on that scale until April of 1964, when a severe financial crisis forced a reduction of the working crew to 100 men. Thereafter excavation necessarily proceeded more slowly, but by keeping the dig going until 11 June, 1964, we did indeed succeed in reaching and fully clearing Level 18. A series of test pits revealed the welcome news that there was nothing beneath but clean, white sand. Nature happily and unexpectedly favored our enterprise, for instead of the usual blistering temperatures of May and June, we had a succession of unusually moderate days, with temperatures in the middle 30s and with a continual slight breeze. We were, as a result, able to complete an excavation season of nine months and two days—perhaps the longest uninterrupted excavation season ever undertaken in Nubia.

In addition to the force of Nubian laborers, the work at

Meinarti was assisted throughout by a group of seven *Qufti* supervisors, under the highly capable direction of Reis Youssef Mohammed Youssef. The success of the Meinarti excavations owes a great deal to the genius of this extraordinary foreman, to whom I have paid tribute in the Preface. Without his continual forethought and his managerial skills, I could certainly never have managed, single-handed, the supervision of 250 laborers, along with all of the other duties of mapping and recording.

The methodology employed at Meinarti developed in part as the dig went along, and it was an adaptation to what I can only call "emergency" circumstances. It was quite unlike anything in my previous or subsequent experience, and also unlike anything familiar to me in published literature. For that reason I have thought it desirable here to describe the methodology in considerable detail, so that readers may judge for themselves how much confidence they want to place in the results. However, persons uninterested in methodological questions may wish to skip the remainder of this chapter, and proceed to the next two chapters where substantive data on the Meroitic and Ballaña remains is presented.

Basic excavation philosophy

Textbooks on archaeological method are apt to give the impression that there is only one proper way to dig a site. In fact, there are as many different and legitimate ways of digging as there are reasons for digging. The archaeologist must at the outset ask himself what he hopes to learn, and then decide what is the best way to go about it. Every excavator has his or her own objectives, vis-a-vis any particular site, and at a deeper level it is probably true also that every excavator has his or her own excavation philosophy, based on personal interests plus the accumulated wisdom of previous digs.

One of the most fundamental choices to be made, in the case of townsite archaeology, is that between revealing horizontal pattern and revealing vertical sequence. A maximum vertical exposure, by trenching or pitting, will reveal the sequences of occupation in a site from bottom to top, yet each such exposure will yield relatively little information about the occupation at any one moment in time. Each is, rather, a record only of particularized events at one locality. Even a whole series of disconnected pits or trenches do not furnish a coherent, overall view of the community at any particular moment in its history. A maximum horizontal exposure will much more adequately reveal concurrent patterns of occupation, but will not reveal the sequence of development from age to age. The only way to combine the two objectives is to clear each level fully, but then to dismantle it and do the same for the next level down. Fortunately, this proved to be possible at Meinarti.

My approach to the excavation and recording of Meinarti was shaped by four factors: my early experience and interests as an ethnologist (see Adams 1992, 6-7; my experience in archaeological salvage work in the American Southwest (ibid, 5-7); my previous experience in the excavation of Nubian sites;[14] and the nature and limita-

---

[13] The Faras Potteries were the main exception; see Adams 1961b, 31-3.

[14] See Adams 1961b; Adams 1962c; Adams 1964, 218-22; and Adams and Nordström 1963.

tions of the Meinarti site itself. As a "once and future" ethnologist, I always approached townsite archaeology as nearly as possible like ethnography; that is, I sought to develop an integrative, overall view of the community at each moment in its history. This meant digging most or all of the structures and recovering all of the artifacts that had been is use at any one moment in time. I always abhorred the all-too-common practice of selective trenching or pitting that would result in the partial excavation of houses. Very few archaeologists would have the discourtesy to uncover half a burial, while leaving the other half unexcavated, and a house is in every way as much an organic unit as is a skeleton. To be fully understood it must be seen in its entirety. In the broadest sense the same is true of the community as a whole, although the total excavation of a community is not always a practical possibility. I always felt however that a maximum contiguous exposure was preferable to a series of disconnected excavations that could be connected up only by considerable leaps of the imagination.

As a director of archaeological salvage in the Glen Canyon Reservoir area[15] of Arizona and Utah from 1957 to 1959, I had also learned that, under the time constraints of reservoir salvage, certain departures from ideal practice were essential. Bill Lipe has recently summarized some of the basic principles that were developed in the course of the Glen Canyon work:[16]

"1. Use the largest tool that will do the job.

2. Recovering 90 percent of the data from 10 sites is far better than using the same time and money to recover 99 or 100 percent of the data from one or two sites.

3. Excavation with trowels and screens instead of shovels and no screens is usually a waste of time, in terms of the added yield of artifacts.[17]

4. Maintaining data quality is essential, but the level of quality sought should be appropriate. Perfection is not achievable, and the attempt to achieve it is a waste of time.

5. In the area of data quality, the field record is preeminent. A researcher can always reclassify the artifacts that have been collected, but he or she cannot go back and re-excavate the portions of a site that have already been dug.

6. Fieldwork unreported is fieldwork never done; furthermore, it has resulted in destruction of a site with no resulting gain in information about the past."

Previous work in Nubian townsites, particularly at the Faras Potteries (Adams 1961b) and at Kasanarti (Adams 1964, 218-22), had also made me familiar with some of the special peculiarities and problems of townsite excavation in the Nile Valley, where the deposit consists largely of drifted sand. This material will not hold any kind of a vertical face; in order to excavate downward for one meter it is usually necessary to extend the excavation out-

ward for two meters. The digging of straight-sided trenches or pits, and the leaving of unexcavated baulks, is therefore out of the question. Given the sheer volume of overburden to be removed, moreover, the bulk of the work must necessarily be done not by trained archaeologists but by relatively unskilled laborers, who are apt to assume that the only object of the excavations is to recover objects. This was even more true at Meinarti than at my previous digs, since the crew was larger than any that I had previously managed.

In keeping with my basic philosophy, then, I had two overriding objectives at Meinarti, which were potentially contradictory. The first was to expose each of the site's stratigraphic levels as fully as possible, in a single contiguous exposure. The second was, at all costs, to reach the bottom of the mound, so as to reveal the full occupation history of the community. In order to achieve both objectives it was necessary to work not only on a very large scale but also fairly rapidly, and this meant "cutting a good many corners" when it came to the niceties of control and recording. Some of the resulting deficiencies in the record will become apparent in later pages, but I am confident that the bottom of the mound could not have been reached in any other way.

Digging methods

The basic digging methods employed at Meinarti were those which, at least up to that time, were universal in Nile Valley archaeology. Digging was done almost exclusively with the use of the *turiya*, after which loosened fill was carried away in baskets to dumps around the periphery of the site. The number of basket-carriers assigned to each *turiya*- man varied according to the distance from the dumps, but averaged about four carriers per digger. There were, consequently, about 60 men actually digging when the force was at its full strength (see Pl. 2a).

When room floors appeared, the *turiya* was usually discarded in favor of the trowel. Most trowel work was done by the *Qufti* supervisors, although a few of the local laborers also became skilled trowel men. When not clearing floors or other detail features, the *Quftis* also worked with the *turiya*, in addition to supervising the work of from 10 to 20 of the Nubian diggers each.

Two collection baskets were always placed in front of each digger: one to receive potsherds, and one to receive all other artifactual finds. Labels attached to the handles of each basket identified the house, room, and level from which the finds came. In theory all sherds were collected, washed, and examined, but in most cases only the decorated wares were counted, because of constraints on the excavator's time. It should be added too that not all the *turiya*- men were equally skilled in their use of the instrument, or equally diligent in the collection of sherds and artifacts. As a result, a good many sherds and some artifacts were inadvertently carried to the dumps, from which they were sometimes later rescued. In all such cases, the proveniences were of course lost.

My reasons for collecting and counting potsherds at Meinarti require a word of explanation. First of all, in the course of excavation they always served as a kind of gross stratigraphic control. They could tell me if the diggers in

---

[15] Now Lake Powell. For reports see Adams and Adams 1959, and Adams, Lindsay and Turner 1961.

[16] Paraphrased from Lipe 1997. These principles were actually enunciated by my Glen Canyon colleague Jesse D. Jennings, but I was in general agreement with all of them.

[17] I was later able to verify this by actual experimentation at Qasr Ibrim, comparing the yield of potsherds and of artifacts from deposits that were and were not screened.

a certain area were getting down into Early Christian deposits when they were supposed to be clearing a Classic Christian level, for example. This was particularly important when working in deposits where no architectural features (i.e. wall tops) had yet appeared. However, at this stage of my ceramic analysis, I was not really "using the pottery to read the site," as I later did at Kulubnarti and Qasr Ibrim,[18] because I had not yet worked out the sequence and the frequency of the wares in detail. It was rather the other way around: I was "using the site to learn the pottery." It was precisely the stratigraphic levels at Meinarti, and the ceramic counts obtained from them, that helped me later to work out the sequence and frequency of wares.[19]

Strategy and tactics

Throughout the Meinarti excavations, then, my hope and basic objective was to strip the mound one level at a time, and not to begin work at any new level until the overlying level had been fully cleared and recorded. In practice, however, this was easier said than done. For purely logistic reasons it was rarely possible to keep the whole labor force working within one contiguous area; usually there were different teams working simultaneously in different parts of the site. Until floor surfaces were actually reached, it was never certain "what went with what;" in other words that the different teams were working in deposits of the same age. Although remains of the seven major phases could be clearly distinguished from one another on the basis of stratigraphy alone, this was not always true in the case of subphases. It sometimes turned out that different teams were working on remains of different subphases (e.g. 4a, 4b, and 4c) at the same time.

To deal with this problem, I never made a final assignment of any building or its contents to a phase or subphase until I was certain of its proper placement. In the meantime I compiled from day to day a base plan, at a scale of 1:100, showing whatever walls and features had actually been excavated, without any *a priori* decision as to what level they belonged to. Only when the proper level for each building and room (i.e. "what went with what") had been determined, through the excavation of floors and the study of recovered pottery, were the mapped walls and other features then transferred from the base plan onto a tracing, of which a separate one was made for each level. At any given time in the excavations I was usually working on two or even three tracings, of different levels, onto which remains were being mapped.

In the day-to-day conduct of the excavations, there were always two practical challenges: to keep all of the *turiya*-men meaningfully employed, and to keep the basket carriers from getting in each others' way. Achieving the first of these objectives required a good deal of forethought and prioritizing. Whenever work was finished in a particular house, or when the potsherds revealed that the excavations were reaching a lower level than I was ready for, it was necessary to transfer the men working on that job to another area. I had therefore always to have another job ready; that is, to decide in advance what the next target or targets should be. In these cases I was often greatly aided by Reis Youssef, who was thinking ahead just as I was.

Keeping the traffic of the basket-carriers moving smoothly was chiefly a matter of keeping open a number of different routes from the worksites to the dumps. This problem was alleviated at Meinarti by the fact that it was possible to deposit the spoil on all sides of the mound, except at the unexcavated north. Indeed, at the end of the excavations Meinarti had the appearance of a kind of "inverted mound," the dumps on all sides being considerably higher than the excavated area itself.

In the excavation of any level, I tried as much as possible to have the work of clearing begin in the center of the site, and proceed from there outward. That way, the basket-carriers would not have to be passing back and forth over finished work or cleared floors, and would not have to step over standing walls, on their way to the dumps. Moreover, as the central area was cleared, I could write field notes and take measurements without being in the way of the laborers. When the remains at any level were to be demolished, on the other hand, the work for obvious reasons proceeded from the outside inward—again so that the laborers would not have to be stepping over walls.

The excavation of buildings. The major remains at Meinarti were almost entirely those of buildings, which for purposes of uniform nomenclature were always designated as "houses," although a number were not actually dwellings. As soon as its wall tops had been exposed and its limits defined, each house was given a number. Roman numeral designations, from I to LX, were employed to avoid any confusion between house numbers and level numbers. During the first season individual rooms were also numbered, with Arabic numerals, as soon as all of their wall tops had appeared. Cardboard tags were nailed to the north wall of each room, identifying the house and room number; they can be seen in Plate 2b.

My usual procedure, when a house had been identified and numbered, was to complete the excavation of the whole building in one continuous operation, down to the uppermost preserved floor surfaces. This was chiefly for the convenience of mapping, note-taking, and photography, since I did not attempt a comprehensive documentation until a house had been fully cleared. Under the circumstances, several *turiya*-men were usually at work in any house simultaneously, sometimes one in each room. Apart from the matter of convenience, there was also a very practical reason for this procedure. Because a great many of the brick walls at Meinarti were thin (mostly about 20cm), it was necessary to remove more or less equal amounts of sand deposit from both sides of them, in order to avert the danger of collapse from the thrust of sand against one side. For the same reason, the deposit adjoining the outside house walls had to be removed at the same time when the interior was being excavated.

Once a house had been cleared to its uppermost floors, the diggers were dispatched to another location while mapping, photography, and note-taking were carried out.

---

[18] For discussion see especially Adams and Adams 1991, 136-9.

[19] For extended discussion see Adams 1986, 601-16.

Then, test probes were made below the floors in each room, to see if earlier floors were present, as in most cases they were. The clearance of earlier floors often revealed at the same time the remnants of older floor features such as bins, fireplaces, and mastabas, which would have to be separately noted and mapped, and in time transferred from the base plan onto the appropriate tracing. When probes revealed that the lowest (i.e. original) floors had been uncovered, and when recording procedures were complete, the house was then left until such time as it, along with all of the neighboring structures of the same age, could be dismantled, preparatory to the excavation of the next level.

The excavation of the cemetery. The presence of the Meinarti cemetery was not apparent when excavations began, because no superstructures were preserved at the uppermost levels. Moreover the grave shafts had been dug into soft sand, and subsequently refilled with the same material, so that shaft outlines could rarely be made out. The presence of the cemetery became apparent only when routine clearing operations alongside the church began encountering burials. Once encountered they were of course carefully exposed with trowel and brush, and documented with notes and photos in the traditional manner.

At deeper levels (Phase 4) the excavations began encountering tomb superstructures, mostly in the form of brick mastabas, which had later been entirely sanded over. Altogether, 119 superstructures were recorded. When these were removed, however, it was still not possible in most cases to recognize the outlines of the underlying grave shafts, because of the soft sand deposit. It would not in any case have been possible to dig the graves shaft by shaft, in the manner usually followed, because of the probability that the side walls would have collapsed. Instead, the whole cemetery area was scraped down in a series of careful, horizontal clearances, each clearance taking off about 25cm of deposit. Whenever burials were encountered, the *turiya* was laid aside in favor of trowel and brush.

Burials without superstructures were given numbers preceded by the letter B, and those with superstructures were given numbers preceded by T. Whenever a superstructure had been encountered and recorded, and before it was dismantled, a stake with the appropriate tomb number was driven into the ground just to the west of the structure. Then, as the superstructure was dismantled and the excavation proceeded downward, the numbered stake was also driven downward until, at a depth usually of about 120cm below the superstructure, the associated burial was encountered. It was this procedure that made possible the proper identification of the burials associated with each superstructure. The Meinarti cemetery and its contents will be more fully discussed in a later volume (*Meinarti IV*).

Conservation work

Fragmentary painted murals were found in the Meinarti Church and in two other buildings of the Late Christian period. Full-size as well as miniature colored copies were made of all of them by the artist Abdel Rahim Hag el Amin,

who at that time was a member of the Antiquities Service staff. He is shown at work in Plate 2c. Subsequently, all but a few of the paintings were conserved and physically removed by Mr. Jozef Gazy, whose services were kindly loaned by the Polish Expedition at Faras. He is shown at work in Plate 2d. All the conserved paintings are now in the Sudan National Antiquities Museum in Khartoum.

The daily routine

Because the site of Meinarti was fairly close to the town of Wadi Halfa, I "commuted" daily to the dig from our Antiquities Service "town house" in Wadi Halfa rather than renting a dwelling in a nearby village. The advantage of this arrangement was that our Wadi Halfa house had electricity, which meant that jobs like the transcribing of field notes, the inking of maps, and object registration could be carried on at home during the evening hours.

Although work at Meinarti began at 6:00 AM, I usually did not arrive on the site until between 6:30 and 7:00. My first activity then would be to make a complete tour of the excavations, to see how the work was progressing and what had been done during my absence, and often to set out new numbered baskets for sherds and artifact finds. Sometimes I would give specific instructions to the *Qufti* sub-foremen working in particular areas, although for the most part my orders were transmitted entirely through Reis Youssef. Having completed the tour of inspection I would have a general discussion of the day's work with the Reis, and we would agree on priorities and alternative possibilities for upcoming work.

To aid in the supervision of the Meinarti excavations, I had a *rakuba* built just to the north of the excavation area, with an open side facing the excavations (see Pl. 2b). Here, when not actually working on-site, I could keep one eye on the excavations while tracing plans, writing field notes, or registering artifacts. This work was done on either of two large tables, one situated within the *rakuba* and one just in front of it. The latter table was needed for jobs requiring strong sunlight, such as the tracing of maps and the examination of potsherds. Against the back wall of the *rakuba* there were shelves where I kept field notebooks and the tracings of the different levels, as well as various supplies. A small inner room, accessible only from the outer room, was equipped with additional shelves were artifacts were stored until such time as they could be taken to Wadi Halfa. Baskets of accumulated sherds however were too numerous to collect within the *rakuba;* they were piled up against the outside wall, awaiting my examination.

The largest part of my time, nearly every day, was spent in mapping and writing field notes for those houses and areas where excavation had been completed. This work had necessarily to be done within each excavated structure, and I could very often be seen trotting around the site with a plane table balanced on my head, as I moved from one mapping locality to another. As previously noted, all walls and features were plotted originally on a base map; they were subsequently taken off onto tracings when I had determined with certainty which level they belonged to.

Photography was done by choice at times and in places

where there were no men actually working. If I needed any area or feature photographed with a low eastern light, I would have that area cleaned up, and all working instruments removed, just before the break for breakfast at 9:00 AM. This would then leave a half hour free for photography, before the workers returned at 9:30. For photos requiring overhead light, I would have the requisite area cleaned up just before the conclusion of work at 2:00 PM, and would take the pictures just after the men had departed. If a low western light was required I would have to stay on the site, after the conclusion of work, until late afternoon. The intervening hours however could always be spent in sorting and tallying potsherds, or in registering artifacts.

The week's accumulation of photos, which typically amounted to several rolls, was always developed and printed on Fridays, our regular day of respite from the digging. This was a job that could rarely be postponed, because I had learned from unhappy previous experience never to dismantle any feature until I was sure that I had good photos. Under the rather primitive field conditions prevailing in Nubia, it was inevitable that occasional films were spoiled, usually due to overheating or to sand in the camera shutters.

In the intervals of mapping and note writing, I tried to tour the site at least every hour, partly to see how the work was progressing and partly to set out new sherd and artifact baskets, as the previous ones became filled. On these occasions I always took at least a quick glance at the sherds that had been collected at each worksite, to satisfy myself that the crew was indeed working at the proper stratigraphic level. It was also common at other times, while I was mapping or tracing, for the Reis to come and ask me to look at the work in a particular area, to give fresh instructions to a particular crew, or to label new sherd baskets.

Just before the work concluded at 2:00 PM, I would give Reis Youssef instructions for the next morning's work, since I would not be arriving at the start of the workday. Sometimes, as previously noted, I would also stay after working hours to take photos. Very often too I had to stay for some time to sort and tally potsherds—a time-consuming process for which I could rarely find time while the dig was actually in progress.

The major, but unavoidable, deficiency in my operating procedures was that I could not maintain close and continuous supervision over the work going on simultaneously at several different worksites. As a result some teams at times worked more carelessly than they should have, and a good many sherds and some artifacts went uncollected until they turned up on the dumps. A good deal of material was recovered in this latter fashion, because one man was always stationed on each dump to look over the basket contents as they were unloaded.

Logistic support

The proximity of the Meinarti dig to Wadi Halfa, and the fact that I could "commute" daily to the site, made it much easier to bring supplies to and from this dig than to most others. If I was able to run so large an operation single-handed, however, it was also because at Meinarti I en-

joyed a privilege rarely given to dig directors: that of being a full-time archaeologist. All the tasks of buying equipment; of recruiting, transporting, housing, and paying the laborers; of arranging my own transport and housing; and a hundred other annoying chores that consume so much of a director's time, were taken off my hands and superbly managed by the Sudan Antiquities Service, leaving me free for the work that I have detailed in the previous pages. Whatever I asked for in the way of support I got, without question and usually without delay. On subsequent digs, at Kulubnarti and at Qasr Ibrim, I felt lucky if I could devote even 50% of my time to purely professional activities, in the intervals of attending to basic logistic needs. The contribution of the Antiquities Service to the ultimate success of the Meinarti dig cannot be overstated, and I have registered my appreciation in the Preface.

Controls and documentation

Horizontal controls. For both practical and theoretical reasons, I did not lay a mapping grid over the Meinarti site, as I have done on some previous and some subsequent excavations. Since the whole area of the mound, or rather of its southern half, was to be excavated simultaneously, there could be no permanently fixed datum points. It would have been very cumbersome to keep continually repositioning the grid corner markers as the excavations proceeded downward, as well as involving some risk of horizontal displacement. More importantly, however, there is no real justification for the use of arbitrary control points where natural ones, in the form of house and room walls, are available. On this point again I agree with my Glen Canyon colleague, who "...abhorred excavation by grid square and arbitrary level, seeing it as an excuse for not thinking about how best to expose and understand the archaeological record" (Lipe 1997). To record an artifact as coming from "Unit G3, northwest corner, Level 3" conveys no cultural or historical meaning, while to say that it comes from "House XIV, Room 3, Floor 1" provides an immediately meaningful cultural context. Throughout the Meinarti excavations, standing structural features were used as datum points for both mapping and cross-sectioning, and the location of finds was recorded with reference to numbered houses and rooms. This system of documentation was not of course entirely successful for finds made in plazas or street deposits, which were usually recorded only with some such designation as "outside north of House XXV" or "west end of Street C."

Building numbers. All buildings at Meinarti were given Roman numeral designations, usually as soon as their wall tops had been defined. For simplicity of recording, all buildings were labeled as "houses," though some of course were churches, or served other non-domestic purposes. Readers will however discover certain discrepancies in the system of house numbers, resulting from the fact that numbers had to be assigned as soon as the buildings began to appear, in order that the provenience of potsherds and artifacts could be recorded. Since work was often going on simultaneously in several non-contiguous areas, it sometimes happened that separate numbers were assigned to clusters of rooms which afterwards were found to belong to the same building. This was particularly true at Phases 2 and 4, where the principal remains in each case were huge, contiguous room clusters. Because large numbers of sherds and artifacts had already been recorded by the time these junctures were recognized, it was not considered feasible to re-number the houses. The result is that some buildings, particularly in Phases 2 and 4, carry two, three, or even four different numbers in different parts of the building.

The opposite sometimes also happened. That is, room blocks which were assumed to be parts of the same building, and were given a single house number, later proved to belong to separate buildings. Sometimes it was found that two or more once-separate houses had been joined together at a later date by the building of additional rooms, meaning that they could be given a single house number in their latest phase, but had to be given separate numbers at an earlier phase. To take care of this problem, a certain number of houses were re-numbered long after their original discovery, and some were not re-numbered until final maps were drawn after the conclusion of the dig. Therefore, the house numbers appearing on the plan of any one level do not always form a continuous or a logical series. On the published plans (Figures 8-12 and 23-26 in this volume), the outlines of separately numbered houses are indicated by heavy black lines.

Suite numbers. Obviously, the house numbers assigned at Meinarti were first and foremost a heuristic convenience. They reflect the practical and immediate need to record data, not a reasoned, functional analysis of living and working arrangements. Since houses had to be numbered immediately at the time of their discovery, there was no guarantee that each separately designated house would turn out to be a meaningful functional unit. Many "houses" were in fact large, irregular aggregations of rooms that had grown by accretion, with only a limited amount of interconnection between the rooms. After excavation and mapping had been completed, however, it was often possible by careful examination to divide these large clusters into separate suites, each comprising a set of interconnected rooms (usually from three to five rooms) with a single exterior doorway. These are believed to represent functionally meaningful units; in most cases family dwellings. Suites within each house were designated by the capital letters A, B, C, etc.

Suite designation letters and suite boundaries (indicated by dotted lines) can be seen on many of the Meinarti site plans. It has to be emphasized however that this analytical device was applied only after the completion of the excavations. Thus, no potsherd or artifact locations were recorded with reference to any suite, but only with reference to house and room numbers.

Room numbers. During the first excavation season, rooms within each building were given Arabic numeral designation, which in most but not all cases involved a separate number sequence, beginning with 1, for each house. Sherd and artifact locations were then usually recorded separately for each room. Normally, any space enclosed within brick walls was designated as a room, unless it was evident that the walls had not reached to full room height.

However, this latter circumstance could not always be determined with certainty, especially in the case of badly denuded houses. It is possible in a good many cases, and certain in a few, that enclosures which were numbered as "rooms" were actually no more than interior bins.

As in the case of house numbers, readers will discover inconsistencies in the numeration of rooms. It was necessary to assign room numbers as well as house numbers virtually at the moment of first discovery, when only the tops of the walls were showing, in order that any finds in the fill could be recorded. At this point, to keep track of the numbers, I would draw a preliminary sketch plan of each house in my field notes, showing the layout of the rooms. Tags specifying the house and room number would then be attached to the north wall of each room. Since they were numbered simply in the order of discovery, however, the room numbers in any one house do not necessarily follow in a logical geographical order. After further excavation, some apparent "rooms" did not turn out to be separate rooms, with the result that their assigned numbers were discarded. It was also sometimes found that a single late room, dating from the final occupation of a house, had been created by the dismantling of a partition and the combining of two or more earlier rooms. In these cases the earlier rooms were given the same number as the later room, but were distinguished from each other by the letters A, B, C, etc. following the room number.

As previously noted, it was sometimes found that large contiguous clusters of rooms, treated initially as forming a single "house," had actually developed when two or more older houses had grown together. As a result, a common sequence of room numbers was sometimes assigned to what in the beginning were several different houses. At Phase 4, for example, a common sequence of numbers, from 1 to 190, was assigned to all the rooms comprising Houses V, XXI, XXVII, LI, LII, and LIII, which at Subphase 4c had grown together to form one single cluster. In consequence, several of these houses have only high-numbered rooms.

Throughout the first season's excavations at Meinarti, embracing Phases 4, 5, 6, and 7 (Levels 1-7), room numbers were routinely assigned, and the provenience of all sherds and artifacts was recorded with reference to a room as well as to a house and a level number. This practice was resumed at the beginning of the second season, but the scale of the operations, together with the complexity of the remains, soon made it a practical impossibility to keep numbering individual rooms. Sherd and artifact proveniences thereafter were recorded with reference only to house and level numbers, and not to rooms. Room numbers will be found on all the site plans (Figures 8-12 and 23-26 in the present volume), but those for Phases 1 through 3 (Levels 8-18) were assigned after the completion of the excavations, and they do not appear in the field notes.

Directional notations. The directional notations "north," "east," "south," and "west" have been employed in describing the geographical orientation of all Meinarti buildings, in the field records and in this volume. Readers should note however that these directions are calculated with respect to the direction of the river's flow, rather than to the points of the compass. In other words, "north" means Nile north, "east" means Nile east, and so on. The buildings at Meinarti, like nearly all others in Nubia, were oriented parallel to the course of the river. Nile north at Meinarti was about 35 degrees east of magnetic north.

Vertical controls. Because my overriding objective throughout the Meinarti excavations was to assign each building and each artifact to its proper place in the chronological sequence, the most basic unit of control and documentation was the level. It is necessary at this point, and before going further, to consider the bases on which levels were differentiated, for the term is used in a variety of ways by different archaeologists, and in different contexts. My usage throughout the Meinarti dig, and throughout these volumes, does not necessarily conform to that of other archaeologists, and indeed was to some extent idiosyncratic. It was a heuristic necessity dictated by the very large scale and rapid procedure of the excavations.

What is a level? The important point to note at the outset is that the level is, for most archaeologists, the basic unit of vertical control, just as the grid square or house or room is the basic unit of horizontal control. It is, therefore, a heuristic device, devised to suit the needs and/or the preference of the archaeologist. But whatever system of level designation is employed, it must be employed from the start of the excavations, because the location of artifacts and other features must be recorded at the time of finding.

Like all heuristic devices, levels can be designated in any of several ways. Which system is employed may to some extent reflect the archaeologist's habitual preferences, but it will also depend a good deal on the nature of the site, and even more on the way in which it is excavated. Some excavators prefer to employ purely arbitrary levels, measured in terms of a certain increment of centimeters (say, 25-50cm.) below the site surface; this is a common practice where there is no observable natural stratigraphy. Where stratigraphy is present, however, most archaeologists prefer to let levels "define themselves," in terms of observable natural or cultural features.

There are nevertheless many different kinds of stratification which may serve as a basis for the designation of levels. Much depends on the method of excavation that is employed. Excavation that proceeds by vertical trenching or pitting (the so-called Wheeler-Kenyon Method) will reveal a great deal about depositional episodes (burning, midden accumulation, wall collapse, at the like), but much less about architectural features, since walls and floors are cut through without giving much information about their horizontal extent. Consequently, archaeologists who proceed by trenching or pitting generally designate "levels" on the basis of depositional rather than or cultural features. Levels thus designated must of course be identified and numbered separately for each pit or trench, since depositional features are seldom uniform over large areas of a site.

Excavation that proceeds by horizontal stripping rather than by vertical trenching, as at Meinarti, will reveal much more about cultural features (the horizontal extent of buildings, etc.) but less about depositional features. Consequently, levels are likely to be defined on the basis of cultural features: occupation surfaces, building clusters and styles, or even uniformity of sherd content. Levels thus defined are very commonly site-wide, rather than confined to specific areas.

This is nevertheless a more complex matter than it might appear, because different kinds of remains may be stratified in different ways. From bottom to top of the site there will be, predictably, a changing succession of pottery types in the deposits, a superposition of floor surfaces, and a succession of architectural overbuildings, but the three do not necessarily "march to the same beat." There may be a buildup of floor deposits without any changes in the structures surrounding them, and there may also be a rearrangement of walls and doorways without any raising of the floors. Pottery styles of course follow their own, usually region-wide dynamic of change, without any reference to concurrent architectural developments (cf. especially Adams 1979).

Culturally defined levels can thus be designated in at least three ways: on the basis of artifacts (usually potsherds) found in the deposits, on the basis of the superposition of floor surfaces, or on the basis of architectural layering. When, in East Mediterranean site reports, levels are designated as Early Bronze I, Early Bronze II, etc., there is a strong probability that these have been differentiated on the basis of their potsherds and other artefactual content. When levels are given ad hoc numeration with reference to a single site, as with Troy III, IV, and V, it is probable that they have been differentiated on the basis of architectural superposition. Where there are no surviving structures and few artifacts, as in the case of many eastern North American mounds, levels are likely to be differentiated and numbered on the basis of a succession of compacted floor surfaces. The criteria employed for level differentiation will depend partly on the nature of the site, but also on what the archaeologist most wants to record.

However they are designated, the system of levels becomes reified in the same way as do pottery and artifact typologies; it becomes a categorical framework into which all kinds of data must thereafter be fitted. Here lies the archaeologist's problem, because, no matter how the levels are defined, not all of the different kinds of data will fit equally well into them. Levels defined on the basis of pottery types may not accurately reflect the succession of architectural changes, and levels defined on the basis of architecture alone may not coincide with the succession of floors or of refuse deposits.

Levels at Meinarti. At this point, the problem may be considered with reference to the specifics of the Meinarti dig. From the beginning, I wanted to keep vertical control (that is, to record the vertical positioning) of four things: potsherds and artifacts, fill deposits, floor surfaces, and architectural constructions and reconstructions. The system of levels which I designated was intended to do all of those things. Artifact and sherd proveniences were recorded, in terms of a numbered level, on data cards (and subsequently in Tables 9, 10, 12, and 13 in the present report); the stratification of fill deposits was recorded on cross-sections (Figures 5-7 and 22 in the present report); floor surfaces were recorded as a succession of numbered lines on the cross sections; and architectural changes were recorded on a succession of plans, one for each level (Figures 8-12 and 23-26 in the present report). The same set of 18 level designations was employed throughout all these records.

My system of level designations was not, however, developed on the basis of any uniform criteria that I had thought out in advance. Rather, it took shape ad hoc as the excavations proceeded, in response to the practical and immediate necessities of recording. As a result, it was never totally consistent. The practical difficulty, which all archaeologists face, is that the history of a site does not disclose itself in the order of its actual development, but rather in reverse order. Therefore, as a recording necessity, the excavator has to assign level numbers to newly appearing remains long before a level has been fully cleared or defined.

The actual process of level designation at Meinarti can best be illustrated with reference to a specific case: that of the three Levels 14, 15a, and 15b, which collectively comprise Phase 2 of the occupation of the site (described in a later chapter). After the remains of Level 13 had been fully cleared away, and the excavation proceeded downward, the first thing to emerge was of course a new set of wall tops. When these had emerged sufficiently to reveal a building pattern, house numbers and room numbers were assigned, and the horizontal provenience of all sherds and artifacts was then recorded with reference to these numbered units. Vertical proveniences however were simply recorded, a priori, as Level 14. Then, when the uppermost floor surface (i.e. a compacted surface exhibiting a scatter of sherds, charcoal, and other material) had been exposed in each room, the entire complex of buildings was mapped, and was given the designation Level 14 (Figure 25 below). The Level 14 floor levels were also entered on each of the intersecting cross-sections, as shown in Figure 22.[20]

The Level 14 floor levels were next dug through, without at the same time dismantling walls, because it had been well demonstrated by this time that most Meinarti rooms had at least two or three floor levels within the same walls. Sherds and artifacts encountered below the Level 14 floor levels were now given (initially) the designation Level 15. But while most house walls could indeed be followed downward to lower floor levels, some did not extend below the uppermost floors, because they had been late architectural additions. Those walls were consequently dismantled. At the same time however some new wall tops appeared beneath the Level 14 floors; they were the stumps of older walls that had been dismantled in the course of building modifications.

When a new set of floor levels had been reached throughout the site, the whole complex was re-mapped to show the older walls that had been uncovered, and to eliminate the late walls that did not extend below Level 14. The

new plan was designated as that of Level 15 (cf. Figure 23), and the Level 15 floor surfaces were also entered on the cross-sections (cf. Figure 22).

The same procedure was followed again after Level 15 had been fully recorded, but in this instance the amount of change encountered was not very great. Older, mostly original floor surfaces were encountered at no great distance (generally 10 to 25cm) below those of Level 15, and there were only a few new walls to be mapped, and old ones to be deleted. In some parts of the site it was found that there had been no change at all, and no buildup of deposit, at the same time when there was a buildup of floors and a modification of walls in other parts. Under these circumstances, the newly exposed floors and their associated walls were recorded and mapped as Level 15b (cf. Figure 23), and the overlying Level 15 was redesignated as Level 15a. A glance at the two plans (Figures 24 and 23) will confirm that the architectural differences between the two were not large, and a glance at the cross-sections (Figure 22) will show that some floor surfaces were identified as belonging to both Level 15a and Level 15b, in areas where there had been no change. (They are shown on the published cross-sections as Subphase 2b and Subphase 2a levels).

Below Level 15b there was a major "unconformity" in the archaeological record. The vast majority of Level 15b walls did not extend downward to any lower level, while only two houses and a few remnants of others were found to be survivors of a previous occupation (cf. Figures 23 and 12). It seemed clear that there had been a considerable hiatus in the occupation of the site, followed by wholesale rebuilding. As a result it was possible to dismantle and clear away nearly all the building remains from Level 15b, and to begin the process of uncovering and defining Level 16.

In summary, several points should be made. First, since the system of levels was employed to record both the buildup of floors and the modification of walls, it was necessary to designate a new level whenever either new floor levels or a set of architectural modifications was encountered. As a result, a level at Meinarti was not defined exclusively either by deposition or by architecture, but by a combination of the two. Some levels were distinguished from those above and below mainly by architectural changes, and others by depositional buildup. Second, and following logically from the foregoing, levels were not equally different from one another. There were very conspicuous differences between the levels in different major phases (e.g. between Level 14 and Level 13, which belong respectively to occupation Phases 2 and 3), but often only minor differences between levels within the same phase (e.g. especially Levels 15b and 15a, reported here). Third, and for the same reason, not all levels were equally clearly recognizable, especially in cases where walls were denuded and floors poorly defined. This will become clear especially in the discussion of the Phase 3 levels (Levels 13, 12, 11b, and 11a) in the volume *Meinarti II*.

Finally and importantly, level attributions are more accurate when applied to walls and floors than they are when applied to sherds and artifacts. Note that the provenience of sherds and artifacts had to be recorded in most cases

---

[20] On the published cross-sections, however, floor surfaces are identified by phase numbers rather than by level numbers. For the conversion of the numbers see Table 1.

19

before the underlying floor level had come to light, since most were in fill deposit rather than lying on floors. As a result, it was not always clear whether the objects had been deposited at an early or a late stage during the occupation of a room, or even after its abandonment. In this and later reports, I stand with a good deal more confidence behind the level attributions of walls and floors than I do behind the level attributions of sherds and artifacts.

To sum it all up, a Meinarti level is really a rather complex mental construct, embracing several things. As applied to deposits, it designates a layer of material intervening between two numbered floor surfaces, and bearing the number of the underlying surface. As applied to sherds and artifacts, it serves to label everything found within the aforesaid layer. As applied to floors, it designates a set of contiguous occupation surfaces that were in use at one time, which however may have been an interval of long or of short duration. As applied to walls, it designates a complex of walls articulating with the aforesaid floors, including some walls surviving from earlier times and some newly built—not necessarily all at once.

What I have described, in sum, is an ad hoc system of level designation that developed under the exigencies of the Meinarti dig situation, and that represents my best effort at the time to maintain vertical control over several things at once. I do not necessarily recommend this as a model for other archaeologists to follow, and indeed I have not entirely followed it myself in subsequent digs at Kulubnarti (Adams 1994b; Adams and Adams 1998) and Qasr Ibrim (Adams 1996). In neither of those places was it possible to follow occupation surfaces from house to house and from room to room throughout the site, as was the case at Meinarti. Consequently I relied much more on the sherd content of houses and floor deposits, rather than on architectural continuity per se, to determine the contemporaneity or the sequence of structures.[21]

In view of what I have said above, readers should be clear that my usage of the term *level* in this and subsequent volumes on Meinarti is in some sense idiosyncratic, and does not necessarily correspond to the usage of other archaeologists.

The temporal dimension. One may tend to think of a level, like a natural stratum, in purely spatial terms—that is, as having only horizontal and vertical dimensions. However, the foregoing discussion should make it clear that a level has also an implied dimension of time. That is, it embraces an accumulation of deposit buildup and of architectural modifications that took place during an increment of time; specifically, the time since the endpoint of the last previous level. As Table 1 shows, the time increment estimated for most Meinarti levels is between 50 and 200 years.

The length of time estimated for any level is based on two things: the extent of deposit buildup overlying the floors (as shown for example in Figure 22), and the extent of architectural modification that took place. Thus, for example, the increment of time estimated for Level 15b (shown in Figure 23) is only 25 years, because there was only a slight buildup of deposit (shown in Figure 22), and

relatively minor architectural changes (compare Figures 24 and 23) between it and Level 15a. The increment of time estimated for Level 15a is 75 years, because there was more buildup of deposit and more architectural modification, before the beginning of Level 14. The amount and the kinds of architectural modification that took place at the each of the successive Meinarti levels is shown in Table 3.

Throughout the time period assigned to any level, architectural rearrangements and the buildup of deposits were probably taking place more or less continually. A person living at Meinarti during the 75 years or so assigned to Level 15a (*c.* A.D. 500-575) could presumably have mapped the community at every decade, and found a slightly different arrangement of walls each time. But the archaeologist cannot afterward tell, most of the time, in what order the walls were added. He can only map the aggregation of architectural changes at the end of a certain interval of time, just before a new set of floors was installed (marking the beginning of a new level). This in essence is what each of the site plans does. Similarly, the cross-sections show floors that were all in use at one time, but some of them might have remained stable for decades while others were recently established. A level, in sum, encompasses an interval of time during which certain empirically recognizable changes took place, but the site plans and the cross-sections show only what was in existence at or near the end of that period. Consequently, the specific dates that appear on the various plans (Figures 8-12 and 23-26 herein) are in most cases dates near the end of the period in question.

The dating of levels. It will be apparent, from what has been said in foregoing pages, that pottery types did not play a defining role in the designation of levels at Meinarti. They served, at best, as a cross-check on the stratigraphic and architectural evidence. That is, the consistency with which the same types were present and absent at any level served to confirm the contemporaneity of the walls and floors. But If pottery types were not used as a basis for defining levels, they nevertheless played a major role in assigning historical dates to them.

In a few instances there was other evidence, such as inscriptions and the evidence of historically recorded incursions, that could assist in the dating of deposits and structures, but the majority of level dates were calculated on the basis of ceramic evidence alone. And since my calculated dates for pottery types have been revised several times on the basis of subsequent digs, it follows that the estimated dates for the Meinarti levels have also had to be revised. The dates I published in a 1968 book chapter (Adams 1968) were different from those originally announced in the preliminary excavation reports (Adams 1964c and Adams 1965c), and the estimated dates appearing in the present volume are somewhat different again. And as long as excavation continues in Nubia, and new ceramic data comes to light, there will always be a prospect for further revision. The procedures employed in dating will be more fully considered in the concluding pages of this chapter.

Level numbers. The site-wide levels at Meinarti were as-

---

[21] For the methodology see Adams and Adams 1991, 136-9.

signed Arabic numbers, from 1 to 18, in the order of their discovery (i.e. from the top down). The system of numbers however is not wholly consistent; for example, there is no Level 10. When the Early Classic Christian remains of Level 11 (Subphase 3d) were encountered immediately below the Late Classic remains of Level 9 (Subphase 4a), the discrepancy, or unconformity, between the two was so great that I assumed that an intermediate phase between the two must be present somewhere on the site. Accordingly Level 11 was assigned to the newly emerging remains, while Level 10 was reserved for the expected intermediate phase that in fact never emerged. In two cases, at Levels 11 and 15, there were minor architectural changes affecting some parts of the Meinarti village but not others, and in order to document these the two levels were subdivided into a and b phases.

Phases and phase numbers, In this and subsequent volumes, the story of Meinarti is to be told not in stratigraphic but in chronological order; that is, not in the way that it revealed itself to the archaeologist but in the way the community actually developed historically, as nearly as I can reconstruct it. To facilitate such description, the various levels have been correlated with a series of phases, which are numbered from the bottom up (that is, chronologically) rather than from the top down. The complete 1800-year history of the site can quite readily be divided into seven major continua of occupation, each of which began with a wholesale rebuilding and ended with an episode of major destruction and/or of abandonment. These continua have been designated as phases, from Phase 1 (Meroitic) through Phase 7 (Turco-Egyptian).

Within each major phase it has also been possible to recognize from two to four developmental subphases, each corresponding to one of the numbered levels. The subphases within each major phase have been designated by the letters a, b, c, and d, attached to the basic phase number. Although phase numbers rather than level numbers are employed at various times throughout this volume, it is necessary to reiterate that these do not represent field documentation; they were assigned in all cases after the end of the excavations. The vertical controls that appear on all of the Meinarti field records (notes, photos, maps, and artifact registers) are level numbers rather than phase numbers. Tables 1 and 4 show the correspondence of phase designations to level designations.

Both levels and phases were designated purely on the basis of the internal, stratigraphic and architectural evidence at Meinarti. They were not defined in any case by ceramic or artifactual finds. It should not be supposed therefore that they correspond in a close way to the general periods of Nubian cultural history that have previously been designated as Meroitic, Ballaña, Early Christian, Classic Christian, and so on.[22] On the contrary, some major phase changes were evidently the result of purely local events, like the total rebuilding of the community at the beginning of Phase 4, which followed an episode of major flooding in the middle of the Classic Christian pe-

riod. Pottery finds in fact indicate that Phase 1 covered not only the last years of the Meroitic period but also the earliest years of the Ballaña period; Phase 3 covered the Early Christian and part of the Classic Christian period; and Phase 6 covered the Terminal Christian and the early Post-Christian period. The correspondence between Meinarti phases and the Nubian cultural periods is shown in Table 4.

The finds

Altogether, 1507 artefactual finds were registered from the Meinarti excavations. As in all townsite archaeology, the great majority were objects that had been discarded, lost, or accidentally buried, and the largest number were in fragmentary condition. There were, nevertheless, a good many more complete pottery vessels and other artifacts than can usually be expected, thanks mainly to the caches of deliberately buried goods at Level 5, and the numbers of carelessly discarded wine goblets at Levels 14 and 15, mentioned earlier. In addition to registered items, there were 45 large objects of stone—mostly architectural fragments—that were recorded and photographed but were not numbered, since they were eventually left on the site. A complete numerical tabulation of the registered finds is given in Table 5, and the percentage distribution of finds by level and by material is given in Table 6. All the registered finds from Meinarti are now in the Sudan National Antiquities Museum in Khartoum, except for a few items that were loaned to other institutions for study purposes.[23] However, only a small percentage of the finds are on exhibition in Khartoum. (Sudan Museum accession numbers for all objects are listed in the Appendix at the end of the volume.)

It will be obvious from the tabulations that perishable materials of all kinds (wood, leather, basketry, textiles, etc.) were very scarce at Meinarti, due to the moisture that had affected all of the deposits. Three-quarters of all the perishable finds came from the single Level 5 (Subphase 5b). Most were found among the caches of goods that had been deliberately buried at the end of Subphase 5a, and their preservation can be attributed to the fact that those deposits were both underlain and overlain by densely compacted floor surfaces.

In the following paragraphs, finds will be briefly discussed in the order of their frequency of occurrence. It has to be stressed however that the numbers cited here refer to separate registrations and not necessarily to individual items, since several items were sometimes registered under the same number.

Pottery. As can be seen in Tables 5 and 6, pottery vessels and their fragments comprised just over two-thirds of all the registered finds from Meinarti. They were distributed in abundance through all the levels, and were the single most frequently occurring category of material in all of them. The exceptionally high percentage of pottery recorded at Level 5 (Subphase 5b) reflects the several caches

<hr>

[22] For my periodization see Adams 1964c, 241-7. The dates appearing there have however been somewhat revised as a result of later research.

[23] Several Meroitic *ostraca* and one fragmentary offering table were loaned to the late Bryan Haycock at Khartoum University, but after his untimely death they were not found among his effects. Their present whereabouts is unknown.

TABLE 4. CORRESPONDENCE OF MEINARTI PHASES, LEVELS, AND HISTORICAL PERIODS.

Dates, A.D.	Levels	Phases	Ceramic index*	Historical periods	Historical events
1600	2	6b	PC	Post-Christian	
1500	3	6a	TC	Terminal Christian	End of Nubian Christianity, c. 1500
1400	4	5c	LC2	Late Christian 2	Occupation by Beni Ikrima. c. 1367
1300	5	5b	LC1	Late Christian 1	Evacuation of Lower Nubia, 1268
1200	6	5a		Late Christian 1	Invasion by Shams ed-Dawla, 1172-4
1100	7	4c	CC2		
	8	4b		Classic Christian 2	
1000	9	4a			
	11a	3d	CC1b		
900	11b	3c	CC1a	Classic Christian 1	
800	12	3b	EC2	Early Christian 2	
700	13	3a		Early Christian 1	
600	14	2c	EC1		Arab invasions, 642 and 652
	15a	2b	XC2	Transitional	Christianization of Nubia, c. 550
500	15b	2a	XC1		
			X2	Ballaña	
400	16	1c	X1		
	17	1b	MX		
300	18	1a	M2	Meroitic	Fall of Kushite Empire, c. 320
200					

of buried vessels found at that level; the high numbers for Levels 14, 15a, and 15b (collectively Phase 2) are indicative the large quantities of wine goblets that were discarded in Ballaña times. The relatively large numbers at Levels 7-9 (collectively Phase 4) reflect the fact that many very large and attractive sherds were found in the latrine deposits peculiar to that phase. Pottery vessels and their fragments, sometimes including relatively small sherds, were registered if in my judgment they had either display or study value — of if I was asked to register them by Antiquities Service personnel.

As everywhere in Nubia, and at all times, a high percentage of the pottery consisted of undecorated utility vessels, both wheel-thrown and hand-made. A great many vessels of the latter type were found buried in house floors, where they had served both for the storage of small items and, at times, as fireplaces. There is nevertheless a much higher percentage of fine decorated wares than is usually found in Nubian habitation sites, and it is almost wholly a reflection of the large caches of complete vessels found at

Level 5. It is probable in fact that the Meinarti finds, now housed in the Sudan Antiquities Museum, comprise more than one-half of all the decorated pottery from the Classic and Late Christian periods that is to be found anywhere in the world.

Copper, copper-alloy, and brass. At least a few objects of copper and/or copper-alloy were found at every level, and there is some evidence, in the form of wasters, of local copper-founding activity. The special abundance of copper-alloy items at Level 17 is due to the fact that the Meroitic wine press, after abandonment, had been filled with dense refuse which included a great many copper-alloy scraps. By far the most common use of copper-alloy was for small ornaments, but kohl sticks were also fairly common. There were also fragments of several large vessels, and a few complete small ones. Only two or three items could be specifically identified as made of copper or brass rather than of copper-alloy.

Stone is not very meaningful as a functional category, since it includes everything from carnelian beads to slate palettes to sandstone tombstones. Objects of stone occurred in small quantities at every level; the most common were

TABLE 5. TABULATION OF REGISTERED FINDS FROM MEINARTI, BY MATERIAL

					Materials					
Levels	Stone	Pottery	Faience/ceramic	Mud	Glass	Iron	Copper-alloy	Lead	Gold/silver	Leather
Surf.	2	5		1			1	1		
1		7	1					1		
2	1	10		2	1	4				2
3		14				1	1			
4	5	26		3	2	1	4			3
5	7	150	1	6	9	7	13		1	20
6	8	19			1		6			
7	12	59	2	2	3	4	2		2	
8	8	57	2	1	3	4	4			
9	5	41	1	1	3	4	10			1
11a	2	29			2	3	15			
11b	2	6			2	1	2			
12	4	34	1		1	2	8			
13	1	42			1	2	7		2	
14	4	81	8		1	1	2			
15a	15	82	4			5	7			
15b	2	65	4			1	3			
16	8	11	1			3	3			
17	15	41	5			9	18			
18	2	5	1			1				
???	13	190	12	15	7	2	5	1		3
Totals	116	990	43	31	36	56	118	3	5	29

					Materials					
Levels	Horn/ hoof	Bone	Shell	Ivory	Gourd/wood	Fiber/hair	Basketry	Textile	Parchment	Totals
Surf.	1									11
1										9
2										20
3										16
4	1		1					1	2	49
5	4	1	9	1	6	4	4	16		259
6	2	1			1			3		41
7		1						1		88
8				1						80
9				1						67
11a		2	1							54
11b										13
12										50
13		1								56
14										97
15a			1							115
15b				1						76
16										26
17				1						89
18										9
???	2		5	3	1				1	260
Totals	10	5	18	8	8	4	4	22	2	1507

TABLE 6. PERCENTAGE DISTRIBUTION OF MEINARTI FINDS BY LEVEL AND BY MATERIAL

Level	Pct.*	Material**	Pct.*
1	0.7	Pottery	67.0
2	0.6	Copper-alloy, copper	7.8
3	1.3	brass	
4	1.7	Stone	7.7
5	17.2	Iron	3.7
6	2.7	Glass	2.4
7	5.8	Mud	2.0
8	5.3	Leather	1.9
9	4.4	Ceramic	1.5
11a	3.6	Textile	1.5
11b	0.9	Shell	1.2
12	3.3	Horn, hoof	0.6
13	3.7	Wood	
14	6.8	gourd	0.5
15a	7.9	Ivory	0.5
15b	5.4	Gold, silver	T
16	1.7	Lead	T
17	4.3	Bone	T
18	2.0	Fiber	T
???	18.0	Basketry	T
		Parchment	T

* Percentage of all registered artifacts (i.e. n/1507)
** Listed in order of frequency of occurrence

mortars, palettes, weights, and jar stamps, as well as several whole and fragmentary tombstones. In addition to registered objects, there were several large and heavy items of stone that were recorded but subsequently left on the site. They consisted mostly of lintel, jamb, and column fragments, and perforated weights that were probably boat anchors.

Iron occurred in small quantities at nearly every level, but was not abundant in any of them. Nearly all the finds that could be identified were small utilitarian implements such as knives and sickles, plus a number of hoe and *turiya* blades found in the uppermost levels. However, many iron objects were unidentifiable due to their extreme corrosion and/or fragmentary condition.

Glass fragments were found in all levels, but only a few were well enough preserved to merit registration. By far the most common use of glass was for beads, but there were also remains of several small to medium-sized vessels, especially in the Classic and Late Christian levels (Levels 11-4). However it should not be supposed, from the relatively small number of registered artifacts, that glass was scarce at Meinarti. In addition to the registered items there were several hundred small sherds, mostly from the Classic and Late Christian levels, that were bagged according to level and saved as a study collection.

Mud. Objects of unfired clay or mud were found almost entirely in the upper levels (Phases 4-6). They consisted mainly of jar seals, and animal figurines.

Leather. Of the 29 registered items of leather, 20 were found at Level 5 (Subphase 5b). Most were included in the caches of goods that had been deliberately buried at the end of Subphase 5b. However, very few of the items

could be specifically recognized as parts of garments or bags; most were simply scraps or strips. In a few cases the skin could be identified as that of a goat or sheep; in most others the source of the skin was not identified, but was most probably bovine. Two strips of thick hide are evidently crocodile skin, and one extremely thick specimen may be either of elephant or of rhinoceros.

Ceramic is a category including all objects of fired clay other than pottery vessels. By far the most common items were whole and fragmentary female figurines and horse figurines, found exclusively in the Ballaña levels (Phase 2). Ceramic bells were another occasional item, found only in the Ballaña levels. Other items were jar stamps, ostraca, and ground-down potsherds that had been used mainly for spindle whorls.

Textiles. Twenty of the 22 registered items of textile were found in the Late Christian levels (Phase 5), and 16 of these had been included in the buried caches at Subphase 5b. The largest number were brilliantly colored woolen robes or blankets, having stripes or checks in a variety of colors. There were also textile pieces having a solid brown color, a solid blue color, and in one case undyed. All these latter were identified at the time of finding as linen,[24] but this is almost certainly an error. On the basis of comparable finds from Qasr Ibrim (N. Adams 1986) and from Kulubnarti (Adams and Adams 1998, 69-80), an identification as cotton seems much more likely. None of the Meinarti textiles exhibited any surviving traces of sewing.

Shell. Finds of shell were scattered through a number of levels, but again were heavily concentrated at Level 5. Nearly all were spoons, made either from Nile oyster or Nile mussel. Oyster shells had usually been ground smooth around the edges, while most mussel shells were unmodified. One group of seven mussel shells had been bound together with a strand of palm fiber.

Horn. Items of horn that could be securely identified were found only in the Late Christian levels (Phase 5). With a couple of exceptions, they consisted either of funnels, made from cut-off horn tips, or of bracelet fragments. The horns employed in funnels were those of short-horned cattle (*Bos taurus brachyceros*).

Wood and gourd. Even allowing for destruction by moisture, the scarcity of wooden articles from Meinarti is remarkable; they were substantially less common than either textiles or leather, for example. Of the eight registered items, seven came from the Late Christian Levels 6 and 5 (Subphases 5a-b). They consisted of a comb, several fragmentary and two complete vessels, and an apparent implement. The finds also include two small, complete gourd shells, and two gourd fragments with fancy, incised decoration.

Ivory. Fragments of carved ivory were found at several

[24] At the time of the Meinarti excavations, Mrs. Nettie Adams had not yet acquired the expertise in the study of ancient textiles for which she is now widely recognized. We attempted to identify the fiber in each textile specimen by means of a simple burning test, recommended to us by a friend in Khartoum. A small corner of each piece was burned with a match, and the identification of fiber was made on the basis of the smell that ensued. We now know that

24

levels; they consisted of bracelet fragments, a die, a button, a piece of decorative inlay, and some apparent pieces of implements.

Precious metals. The five items of gold and silver found at Meinarti were certainly things that had been accidentally lost or forgotten, rather than discarded. The only example of gold occurred in a small medallion having the repoussé head of a holy figure in sheet gold on one side, and the same design in sheet silver on the opposite, the two being held together with a band of silver around the edge. This item was found in the fill of a grave shaft, about half way down, and had almost certainly fallen in by accident. Other items of silver were a very thin pendant medallion, again bearing the repoussé design of a holy figure, and a small reliquary box. Both were found, together with a large collection of beads, cached in a pot below a house floor. There was also one small ingot of unworked silver.

Lead was found only in the form of bullets, a musket ball, and two cylindrical slugs, all found on the surface or in the Anglo-Egyptian Level 1.

Bone occurred in only five finds, of which one was a finely turned kohl tube, one an implement with incised decoration, and one a disc ground from a crocodile scute. The other two items were polished shafts whose function was unidentifiable.

Fiber. The only registered items in this category were a mass of fine yarn, probably cotton, wound around a conical shuttle, a mass of brown yarn which might be a very decomposed net, and two other masses of hair. The total absence of rope fragments is remarkable, given the abundance of this material at Qasr Ibrim (Adams 1996, 140) and Kulubnarti (Adams and Adams 1998, 50-51).

Basketry. The scarcity of basketry fragments is perhaps the most remarkable of all the absences at Meinarti, even allowing for destruction by capillary moisture. Only four specimens were recorded, comprising one small but complete coiled basket, one fragment of a coiled basket, and two small fragments of plaited mats.

Parchment. The only examples of parchment were uninscribed scraps, one of which may have been a book cover. There were no preserved specimens of paper. *Ostraca* and tombstones were thus the only examples of written material among the Meinarti artifacts.

Curation
In the summer of 1964, when the flooding of Wadi Halfa was imminent, all of the finds from the Unesco Archaeological Survey, including those from Meinarti, were shipped by rail to Khartoum, and deposited in the new Sudan Antiquities Museum which was then under construction. It was there that detailed measurement, recording, photography, and a certain amount of restoration was undertaken. Readers should be aware however that in the 1960s we had no conservation laboratory facilities in Khartoum. Objects of iron and copper-alloy, in particular, could only be photographed and drawn in the corroded condition in which they were found, and they are mostly illustrated as such in the pages that follow.

Except for a few objects loaned to other institutions for study purposes, all the registered objects from Meinarti remain in the Sudan National Antiquities Museum, although only a small number are on display. Sudan Museum accession numbers for all of the objects found in the Meroitic and Ballaña levels are given in the Appendix at the end of this volume.

The records
There is considerable variability both in the quantity and the quality of field records from Meinarti, reflecting both the exigencies of the field situation and the author's personal predilections. I am not much interested in material acquisitions, and in my days as an ethnologist I was always more interested in social relations than in economics or technology. This means that, in archaeology, the architectural remains "speak to me" more than do artifacts. Readers will find therefore that the architectural record from Meinarti is a good deal more complete and precise than is the artifactual record. This is a deficiency that I have many times regretted; particularly since the objects themselves are no longer accessible to me. In this and subsequent volumes I have to describe them entirely on the basis of registry cards and photos, which are often less detailed than I could wish.

Original field notes
When I first began fieldwork in Nubia, I tried keeping excavation records primarily on standardized forms, following a procedure that is usual in North American archaeology.[25] I soon found however that, while the procedure works well enough in the case of burials, standardized forms are entirely inadequate to deal with the complexity and variability of Nubian architectural remains. The various blanks or boxes are simply not large enough to hold all the relevant information, and I found myself writing all over the backs of the forms, and adding many supplementary sheets. Eventually, well before I began work at Meinarti, I abandoned the use of forms in favor of notebooks, using a comprehensive checklist of all the categories of information that I might conceivably be able to observe and record for each house, room, or other feature. A copy of the checklist was pasted in the front of each of my field notebooks. By choice I use 8 x10" "botany" notebooks, having lined paper on the right-hand sheets and a millimeter-grid on the left-hand sheets, since this latter facilitates the drawing of sketch plans. Four such books, each numbering 150 pages, were filled by the Meinarti notes.

The quality and comprehensiveness of my field notes nevertheless varies considerably, depending largely on how much time was available and how much there was to be described. My intention in principle was to write a separate paragraph or more on each room in each house, describing all the floor and wall features as well as conditions of preservation, but there are a good many instances in which I have only summary notes for a whole house, and not for the individual rooms. There are two or three houses for which I have no notes at all, because I felt that

---

[25] Surprisingly, however, it was actually originated by Reisner in the First Archaeological Survey of Nubia. See Rowe 1961, 1380.

everything of importance was captured by the plans and cross-sections. In general, my notes are most complete and comprehensive for Phases 4 and 5 (Levels 9-4), and least so for Phase 2 (Levels 15b-14).

Revised notes

Original field notes, compiled on a day-to-day basis as features emerge, are necessarily full of lacunae as well as a fair number of mistaken ideas and observations. Moreover, the entries for any particular house are apt to be scattered over many pages in a number of disconnected segments, separated by passages describing other houses. It is necessary after excavation to pull together, synthesize, and summarize the original notes for each level and building, and this has been done in the case of all the Meinarti notes. The revised notes, which incorporate also information from the plans and from photos, comprise 483 pages of single-spaced typescript. These notes are available on disc, and may be sent on request to anyone having a scholarly need for them. Application should be made to the author at 957 Wolf Run Road, Lexington, KY 40504, USA, or by e-mail to wadams@pop.uky.edu.

Plans

Plans are without doubt the most complete and most comprehensive aspect of the Meinarti field record, reflecting my belief that, in the case of townsites, they are really "what we are after." Separate plans, showing all floor features as well as walls, were compiled for each of the 18 Meinarti levels, and no wall or floor feature was ever found that was not recorded on one or another of the plans. Given the scope of the operations, however, mapping at the usual scale of 1:50 was out of the question. All levels and buildings were mapped at 1:100 except in the case of the church, which was mapped both at 1:50 (as a separate building) and at 1:100 (as part of the more general, level-wide plans). The plans of Levels 18 through 13 appear in the present volume (Figures 8-12 and 23-26).

Initial mapping, of Levels 1-3, was done mostly by triangulating from a series of fixed datum points along a previously surveyed line. As the excavations proceeded downward, however, it would have been difficult and cumbersome to continually re-position the original datum points. Instead, mapping was done largely by triangulating from previously mapped architectural features, which in most cases were room corners. Such a procedure will of course result in a gradual multiplication of small errors, and in order to correct for this I periodically checked certain points on the map by "shooting" their position from a single fixed datum point just in front of my *rakuba,* using an alidade and stadia rod. It should not be supposed however that the plans appearing in this and subsequent volumes are accurate to the last centimeter, especially since a great many of the walls at Meinarti were far from straight.

In the preparation of site plans, as in other aspects of archaeology, there are certain differences of philosophy to be observed. There are, in effect, "idealist" and "realist" schools of thought. The idealist uses a straight-edged ruler to map walls that were undoubtedly meant to be straight—not because they were actually found that way but because that is what the builder no doubt intended.

The realist at the other extreme insists on showing exactly what was actually found, which means mapping *in situ* every fallen stone and brick. In the case of badly decayed walls, this may produce a plan in which it is hard to recognize the original wall alignments. I have always attempted to steer a middle course between these two extremes; to produce a plan that shows the village as nearly as possible as it would really have looked at the time of occupation. I try to show sagged, buckled, or otherwise irregular walls where I think they actually occurred, but to eliminate anything that seems attributable to post-abandonment decay. As a matter of personal preference I do not use a straight-edge—not because I believe that my hand-drawn lines are more accurate than ruled lines, but simply because they look more "natural" to my eye.

Cross-sections

Vertical mapping of the Meinarti site is in the form of a series of cross-sections along fixed lines. From the beginning of the excavation I maintained one north-south[26] section (B-B'), four east-west sections (G-G', J-J', K-K', and L-L'), and one section running diagonally through the church (F-F'). Section G-G', at the northern edge of the excavated area, was carried down only as far as Level 9, for below that point the remains at the north end of the dig were not excavated. The five other original sections continued to be recorded until the end of the excavations, and therefore show the stratigraphy through all 18 levels of the mound. Beginning at the start of the second season I added two more north-south sections (A-A' and C-C') and one additional east-west section (H-H'); these sections therefore show the stratigraphy only from Level 7 downward. In addition to sections across the full mound, I recorded one section across the "castle-house" at Level 3 (M-M'), two north-south sections across the church only (D-D' and E-E', recorded for Levels 4-13), and two sections across the Meroitic buildings at Level 18 (N-N' and P-P'). All of the cross-sections except D-D', E-E', G-G', and M-M' appear in the present volume (Figs. 5, 6, and 22).

The cross-sections show all of the walls and floors which they intersected, but for the most part they do not show interior features such as bins and fireplaces. Their major insufficiency however is simply in their number. That is, I did not maintain nearly enough cross-sections to intersect every room, although all but one of Meinarti's 60 houses is intersected by at least one cross-section. As a result, there is no recorded level information for a good many rooms, other than what appears in my field notes.

Levels were "shot" in many cases by the use of a level and stadia rod, from a fixed datum point in front of my *rakuba.* That is, they were measured downward from a point about 8 m above the floodplain. But wherever possible, to save time, the levels of floors were determined simply by tape-measuring downward from the tops of previously recorded walls, rather than by the use of surveying instruments. After the completion of excavation, the recorded level information was converted into figures

[26] That is, "north" and "south" with reference to the orientation of the buildings, or in other words "Nile north and south."

measuring upward from the floodplain, as shown in the scale bars accompanying the drawings.

Photographs

Site photographs are, along with plans, the most complete and most satisfactory component of the Meinarti record, since I believe that archaeological reporting must often stand or fall on the photographic record. Altogether 96 complete 36-exposure rolls, representing more than 3,000 individual photos, were taken. Nearly every house is well documented, as are a great many interior details, most tomb superstructures, and most burials. As previously noted, I always made sure that I had good photographs before any remains were dismantled.

The photographs of artifacts, taken in Khartoum subsequent to the dig, are also generally very satisfactory. Like everything else connected with the Meinarti dig, however, the photography of objects had to be carried out under severe constraints of time. To save time, most finds were photographed in groups rather than individually. Moreover they were grouped, for photographic purposes, purely on the basis of their similarities of form or type (knives, awls, palettes, etc.), and without reference to provenience. Consequently, readers will find that many of the plates in this and subsequent volume show objects belonging to more than one phase of occupation.

Artifact records

Artifact records are, by any reckoning, the least satisfactory aspect of the Meinarti documentation. For all of the levels excavated in the first season, I tried to record the provenience of each find by both house and room, though not in any case by an exact location within the room. In the second season, pressed as I was for time, I generally recorded proveniences by house only. My lack of insistence on a more precise recording reflects my belief that, in townsite excavations, horizontal locations are usually not very meaningful, since most items were haphazardly discarded.

Regardless of horizontal provenience, I tried in all cases to record the vertical location (that is, level) for every artifact, believing that this is always meaningful information. Where an attribution to one of the 18 site-wide levels was initially uncertain, the vertical provenience of an object might be recorded originally in terms of *ad hoc* levels assigned to a particular house or room. However, these entries were later converted to correspond to the site-wide system of 18 levels. These are the level allocations appearing in Tables 5 and 6. As I have stated in previous discussion, they are not totally reliable, since at the time when artifacts were registered it was not always clear "what went with what."

It will be noted too, in Tables 5 and 6, that 271 items (representing 18% of all registered finds) are without recorded provenience. Some of these were items brought to me from the dumps, where they had been unintentionally discarded in the baskets of sand. The largest number however are my type collection of sherds, which I registered at the request of the Sudan Antiquities Service, after the dig was over. During excavation, after sorting and counting sherds, I selected a certain number of specimens of each type to form a study collection, but after they had been tallied I did not keep a record of their provenience. Instead they were boxed simply according to type, with the result that, when I came to register them, there was no available provenience information.

At the time of their discovery, artifacts were simply numbered and entered in a register book, which in addition to provenience listed only their material, color, condition (whole or fragmentary), and shelf location. There was no time for full cleaning, or restoration. It was not until after the conclusion of the excavations, and after all of the collections had been removed from Wadi Halfa to Khartoum, that proper curation and a fuller documentation could be undertaken. At that time every object was recorded on a separate register card, giving a brief description and measurements, and in a good many cases a drawing. Nearly every object was also photographed in black and white, and a few were photographed in color. (Color photography in 1964, it should be recalled, was not nearly as advanced or as inexpensive as it is today, and every film had to be sent to England for development.) To save time and expense, however, most smaller objects were photographed in groups rather than individually.

The photographs are perhaps the most satisfactory aspect of the artifact record, and the drawings the least satisfactory, since my artistic talents are somewhat limited. The verbal descriptions are also less detailed, in many cases, than a fully professional curator would have compiled. At the time of their preparation we did not fully realize that the objects themselves would not be accessible to us, when the time came to write up final reports on the Meinarti excavation.[27] Such however is the case, and the discussion of artifactual finds in the present and subsequent volumes is based entirely on the photos and cards.

Sherd tallies

At the time when I began the Meinarti dig, I had just about completed the typology of Meroitic, X-Group, and Christian wares which first appeared in complete form in *Kush* 15 (Adams 1973). All vessels and sherds could therefore be assigned to one of the 102 types that I recognized at that time, and the collection and typological sorting of sherds became one of my principal objectives at Meinarti, in order to determine their proper chronology. I had not yet, however, developed the standardized tally sheets that I have employed on all subsequent digs (see especially Adams 1986, 618-22), and for that reason sherd tallies are another aspect of the Meinarti record that is less than satisfactory. In principle all sherds from all proveniences were supposed to be saved, although some of the *turiya* men were more assiduous than others in this regard. When a sherd basket was filled it was taken to the river, where the contents were washed and then returned to the basket, to await my inspection. I could not often find time to sort and tally sherds while the dig was in progress, which meant that the baskets tended to accumulate until I could

---

[27] This was because we had expected to write up our reports while still resident in the Sudan, but time and events forestalled that possibility.

spare an afternoon to look at them. (The pile of sherds that were eventually examined and tallied, from beginning to end of the dig, is shown in Plate 2e).

Although the Meinarti collection baskets were labeled to identify in each case the house, room, and level from which the contents came, tallies of the different types were recorded only in summary form, for each house and level, in the first season, and only by levels in the second season. Moreover, I made accurate numerical tallies only for the decorated wares. When the number for any ware mounted up into the hundreds, they were simply recorded as "abundant," without being actually counted. This was conspicuously true in the case of the unslipped utility wares, which made up more than 75% of the ceramic total at nearly every level. As a result, I do not have accurate frequency statistics that I can compare with the data from other sites that I have since excavated.[28]

Other records

Paintings. Fragmentary wall paintings were found in the Meinarti Church and in two other buildings, all dating from the Late Christian Phase 5. All were numbered and described in a special register book, and all but the most fragmentary were photographed and were also copied by an artist. The best preserved paintings from two of the buildings were conserved and were physically removed from the walls by Mr. Jozef Gazy; they are now housed in the Sudan National Antiquities Museum in Khartoum.

Mural inscriptions. More than 30 painted and incised inscriptions were found on house walls of the Classic, Late, and Terminal Christian periods (Phases 4-6). Like the paintings these were recorded in a separate register book, and many were photographed. Translations of several of the inscriptions were later provided by Mr. A. F. Shore, then of the British Museum and Prof. G. M. Browne of the University of Illinois.

Potmarks. A great many pottery vessels in the Classic and Late Christian periods (Phases 4 and 5) had scratched owners' graffiti, and a separate register of these was made, including the frequency of occurrence of each. More than 100 designs were recorded, of which the most common were cabalistic monograms on the name MIXAHL.

Burials. A separate burial register book was kept, recording information about each of the 323 graves uncovered. The entries include information about superstructure types and condition, shaft types, body coverings, body positions, age, sex, and condition of the bones. Age and sex information was provided by the three University of Colorado physical anthropologists who supervised the cemetery excavation and examined each of the bodies.[29] Most burials were also photographed.

Diaries. I always keep a daily record of activities on a dig, but I do not use it to record basic archaeological information, as was once common practice in the Nile Valley (cf. Adams 1966a, 159). The diary entries are no more than brief notations of what was done each day, not of what

was found. Their chief interest today is biographical.

Historical records

So far as is currently known, there are no historical records relating to Meinarti before the late medieval period. It seems a virtual certainty however that Meinarti can be identified with the "Island of Michael" mentioned by a number of Arab historians and geographers in the 13th and 14th centuries. Identification is based on the fact that the Island of Michael is specifically placed by several of the authors at the foot of the Second Cataract. It has generally been assumed in fact that the modern name is a corruption of "Mixael-n-arti," which would be "Island of Michael" in medieval Nubian. The Arab records have been of enormous value in interpreting the archaeological finds from the Late Christian periods (Phase 6), but they will be discussed in *Meinarti III* rather than in the present volume.

From archaeology to history:

the interpretation of the record

In the excavation of any stratified *tell* site, the archaeological record reveals itself as a succession of occupation deposits and floor surfaces, each accompanied by a set of associated structures and artifacts. These will be duly recorded on level plans, cross-sections, sherd tallies, artifact registers, and other documents.

The archaeological purist may perhaps be content to leave the matter at that, publishing his plans and cross-sections without attempting to suggest what they mean in culture-historical terms. However, the archaeologist who is also a historian, and for whom excavation is a means to an end rather than an end in itself, will try to reconstruct, from his mostly static records, a narrative picture of what really happened when the community was occupied. If he was forced, as a heuristic necessity, to reduce the evidence of ongoing occupation to a series of static records, his problem now is to get back from statics to dynamics. It is a process of translating archaeological levels into historical phases, as I have defined those terms in earlier pages. The process is likely to be a humbling one, for it will make the archaeologist aware, as nothing else can, of the limitations, the ambiguities, and the arbitrary categorizations in the record as he has documented it.

To begin with, the archaeologist-turned-historian may need to reverse his dynamic perspective. In the excavation of a stratified site it is all too easy to begin thinking of the site as "evolving" downward, because that is what seems to be happening before one's eyes. Level 4 gives way to Level 5 as new walls and new floor surfaces appear, and old ones disappear. Eventually, Level 5 is mapped to show a series of changes from previously mapped Level 4, whereas it actually developed through a series of changes from Level 6—which however has yet to make its appearance to the excavator. What the excavator has actually recorded on each site plan is the end point of a succession of architectural changes, of which he is not yet aware.

---

[28] For explanation of frequency seriation Adams 1986, 626-32.

[29] Drs. George Armelagos, George Ewing, and David Greene.

Second, the archaeologist will have to recognize that what his plans, cross-sections, and artifact registers add up to is not a historical record in any direct sense; that is, it is not a record of ongoing processes. Each of the documents records a fixed point, or a connected series of fixed points, in time and space, but none of them in and of itself is a record of change.

A generation ago, in the heyday of self-proclaimed "New Archaeology," there was a good deal of talk about "processual archaeology." It was asserted that we ought to be studying cultural processes, not cultural history (cf. especially Flannery 1967). The distinction is of course a spurious one: processes, extending over time, are nothing if not history, and history is nothing if not process. More important, however, is the fact that the argument is epistemologically flawed. In archaeology, one cannot study process empirically, because process is motion or change, and the inert objects that make up the archaeological record do not move or change, once they are buried. Process in archaeology is an inference, not an observation: it is an inference of change based on the measurable difference between two or more fixed points. At Meinarti, to get down to specifics, the processes of change that led from Level 15a to Level 14 are *inferred* from the totality of differences between the two levels, as recorded in plans, cross-sections, sherd tallies, and artifact records.

The business of translating levels into phases, then, is quintessentially a matter of inference. As such, it can never be a strictly scientific matter; it involves both imagination and speculation. It should also, obviously, make maximum use of evidence external to the site itself: the recorded evidence of parallel changes in other sites, and their interpretation.

The archaeologist/historian must recognize finally that the evidence meticulously documented in his plans and notes is at best a very incomplete record, even archaeologically. In the case of houses, there were certainly walls built, and later destroyed, such that no trace of them remained for the archaeologist to find. It is sufficient to point out that the houses shown at the outermost limits of all of the Meinarti site plans (Figures 8-12 and 23-26 in this volume) are incomplete as mapped, because they had been partially carried away by flooding long before the time of excavation. In the case of floor surfaces, the surfaces recorded in the cross-sections are only those that were well defined, and that could be related to changes in architecture. In the case of artifacts, what is left (in a townsite) is largely what the inhabitants threw away or accidentally lost, and this does not by any means embrace all of the categories of material culture that were in use.

It is from these fragmentary records, then, that I have attempted to reconstruct the actual history of occupation and of cultural development at Meinarti. My interpretations will be found at the conclusion of each subsequent chapter, in this and the next three volumes. The final volume, *Meinarti V,* will attempt to place the occupation at Meinarti more generally within the context of Nubian cultural history, and that of neighboring areas.

The dating of phases
Phases, no less than levels, are a heuristic device of the author. They constitute, collectively, a system of relative dating: a division of the occupation record into successive periods based on the various kinds of evidence discussed earlier. The assignment of absolute dates to both levels and phases is however a separate and more difficult problem, for it cannot be based strictly on internal or direct evidence. Like the designation of phases, it is largely a matter of inference.

Direct evidence. Of the 1507 registered artifacts from Meinarti, only one not only bore a direct date, but was in its proper, original context. This was the tombstone attached to Tomb 12 in the cemetery. It bore a date equivalent to AD 1045, and it could be assigned with confidence, on stratigraphic grounds, to Level 9.[30] Several other dated tombstones were discovered by us and by previous visitors to Meinarti, but none was found in its original context.[31] Four datable coins were also found, two of Ptolemaic and two of Roman issue, but all were found in substantially later contexts.

Historical plus archaeological evidence. Three historical events, recorded by medieval Arab chroniclers, can be correlated with the archaeological conditions encountered at Meinarti:

In or around the years 1172-1174, the emir Shams ed-Dawla Turan Shah (brother of the famous Salah-ed-Din, or Saladin), invaded Nubia, sacked Qasr Ibrim, and ravaged the country as far south as the Second Cataract (Monneret de Villard 1938, 197; Vantini 1975, 532). This may well account for the temporary abandonment of Meinarti at the end of Phase 4, although the evidence is of course not conclusive.

In the year 1286, the Nubian King Shemamun ordered the complete evacuation of Lower Nubia in the face of a Mamluk invasion (Vantini 1975, 478-9 and 687). Almost certainly, this accounts for the caches of undisturbed goods that were found buried under house floors at Level 5 (Subphase 5b), the inhabitants having hidden them before they fled (Adams 1964c, 236-7). The year 1286 can therefore be taken with some confidence as marking the end of Subphase 5b, although how much time elapsed before the inhabitants returned at Subphase 5c is uncertain.

In or around the year 1366 another Mamluk army attacked the "Island of Michael" in order to drive out the Beni Ikrima nomad raiders, who had previously established themselves there (Vantini 1975, 701). It was almost certainly these Muslim intruders who defaced the murals in the Meinarti Church and in another public building (Adams 1964c, 235), as well as stabling their animals in several of the houses. Meinarti was reoccupied at some point subsequent to their expulsion, but neither the church nor the other decorated building was ever restored to use. The year 1366 can therefore be taken with almost complete confidence as marking the end of Phase 5, though not necessarily the beginning of Phase 6, since there was evidently a considerable hiatus before the community was reoccupied.

[30] 6-K-3/832; see Adams 1965c, 172.
[31] They are enumerated in Adams 1964c, 248.

It might have been supposed that the defacement of murals at Meinarti took place at a time following the final demise of Nubian Christianity, and the establishment of Islam, since this is what apparently happened at other Nubian sites. At Meinarti however such a dating is disproved by the fact that the sanded-up public building, with its defaced murals, was overbuilt by a massive "castle-house" which itself contained Christian inscriptions (Adams 1964c, 232).

Ceramic evidence. In the general absence both of dated material and of historical records, potsherds provided the main evidence for dating the Meinarti phases. As previously noted, all sherds were collected from all levels,[32] and the frequencies of the different decorated wares were tallied. At the time of the dig, however, I had not yet calculated dates for most of the wares with any degree of accuracy. Consequently, the dates that I originally published for the Meinarti levels were little more than educated guesses (Adams 1965c, 150). In subsequent excavations at Kulubnarti, and particularly at Qasr Ibrim with its wealth of independently datable material, I have been able not only to refine the dating of individual wares, but also to recognize what I call index clusters, each representing a unique combination of wares occurring in more or less the same frequencies over a specifiable period of time.[33] At Qasr Ibrim, the index clusters have allowed me to date many deposits, especially from the Ballaña and Early Christian periods, within brackets of no more than 50 years.

The system of index clusters, although developed entirely on the basis of ceramic distributions at Qasr Ibrim, appears to fit fairly well at Meinarti also, in those instances where there is enough recorded sherd frequency data to permit its application.

The calculated ceramic index clusters for each of the Meinarti levels are shown in Table 4. It has to be stressed however that the system of index clusters is more reliable for the chronological ordering of deposits (i.e. relative dating) than it is for absolute dating, since the dates for the various clusters can still only be estimated on the basis of their association with other, datable artifacts or texts.[34]

In default of all other evidence, ceramic counts have provided the sole basis for dating all of the pre-Christian and Early Christian phases at Meinarti (Phases 1-3; Levels 18 to 11a). The system is relatively satisfactory for the later Ballaña and for the Early Christian periods, where the evidence from Meinarti can be correlated with that from numerous other Lower Nubian sites. However, it remains far from satisfactory for the Meroitic period, where I have nothing concrete to guide me in calculating dates. In the excavation of several stratified Meroitic sites in Lower Nubia, including Meinarti, I have never been able to observe any change in the pottery from the earliest to the latest levels, nor enough depth of deposition to suggest a long occupation (see Adams and Nordström 1963, 24-28, and Adams 1964c, 220). Consequently I have

postulated, and continue to postulate, a fairly short occupation for the sites I have dug, covering a period of perhaps no more than two centuries prior to the final disappearance of Meroitic culture. But the date for that disappearance is itself a matter of dispute among scholars; it is uncertain both when the Kushite Empire finally collapsed, and how long after that date (or even before it) Meroitic pottery remained in use, and Meroitic burial ritual persisted, in Lower Nubia.[35] Consequently the dates that I have given for Phase 1 (Levels 18-16) in this volume, are still little more than educated guesses, and they are based wholly on my interpretation of internal evidence from this one site.

It should be reiterated in conclusion that the dates and time estimates appearing in this and subsequent volumes are not always those that I made at the time of excavation, or that appear in the earlier preliminary reports (Adams 1964c, 225; Adams 1965c, 150). They have been revised partly after a more thorough and mature analysis of the archaeological evidence, partly based on historical evidence that was not available to me at the time of the excavations,[36] and partly by using methods of ceramic analysis that I have perfected since the Meinarti dig, especially at Kulubnarti and Qasr Ibrim (Adams 1986, 601-33). They are still, however, far from precise, particularly for the earlier phases of occupation.

Summary

In order that readers may properly understand and evaluate the findings presented in this and subsequent volumes, I have tried here to describe all of the different aspects of the Meinarti excavation, including both its strengths and its weaknesses. The dig remains, so far as I know, unique in the annals of Nile Valley archaeology, involving as it did the total excavation of one contiguous area in a stratified *kom*, from top to bottom. The entire project had to be completed in a period of no more than 18 months, and this required not only a massive effort, in terms of labor, but also a great many compromises with usual archaeological practice.

Some compromises, like the practice of mapping from point to point rather than from a fixed datum line, and the failure to screen the deposits, were justifiable on both theoretical and practical grounds, and resulted in no real sacrifice of data. I would have employed them whether or not there were time constraints, and have continued to do so in later digs. Others, like the failure to maintain close supervision over all the worksites, did result in some loss of data, but they were an unavoidable consequence of the severe shortage of supervisory personnel. Others again, like my failure to make total sherd counts and my failure to record accurately the horizontal provenience of artifacts, particularly in the second season, can be blamed partly on time constraints, but also on my lack of appreciation for the importance of this data.

Insofar as there is any ultimate vindication for my meth-

[32] Except Level 17.
[33] For the methodology see Adams 1986, 627-32.
[34] Pamela Rose, in her unpublished dissertation, has suggested certain revisions in the scheme of index clusters as originally published. See Rose n. d., 152-62.

[35] This issue will be further discussed at the end of the next chapter.
[36] Especially as adduced by Fr. Giovanni Vantini in his invaluable *Oriental Sources Concerning Nubia* (Vantini 1975), pp. 324, 471, 478-479, 487-489, 532, 539, 648-649, 680, 684, 687-688, 701, and 737.

odology at Meinarti, it lies in the fact that I did indeed reach the bottom of the mound, just weeks ahead of the rising water. I have as a result been able to present a somewhat imprecise record of the whole history of the community, rather than a more accurate record of only a part of its history. On this point I am in agreement once again with the methodological precept of my Glen Canyon colleague Jesse Jennings, who contended that "Recovering 90 percent of the data from 10 sites is far better than using the same time and money to recover 99 or 100 percent of the data from one or two sites" (Lipe 1997). The same principle surely applies to the excavation of 10 or more levels, as opposed to one or two levels.

Meinarti was for me very much a learning experience, as indeed has been every other dig of mine. Many of my procedures were developed as I went along, and some at least improved with experience and familiarity with the site. At the same time, some of the gains were canceled out by the incremental increases in the size of the labor force, which obliged me to "cut more and more corners" just to keep abreast of the work. The lessons learned at Meinarti have however been applied in my later digs at Kulubnarti and at Qasr Ibrim, for both of which I have a more precise record than I was able to compile at Meinarti (see Adams 1994b; 1996; and Adams and Adams 1998).

PHASE 1:
THE LATE MEROITIC AND EARLY BALLAÑA OCCUPATION

Phase 1 designates the earliest occupation at Meinarti, beginning perhaps around A.D. 200, and ending perhaps around 425. These dates are however hardly more than rough approximations, based mainly on ceramic evidence. The dates and their probable historical significance will be further discussed at the end of the chapter.

Phase 1 comprises the three Subphases 1a, 1b, and 1c, represented respectively by stratigraphic Levels 18, 17, 16. These were, collectively, among the most poorly preserved remains at Meinarti, covering an area of no more than 1600m² at Level 18, and 1100m² at Levels 17 and 16. A few walls stood as much as 120cm high, but the average height of preserved walls was no more than half that figure. It was clear too that the preserved remains represented only the central and highest portion of a community that had once extended considerably further to the south, east, and west, the outlying portions having been destroyed entirely by flooding.

The remains uncovered at Level 18 were the oldest that had survived at Meinarti, but they did not in all cases represent the original plan of the various buildings. In particular the plan of Building XLVII, as found, shows fairly conclusively that this structure had previously been attacked by floods, and then rebuilt in somewhat haphazard fashion, so that the plan of Level 18 (Fig. 8) shows the rebuilt form and not the original form.

There seems little doubt that Subphases 1a, 1aa, and 1b represent a continuum of occupation, though with temporary interruptions due to flooding of the site. The changes that took place between the three subphases were mainly of a degenerative nature, the result both of flood damage and of a fire in the largest building. The case of Subphase 1c is more problematical, since there was at that time a considerable amount of rebuilding, as well as a notable change in the ceramic complex. The possibility of some hiatus in occupation between Subphases 1b and 1c therefore cannot be wholly ruled out. Subphase 1c is nevertheless included for descriptive purposes as the final stage of Phase 1 because it was not marked by a wholesale rebuilding; most of its preserved structures involved the restoration or the continued use of older buildings. Moreover, Subphase 1c (and therefore Phase 1) seems to have been followed by a general abandonment of the site, perhaps for half a century or more. However, the evidence for this is based more on ceramics than on stratigraphy; it will be considered further at the end of the chapter.

Because of the denuded condition of the remains, it was not easy to maintain accurate stratigraphic controls during the excavation of the Phase 1 levels. This is particularly true as between Subphase 1a (Level 18) and Subphase 1b (Level 17), since the change that took place between the two was almost wholly degenerative, and since much of the intervening deposit was flood-borne. As a result, no effort was made to count sherds separately for the two levels, and the great majority of artifact finds were attributed to Level 17 simply because, at the time of their discovery, Level 18 had not yet been identified.

Subphase 1a (Level 18)

Remains from this earliest level of occupation consisted of four identifiable buildings and remnants of a fifth, covering a total area of about 1600 m². (Figure 8 and Pl. 3a). This was by no means the full original extent of the settlement, for its outer limits at the southern, eastern, and western sides had all been destroyed by flood action, while at the north at least one building extended beyond the limit of the excavated area. The original buildings were constructed on a small accumulation of sand, between 50 and 150cm deep, which overlay the island's alluvial substratum (cf. Figures 5-7). They were all, originally, heavy-walled structures of brick, and at least three of them were "public" or at least non-domestic structures, which may have been built at one time and as an integrated complex. The extent of preservation was variable, but generally poor. All construction was in brick, though the two largest buildings had rough stone foundations. All of the public buildings had a thick, smooth mud plaster, with a pale cream or light yellow wash on both interior and exterior surfaces.

Building XLVIII: the Administration Building (Plate 3)

This was the largest, probably the most important, and certainly the most enigmatic of the Subphase 1a structures. It occupied the northwestern portion of the community, and was separated by a narrow alleyway from Building XLIII to the east, and by a wider street from Building XLVI to the south. It was constructed on slightly higher ground than the neighboring buildings, so that its floors were at a level about 120cm higher than those in Buildings XLIII and XLVI (cf. Figure 7).

The preserved remains were those of an irregularly rectangular building, measuring at least 22m from north[1] to south and 16 m from east to west. The full northern extent is however unknown, since the building extended beyond the limit of the excavated area. The structure was approached from the east by a broad flight of steps leading up to a stone-flagged landing, which gave access in turn to a large square antechamber (Room 14; Pls. 3b and 3c). This was separated from the main building by a stoutly

---

[1] "North" means of course Nile north. The buildings at Meinarti, like nearly all others in Nubia, were oriented parallel to the course of the river rather that to the points of the compass. Nile north at Meinarti was about 35 degrees east of magnetic north.

SECTION N - N'
Through the "Temple"

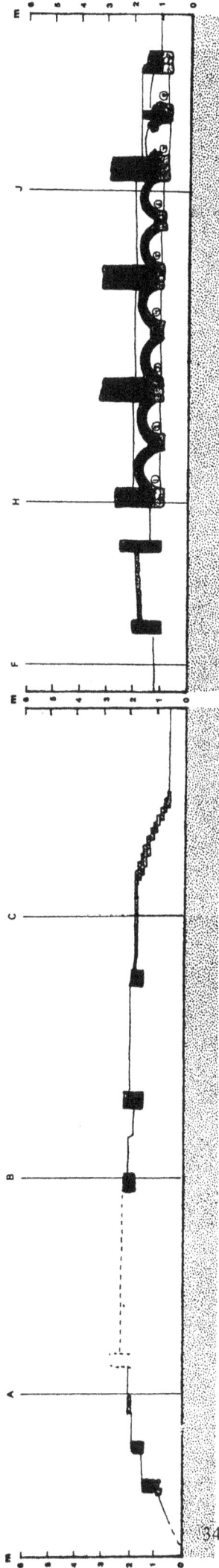

SECTION P - P'
Through the Magazines

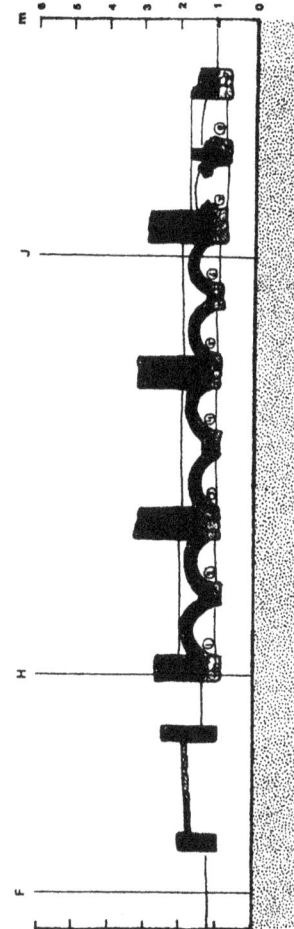

CROSS-SECTIONS THROUGH MEROITIC LEVEL 1a

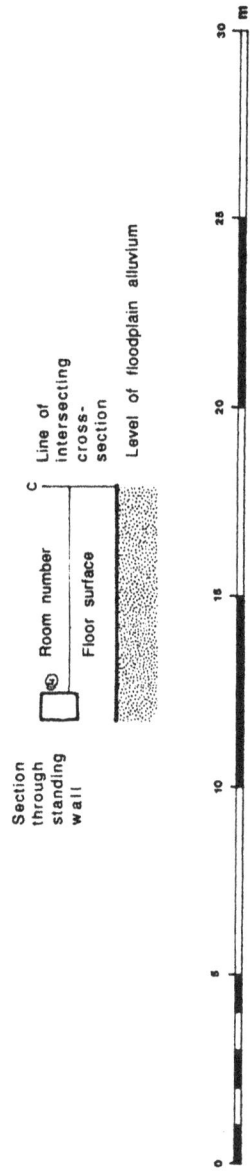

6-K-3 - MEINARTI

Section
through
standing
wall

Room number

Floor surface

Line of
intersecting
cross-
section

Level of floodplain alluvium

34

Figure 7. Cross-sections through Meroitic Buildings XLVIII (the Administration Building) and XLIII (the Market Compound), at Phase 1.

walled gateway, within which there were three steps ascending to the level of the building interior. From the antechamber there was also a narrow passageway (Room 15) leading southward and ending in a flight of steps ; these may have led up to a second storey, or to the roof. In addition to the "monumental" entryway at the east, there was a second doorway to Building XLVIII near the east end of the south wall, opening into Room 13. Whether this was an original feature or was cut through at a later date could not be determined.

Although the excavated portion of Building XLVIII seemed to exhibit a rough bilateral symmetry, there were nevertheless certain anomalies that are not easily explained. The eastern outside wall, from the antechamber northward, was on a line considerably further west than was the southern half of the same wall. Wall thicknesses throughout the building were curiously variable, the eastern outside wall being 65cm thick, the western wall 50cm thick, and the southern wall no less than 1 m thick. Interior partitions were variously 50 and 65cm thick.[2] Floors were at slightly different levels in different parts of the building, as can be seen in Cross-section N-N' (Figure 7). Finally, the entryway at the east side, rather than in line with the long axis of the building, represents a further example of asymmetry.

Interior arrangements in Building XLVIII are very difficult to reconstruct, due to poor preservation. At the conclusion of the Subphase 1a occupation the whole structure was burned and largely destroyed, and the resulting fallen debris must have been mostly carried away, since very little of it was found in situ. What survived were the lowermost courses of the outer room walls, but for the most part only the foundations of the inner walls. These foundations were of an unusual nature: they were clusters of large and roughly shaped sandstone blocks, set in straight rows at intervals of between 100 and 120cm from one another (Pls. 3d and 3e). Since these groups, mostly comprising from 2 to 6 individual stones (Pl. 3e), were uniformly spaced with respect to both the north-south and the east-west axes of the building, the possibility exists that they were foundations for columns rather than for walls. However, in several places where the bases of brick walls were preserved, they were found to rest on exactly similar foundations of spaced blocks. Moreover, in at least some cases the spaces between the stone block groups had been bridged across with unshaped timbers, of which only the charred remnants were preserved.[3]

It is worth noting that there were no sandstone outcrops on the island of Meinarti; the foundation stones must therefore have been carried across the river from a nearby point on the west bank. This perhaps explains why the

builders of Building XLVIII "cut corners" by installing the blocks only at intervals, rather than in continuous rows like the granite foundations of Building XLIII (see below), which could have been quarried on the island.

As nearly as can be determined from the denuded remains, the interior of Building XLVIII seems to have comprised an outer group of fairly large rectangular rooms (Rooms 1-4 and 8-13 on the plan) surrounding an inner cluster of much smaller rooms. Since these latter were mostly preserved only as foundations, and since the foundation blocks were laid in orderly rows along both north-south and east-west lines, it is possible to visualize the major interior walls as running in either of the two directions.

At the south end of Building XLVIII were three rooms (Rooms 11-13), whose floors were at levels about 1 m lower than those in the adjoining rooms. A set of steps (visible at lower left in Plate 3f) descended from a doorway in the north wall into the middle room of the three (Room 12), which was probably though not certainly connected by a doorway with Room 11 to the west of it. It seems probable that these rooms were storage cellars.

Doorways within Building XLVIII were highly variable in width, but none was equipped with a buttress or a rebated jamb, nor were any socket stones found. There is consequently no evidence that pivoting, closing doors were installed anywhere in the building. Fragments of *Uraeus* lintels and sculptured stone jambs (Pl. 12f) found here and there in the fill at higher levels, probably came originally from doorways in this building, since none of the other Meroitic structures at Meinarti were similarly monumental. Alone among all the doorways in the building, the one leading from the antechamber (Room 14) into the adjoining southern passageway (Room 15) had a cut stone threshold as well as the remnants of cut stone jambs preserved *in situ*. Roofs in the large outer rooms of the building may have been brick vaults, while the small inner rooms could have had either vaulted or flat, timbered roofs. The fact that so much burning took place at the end of Subphase 1a argues in favor of timbered rather than brick roofs.

There were no interior features in Building XLVIII that might help to explain its function. Floors throughout the building were of hard-packed mud, the only stone flagging being found on the approach platform outside. A large ceramic oven and the base of a *quseba* (conical mud silo) were found in the northeastern part of the building, close to the east wall, but these might have been installed at a date considerably later than the original construction. The only other floor feature in the building was a large mastaba adjoining the south wall in the large southern Room 8, suggesting the possibility that this was either an audience chamber or, more probably, a waiting room. The mastaba, with a length of 320cm, was considerably longer than the typical sleeping mastabas found in Nubian houses. A large Meroitic painted jar (6-K-3/1212; Pls. 9d-e) buried under the floor of the store Room 12, was the only other floor feature datable to the original construction of the building.

In the original excavation report I suggested that Building XLVIII was a temple (Adams 1965c, 162-3), but I no longer favor this interpretation, in view of the obvious

---

[2] Brick sizes at Levels 18 and 17 were typically 33cm long, 16cm wide, and 9cm thick.

For convenience, walls having a thickness of two stretcher bricks or one header brick are described as 35-cm walls; those with a thickness of one stretcher plus one header brick as 50-cm walls, those with a thickness of two header bricks as 65-cm walls, and those with a thickness of three header bricks as 100-cm walls.

[3] Similar foundations were encountered by Derek Welsby in a building of Kerma age in the Dongola Reach; see Welsby 1997, 88 and 93. Apparently, the Napatan age magazine at Sanam also had such foundations; see Welsby 1996, 130.

asymmetries in the design. At one time also I entertained the possibility that the building might never have been finished, because of the scarcity of fallen building material overlying its floors. However, fragments of a carved *Uraeus* lintel and two stone jambs of Meroitic type were found in the refuse fill elsewhere on the site, and it seems likely that they were installed originally in this building, although they could also have come from some other, unexcavated building. If they came from Building XLVIII, they would presumably not have been made unless or until the building was nearing completion. Finally there is the evidence of burning throughout the building, which, in view of its completeness, appears to have been deliberate. Such an act of destruction would hardly have been considered necessary in an unfinished building.

But if Building XLVIII was not a temple, it surely had some kind of official, probably administrative function. Its closest resemblance is to various Meroitic "palaces," so-called, at Wad ben Naqa (Vercoutter 1962) and Meroe (Garstang 1914, 1-8 and pls. II-III), and especially to recently excavated structures at Jebel Barkal.[4] Conventional usage has labeled these buildings as palaces, but since the word "palace" normally carries a certain residential connotation, I prefer to label Building XLVIII simply as an administration building. I assume that it was the administrative command center for the various activities carried on at Meinarti, and possibly for a larger surrounding area as well.

Building XLIII: the Market Compound (Plate 4)

This large structure, the best preserved of the Subphase 1a buildings, stood immediately to the east of the Administration Building XLVIII, from which it was separated by a narrow alley. The surviving remains were those of two symmetrical rows of rectangular, vaulted rooms, which had faced each other across an open courtyard. The whole comprised a single walled compound, originally entered through two doorways in the north courtyard wall. The more westerly line of rooms, designated as the Western Range, was by far the better preserved of the two (cf. Pls. 4a-4d); indeed most of the eastern rooms were preserved only at the level of their stone foundations (Pl. 4f). Since the floor plan of the eastern room foundations exactly duplicated that of the western rooms, however, it is assumed that the arrangements were basically the same on the two sides of the courtyard. All of the original walls in Building XLIII were 65-cm brick walls,[5] resting on foundations of irregular granite blocks. All of the rooms, like those in the Administration Building, had originally been smoothly plastered with a thin coat of pale cream or yellow wash inside and out. From their size and shape it is presumed that all of the rooms had vaulted ceilings, although no part of these had survived.

The Western Range in Building XLIII consisted of four rooms, all identical in size, arranged in two interconnected pairs. The northern pair, Rooms 1 and 2, were entered from the courtyard through a doorway into Room 2, from

which an interior doorway opened into Room 1. Likewise the two southern rooms were entered from the courtyard through a doorway into Room 3, from which an interior door opened into Room 4. All of these doorways were without rebates, buttresses, or recessed jambs, and none originally had a raised threshold. It is therefore not clear what kind of closure they had, if any. It is presumed, though of course it cannot be demonstrated, that the arrangement of rooms and doors was the same in the Eastern as in the Western Range of rooms. The intervening courtyard was originally devoid of features, although at Subphase 1aa it underwent considerable modification, as described below.

The hard-packed mud floors in the four western rooms were at a level substantially higher than the floor in the courtyard. This was because the floor in each room was underlain by a pair of low, vaulted cellars, 120cm wide and 60cm high, running the full length of the room (Figure 7 and Pls. 4c and 4d). These structures were found fully intact, except in the case of Room 4. Curiously, the cellars were not originally entered from the rooms above; they were entered through low, arched doorways at their eastern ends, from the courtyard outside (visible especially in Plates 4c and 4e). There was no indication as to how these entrances were closed, if they were. At some later date, holes (visible especially in Plate 4d) were rather crudely knocked through the tops of the vaults, allowing direct access from the rooms above, but this appears to have been done at the time of Subphase 1b, when the original entryways were no longer accessible.

All the floors in the western rooms as well as the underlying cellars were devoid of any features that might have identified their function. Fortunately, however, the excavations in the courtyard yielded a complete steelyard scale and parts of three balance-beam scales (Plates 13c-d), which had been buried in mud when the place was ravaged by a flood at the end of Subphase 1aa. These finds suggest fairly convincingly that Building XLIII was a market compound, in which each of the pairs of rooms represented a shop, with storage cellars below the floors. The rooms were presumably for the storage and display of goods, while actual transactions were carried on largely in the courtyard outside.

As the plan (Figure 8) shows, the north wall of Building XLIII extended eastward for almost 7 m beyond the northeast corner of the building, indicating almost certainly the presence of an adjoining structure, of which no trace remained except this one wall.

The Meinarti Market Compound is not exactly duplicated at any other known Meroitic site. The closest parallel is found in the building at Faras which Griffith called the Western Palace (Griffith 1926, 21-2 and pls. XIII-XIV). This was however a considerably larger structure, measuring about 38 m square. It had small rooms ranged around three sides of a courtyard, with a free-standing building in the middle of the courtyard. The size of the individual rooms is however roughly comparable to those at Meinarti, and the fact that Griffith's plan shows no lateral entryway into any of them suggests that they might have been subfloor cellars (ibid., pl. XIII).

---

[4] See Donadoni 1993
[5] See n. 2.

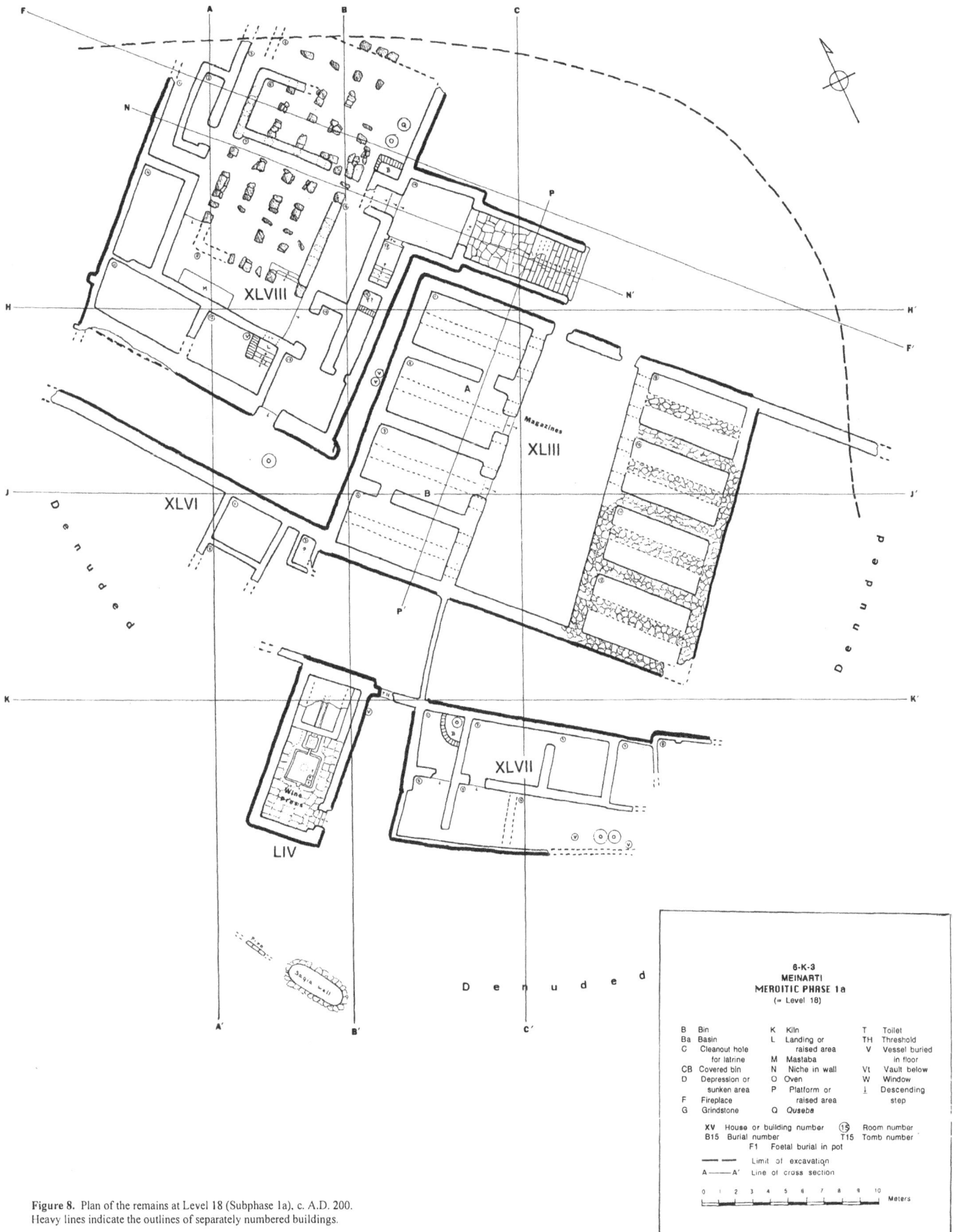

Figure 8. Plan of the remains at Level 18 (Subphase 1a). c. A.D. 200.
Heavy lines indicate the outlines of separately numbered buildings.

Building LIV: the Wine Press (Plate 5)

This one-room structure stood a short distance directly to the south of the Market Compound. As preserved it was a single large room with a stone-flagged floor, having within it three sunken basins lined with red *opus signinum* cement (Figure 9) (see Daremberg and Saglio,

lation, like all the others, was a foot-press of the type illustrated in ancient Egyptian tomb scenes.[7] It consisted of three features: a slightly elevated upper basin with a sloping floor, a small middle basin set into the room floor, and a much larger lower basin, also set into the room floor.

As preserved, Building LIV was a single large, rectan-

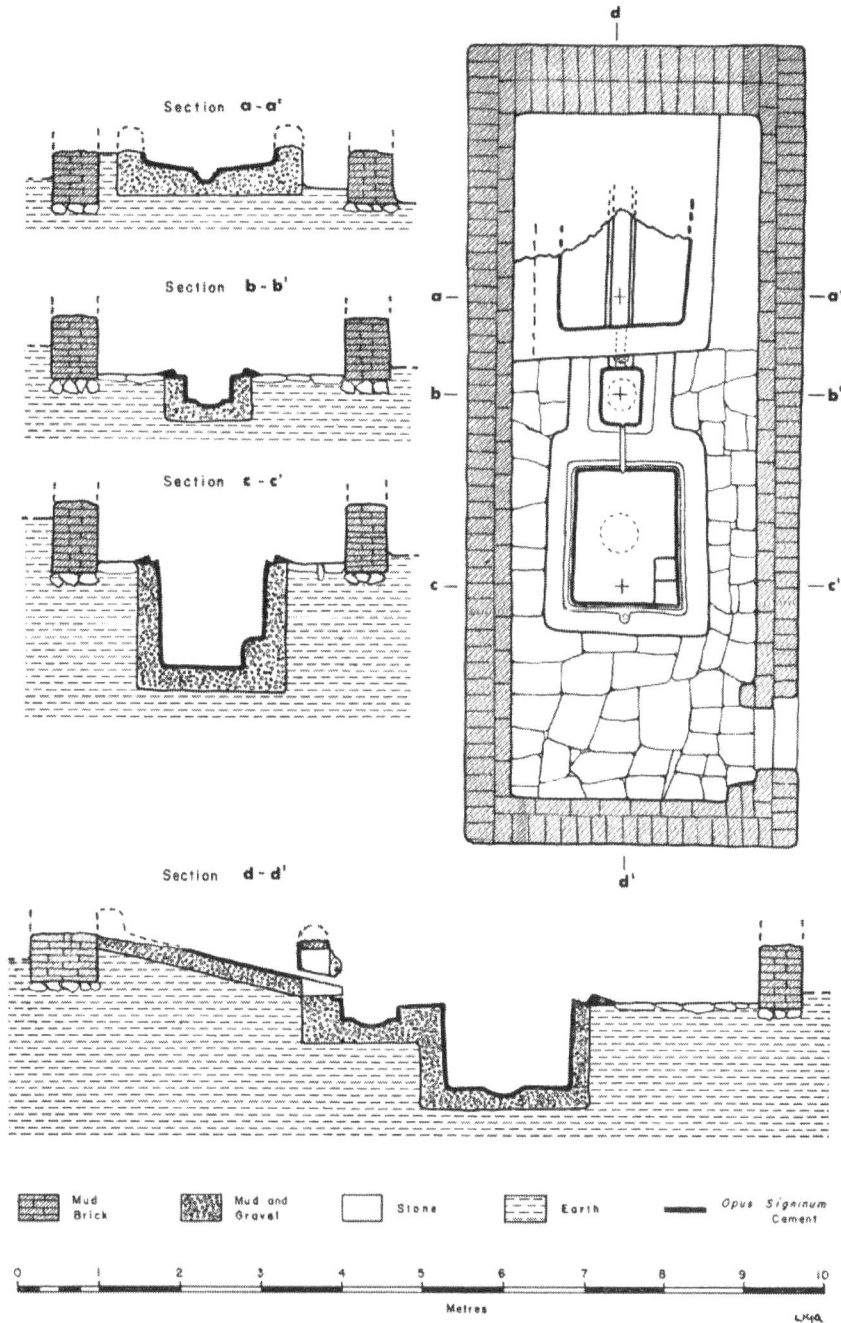

Figure 9. Plan and cross-sections of the Wine Press (Building LIV) at Subphase 1a.

1919, 213). While I suggested in the original excavation report that the basins in Building LIV might have been some kind of public bath (Adams 1965c, 164), subsequent research has demonstrated at least to my satisfaction that they are the remains of a wine press—one of twelve such installations built in Meroitic times between Ikhmindi in the north and Meinarti in the south.[6] The Meinarti instal-

gular room enclosed by a 65-cm wall on the north, and by 50-cm walls on the other three sides. All the walls, like those of the Market Compound, rested on foundations of irregular granite blocks. The walls had a smooth but somewhat uneven mud plaster; they were not whitewashed as were the walls in Buildings XLIII and XLVIII. Entry to the room was by means of a fairly wide doorway at the south end of the east wall (visible at lower right in Plate 5a), from the open space between Buildings LIV and

---

[6] See Adams 1966b, 262-83. My friend and colleague Jean Vercoutter originally identified these structures as gold washing stations of Pharaonic age, and informs me that he still prefers this interpretation. See Vercoutter 1959.

[7] For the numerous references see Adams 1966b, 271.

XLVII. On its northern side, the doorway had a recessed jamb on the outer side, and a small adjoining buttress on the inner side. Within the doorway itself, there were two very narrow ascending steps, from the outside ground surface to the floor in the room.

Approximately the northern two-fifths of the room was occupied by the upper (pressing) basin, which was at a level considerably higher than the rest of the room. The remaining three-fifths of the room had a flagged floor of irregular sandstone slabs, surrounding the middle and lower basins. This floor was found intact except at the northwest corner, where one or more flagstones were missing (Pls. 5a and 5b).

The walls on all sides of the room were preserved to a uniform height of about 50cm, but this was certainly not their full original height. Their upper parts appear to have been deliberately dismantled, along with the upper end of the pressing tank, at the time of Subphase 1b. Whether the walls were ever of full room height, and supported a roof, is nevertheless problematical, given that most of the other Meroitic wine presses were demonstrably open-air affairs (Adams 1966b, 266).

The basins
The pressing apparatus at Meinarti, as in all Meroitic wine presses, consisted of three cement-lined basins in a descending series. At the upper (north) end was the pressing basin, with a floor sloping to the south. The pressed juice flowed from the lower end of this basin through a spout in the wall, then dropped about 40cm into a small, square settling basin. When this was filled, juice flowed through a narrow channel at its south side into the much larger fermentation basin at the south end of the series.

The basins were not constructed of masonry; their walls were formed of very dense coursed adobe, containing a good deal of fine gravel. The inner sides were then faced with 1 to 2cm of *opus signinum* cement, made from burned lime and crushed red brick. The two lower basins (i.e. those below floor level) were evidently made by digging large holes in the underlying sand, laying a thick floor of adobe at the bottom of the holes, then building up the basin side walls with more adobe, after which the area around the outside of the walls was refilled with sand and refuse. Finally, the inner sides of the walls were faced with cement. The upper basin was similarly constructed except that it was not built within a hole in the ground; its floor and side walls were built up of coursed adobe above floor level.

The cement lining of the three basins was naturally a pale pink color, but its surface had been painted a dark maroon in all three basins. In the case of the middle and lower basins, the cement lining covered not only the inner faces but also the tops of their side walls. That is, it formed a kind of flooring, about 20cm wide, extending a short distance away from the rims of the two basins. Beyond its 20-cm limit it was adjoined by the stone flags that made up most of the floor. The lining in the lowermost basin had been damaged by long cracks, and subsequently repaired in several places with additional plaster, as can be seen in Plate 5c. The lining of the upper basin, which had to sustain the weight of the grape-pressers, had been

entirely renewed twice.

The upper (pressing) basin. This basin when complete occupied about the northern 2/5 of the floor area in Building LIV. It was at a level considerably higher than the remainder of the house, so as to allow the pressed juice to flow downward from its floor into the basins below. However, only the southern half of the basin was preserved. When complete it would have had original inside dimensions of about 215cm from north to south, and 160cm from east to west. The basin was enclosed on all sides by its own adobe walls, of which the west and north walls were built directly against the inner faces of the house walls. The east wall however was separated from the east house wall by a passage about 45cm wide. This was a sloping, mud-floored ramp which ascended from the level of the flagged house floor to the level at the top of the pressing basin; evidently it was meant to allow the grape-treaders to gain access to the basin without having to step over a high wall.

The south wall of the upper basin was the wall separating it from the remaining part of the house; it was preserved to a height of about 40cm above the adjoining flagged floor on the south side. The outer (south) face of this wall, as well as that of the east wall, adjoining the sloping ramp, was faced with the same red-painted cement as that used in the inner lining.

The floor in the upper basin had a considerable slope from north to south. The upper end, if fully preserved, would have been at a level about 50cm higher than the lower end. The lower end was itself about 35cm above the level of the neighboring house floor to the south. Additionally, from the east and west walls, the floor sloped downward toward a narrow central channel or gutter, about 20cm wide, which had the same north to south slope as had the adjoining portions of the floor. This served to collect the pressed juice and conduct it to the exit port at the lower end of the basin.

Lion spout. The exit port from the upper basin was a round hole 8cm in diameter in the middle of the south wall, from which juice flowed out of the upper basin and then dropped into the middle basin (Pls 5d and 5e). The hole was carved through the middle of a large, rectangular sandstone block, which extended through the full thickness of the upper basin wall. On its outer (southern) side, the block was carved in the form of a lion head, with the two front paws immediately below. The exit hole was directly under the lion's chin and between the paws. The head and paws projected outward like a spout, for about 15cm beyond the face of the wall, so as to allow the juice to drop directly into the middle basin below, without running down the wall. Lion-head spouts were also present at most of the other known Meroitic wine presses (Adams 1966b, 264-5).

The middle (settling) basin was a small square basin set into the flagged room floor at its north end, directly underneath the lion spout (Pls 5d and 5e). The basin was 65cm long from north to south and 55cm wide, with a depth of 30cm. In the middle of the floor of the basin however was a round concavity that was slightly deeper.

The total drop from the lion spout to the floor of the middle basin was 40cm. The immediate rim of the basin was adjoined by a narrow gutter, formed of cement, and beyond this the cement "skirt" extended outward for another 20cm or so, beyond which it gave way to flagstones. Since in all of the known wine presses there was always a plunge from the pressing basin to the middle basin, it is surmised that the purpose of the middle basin was for the settling out of impurities, possibly including sand and mud from the pressers' feet.

From the midpoint along the southern rim of the middle basin, a short, cement-lined channel led southward for 55cm, and emptied into the large lower basin at the midpoint on its north rim. The channel was about 10cm wide and 10cm deep, and had a very slight projecting lip at the south end, where the juice poured into the lower basin.

The lower (fermentation) basin measured 160cm from north to south and 130cm from east to west, with a depth of 105cm. As in the middle basin, there was a shallow, round concavity in the middle of the bottom. The basin, like those in all other Meroitic wine presses, had two descending steps built into the southeast corner (visible in Plates 5b and 5f); they were covered with the same red cement found on the adjoining walls (see Adams 1966b, 264-5). The top of each step measured approximately 25 x 25cm, and the treads were respectively 20 and 40cm above the floor.

The lower basin, like the middle basin, had a narrow gutter surrounding its rim, with a raised outer edge. In the middle of the south side, however, there was a slight southward projection of the gutter. It is a possibility that the gutter was designed to allow a cover to fit tightly over the tank, and down into the gutter, while the southward projection would allow someone to hook a finger under the edge of the cover, and lift it.

The cement lining of the lower basin, and the fact that it was patched when cracks occurred, indicates conclusively that wine was intended to stand for some time in this tank; it was not merely a place for the filling of amphorae. It seems probable therefore that this was for the fermentation of the wine.[8]

Building LIV was connected to the neighboring Building XLVII by a wall which ran eastward from its northeast corner to the northwest corner of Building XLVII. A doorway in the west end of the connecting wall suggests the probability that the area between the two buildings was itself once fully enclosed, and indeed in the original excavation notes the two were treated as parts of a single building. The two parts however were probably not built at the same time, since the alignment of their north-south walls was not quite the same. The north wall of Building LIV also extended westward for about 3 m beyond the northwest corner of the house, beyond which it was not preserved. Presumably therefore there was another

adjoining structure here, of which nothing survived except this one remnant of wall.

The Meinarti press must have been used for some considerable time, for the upper (pressing) tank had twice been refloored in its entirety, and cracks in the lower (fermentation) basin had also been repaired. By the time of Subphase 1b however the installation had already been abandoned, and the basins filled with refuse.

Building XLVII: the domestic (?) structure (Plate 5f)

This building, at the southern end of the mound, was the most poorly preserved of the four main Meroitic structures, with no wall surviving to a height of over 35cm. (It is visible in the background in Plate 5f). The surviving remains constituted, in all probability, only the northwest corner of the original building, the remainder having been carried away by flooding. A glance at the plan (Figure 8) will show that the building as preserved had three heavy-walled rooms at the northwest, which were adjoined to the south and east by rooms having thinner walls. Almost certainly this does not represent the original plan of the building. It was probably built originally with walls uniformly 50cm thick,[9] but later, after flood damage, was rather haphazardly repaired with walls of thinner masonry. This was a process that was to be repeated again and again in the subsequent history of Meinarti.

The house as preserved included all or parts of six interconnected rooms (Rooms 1-6), plus two others (Rooms 7-8) that may or may not have been interconnected. The three northwestern Rooms 1, 3, and 4 retained all of their original 50-cm walls, while the other rooms had been partially or wholly rebuilt with thinner and more irregular masonry. There was no doorway in the surviving walls to show where the house had been entered from the outside. Floors were apparently of hard mud, though they were not well defined, due to flood damage. The floors in the two southern Rooms 2 and 5 were apparently at a slightly lower level than those in the northern rooms; there was consequently a step down into these rooms from those that adjoined them on the north.

While the original function of Building XLVII could not be determined from its very denuded remains, it was the only Subphase 1a structure that exhibited any domestic features. These included a ceramic oven enclosed within a quarter-round corner bin in Room 1 (visible in Plate 5f), two other ceramic ovens side by side in Room 6, two pottery vessels buried to their rims, also in Room 6, and corner fireplaces (not shown on the plan) in three rooms. These latter, like so many Meroitic fireplaces, consisted of the broken bases of very large pottery vessels, stacked one above another in dense beds of ash.

Other remains at Subphase 1a

In addition to the four buildings just described, there were remnants of a few other structures at Subphase 1a, or at least hints of their former existence. The north wall of Building XLIII (the Market Compound) extended east-

---

[8] Egyptian tomb paintings do not show a lower basin like those in the Nubian presses; they show the wine being collected directly into amphorae as it issued from the lion-head spout (for the references see Adams 1966b, 271). This must mean that in Egypt fermentation took place within the amphorae themselves. The presence of a fermentation tank in the Nubian basins may reflect the absence of suitable amphorae in the southern region.

[9] Walls having a width of one header and one stretcher brick would have a thickness, including mortar, of 49cm; they are here designated for convenience as 50-cm walls.

ward for about 7 m beyond the northeast corner of the compound itself; beyond that point it was not preserved. There is therefore a suggestion of an adjoining structure on the east side of the compound, although nothing survived except this one segment of its north wall. Similarly, the north wall of Building LIV (the Wine Press) extended westward beyond the corner of this building, suggesting again the presence of an adjoining room or rooms.

From the southwest corner of the Market Compound, a very stout (65-cm), straight wall extended westward for no less than 17 m, beyond which it was not preserved. This wall exactly paralleled the southern outside wall of Building XLVIII (the Administration Building), at a distance of 4 m from it. The size and length suggest the probability that this was the northern enclosing wall of another major, probably public building. However, only a few small remnants of rooms adjoined it on the south side; these were designated as Building XLVI.

At a point 7 m to the south of the Wine Press, a small, stone-lined *saqia* well was discovered. It measured 340cm in its long dimension, from northwest to southeast, and 120cm across, and was faced with a masonry of rough granite blocks. The original depth was not determined. Water from the *saqia* apparently fed into a channel comprised of ceramic pipe, of which three sections were found *in situ*, to the northwest of the well. The *saqia* was certainly not needed as a domestic water source; most probably it irrigated a small area of fields at the southwest side of the settlement.

Summary and interpretation of Subphase 1a

The remains of Subphase 1a were those of a complex of mostly large, heavy walled buildings whose function was not domestic. Their stout, straight walls and finely finished surfaces suggest the probability that they were the work of professional builders. The juxtaposition and alignment at least of the Administration Building, the Market Compound, and the largely vanished Building XLVI suggest that they were built at one time and as an integrated complex. Whether or not the Wine Press was part of the same original complex, or was added later, is uncertain. Building XLVII, whose alignment deviated somewhat from that of the other buildings, was probably a later addition. In the original community there may well have been ordinary residences surrounding the public buildings, but no trace of them survived at Level 18.

The general impression is that of an administrative and commercial center, taking advantage of Meinarti's strategic location at the foot of the Second Cataract. Very probably it was developed under the aegis of the Kushite state, and was part of a more general program to reassert and strengthen Kushite sovereignty in Lower Nubia. This issue will be further considered at the end of the chapter.

As I have indicated earlier, there is no secure basis on which to date the beginning of Subphase 1a, which is to say the beginning of the occupation at Meinarti. I have very tentatively fixed the date at A.D. 200, based mainly on the lack of developmental change between the beginning and the end of Subphase 1a, which took place around A.D. 350. This nevertheless must remain conjectural, since Subphase 1a was terminated by a flood that washed away

most of the ceramic and depositional evidence on which such a dating might have been based. The relatively few ceramic finds that can be dated unequivocally to this subphase are purely of Meroitic types, with no admixture of early X-Group wares, and thus appear to belong to Ceramic Index Cluster M2 (see *Introduction* and Adams 1986, 629). This, if reliable, would suggest a terminal date around the middle of the fourth century. However, the ceramic sample is too small to be completely reliable. The pottery finds will be more fully discussed in a later section.

Subphase 1aa

At some time after its original building, at a time designated (for this one building only) as Subphase 1aa, the Market Compound (Building XLIII) underwent certain modifications which are shown in Figure 10 and Plate 4e. The central courtyard was divided by a long north-south wall into separate eastern and western sectors, adjoining respectively the Eastern and Western ranges. At the same time the original eastern door in the north courtyard wall was blocked, while a new door was cut through the south courtyard wall, with the result that the western rooms were reached (as before) only from the north, while the eastern rooms were now reached only from the south.

At least in the case of the western rooms, the area of courtyard in front of each room was further partitioned off by cross-walls, with the result that Rooms 1, 2, 3, and 4 were each adjoined by their own partially enclosed patios, which may have been vending areas (visible in Plate 4e), within the former courtyard. The partitions were only 33cm thick,[10] and it is not at all certain that they ever stood to full room height. Perhaps this partitioning was meant to resolve disputes over market floor space, between neighboring shopkeepers. There was no surviving evidence of similar partitioning in the eastern half of the courtyard, but this might have been due to flood destruction.

Concurrently with the partitioning of the courtyard, one further change was effected, which destroyed the original perfect symmetry of the Market Compound. A doorway was cut directly through from the courtyard into Room 1, which had formerly been entered only from Room 2. The new doorway, unlike all of the original ones, was rebated on the inner side. On its outer side, the doorway was adjoined by a raised stoop and two ascending steps—a construction which effectively blocked the entryway to one of the sub-floor cellars under Room 1. This feature is visible in the right background in Plate 4e.

Subphase 1b (Level 17)

The scanty surviving remains at Level 17 were those of a badly damaged and only partially rebuilt community, which had perhaps lost many of its public functions. Flood action had entirely destroyed the Wine Press, the neighboring Building XLVII, and more than half of the Market Compound, while the Administration Building seems to have been destroyed by fire. To the north of the older buildings, however, there now appeared a group of mostly small and very irregularly constructed rooms, having the typi-

---

[10] i.e. having the width of one header brick.

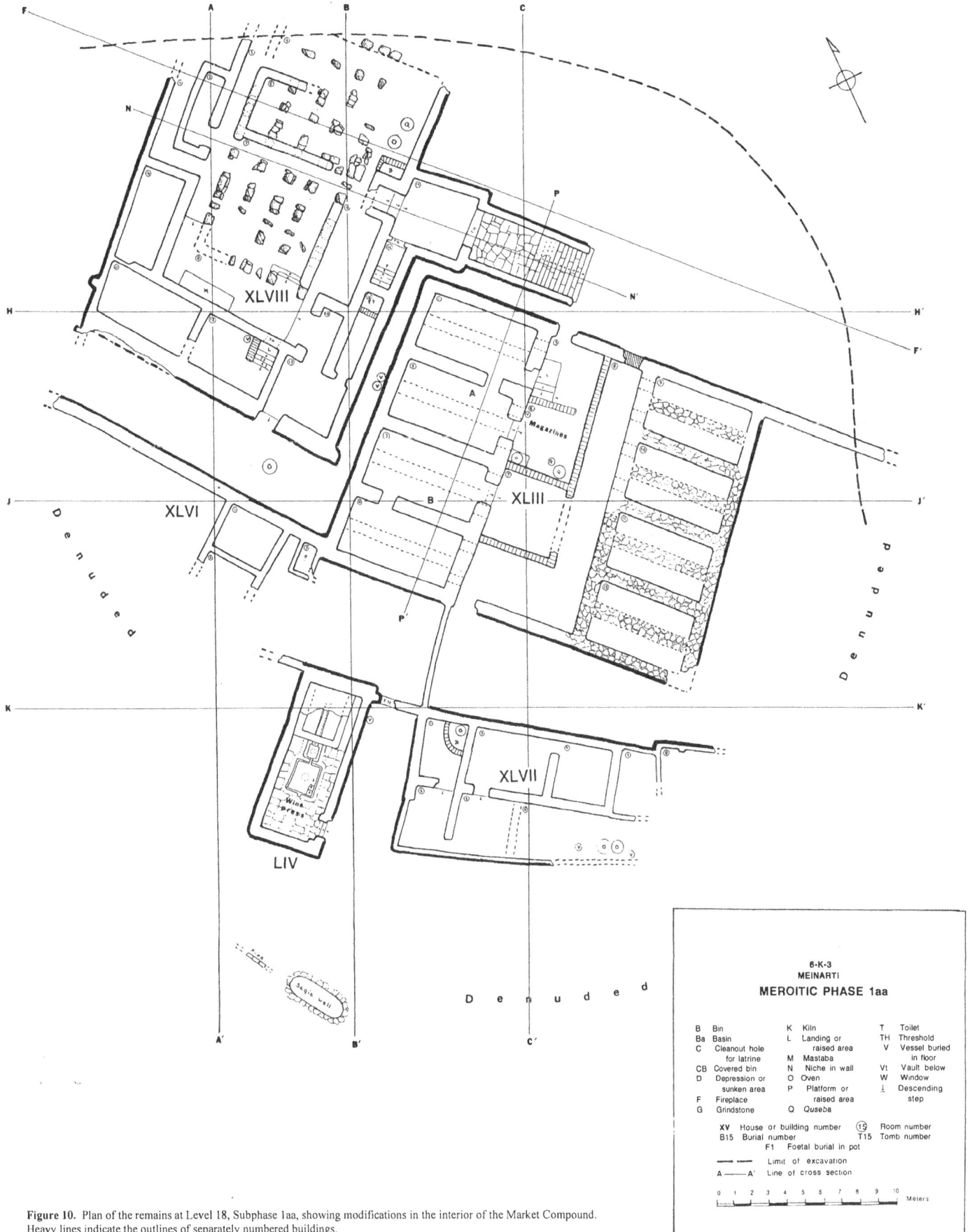

Figure 10. Plan of the remains at Level 18, Subphase 1aa, showing modifications in the interior of the Market Compound. Heavy lines indicate the outlines of separately numbered buildings.

6-K-3
MEINARTI
MEROITIC PHASE 1aa

B	Bin	K	Kiln	T	Toilet
Ba	Basin	L	Landing or	TH	Threshold
C	Cleanout hole		raised area	V	Vessel buried
	for latrine	M	Mastaba		in floor
CB	Covered bin	N	Niche in wall	Vt	Vault below
D	Depression or	O	Oven	W	Window
	sunken area	P	Platform or	⊥	Descending
F	Fireplace		raised area		step
G	Grindstone	Q	Quseba		

XV   House or building number   ⑮   Room number
B15   Burial number   T15   Tomb number
F1   Foetal burial in pot

— — —   Limit of excavation

A ——— A'   Line of cross section

0 1 2 3 4 5 6 7 8 9 10   Meters

cal earmarks of squatter occupation. Nevertheless, they appear to have been the scene of a good deal of manufacturing as well as food preparation activity. The surviving remains covered an area of no more than 1100m² (Fig. 11).

Building XLVIII: the former Administration Building

There can be no doubt that this building was burned at the end of Subphase 1a; by whom and for what reason is unknown. The fire was sufficiently hot so that in places the surviving remnants of brick wall were burned red all the way through. Subsequently, however, it seems that most of the fallen debris was cleared away, after which a part of the former interior area may have become an outdoor working area.

The history of Building XLVIII at Subphase 1b is however difficult to reconstruct from the scanty surviving remains. A new, rather uneven mud floor was established throughout the central area, on top of the stumps and foundations of the original walls, and of a shallow layer of destruction debris that had not been carried away. This seems to have become an outdoor working area in which some activity was carried on that involved a lot of burning, as evidenced by reddened areas and accumulations of ash at various points on the floor. There was at the same time some continued use of rooms at the southeast corner of the building, where some new and irregular partitions were built, several earlier doorways were blocked, and small bins were installed in the floor. These are typically features of domestic architecture at Meinarti, and they suggest that squatters may have taken possession of the still-standing remnant at the southeast corner of Building XLVIII, turning it into a somewhat ramshackle domicile. How it was entered is uncertain, for the original entryways to Building XLVIII, both at the east and at the south, were now blocked by new masonry. At the east side of Building XLVIII, the former stairway and the stone-flagged landing which had provided the principal approach to the building were now largely buried under drifted sand.

Outside the building, the former narrow alley that had separated the Administration Building from the Market Compound was walled off at the southern end, so that it became a cul-de-sac. It seems to have served for a time as a latrine, then more generally as a refuse dump, and finally to have been walled off at the north as well as the south end.

Building XLIII: the Market Compound

Of the four or five original buildings from Subphase 1a, only the northwestern portion of the Market Compound seems to have survived in anything like its original form. Rooms 1 and 2 retained all of their original walls, but both were now subdivided into two rooms by thin interior partitions. There is inferential evidence for the continued use of the vaulted cellars beneath these rooms, in that holes had been knocked through the overlying room floors, giving access to them from above. Presumably this became necessary when the level of refuse accumulation in the adjoining courtyard had reached the point where it blocked the original doorways to the cellars. When found,

however, all of the cellars except the most northerly one were themselves filled with sand and refuse, which must have accumulated in the course of Subphase 1b.

In the case of Room 3, its original eastern wall had been destroyed, and it was rebuilt with thinner masonry at a point considerably to the west of the original location, resulting in a smaller room. The former doorway from Room 3 to Room 4 was blocked, for Room 4 had been wholly destroyed, as had the entire Eastern Range of rooms in Building XLIII. Two new, very narrow rooms (Rooms 4a and 4b) were created within the former area of Room 4, by the building of a thin dividing partition.

When found, the outside doorways to Rooms 1 and 2 were solidly blocked with brick masonry, but this probably was done at the end of the Subphase 1b occupation rather than earlier.

New Buildings XLIX and L

The changes that took place at Subphase 1b were not wholly degenerative. At the north side of the excavated area, where there were no surviving traces of buildings at Subphase 1a, several new structures made their appearance. They were very irregularly shaped, mostly thin-walled structures, built on top of the sand that had been steadily accumulating at the northern side of the settlement, and had buried the more northerly remnants of the Administration Building. The two most complete, and most completely excavated, structures were designated as Buildings XLIX and L, but there were remnants of several others as well.

The functions of these new buildings, which were themselves very denuded, were difficult to interpret. House XLIX consisted of three contiguous thin-walled (16-cm) rooms which were not interconnected, and which contained no interior features. However, the smallest of the rooms had a continuous flooring of mud bricks laid horizontally, while the two other rooms had a very thick flooring of hard mud, 20 to 30cm thick. The inner faces of many walls showed considerable erosion, apparently from the splashing of water that may have been stored here.

House L, adjoining House XLIX on the east, was very irregular in plan. It comprised an interconnected group of three (or possibly four) western rooms having 35-cm walls, and an adjoining group of eastern rooms having mostly 16-cm walls. Almost certainly the building as preserved does not represent the original plan; the thin-walled eastern rooms perhaps were added after flood damage to the original walls. House L contained several ceramic ovens and a granite oil press, but it was also the scene of some activity that involved a great deal of water. Not only were the walls in the western rooms considerably eaten away by splashed water, but there were extensive, irregular deposits of mud on the room floors. It seems clear therefore that neither House XLIX nor House L was an ordinary domicile. On the other hand a detached suite of three rooms (shown on the plan as Suite C) had more nearly the appearance of an ordinary dwelling, although no interior features were preserved.

Summary and interpretation of Subphase 1b

Although the scanty ceramic remains at Subphase 1b were

still of Meroitic types, the state of the architectural remains would seem to signalize the collapse of Kushite authority, at least in this area. Political events obviously cannot be blamed for the flood that so severely damaged the community; on the other hand a still-powerful state would probably have made a more systematic effort to rebuild. The burning of the administration building is, moreover, a fairly convincing evidence of the fall of the state. At the same time I do not see this as evidence of an "X-Group invasion"—something against which I have repeatedly argued in earlier writings (e.g. Adams 1965b, 163-9; Adams 1967, 12-13; Adams 1977, 391-2). I think it represents simply an act of repudiation, by independent-minded locals, of an imperial yoke that was never congenial.

Though its administrative function was clearly gone, Meinarti may still have hummed with commercial activity, now in the hands of private entrepreneurs. Certainly it hummed with some kind of activity, for nearly all of the preserved remains at Subphase 1b were those of activity areas of one sort and another. The community was still not, at this time, the ordinary farming village that it later became.

Ceramic finds from Level 17 (Subphase 1b) fall quite clearly into Index Cluster MX, involving a mixture of Meroitic and X-Group wares (see *Introduction*). At Qasr Ibrim, this cluster was dated, approximately, at A.D. 350-400 (see Adams 1986, 629), and the fifty-year time span thus suggested would not be inappropriate for the remains at Level 17. The pottery finds will be much more fully discussed in a later section.

Subphase 1c (Level 16)

The surviving remains at Level 16 suggest a kind of small-scale, and perhaps short-lived, renaissance. The Market Compound was restored to something approximating its original form, and two stout new residential buildings were added at the south side of the community, directly overlying the sanded-up remains of the old Wine Press and the neighboring Building XLVII (Figure 12 and Pl. 6b). The remains were generally better preserved than in the two previous subphases, at least in their vertical dimension, with some walls in the newly built House XXXIV standing to a height of 160cm. However, the remains once again covered an area of no more than 1100m². The pottery found at this level was mainly of early "X-Group" (Ballaña) rather than of Meroitic types, opening the possibility that there may have been some hiatus in time between the Subphase 1b and 1c occupations. However, this is very far from a certainty.

Buildings XLIII and XLIV: the Market Compound
The former area of the old Meroitic Market Compound was now occupied by two separately designated houses, which faced each other across a broad street or a small plaza. Access to this was however limited both at the north and south ends, and the two houses, together with the plaza, can again be viewed as forming a single walled compound. The rooms on the west side of the street largely retained the plan of the old Western Range (as it had ex-

isted at Subphase 1b), and for that reason they are still designated at this subphase as Building XLIII. The rooms on the eastern side however did not retain the plan of the underlying Eastern Range (which had been wholly abandoned at Subphase 1b), and for that reason they were given a separate designation, as House XLIV.

Building XLIII. In the original Western Range of the Market Compound, Rooms 1, 2, and 3 remained in use, or more probably were restored to use, at Subphase 1c. They were the only components of the original, Subphase 1a building that survived in anything like their original form at Subphase 1c All the rooms however underwent some remodeling, as their walls were built upward upon the stumps of the earlier walls. The new masonry exhibited a great deal of variability from room to room. Generally speaking the new walls were thinner than the stumps that they rested upon, but the wall separating Rooms 1 and 2 was made thicker than the original. The east wall of Rooms 1 and 2 was entirely rebuilt, on an alignment slightly different from the original, and the more southerly part of it was rebuilt in rough stone rather than in brick masonry. It was almost the only occurrence of stone masonry in the entire Meinarti site. None of the three rooms were interconnected, as the former doorway between Rooms 1 and 2 was sealed up.

As before, Rooms 1, 2, and 3 all had doorways opening eastward, into the central street or plaza. However, Room 1 now also had two new outside doors, respectively in the north and west walls. Drifted sand by this time had accumulated around the outside of the building to such an extent that in the north doorway there were three descending steps from the outside street level to the floor level in Room 1, and in the west doorway there were two descending steps. There were no interior features which might suggest whether these rooms did or did not retain their original commercial function.

House XLIV. To the east of Building XLIII, an entirely new set of rooms (visible in the background in Plate 6a) was built upon the denuded remains that had once been the Eastern Range of the Market Compound. Although the new rooms mostly occupied the same area as the old Eastern Range, they did not retain any part of its original plan, and only in a few places were they built up on the foundations of the older walls. Here again, as in rebuilt Building XLIII, the masonry was highly irregular, with 16-cm walls, 35-cm walls, and 50-cm walls combining in a not very coherent fashion. The complex gave the appearance of having grown by accretion, the eastern Rooms 15, 17, and 18, with their fairly straight walls, having been built first, and the western Rooms 13 and 14, with their thin and curving walls, added later. This could explain why the west wall of Room 15 was breached by two small windows that only opened into the adjoining Room 14, but that probably originally opened onto the street outside.

Unlike the rooms in Building XLIII, those in House XLIV resolved themselves quite evidently into two suites of interconnected rooms, Suites C and D, each of which was probably a family residence. Interior features included a mastaba and several pots buried up to their rims in the

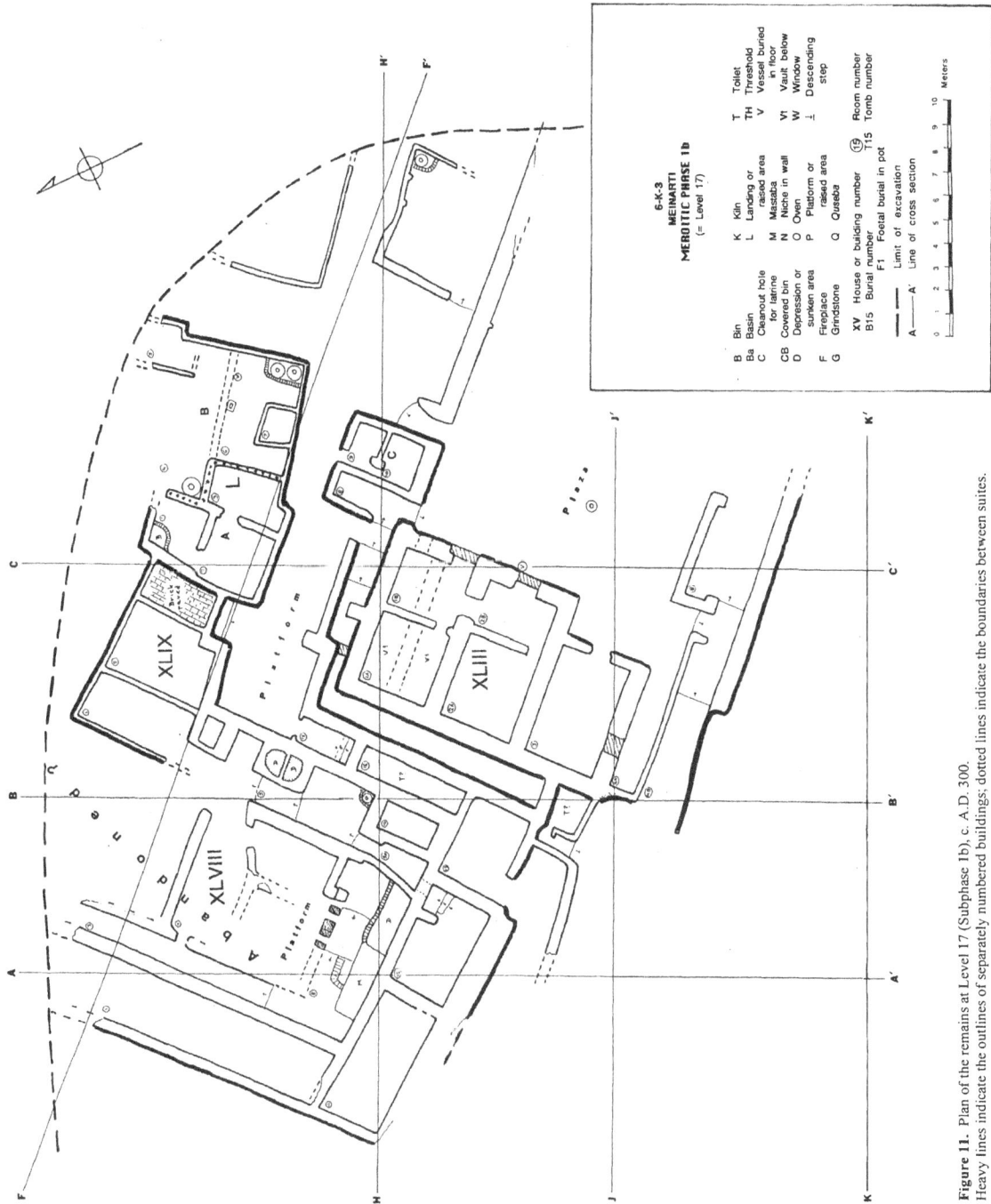

Figure 11. Plan of the remains at Level 17 (Subphase 1b), c. A.D. 300.
Heavy lines indicate the outlines of separately numbered buildings; dotted lines indicate the boundaries between suites.

floors—typical features of Nubian domestic architecture at all times. Adjoining the more northerly Suite C, but not interconnected with it, was a single room (Room 16) enclosed only on three sides, and having a brick-paved floor. The function of this feature is unknown.

Central street area. The area between Houses XLIII and XLIV was a kind of open street or a small plaza, but it was partially walled off both at the north and at the south, so that access was limited. It therefore functioned as a kind of courtyard between the two houses, much as had the original courtyard in the Market Compound. The area of the street or plaza was encroached upon at several places by structures, which were not properly part of either Building XLIII or House XLIV. At the northwest corner, adjoining the outside wall of Building XLIII, there was a small quarter-round bin or room (Room 5 on the plan), containing the base of a *quseba*. The whole southern end of the plaza was partitioned off to form a separate three-room residential suite of irregular shape. It was designated for convenience as Suite D of Building XLIII, but in fact was not connected with the other suites in that house. There were also traces of masonry encroaching on the middle part of the street, but not enough was preserved to allow the reconstruction of a room or rooms.

Complex XLII (Plates 6c and 6d)
The restored Market Compound was adjoined, all along its southern side, by the newly built Complex XLII. This consisted of two units: a square, three-room house (designated as Suite A) at the west, and a large walled courtyard (Suite B) adjoining it to the east. Unlike the rebuilt Market Compound, these buildings had stout, straight walls, and were probably the work of professional builders. All of the house walls, and the exterior courtyard walls on the east, west, and south, were 40cm thick. Most of the north courtyard wall however was 75cm thick, as it was built upward upon the stump of the original south wall of the Market Compound. Interior partitions in the courtyard were 20-cm walls, formed of stretcher bricks only.[11] Most of the walls in the house were preserved to a height of between 80 and 120cm, as was the north courtyard wall. The other courtyard walls, including the interior partitions, were much more denuded, surviving in most places to a height of between 30 and 40cm. The house walls were very smoothly plastered, but were not whitewashed.

The house (Suite A) was an almost perfectly square building, measuring 7 m on a side (Pl. 6c). It was entered from the adjoining courtyard (Suite B) through a wide doorway at the south end of its east wall. The doorway had recessed jambs on the outer side, and was equipped with a cut stone threshold. There were two steps down from the floor level in the courtyard to that within the house.

[11] The typical brick size in the Ballaña and Early Christian periods was 36 x 18 x 9cm. For convenience, and allowing for the thickness of plaster, walls having the thickness of a single stretcher brick are described as 20-cm walls; those with the thickness of two stretcher bricks or one header brick are described as 40-cm walls; those with a thickness of one stretcher plus one header brick as 55-cm walls; and those with a thickness of two header bricks as 70-cm walls.

Floors were at the same level throughout the house, and were of smooth, wet-laid mud.

The outside doorway led into the very large front Room 3, which occupied slightly more than half the total floor area of the house. This room had buttresses, 40cm square, adjoining the middles of both the east and the north wall, and had also a free-standing, 40-cm pilaster in the center of the floor. These features suggest the probability that the house, or at least this room, had a flat, timbered ceiling. The central pilaster, found very commonly in large rooms at Meinarti, was necessary to support a master ceiling beam, because palm logs (the only timber available) were not strong enough to span a wide room. A handmade pot was buried in the floor at the base of the north wall, but Room 3 was otherwise devoid of features.

From Room 3, a doorway at the north end of the west wall opened into Room 1, which occupied the northwest corner of the house. Another rather narrow doorway, in the south wall of this room, opened in turn into Room 2. Both interior doorways were adjoined by buttresses on their inner sides, suggesting the probability that they were equipped with closing doors. The floors of Rooms 1 and 2 were featureless, but the northeast corner of Room 2 was occupied by a short, steep flight of three steps, enclosed behind a 20-cm retaining wall (shown in Plate 6c). The height of each riser was about 35cm, and the two upper treads were each 60cm wide, while the lowermost was 30cm wide.

It is difficult to suggest any function for the stairway except to provide access to a second storey or to the roof. Since the level of the top step was only about one meter above the floor, however, while the roof would probably have been another meter above that, it seems that a ladder or rope would have been necessary to climb above the level reached by the stairs. It is noteworthy that, at Subphase 2a, House XLII was equipped with a broad outside stairway which ascended to the full height of the south wall; presumably this was meant to simplify the access to the second storey or to the roof.

The courtyard (Suite B, visible in the background in Plate 6d) was almost certainly built concurrently with the house (Suite A), since a single doorway gave access to both. The doorway, which was not rebated, was at the extreme south end of the west wall, just alongside the south house wall. A short section of wing wall, on the north side of the doorway, provided a kind of baffle wall for the house door, which was just to the north. There was a single step up from the outside ground level to the floor level within the courtyard. The floor surfaces throughout the courtyard were mostly rather soft and poorly defined, in contrast to the hard mud floors within the house.

Most of the courtyard (Room 7) was an open area, within which there was a good deal of evidence of fires and cooking. A very large, round ceramic oven was situated in the northeast corner, and a somewhat smaller oven was located further to the south, along the base of the east wall. The whole southeastern portion of the courtyard seems to have been occupied by a slightly raised platform or dais, enclosed by a brick wall, although this was very poorly preserved. At the north side of the courtyard, two large rooms of about equal size (Rooms 4 and 5) were partitioned off by thin (20-cm) walls. These structures were probably roofed. The more westerly Room 4 was entered from the open area through a doorway in the west end of its south wall. Room 5 however had no lateral entrance, and can only have been accessed from above. In later centuries, "strongrooms" without lateral entrances were to become a regular feature of Meinarti architecture, but this was the only instance of such a feature at Phase 1. Room 5 had a hand-made pot buried to the rim in its northwest corner.

It seems likely that House XLII was the residence of an important functionary—most probably an entrepreneur of some kind—while the courtyard was the scene of commercial and/or manufacturing activity carried out under his supervision. However, it might also have been a storage area for goods in transit.

House XXXIV

House XXXIV, another new building, was the best preserved structure from Subphase 1c. It stood just to the west of House XLII, from which it was separated by a narrow passage. The two houses were nearly identical in size and in plan, but House XXXIV was built throughout with heavier (55-cm) walls (Pls. 6b, 6e and 6f). The house was smoothly plastered throughout, and was apparently whitewashed. The walls were preserved to a sufficient height to show unmistakably that the building had vaulted ceilings, whose springings were 140cm above the level of the original floor. However, there was no trace of a stairway to suggest the presence of a second floor. Unlike its neighbor, House XXXIV was never adjoined by a courtyard; at Subphase 1c it was a completely free-standing structure.

House XXXIV, like House XLII, was entered through a doorway at the south end of its east wall, which is to say on the side farthest from the prevailing wind direction. The doorway had slightly recessed jambs on the outer side, but there was no raised threshold. The smooth, hard mud floors throughout the house were at the same level as that of the ground outside. The outside doorway led into the large Room 3, which occupied slightly more than half the total area of the building. This room was entirely featureless; it had no wall buttresses or central pilaster like those found in House XLII. The explanation for their lack undoubtedly lies in the fact that this house had vaulted rather than timbered ceilings, so that interior supports for the roof were unnecessary.

A door in the north end of the west wall of Room 3 opened into Room 1, and a door in the south wall of that room led in turn into Room 2, exactly as in House XLII. Both the interior doors were buttressed on their inner sides. There were no floor features in any of the rooms, but Rooms 1 and 2 both had arched niches in their east walls, at a level about 1 m above the floor. The niches in each case were 45cm wide and 40cm deep. Presumably they were meant for lamps, although no evidence of burning or oil-staining was noted on the adjacent walls.

The quality of construction, notably including the vaulted roof, indicates that this house was the work of professional builders. Presumably it, like House XLII, was the residence of someone important, although in this case there was nothing to indicate what role that individual might have played. The house was to have a very long history, extending through the whole of Phase 2 and even into the beginning of Phase 3, although it may in the end have been no more than a refuse dump.

Other remains at Subphase 1c

There were remnants of several 20-cm walls adjoining the east side of the Complex XLII courtyard, indicating the presence of one or more additional structures here. One room had a pot buried to the rim in the floor. However, not enough survived to permit designation of an additional house.

At the north end of the excavated area, there were surviving remnants of the two Houses XLIX and L, built originally at Subphase 1b. Both however had had their interior partitions very substantially rearranged, almost entirely with 20-cm masonry. One small room in House L (Room 1) had in the center a brick enclosure containing no fewer than four ceramic ovens.

Summary and interpretation of Subphase 1c

The principal surviving remains at Subphase 1c were those of the partially restored Market Compound, and of two new, stoutly built houses to the south of it, one of which was adjoined by a large walled courtyard. Adjoining and to the north of these were remnants of other, flimsier buildings that may have been ordinary peasant domiciles. The two stout houses were not typical of either Meroitic or Ballaña sites in Lower Nubia, but a few similar examples have been found in other Meroitic sites,[12] as well as in the Ballaña levels at Qasr Ibrim (cf. Plumley and Adams 1974, 214-25). In several of these places they stood cheek-by-jowl with much flimsier houses, and they are believed therefore to represent the homes of a ruling upper class (cf. Adams 1977, 356-7). Their presence at Meinarti suggests the probability that the island was now home to two prominent individuals, at least one of whom was apparently engaged in commercial activity. Very possibly Meinarti at this time had regained some of its former importance as a commercial entrepôt, for cargoes destined for upriver trade.

The rather limited ceramic finds from Level 16 (Subphase 1c) seem to belong quite clearly to Index Cluster X1, consisting entirely of early X-Group wares, with no admixture of Meroitic wares (see *Introduction* and Adams 1977, 629). This cluster corresponds to the Early Phase of X-Group ceramics, as defined by Rose (n.d.). At Qasr Ibrim, the beginning date for the cluster was estimated at A.D. 400, and this appears consistent with the evidence from Meinarti. That is, it furnishes a satisfactory starting date for Subphase 1c.

Nevertheless, the occupation of Meinarti at Subphase 1c did not by any means continue through the full time

---

[12] e.g. Wadi el-Arab, Karanòg, Arminna, and ash-Shaukan. See Emery and Kirwan 1935, pl. 17; Woolley, 1911, pls. 26-29; Trigger 1967, fig. 23; Jacquet 1971, 121-31.

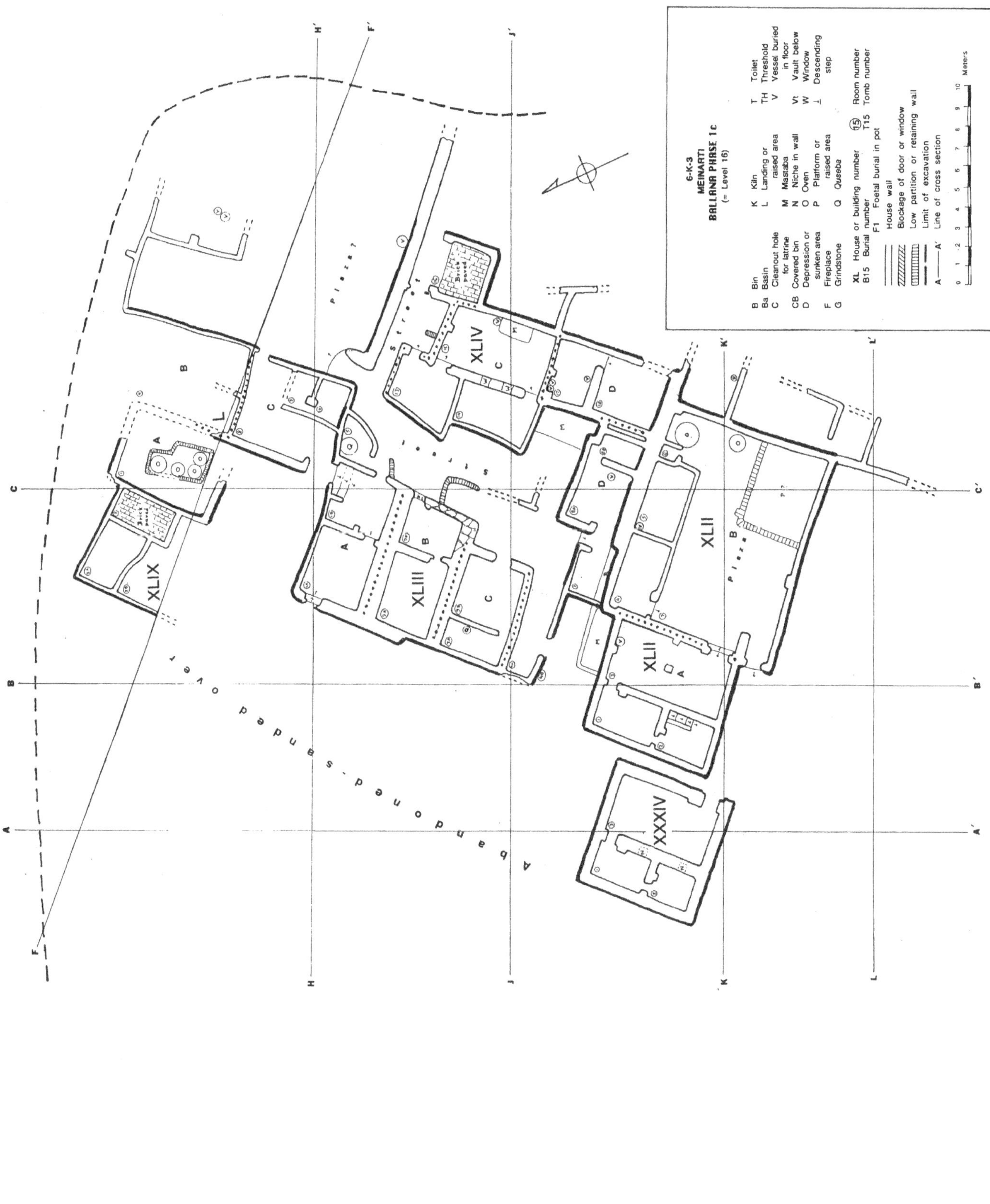

Figure 12. Plan of the remains at Level 16 (Subphase 1c), c. A.D. 375.
Heavy lines indicate the outlines of separately numbered buildings; dotted lines indicate the boundaries between suites.

Please note that a full-size version of this image is available to download from www.barpublishing.com/additional-downloads.html

span of Index Cluster X1, which may have endured for more than a century.[13] On the contrary, the very limited artifactual finds and sherds suggest a short occupation, followed by a considerable hiatus. Had Subphase 1c been terminated by a flood, the lack of finds might have been attributable to flood damage, as was the case at Subphase 1a. This was not the case, however; the remains of Subphase 1c were buried only under drifted sand, and several of the buildings survived without much damage into Subphase 2a. Accordingly I have estimated the terminal date for Subphase 1c at A.D. 425, partly because there are so few finds, including sherds, and partly because any later dating would allow insufficient time for the very significant ceramic change that took place before the beginning of Phase 2. The pottery finds will be much more fully discussed below.

The finds

Finds were not numerous in any of the Phase 1 levels—a reflection of the generally limited extent and poor preservation of the remains at those levels. More than two-thirds of the registered finds came from Level 17 (Subphase 1b). Readers should be reminded again, however, that the attribution of Meinarti artifacts to particular levels and subphases is not absolutely reliable, for reasons discussed in the Introduction. In many parts of the site where buildings were denuded, it was impossible to differentiate between Subphase 1a and Subphase 1b deposits at the time of excavation, and the attribution of so many objects to Level 17 simply reflects the fact that at the time when they were registered, the existence of Level 18 had not yet been recognized.

The pottery

Classificatory terminology

Throughout the discussion that follows, pottery finds are described in accordance with the classificatory systems published in *Ceramic Industries of Medieval Nubia*.[14] The classificatory terminology will be briefly explained in the next paragraphs, before the actual finds are discussed. Where registration numbers are cited (generally in parentheses) should be read in all cases as though preceded by 6-K-3/.

Families are the most inclusive unit of pottery classification. They designate groups of vessels having the same mode of construction (wheel-thrown or hand-modeled), the same fabric (paste plus temper), and a recognizable continuum of development over time. They are presumed to represent pottery made by the same people, in the same place or places, over a long period. The families chiefly represented at Phase 1 are Family M (the Meroitic fine wares), Family N (the Nubian wheel-thrown wares), Fam-

ily D (the Nubian hand-modeled wares), and Family A (the Aswan wares).[15]

Ware groups are chronological subdivisions within each family, except Family M. They designate groups of vessels which, in addition to the same method of construction and the same fabric, exhibit common standards of vessel form and of decorative design, which were in vogue during a period usually of one to three centuries. Ware groups represented in the present study are Group N.I (the Meroitic ordinary wares), and its successor, Group N. II (the Ballaña ordinary wares); Group NU (Nubian undecorated wheel-made wares); Group D.I (Meroitic hand-made wares); Group D.II (X-Group and Earlier Christian domestic wares); Group A.I (Graeco-Roman Aswan wares), and its successor Group A.II (Byzantine Aswan wares).[16]

Wares are the minimum unit of classification. In addition to a common fabric, a common group of forms, and a common decorative style, all the vessels in each ware also exhibit the same set of colors, and sometimes also in surface treatment (burnished, polished, or matte). A typical Nubian ware group will include at least three or four different wares, some red-slipped and some white- or cream-slipped, but otherwise identical in forms and decoration. There may also be both polished and matte wares that are otherwise identical.[17] Table 7 gives a complete list of the families, ware groups, and wares found at Phase 1, with their frequencies. Entries in parentheses are previous group and ware designations, as published in *Kush* 10 and 12.

In addition to the synthetic classification of families, ware groups, and wares, there are also separate, analytic classifications of vessel forms and of decorative styles.

Vessel forms have been classified into 27 basic form classes (cups, goblets, bowls, etc.) and 625 individual forms, which are numbered separately, beginning with 1, for each form class. Thus, the various cup forms are A1, A2, A3, etc.; the goblet forms are B1, B2, B3, etc. Thirty-nine vessel forms are represented in the collections from Phase 1.[18]

Decorative styles have been classified according to a very complex scheme that involves seven "general styles" (red-slip only, white slip only, rim stripe only, unslipped, etc.); 23 "horizon styles," each of which is distinctive of a particular ware group; and "individual styles," each of which is found on one ware only. General styles are designated only by Roman numerals, from I to VI plus X. Horizon styles are designated by the name of the ware group on which they are found, followed by a letter A, B, or C if more than one style was associated with the same ware group. Individual styles have the same designation as the ware on which they are found. Table 8 lists the nine styles that are found on the registered vessels of Phase 1.

---

[13] Rose (n.d., 152-62) now suggests that there is no legitimate distinction between Index Clusters X1 and X2, which between them spanned a century and a half. For the original estimated dates see Adams 1986, 629.

[14] Ibid. The classificatory designations do not in most cases correspond to the designations previously published by me in *Kush* (Adams 1962b, 235-88, and Adams 1964a, 126-73.)

[15] For further discussion of families and their designation see Adams 1986, 64-65.

[16] For further discussion of ware groups and their designation see Adams 1986, 65.

[17] For further discussion of wares and their designation see Adams 1986, 65.

[18] For further discussion of forms and their designation see Adams 1986, 63.

TABLE 7. LIST OF FAMILIES, WARE GROUPS, AND WARES FOUND AT PHASE 1 [1]

		Numbers Reg. obj.	Sherds
Family M. Meroitic fine wares			
Ware W26.	Meroitic fine white ware (IA)	6	38
Ware W27.	Meroitic pale pink ware (IC)	1	
Ware R35.	Meroitic fine red ware (IB)	5	29
Family N. Nubian ordinary wares			
Group N. I. Meroitic ordinary wares (Groups II and III)			
Ware W25.	Meroitic ordinary white ware (IIA, IIC, IIIA, IIIB)	3	104
Ware R32.	Meroitic ordinary red ware (IID, IIE, IIIC, IIID)	11	278
Group N. II. "X-Group" wares			
Ware W29.	X-Group ordinary white ware	1?	-
Ware R25.	Early X-Group brown ware (IIH)	7	58
Ware R1	Classic X-Group red ware (1)	7	
Group NU. Nubian coarse utility wares			
Ware U1.	Pre-Christian brown utility ware (IIH; 21)	2	74
Family D. Nubian hand-made domestic wares			
Group D.I. Meroitic domestic wares (Group V)			
Ware H1.	Early domestic plain utility ware (VA)	3	7
Group D.II. X-Group and earlier Christian domestic wares			
Ware H13.	Transitional white-on-red domestic ware	4	1
Family A. Aswan wares			
Group A.I. Graeco-Roman Aswan wares (Group IV)			
Ware R30	Graeco-Roman ordinary red ware (IVA, IVB, IVD)	3	XX**
Ware R31.	Graeco-Roman flaky pink ware (IVC)	1	3
Group A.II. Byzantine Aswan wares			
Ware R4.	Aswan Byzantine polished red ware (4)	5	3
Ware U2.	Aswan Byzantine pink utility ware (22)	1	XX**
Miscellaneous Egyptian trade wares			
Ware U3.	'Saqqara' buff amphora ware (23)	1	2
Ware U4.	Middle Egyptian brown utility ware (IIH; 24)	1	2
Ware U12.	Ballas drab utility ware	-	16
Ware U18.	Micaceous brown utility ware	-	7

[1] Entries in parentheses, following the group and ware names, are the original designations appearing in Adams 1962b, 272-6, and Adams 1964a, 157-61. Roman numeral entries in roman type are Meroitic wares described in Adams 1964a; Arabic numeral entries in italics are X-Group and Christian types described in Adams 1962b.

* Not tallied separately from Ware R25.

** Abundant; not individually tallied. Wares R30 and U2 were not separated in the sherd counts.

In addition to the overall classification of styles, there are two other formal classifications, of design elements and of motifs, either of which may occur in many different styles. Design elements are designated by capital letters, e.g. A, rim stripes; G, continuous friezes; N, radial designs, etc. Meroitic motifs are designated by lower-case letters, e.g. b, connected circles, k, crescents, m, lotus flowers, etc. X-Group and Christian motifs are designated by Arabic numbers, e.g. 5, zigzag, 11, arches, 17, *guilloche,* etc. Within each style, individual designs are classified and designated according to the element and the motif that they represent. For example, the Meroitic cup shown in Plate 7a, no. 9 (1094) exhibits Style N.IA (Meroitic fancy style), Element G (continuous frieze), and Motif f (spots and diagonal lines in combination). Since it is the second of six frieze designs that exhibit the same motif, it is individually designated as f-2.[19] For shorthand convenience, therefore, the decoration can be described as Style N.IA, design G-f-2. Designs are described according to this system on the artifact cards.[20]

Pottery finds, like other finds, were relatively scarce at Phase 1. The 61 registered vessels from Levels 18, 17, and 16 are listed and briefly categorized in Table 9.

Family M: the Meroitic fine wares[21]
These are the famous Meroitic "eggshell" wares, celebrated for their fine paste and elaborate, frequently delicate decoration. There are two principal wares in the family: the white Ware W26, and the red Ware R35.[22] Although they occur in the same vessel forms, Ware W26 commonly (though not always) has fancy painted or stamped designs, while Ware R35 never does; it has only a plain red slip. For this reason, apparently, Ware W26 has been abundantly illustrated in the funerary collections from Karanog, Faras, Meroe, and many other sites,[23] while Ware R35 has received very little attention in published reports.[24] Finds of both wares were relatively scarce at Meinarti, as they are in all habitation sites.

[19] It is illustrated in Adams 1986, 273.

[20] For further discussion of styles and their designation see Adams 1986, 213-35.

[21] For the family description see Adams 1986, 435-6.

[22] There are also two less common white wares, W27 and W30, in Family M. See Adams 1986, 439-40.

[23] For the references see Adams 1986, 439.

[24] For a few references see Adams 1986, 438.

TABLE 8. DECORATIVE STYLES FOUND ON POTTERY VESSELS OF PHASE 1

General styles

I	Red slip only
II	White or cream slip only
III	Red exterior slip; white interior slip
V	Rim stripe only
X	Unslipped

Horizon styles

N.IA	Meroitic fancy style
N.IIA	Classic X-Group style
A.IB	Aswan Roman style

Individual style

| H13 | Ware H13 style |

Ware W26: Meroitic fine white ware[25] is represented by six registered finds, and by an additional 38 tallied sherds. A cup (1094) and two *aryballoi* (1117 and 1434) are illustrated in Plate 7a, nos. 2, 4, and 9, and a footed bowl (1123) is illustrated in Plate 7b, no. 1. Only the cup exhibits any elaboration of decoration, while four of the other vessels have only plain body stripes in dark brown, and the footed bowl is undecorated except for its cream slip. All the vessels except the cup show evidence of extensive use.

Ware W27: Meroitic pale pink ware[26] is a rare variant of Ware W26, used for small vessels that were evidently made in imitation of the Aswan Ware R30, described below. The only example from Meinarti is a fragment of a mold-made lamp (1234), whose upper surface is embossed with a frog figure. Lamps of this type are much more commonly found in Ballaña sites.[27]

Ware R35: Meroitic fine red ware[28] is represented by five registered finds, and 29 tallied sherds. Four of the specimens are cups of essentially the same form, of which three (1438, 1095, and 1439) are shown in Plate 7a, nos. 6-8. The fifth specimen is an *aryballos* (1189), shown in Plate 7a, no. 5.

Family N, Group N.I: the Meroitic ordinary wares[29]
These are the more common Nubian-made wares of the Meroitic period; they are distinguished from the fine wares by their use of Nile mud rather than fine clay in the fabric. They were made in a truly extraordinary variety of vessel forms, some of which occur also in the fine wares. Decoration when present is in the same principal style, N.IA, as that found on the fine ware W26. The finds from Meinarti were entirely of two wares: the white ware W25,

and the red Ware R32. Once again, most specimens were found at Level 17, but a few were also found at Level 18.

Ware W25: Meroitic ordinary white ware.[30] This is the most elaborately decorated of all the Meroitic wares, and is abundantly represented in museum collections.[31] Only three specimens from Meinarti were complete enough to be registered, although sherds were fairly common. The bowl (1198) shown in Plate 7b, no. 8, has no decoration except a red rim stripe with two narrower black stripes below it (Style N.IA, Element A2): a fairly common decorative program in this ware. The very large storage jar (1219) shown in Plate 7c has a shoulder design of a lotus flower (Element H-m-2) on one side, and a trailing vine wreath (Element H-o-17) on the other, with a geometric waist band (Element E-b-13) below. A third, fragmentary specimen (1440), not illustrated, is a small bowl having an interior radial design.

Ware R32: Meroitic ordinary red ware.[32] This is the most common of the Meroitic ordinary wares, used both for large vessels which sometimes have fancy designs, and for smaller vessels which are always undecorated except for the slip. A peculiarity unique to this ware is the use of a red exterior and a white or cream interior slip on the same vessel (designated as Style III), particularly in the case of cups and food bowls. The nine registered specimens found at Meinarti were nearly all small, and all were undecorated. Plate 7b, no. 3, shows one of two cups (1197) having a small, flat pedestal base. In the same plate, no. 4 is a round-bottomed food bowl (1186) and nos. 5, 6, and 7 are three cylindrical food bowls (1188, 1096, and 1097), all having a red exterior and a white interior. Vessels of the same type were found to be rather common at the habitation site of Gaminarti (Adams and Nordström 1963, 26-8), but seem rarely if ever to have been buried in graves. In contrast to the four plain bowls just described, the

---

[25] Designated in Adams 1964a, 157, as Ware IA. For the full ware description see Adams 1986, 437-9.

[26] Designated in Adams 1964a, 157, as Ware IC. For the full ware description see Adams 1986, 439.

[27] See Woolley and Randall-MacIver 1910, 57.

[28] Designated in Adams 1964a, 157, as Ware IB. For the full ware description see Adams 1986, 436-8.

[29] For the ware group description see Adams 1986, 454-5.

[30] Designated in Adams 1964a, 157-8, as Wares IIA, IIC, IIIA, and IIIB. For the full ware description see Adams 1986, 457-8.

[31] For published references see Adams 1986, 457-8.

[32] Designated in Adams 1964a,157-8, as Wares IID, IIE, IIIB, IIIC, and IIID. For the full ware description see Adams 1986, 455-6.

TABLE 9. REGISTERED POTTERY FINDS FROM PHASE 1

Reg. no.	Ware	Form desig.	Form	Portion[1]	Colors[2]	Style	(Phase)	Plate
				Family M: Meroitic fine wares				
1094	W26	A16	Cup	Portion (R)	B/W	N.IA	17 (1b)	7a, 9
1433	W26	C20	Bowl	Fragment (R)	Br/W	N.IA	17 (1b)	7b, 1
1123	W26	D49	Footed bowl	Almost whole (R)	?	I?	17 (1b)	
1117	W26	N10	Aryballos	Almost whole	Br/W	N.IA	17 (1b)	7a, 2
1434	W26	N10	Aryballos	Fragment (R)	Br/W	N.IA	17 (1b)	7a, 4
1435	W26	N2	Oil bottle	Neck portion	Br/W	N.IA	17 (1b)	
1234	W27	P3	Lamp	Fragment	Pink	II	17 (1b)	
1095	R35	A17	Cup	Complete	R-X	I	17 (1b)	7a, 7
1437	R35	A17	Cup	Portion (R)	R-X	I	17 (1b)	
1438	R35	A17	Cup	Portion (R)	R-X	I	17 (1b)	7a, 6
1439	R35	A17	Cup	Portion (R)	R-X	I	17 (1b)	7a, 8
1189	R35	N10	Aryballos	Whole	Red	I	17 (1b)	7a, 5
				Family N : Nubian ordinary wheel-made wares				
				Group N.I: Meroitic wares				
1440	W25	C20	Bowl	Portion	Br+R/W	N.IA	17 (1b)	
1198	W25	C9	Bowl	Portion (R)	Br+R/W	V	17 (1b)	7b, 8
1219	W25	X13	Jar	Almost whole (R)	Br+R/W	N.IA	18 (1a)	7c
1150	R32	A8	Cup	Almost whole	W+R	V	17 (1b)	
1197	R32	A21A	Cup	Portion (R)	R-W	III	17 (1b)	7a, 3
1186	R32	C20	Bowl	Almost whole	R-W	III	18 (1a)	7b, 4
1188	R32	C9	Bowl	Almost whole	R-W	III	18 (1a)	7b, 5
1096	R32	C85	Bowl	Almost whole	R-W	III	17 (1b)	7b, 6
1097	R32	C85	2 Bowls	Almost whole	R-W	I	17 (1b)	7b, 7
1122	R32	C85	Bowl	Portion (R)	Red	I	17 (1b)	
1106	R32	D49	Footed bowl	Almost whole	Red	I	17 (1b)	7b, 2
1441	R32	P12?	Lamp	Almost whole	Red	I	(1)	
1445	R32	U8	Pot	Portion (R)	R-X	I	17 (1b)	
1446	R32	J6?	Jar?	Fragment	R-B	I	?	
				Group N.II: Ballaña wares				
1187	W29?	?	Bottle or jar?	Base portion	Cream	II?	18 (1a)	
1098	R25	C7	Bowl	Almost whole (R)	Red	X	17 (1b)	7d, 11
1099	R25	C18	Bowl	Almost whole (R)	R-W	V	17 (1b)	7e, 7
1105	R25	D66	Footed bowl	Whole	Brown	X	17 (1b)	7d, 6
1151	R25	D82	Footed bowl	Almost whole (R)	Brown	X	17 (1b)	7d, 10
1196	R25	O1	Ointment jar	Whole	Brown	X	17 (1b)	7d, 3
1124	R25	W17	Jar	Almost whole (R)	Red	I	16 (1c)	7f, 1
1203	R25	W16	Jar	Almost whole (R)	Red	I	16 (1c)	8a, 1
1147	R1	A4	Cup	Whole	B+W/R	N.IIA	16 (1c)	17b, 1
1179	R1	B16	Goblet	Almost whole (R)	W/R	N.IIA	16 (1c)	
1193	R1	B17	Goblet	Almost whole	B+W/R	N.IIA	17 (1b)	17c, 3
1194	R1	B17	Goblet	Portion (R)	B+W/R	N.IIA	17 (1b)	
1195	R1	B16?	Goblet	Portion	Red	I	17 (1b)	
1192	R1	G40	Spouted goblet	Mostly complete	B+W/R	N.IIA	17 (1b)	17d, 18
1149	R1	U6	Pot	Almost whole (R)	W/R	V	16 (1c)	

[1] (R) = restored

[2] B=Black; Br = Brown; R = Red; W = White or cream; B/W = Black on white; B+R/W = Black and red on white; B+W/R = Black and white on red; W/R = White on Red; R-W = Red exterior, white interior; R-X = Red exterior, unslipped interior; W+R = White upper body, red lower body; X = Unslipped

48

TABLE 9. REGISTERED POTTERY FINDS FROM PHASE 1 (CONT.)

Reg. no.	Ware	Form desig.	Form	Portion[1]	Colors[2]	Style	(Phase)	Plate
				Group NU: Nubian undecorated utility wares				
1442	U1	P12	Lamp	Whole	Brown	X	17 (1b)	
1152	U1	V2	Qadus	Portion (R)	Brown	X	17 (1b)	8b, 2
				Family D : Nubian hand-made wares				
				Group D.I: Meroitic wares				
1104	H1	Q19	Lid	Whole	Brown	X	17 (1b)	8c, 3
1127	H1	Q19	Lid	Whole	Brown	X	16 (1c)	8c, 4
1443	H1	n/t	Stopper	Whole	Brown	X	17 (1b)	8c, 2
				Group D.II: X-Group and earlier Christian domestic wares				
1126	H13	U11	Small pot	Almost whole	W/R	H13	16 (1c)	8d, 1 19b, 1
1204	H13	U1	Pot	Almost whole	W/R	H13	16 (1c)	8d, 3
1454	H13	U11	Pot	Almost whole	W/R	H13	17 (1b)	
1181	H13	U1	Pot	Whole	W/R	H13	16 (1c)	
				Family A: Aswan wares				
				Group A.I: Graeco-Roman wares				
1148	R30	B16	Goblet	Almost whole (R)	B+W/R	A.IB	?	8f, 6
1403	R30	D11	Footed bowl	Portion	Pink	I?	17 (1b)	
1409	R30	Z5?	Amphora	Upper body	Pink	I	18 (1a)	
1183	R31	M12	Lekythos	Whole	Pink	I	17 (1b)	9a, 6
1125	R31	M9	Lekythos	Mostly complete	Red	I	16 (1c)	19c, 5
				Group A.II: Byzantine wares				
1399	R4	C83	Bowl	Portion (R)	Red	I	17 (1b)	8f, 5
1397	R4	D11	Footed bowl	Portion	Red	I	17 (1b)	8f, 4
1407	R4	?	Miniature bowl	Portion	Red	I	17 (1b)	
1398	R4?	?	Bottle?	Base portion	Pink	X?	17 (1b)	9a, 9
1190	U2	Z6	Amphora	Almost whole (R)	Red	I	16 (1c)	9b, 1
				Family T: Theban wares				
1191	U4	Z2	Amphora	Almost whole (R)	Brown	X	17 (1b)	9c, 2

1 (R) = restored

2 B=Black; Br = Brown; R = Red; W = White or cream; B/W = Black on white; B+R/W = Black and red on white; B+W/R = Black and white on red; W/R = White on Red; R-W = Red exterior, white interior; R-X = Red exterior, unslipped interior; W+R = White upper body, red lower body; X = Unslipped

footed bowl shown in Plate 7b, no. 2 (1106) is clearly a copy of contemporary Roman Egyptian vessels, and like them it has a red slip all over. Other vessels of Ware R32, not illustrated, are a lamp of uncertain form (1441), a fragmentary pot (1445), and a fragmentary jar 1446). The latter of these is unusual in having a black smudged interior.

Family N, Group N.II: 'X-Group" wares.[33]
These were the basic Nubian-made wares of the Ballaña

[33] For the ware group description see Adams 1986, 458-68. In the naming of these wares I retain the unfortunate term "X-Group" because it is so thoroughly embedded in the literature.

period, though their use actually began in the late Meroitic period, and continued well into the Early Christian period. At Subphase 1b (Level 17) they were just about as abundant as were the Meroitic wares of Group N.I, and they were the only Nubian wheel-made wares found at Subphase 1c (Level 16). They were the direct successors of the Group N.I wares, and employed the same fabric of Nile mud, but stylistic continuity is exhibited only in a few vessel forms and a few, very simple decorative elements. The Group N.II wares, unlike their predecessors, were almost wholly modeled on contemporary Roman Egyptian forms, and more specifically on the Aswan Ware R30 which will be described below.

Ware W11: Early X-Group white ware.[34] This was a very uncommon cream-slipped ware, occurring mostly in the same forms as the much more common brown and red wares, R25 and R1. Only a single fragmentary example (1187), not illustrated, was found at Phase 1. It appears to be the base of a thin-walled bottle, having a flat bottom.

Ware R25: Early X-Group brown ware.[35] This very simple, usually unslipped and hastily mass-produced ware represents something of an anomaly: first, because it appears side-by-side with the beautifully finished and decorated Nubian wares of the Meroitic period, and second, because it is the only one of the Nubian wares which is also found abundantly in contemporary Egyptian sites. The explanation seems to lie in the fact that the ware was originally produced only in Roman Egypt, the specimens found in Meroitic Nubia being imports whose appeal may have been their cheapness. Later, and after the demise of the Meroitic artistic tradition, the manufacture of these vessels was taken up in Nubia as well—possibly at first by migrant potters from Egypt. The vessels became, in the earlier Ballaña period, the overwhelmingly dominant Nubian ware, and later they evolved into the distinctive X-Group Ware R1. The Nubian-made and the Egyptian-made representatives of Ware R25 might possibly be differentiated by the use of elaborate and expensive testing procedures, but these were not available to us at the time of the Meinarti dig. Spectrographic analyses carried out by us at the University of Kentucky failed to reveal any differences.[36]

Vessels of Ware R25 occasionally have a thin red wash, but much more commonly are unslipped; hence the designation as a brown ware rather than as a red ware. Either slipped or unslipped vessels may also, very occasionally, have a white rim stripe or simple "splash" designs in white.

Ware R25 is represented by seven registered finds from Meinarti, of which five came from Level 17 (Subphase 1b) and two from Level 16 (Subphase 1c). Among the vessels shown in Plate 7d, nos. 6, 10, and 11 (1105, 1151, and 1098) are food bowls, similar in function but different in form from the prevailing Meroitic forms. The larger bowl shown in Plate 7e, no. 7 (1099) differs from the others in that it has a dark cream rim stripe on the interior, although the remainder of the body is unslipped. Another vessel of Ware R25 is a small ointment jar (1196), shown in Plate 7d, no. 3.

The small pot (1124) shown in Plate 7f, no. 1, and the large jar (1203) in Plate 8a, no. 1 are different from other vessels of Ware R25 in that both are covered with a thin red wash. The gentle ribbing exhibited by both specimens is very characteristic of larger vessels in Ware R25.

Ware R1: Classic X-Group red ware.[37] This ware evolved directly from Ware R25, and became the dominant Nubian ware of the Ballaña period. The process of development was a gradual and continuous one, so that it is not possible to mark a clear dividing point between the two.[38] The main distinction is that vessels of Ware R1 tend to be more carefully finished, to have a polished red slip, and frequently to have simple painted decoration in Style N.IIA. The emergence of this ware, from its rather crude and undecorated predecessor, reflects the consistent Nubian preference for nicely finished and decorated rather than for purely utilitarian pottery. The designs, consisting of grouped vertical lines, festoons, or groups of isolated "blobs," are nearly always executed on both black and white; they are best seen in Plate 17c. A peculiarity of this style is that a rim stripe was never employed, although it was common both in Meroitic (Style N.IA) and in Early Christian (Style N.III) pottery.

The overwhelming majority of vessels in Ware R1 are cups and goblets, which in the beginning were identical in form to their predecessors in Ware R25, and like them were inspired by the late Roman red wares of North Africa. However there was, over time, a gradual evolution in vessel forms, as both cups and goblets became taller and more slender. In Plate 17c, earlier forms are shown in the upper row, and later forms in the lower rows. Unlike the predecessor Ware R25, Ware R1 was a purely Nubian product, and has not been found in Egyptian sites.

Although finds of Ware R1 came overwhelmingly from the Phase 2 levels (15b, 15a, and 14), a few were found in the Meroitic Levels 17 and 16. They include the cup (1147) shown in Plate 17b, no. 1; the goblet (1193) shown in Plate 17c, no. 3; and the spouted goblet (1192) shown in Plate 17c, no. 18. It is noteworthy that all of the cups and goblets (including those not illustrated) were of the relatively low and squat forms characteristic of Ware R1 in its earliest manifestation.

Family N, Group NU: Nubian coarse utility wares
Group NU consists of a number of heavy, undecorated wares whose use in most cases persisted over long periods of time. These wares, like the fine wares, were wheel-made from Nile mud, and it is clear in at least two cases that they were made in the same factories as were the fine wares.[39] Because of their long duration and their lack of decoration, however, it is not possible to assign them to any of the numbered ware groups in Family N, whose distinguishing characteristics are mostly stylistic. Instead, they are lumped together in Group NU, whose only common characteristics are its lack of decoration and its use mainly for large vessels. The only member of the group found at Phase 1 was Ware U1, whose use persisted through the Meroitic and Ballaña and into the earliest Christian period.

Ware U1: Pre-Christian brown utility ware.[40] This ware,

---

[34] For the full ware description see Adams 1986, 472-3.

[35] Designated in Adams 1964a, 159, as Ware IIH. For the full ware description see Adams 1986, 468-9. It is designated as a brown ware because the unslipped surfaces exhibit a color that is more nearly brown than red.

[36] Unpublished laboratory report in the author's possession.

[37] Designated in Adams 1962a, 272, as Ware 1. For the full ware description see Adams 1986, 469-70.

[38] In the case of sherds lacking decoration, it is frequently impossible to distinguish between Wares R25 and R1. Consequently, the two were not distinguished in the sherd tallies shown in Table 7.

[39] At Faras West and at Debeira East; see Adams 1961b, 40-41, and Adams 1962c, 68-70.

[40] Designated in Adams 1962b, 275, as Ware 21, and in Adams 1964a,159, as Ware IIH. For the full ware description see Adams

common throughout the Meroitic and Ballaña periods, is distinguished from the utility ware of the Christian periods (Ware U5) by its thinner vessel walls, frequently ribbed surfaces, and by having a light brown rather than a brick-red color. Although sherds were common in the Phase 1 levels, only two specimens were registered. One is a small lamp (1442), so encrusted with oil that a certain identification of the form is not possible. The other, much more important find is a nearly complete *qadus* (*saqia* pot) (1152), shown in Plate 8b, no. 2. It has the typical gently ribbed walls and angular base knob that are characteristic of *qadus* in the Meroitic and Ballaña periods. Its importance relates to the question of whether or not the *saqia* was in use in Meroitic Nubia, an issue that will be further discussed at the end of the chapter.

Family D, Group D.I: Meroitic domestic wares.[41]
Unlike the wheel-made wares, Nubian hand-modeled pottery exhibits a continuum of development from Neolithic times until the present day. Although partially eclipsed by the wheel-made wares during and after the Pharaonic period, the hand-built vessels continued to be produced and used in very considerable numbers at all subsequent periods. Ethnographic parallels suggest that they were made and largely used by women, while the wheel-thrown wares were the work of male specialists. The use of the hand-made vessels was and is primarily for the preparation, serving, and storage of traditional foods and beverages.

The hand-made wares like most of the wheel-made wares are fashioned primarily from Nile mud, but their fabric tends to be somewhat coarse due to the inclusion of large sand grains and of a certain amount of dung. The fabric is also generally softer than in the wheel-made wares, the result of firing in pits rather than in updraught kilns. The family of hand-made vessels, designated collectively as Family D, includes both unslipped and red-slipped wares at most periods of history. Curiously, however, black-slipped wares were made in Meroitic times (Group D.I) and again in Late Christian times (Group D.III), but not in the intervening centuries (Group D.II). A special peculiarity of the family is that slipped vessels, whether red or black, always have burnished (i.e. pebble-polished) surfaces on which striation marks are clearly visible. There were some painted hand-made vessels, both in Meroitic and in Late Christian times, but incised decoration, usually involving diagonal or criss-crossed lines, was much more prevalent.

Finds of hand-made ware, although common at Gaminarti (see Adams and Nordström 1963, 26-8), were extremely rare in the Meroitic levels at Meinarti. From Ware Group D.I there are only three registered vessels, all in the plain Ware H1.

Ware H1: Early domestic plain utility ware.[42] This is an unslipped and rather coarsely finished brown ware used mainly for pots and jars, but also sometimes for jar lids and other forms. As it happens, none of the three regis-

tered specimens from Meinarti are vessels; they consist of two lids (1104 and 1127) and a stopper (1443), shown in Plate 8c, nos. 3, 4, and 2.

Family D, Group D.II: X-Group and Early Christian domestic wares.[43]
This group belongs to the latter half of the Ballaña period and the earlier half of the Christian period. The undecorated Ware H1, which continued in use for centuries, is included in both Group D.I and D.II. Otherwise, Group D.II is distinguished from its predecessor by the absence of a black-slipped ware, and by the presence of several red-slipped wares not found earlier. However, the only member of the group occurring in the Phase 1 levels at Meinarti is the uncommon white-on-red Ware H13, represented by four examples.

Ware H13: Transitional white-on-red domestic ware.[44] This is a very unusual ware, probably made by a small group of specialized potters at a single locality. It occurs almost exclusively in the form of globular pots, of various sizes, having an inset within the rim to receive a lid. All known specimens have a red slip, and decoration either in broad white lines or in large white dots, which are often executed in rows of overlapping dots. The decorative style (Style H18) is unique to this ware, although it bears a general resemblance to the Classic X-Group Style N.IIA. In addition to other peculiarities, the vessels have an exceptionally soft and rather light-colored fabric, suggesting that they were fired at rather low temperatures. Ware H13 occurs chiefly in deposits of the late Ballaña and earliest Christian periods (hence the name "Transitional"), but four examples were also found at Subphase 1c at Meinarti. Two smaller examples (1126 and 1454) are shown in Plate 8d, nos. 1 and 3. Plate 8e shows two much larger pots (1181 and 1204), whose white decoration is so faded that it cannot be made out in the photographs.

Family A, Group AI: Graeco-Roman Aswan wares.[45]
From Classical times until the end of the Middle Ages, pottery was produced in enormous quantities at or near Aswan, and was widely traded into Nubia. From early Ballaña times until Classic Christian times, the Aswan potters provided the primary models that were copied by the potters of Nubia. The Aswan-made vessels are often identical in form to the Nubian copies, with the distinction however that they have a very hard, light pink fabric instead of a softer fabric of Nile mud. Usually too the Aswan vessels were somewhat more carelessly finished, and generally more carelessly decorated, than were the Nubian copies. Although the specific place of manufacture for these wares has not been determined, their overwhelming prevalence in the *kom* site at Elephantine suggests the probability that they were made somewhere nearby, if not on the island itself. The wares were very widely traded, northward as far as Thebes and southward throughout Lower Nubia, with a few specimens reaching

---

[41] Designated in Adams 1964a, 161, as Group V. For the full group description see Adams 1986, 413-17.

[42] Designated in Adams 1962b, 276, as Ware 27, and in Adams 1964a, 161, as Ware VA. For the full ware description see Adams

[43] For the group description see Adams 1986, 421.

[44] For the ware description see Adams 1986, 424-5.

[45] Designated in Adams 1964a, 160, as Group IV. For the full group description see Adams 1986, 526-34

as far south as Soba.[46] However, it is only in the vicinity of Aswan that they seem to be predominant. Aswan wares nevertheless constitute between 10% and 30% of the pottery found in Nubian sites of all periods from the Meroitic until the Terminal Christian.[47]

Ware Group A.I represents the earliest manifestation of the Aswan tradition, at least as found in Nubia. It is represented at Meinarti by two wares, R30 and R31, of which the first was highly prevalent (in sherd form) and the latter extremely scarce.

Ware R30: Aswan Graeco-Roman ordinary red ware[48] was the basic redware of the late Roman period at Aswan, corresponding in time to the late Meroitic and the earlier half of the Ballaña period in Nubia. It was used for an enormous variety of vessels, from small cups and goblets to very large storage jars, and notably including wine amphorae. The latter were imported into Nubia in great quantities, and account for the very high prevalence of Ware R30 sherds in the Phase 1 deposits (see Table 7). Vessels of any shape might or might not have a thin red wash. However, the great majority do not, and the unslipped surfaces exhibit the same light pink color as is seen in the fabric core. Large vessels, other than amphorae, are often decorated, in a style (Style A.IA) which served as the model for the Classic Nubian X-Group Style N.IIA. Small vessels like cups and goblets are much less often decorated, and are apt to be rather carelessly finished.

The great majority of registered finds of Ware R30 came from the late Ballaña (Phase 2) levels, although amphora sherds were abundant at Phase 1. However, only three objects were registered from Phase 1. A rather crudely finished goblet (1148) is illustrated in Plate 8f, no. 6. Not illustrated are a fragmentary miniature bowl (1403) and a fragmentary amphora (1409).

Ware R31: Aswan Graeco-Roman flaky pink ware.[49] This is an uncommon and a very unusual ware, which seems to have been used exclusively for *lekythoi*, oil bottles, and small jugs. The fabric has the same pink color as that found in the other Aswan wares, but it is less dense, and vessel surfaces have a marked tendency to flake off because of some peculiarity in the paste. Pamela Rose has recently suggested, on the basis of distributional evidence, that the ware was made in Lower Nubia and not at Aswan, and should not be included among the Aswan wares (Rose n.d., 173). The vessels almost never have painted decoration, but *lekythoi* usually have finely incised geometric designs on their upper surfaces. One small *lekythos* (1183) and one large *lekythos* (1125) were found in the Phase 1 levels; they are illustrated respectively in Plate 9a, no. 6 and in Plate 9a, no. 9 The larger specimen has typical incised decoration on the upper body.

Family A, Group A.II: Byzantine Aswan wares.[50]

These wares are the direct successors to the wares in Group A.I, and utility vessels in the unslipped Ware U2 often cannot be distinguished from their predecessors in Ware R30. However, Group A.II includes two new wares, the red Ware R4 and the white Ware W3, that are much better finished than any of the vessels in Group A.I, and that have thick slips and polished surfaces. Some vessel forms are carried over from Group A.I, but in Group A.II the predominant cups and goblets of the earlier group have very largely given way to broad footed bowls and plates. These vessels at a later date served as the models for many of the Early Christian wares (Ware Group N.III), but the earliest imports from Aswan made their appearance in Nubia long before their imitation by the Christian Nubian potters. At Meinarti they were found mostly at Phase 2 levels, but six examples were registered from Phase 1 Levels 17 and 16.

Ware R4: Aswan Byzantine polished red ware.[51] This ware was the successor to the smaller vessel forms in Ware R30. Its most distinctive feature, apart from a new range of vessel forms, is the presence of a dark red slip, which in the case of bowls usually covers the interior surface only. Slipped interior surfaces are always highly polished, while exterior surfaces retain the pink color and the somewhat gritty texture of the fabric.

At Meinarti, the overwhelming preponderance of Ware R4 finds came from the Phase 2 levels. However, four specimens were registered from Subphase 1c (Level 16). A plain bowl (1399) and a footed bowl (1397) are shown in Plate 8f, nos. 4 and 5 respectively. Both these bowls have a red-slipped interior but an unslipped exterior, as does a fragmentary miniature bowl (1407) which is not illustrated. A fragmentary bottle (1398), not illustrated, has also been very tentatively assigned to Ware R4.

Ware U2: Aswan Byzantine pink utility ware.[52] This unslipped ware, a direct outgrowth of Ware R30 in Group A.I, was now used only for larger utility vessels: jugs, bottles, jars, and above all amphorae, which like their predecessors were imported in enormous numbers. Amphorae of Ware U2 can be distinguished from those of Ware R30 by the possession of short loop handles instead of strap handles, and of a "button" base in place of a small ring (cf. Plate 19f), but body sherds of the two wares are often indistinguishable. For this reason, sherds of Ware U2 could not be tallied separately from those of Ware R30 in the sherd counts. A great many amphorae of Ware U2 were recovered from the Phase 2 and Phase 3 levels, but only a single specimen (1190) was found at Phase 1, Level 16 (Subphase 1c). It is shown in Plate 9b, no. 1.

Other Egyptian transport wares
The overwhelming preponderance of the wine enjoyed by the Meroitic Nubians came from Aswan, or at least was shipped in Aswan-made amphorae. However, the presence of other vintages is attested by occasional finds of several other types of amphorae, whose place of manu-

---

[46] Personal communication from Derek Welsby.

[47] For the actual figures for each period see Adams 1986, 630.

[48] Designated in Adams 1964a, 160, as Wares IVA, IVB, and IVD. For the full ware description see Adams 1986, 534-6.

[49] Designated in Adams 1964a, 160, as Ware IVC. For the full ware description see Adams 1986, 536-7.

[50] For the full group description see Adams 1986, 542-3.

[51] Designated in Adams 1962b, 272, as Ware 4. For the full ware description see Adams 1986, 543-4.

[52] Designated in Adams 1962b, 275, as Ware 22. For the full ware description see Adams 1986, 545.

facture in some cases is uncertain.

Family T, Ware U4: Middle Egyptian brown utility ware.[53]

This unslipped ware, dark to medium brown in color, is found exclusively in the form of large and very heavy-walled vessels, most of which are amphorae. Although they were widely traded, their prevalence in the vicinity of Luxor suggests the probability that they were made somewhere in that area. At Meinarti, sherds as well as whole vessels were numerous at Phases 2 and 3, but only a single, very large amphora (1191), illustrated in Plate 9c, no. 2, was registered at Phase 1. This vessel exhibits the same brown fabric and thick walls as do the much more common Ware U4 amphorae of the Ballaña period, but the form, with its elongate tubular base, appears to be unique: it is not illustrated in any other published collection of Nubian or of Roman Egyptian pottery.

Sub-family LB, Ware U12: Ballas drab utility ware.[54]

The distinctive, orange-brown fabric of this ware marks it unmistakably as a product of the Middle Egyptian factories at Ballas. It was imported into Nubia in small quantities throughout the Meroitic, Ballaña, and earlier Christian periods, and then became common in the Late Christian period. In the Phase 1 collections it is represented by no registered finds, but by 16 sherds.

Sub-family LS, Ware U3: Saqqara buff amphora ware.[55]

This easily-recognized ware was used only for amphorae of a highly distinctive form. They must have contained a prized vintage, for they were traded over very long distances, not only into Nubia but throughout the eastern Mediterranean lands. A center of manufacture in Lower Egypt seems most probable, in view of their extreme prevalence in the monasteries at Saqqara. In Nubia they are associated above all with graves of the Ballaña period,[56] and sherds were abundant at the later Ballaña (Phase 2) levels at Meinarti, but only two sherds were found in the Phase 1 levels.

Ware U18: Micaceous brown utility ware.[57] This highly distinctive ware, of unknown origin, is found only in the form of small amphorae having extraordinarily thin walls, and quantities of ground mica in the temper. Examples are not common either in Egypt or in Nubia, and a center of manufacture at Sardis in Asia Minor has been suggested. Most finds in Nubia have come from Ballaña sites, but seven sherds were recorded from the Phase 1 levels at Meinarti.

The principal vessel forms

Of the 27 Nubian vessel form classes that have been designated, examples of 15 have been found in the Meroitic levels at Meinarti:

A: Cups. These small vessels, apparently for wine, were common in both Meroitic and Ballaña times, though rare afterward.[58] Seven examples were found in the Meroitic fine wares, two in the Meroitic ordinary wares, and one in the X-Group ordinary wares. Forms A16 and A17, illustrated in Plate 7a, nos. 6-9, were by far the most common.

B: Goblets. These vessels, apparently also for wine, were almost the "signature" artifacts of the Ballaña period, although their first appearance was slightly earlier.[59] They appeared first in the form of imports in Aswan Ware R30, but were soon widely copied in the Nubian Wares R25 and R1. Dozens of goblets were found in the Phase 2 levels, but only six examples came from the Phase 1 levels: five of Nubian Ware R1, and one of Aswan Ware R30. All the goblets were in the two closely similar forms B16 and B17, illustrated in Plate 17c.

C: Bowls. Although bowls of all sorts became enormously popular in Christian Nubian times, and took a wide variety of forms, the number and variety of forms was limited in Meroitic times.[60] The 12 specimens that were registered were nearly all simple food bowls, of a roughly cylindrical form, as shown in Plates 7b, nos. 4-8, and Plate 7d, nos. 6, 10, and 11. One was in the Meroitic fine Ware W26, eight in the Meroitic ordinary wares, two in the X-Group wares, and one in the Aswan Ware R4.

D: Footed bowls. Bowls having a ring base were made at all times in Nubia, but they were not at all common before Classic Christian times.[61] Only six specimens were registered from the Phase 1 levels. The hemispherical form D49, found in the two specimens shown in Plate 7b, nos. 1 and 2, is a purely Meroitic form. Form D11, found in two specimens of Aswan ware, is no more than a widened version of the common goblet form, B18.

G: Small pots and bottles. The single specimen in this class (1192), shown in Plate 17c, no. 18, is a spouted goblet, of a type (Form G40) that was common in the Ballaña period, but is almost never found either earlier or later.[62]

M: *Lekythoi.* These vessels, essentially miniature jugs, were made and used throughout the Mediterranean world in Greek and Roman times. They are believed to have been containers for oils or scents. They were abundant in Meroitic times, somewhat less so in Ballaña times, and virtually nonexistent thereafter. Although sometimes imitated in the Nubian ordinary wares, the great majority of the vessels found in Nubia are in the Aswan Ware R31.[63] Only two examples, both in Ware R31, were found in the Phase 1 levels; they are shown in Plate 9a, nos. 1 and 6.

---

[53] Designated in Adams 1964a, 159, as Ware IIH. For the full ware description see Adams 1986, 567-8.

[54] For the full ware description see Adams 1986, 574-5.

[55] Designated in Adams 1962b, 275, as Ware 23. For the full ware description see Adams 1986, 580.

[56] For discussion of this ware see especially L. P. Kirwan in Emery and Kirwan 1938, 401-5.

[57] For the full ware description see Adams 1986, 581-2.

[58] For discussion of the class see Adams 1986, 101; for illustrations see ibid., 108-11.

[59] For discussion of the class see Adams 1986, 101; for illustrations see ibid., 112-15.

[60] For discussion of the class see Adams 1986, 101-2; for illustrations see ibid., 116-22.

[61] For discussion of the class see Adams 1986, 102; for illustrations see ibid., 123-9.

[62] For discussion of the class see Adams 1986, 103; for illustrations see ibid., 135-8.

[63] For discussion of the class see Adams 1986, 103; for illustrations see ibid., 147.

N: *Aryballoi*. These are small, more or less round-bodied vessels having a narrow, short neck. Like the *lekythoi* they are believed to have been used for oils. They differ from *lekythoi* in lacking a handle attached to the neck, and usually in lacking a ring base. Like the *lekythoi* they appeared first in the form of imports from Aswan, and later were imitated by the Nubians.[64] The three specimens registered from Phase 1 are all in the Meroitic fine wares; they are shown in Plate 7a, nos. 2, 4, and 5.

O: Ointment jars. These very small, flat-bottomed vessels without handles were rare at all times, and occur mainly in imported forms.[65] The single specimen found in Phase 1 levels at Meinarti is in Ware R25; it could be either locally made or an import. It is shown in Plate 7d, no. 3.

P: Lamps. Lamps were always needed to some extent for illumination, but in the Christian period they were much more commonly used in votive contexts. Consequently lamp finds are rare in Meroitic sites, become common in late Ballaña sites, and are abundant at all later periods.[66] Only one lamp, apparently of the common Meroitic form P12, was found in the Phase 1 levels. It was heavily encrusted with oil, and is not illustrated.

Q: Lids. Round lids, to fit over pot or jar mouths, were made at all periods, but were never common. Those found in the Meroitic period are nearly always in the hand-made Ware H1.[67] Two examples were found in the Phase 1 levels at Meinarti, and are illustrated in Plate 8c, nos. 3 and 4.

U: Pots. Wide-mouthed pots, usually having a more or less globular form, were common at all periods, and were certainly the primary cooking vessels. Before the Late Christian period nearly all were in the hand-made wares.[68] The four specimens registered from Phase 1 levels are all in the unusual painted ware H13; two are illustrated in Plate 8d, nos. 1 and 3. However, at least two dozen additional globular pots in the undecorated Ware H1 were found buried in house floors; these vessels were not registered, and were left on the site. For an illustration of nearly 50 of these vessels, found at Phases 2 and 3, see Plate 19a.

V: *Qadus*. The *saqia*, and hence its distinctive and easily recognized pots, called *qadus*, were used in Nubia from Meroitic times onward. The pots were always of locally made utility wares: Ware U1 in the Meroitic and Ballaña periods, and Ware U5 in the Christian periods. Since their locus of use was necessarily at the riverbank, however, these vessels are not commonly found either in townsites or in graves.[69] A single, fragmentary specimen, shown in

Plate 8b, no. 2, was found at Subphase 1b. The potential historical importance of this find will be discussed in the last part of the chapter.

W: Jars. Jars are large vessels, distinguished from pots only by the possession of a neck. While the overwhelming majority of pots are in the hand-made wares, an equally high percentage of jars are in the wheel-made wares, both locally made and imported. They were probably used mainly for storage, rather than for cooking.[70] Three specimens, all in the Meroitic ordinary wares, were registered from the Phase 1 levels; two are illustrated in Plate 7f, no. 1, and Plate 8a, no. 1.

X: Footed jars are distinguished from the vessels of Class W by the possession of a ring foot. These vessels were most common in Ballaña and Early Christian times, but some were locally made and some were imported in Meroitic times as well.[71] The single very large specimen found at Phase 1 is in the Meroitic painted Ware W25; it is illustrated in Plate 7c.

Z: Amphorae. From Meroitic times onward, the Nubians had an enormous taste for wine, which reached them in foreign-made amphorae. The vast majority of these were in the Aswan Ware R30 and its successor, Ware U2, but many other amphora wares, some of trans-Mediterranean origin, have also been recognized. Because the vessels were very large, they seldom survived intact, so that finds of complete amphorae are comparatively rare while sherds of the amphora wares are abundant.[72] Of the three registered specimens from Phase 1, the one shown in Plate 9b, no. 1, is in Form Z5, which is the typical Aswan amphora form of Meroitic times. A second amphora, also of Aswan ware, is too fragmentary for positive identification. The amphora of Theban Ware U4 shown in Plate 9c, no. 2, is of a unique form (Z2) not otherwise known from Nubia.

The non-pottery finds
Table 10 lists the 69 registered non-pottery finds from Phase 1, plus 14 "stray" finds from later levels that are obviously of Meroitic origin.

Ceramic objects
This designation is given to objects of fired clay that do not exactly fit the category of pottery vessels.

Quseba. Plates 9c and 9d show a very large, hand-made storage vessel (1212), which is like a *quseba* except that it is made of fired pottery rather than of mud, and is slipped and decorated. The exterior surface has a slip ranging in color from buff to orange-brown, on which are painted two writhing snakes with heads facing each other, as shown in Plate 9d. The bodies of the animals are outlined in very dark brown and filled with red-brown. The vessel has four pairs of holes symmetrically arranged around the rim, also visible in Plate 9d. They were presumably meant as an-

---

[64] For discussion of the class (under the name "Oil bottles") see Adams 1986, 103; for illustrations see ibid., 148.

[65] For discussion of the class see Adams 1986, 103; for illustrations see ibid., 149.

[66] For discussion of the class see Adams 1986, 103-4; for illustrations see ibid., 150-54.

[67] For discussion of the class see Adams 1986, 104; for illustrations see ibid., 155-6.

[68] For discussion of the class see Adams 1986, 104-5; for illustrations see ibid., 161-4.

[69] For discussion of the class see Adams 1986, 105; for illustrations see ibid., 165.

[70] For discussion of the class see Adams 1986, 105; for illustrations see ibid., 166-71.

[71] For discussion of the class see Adams 1986, 105; for illustrations see ibid., 172-4.

[72] For discussion of the class see Adams 1986, 107; for illustrations see ibid., 177-82.

TABLE 10. REGISTERED NON-POTTERY FINDS FROM PHASE 1*

Reg. no.	Object	Material	Condition	Level (Phase)	Plate

Ceramic

Reg. no.	Object	Material	Condition	Level (Phase)	Plate
1212	Quseba	Ceramic	Complete	18 (1a)	9c-d
1444	Basin	Ceramic	Fragment	17 (1b	9e
1482	Basin?	Ceramic	Fragment	17 (1b)	
1432	Lamp?	Ceramic	Fragment	17 (1b)	
856	Ba figure head	Ceramic	Portion	15a (2b)*	20e
1110	Animal figurine	Ceramic	Fragment	16 (1c)	20d, 3
1093	Model testicles?	Ceramic	Fragment	17 (1b)	

Stone

Reg. no.	Object	Material	Condition	Level (Phase)	Plate
5	Offering table	Sandstone	Portion	Surf.*	10a, 2
297	Offering table	Sandstone	Portion	5 (5b)*	10a, 4
493	Offering table	Sandstone	Almost complete	7 (4c)*	10a, 1
907	Offering table	Sandstone	Fragment	14 (2c)*	10a, 3
1220	Lion-head spout	Sandstone	Complete	18 (1a)	5c-e
487	Statue base	Hornblende	Fragment	8 (4b)*	11b
1221	Oil press?	Aswan granite	Complete	17 (1b)	10c-d
S9	Oil press?	Aswan granite	Complete	5 (5b)*	10c, 1
1172	Bowl	Alabaster	4 fragments	17 (1b)	
1100	Jar stamp	Sandstone	Complete	17 (1b)	11a, 2
1175	Jar stamp	Sandstone	Complete	17 (1b)	11c
1121	Quern	Lava	Upper unit	16 (1c)	12a
S43	Mortar	Hornblende	Fragment	18 (1a)	
1173	Grinding block	Sandstone	Complete?	17 (1b)	12c, 5
1153	Pestle?	Exotic slate	Fragment	17 (1b)	12b, 7
1141	Pestle	Quartzite	Complete	16 (1c)	
1116	Grinding pebble	Granite?	Complete	16 (1c)	
1174	Sharpening pebble	Ferricrete SS	Complete	17 (1b)	12c, 1
1113	Palette	Greywacke	Portion	16 (1c)	12c, 10
1114	Palette	Greywacke	Portion	16 (1c)	12c, 14
1120	Palette	Granite	Portion	16 (1c)	12c, 13
1154	Whetstone?	Limestone	Complete	17 (1b)	12c, 6
1119	Whetstone?	Greywacke	Complete?	16 (1c)	12c, 16
1202	Whetstone?	Greywacke	Complete	17 (1b)	
S41	Perforated weight	Sandstone	Complete	17 (1b)	12e
S42	Perforated weight	Sandstone	Complete	17 (1b)	12e
S43	Perforated weight	Sandstone	Complete	17 (1b)	12e
S44	Perforated weight	Sandstone	Complete	17 (1b)	12e
S45	Perforated weight	Sandstone	Complete	17 (1b)	12e
1115	Weight?	Sandstone	Complete	16 (1c)	21b, 5
1145	Pendant	Carnelian	Complete	17 (1b)	
1171	Bead	Carnelian	Complete	17 (1b)	12d
S1	Carved lintel	Sandstone	Fragment	Surf.*	12f, 1
S30	Carved lintel	Sandstone	Fragment	12 (3b)*	12f, 2
S47	Carved lintel	Sandstone	Fragment	16 (1c)	12f, 3

Iron

Reg. no.	Object	Material	Condition	Level (Phase)	Plate
1142	Dagger blade	Iron	Complete	16 (1c)	13a, 2
1164	Knife or dagger blade	Iron	Fragment	17 (1b)	
1143	Sickle blade	Iron	Portion	16 (1c)	
1144	Knife or sickle blade	Iron	Fragment	16 (1c)	
1169	Punch?	Iron	Almost complete	17 (1b)	
1166	Pointed object	Iron	Almost complete	17 (1b)	
1167	Problematical object	Iron	Portion	17 (1b)	
1201	Large ring	Iron	Portion.	17 (1b)	
1101	3 spikes	Iron	2 whole; 1 frag.	17 (1b)	13b, 1
1165	Spike	Iron	Complete	18 (1a)	13b, 2
1170	Spike?	Iron	Portion	17 (1b)	
1163	Bent rod	Iron	2 portions	17 (1b)	
1112	Heavy rod	Iron	Fragment	17 (1b)	

* The asterisk identifies finds from later phases that are obviously of Meroitic origin.

55

TABLE 10. REGISTERED NON-POTTERY FINDS FROM PHASE 1* (CONT.)

Reg. no.	Object	Material	Condition	Level (Phase)	Plate
		Copper and bronze			
1130	Steelyard scale	Bronze	Almost complete	17 (1b)	13c, 2
1131	Balance-beam scale	Bronze	Almost complete	17 (1b)	13c-d
1160	Balance-beam scale	Copper	3 fragments	17 (1b)	13d, 2-3
1111	Balance-beam scale?	Copper	Portion	16 (1c)	13d, 4
1139	Needle	Copper	Large portion	17 (1b)	
1159	Awl?	Bronze	Fragment	17 (1b)	
1133	Tripod censer	Bronze	Complete	16 (1c)	14a
1158	Miniature beaker	Bronze	Nearly complete	17 (1b)	14b
1134	Miniature qadus	Bronze	Nearly complete	17 (1b)	14c, 3
1507	Miniature vessel	Bronze	Fragment	17 (1b)	
1132	Lamp	Bronze	Complete	16 (1c)	14e-f
1155	Vessel handle	Bronze	Handle complete	17 (1b)	14d, 2
1156	Vessel handle	Bronze	Nearly complete	17 (1b)	14d, 1
1157	Vessel handle	Bronze	Portion	17 (1b)	14d, 3
1135	Ring	Copper	Nearly complete	17 (1b)	15a, 2
1137	Ring	Bronze	Nearly complete	17 (1b)	15a, 1
1138	Ring	Bronze	Complete	17 (1b)	15a, 4
1161	Ring	Bronze	Complete; 2 pcs.	17 (1b)	15a, 3
559	Ptolemaic coin	Bronze	Complete	11a (3d)*	15b-c
675	Ptolemaic coin	Bronze	Complete	11b (3c)*	15b, 2
1031	Roman coin	Bronze	Complete	15a (2b)*	15b, 1
1048	Roman coin	Bronze	Complete	15b (2a)*	15b, 4
1136	Binding band	Bronze	Complete	17 (1b)	
1140	Binding band	Bronze	Nearly complete	17 (1b)	
729	Scrap with decoration	Bronze	Scrap	12 (3b)*	15d
1505	Thin scraps	Bronze	Numerous scraps	17 (1b)	
		Hippopotamus ivory			
1102	Polished object	Ivory	Fragment	17 (1b)	15e, 9
		Potsherd			
1146	Ostracon	Potsherd	Portion	17 (1b)	15f

* The asterisk identifies finds from later phases that are obviously of Meroitic origin.

chor-holes for cords that would have tied down a lid.

Basins. The object shown in Figure 13, no. 1, and in Plate 9e is one corner of what was apparently a large rectangular basin (1444), elaborately decorated. The vessel has a cream to buff slip both inside and out, and is decorated in dark brown designs with red filling. The larger of the surviving sides has what is clearly a winged *sa* design, while the smaller surviving side has a remnant of what may have been a lotus flower design—both familiar figures on Meroitic decorated pottery (see Adams 1986, 270, fig. 122). The larger side has a small square projecting boss near the top, perforated by two holes, as can be seen in the photograph and drawing. These might have been to permit suspension, but more probably were anchor-holes for a cord that would have tied down a lid. Rather similar basins, some with painted Meroitic designs, were found in the demolished Isis temple at Qasr Ibrim (see Driskell, Adams and French 1989, 20-21 and pl. VI,b).

A second, somewhat problematical item (1482), shown in Figure 13, no. 2, appears to be the corner of a very small rectangular ceramic basin or box. It is made from the Meroitic Fine Ware W26, and may have been painted purple on the outside. As the figure shows, there is a double projecting lip on the interior side, which may have been designed to receive a sliding lid. The vessel has an external projecting knob at the one surviving corner, and there is a small, neat hole through one of the side walls, at some distance below the top.[73]

Lamp. Figure 14, no. 1 shows three views of a fragmentary, apparently boat-shaped ceramic vessel (1436). It appears to be of Meroitic Fine Pink Ware W27, and was hand-made in a mold. The indentation at the pointed end of the rim suggests that it was a lamp.

Horse figurine. Horse figurines are a distinctive feature especially of the later Ballaña period, and will be discussed

[73] Ceramic boxes with sliding lids *in situ* were found in the Isis temple at Qasr Ibrim; see Driskell, Adams and French 1989, 21 and pl. VIII, c. For an illustration of a somewhat more elaborately decorated specimen see Wenig 1978, 271, no. 210.

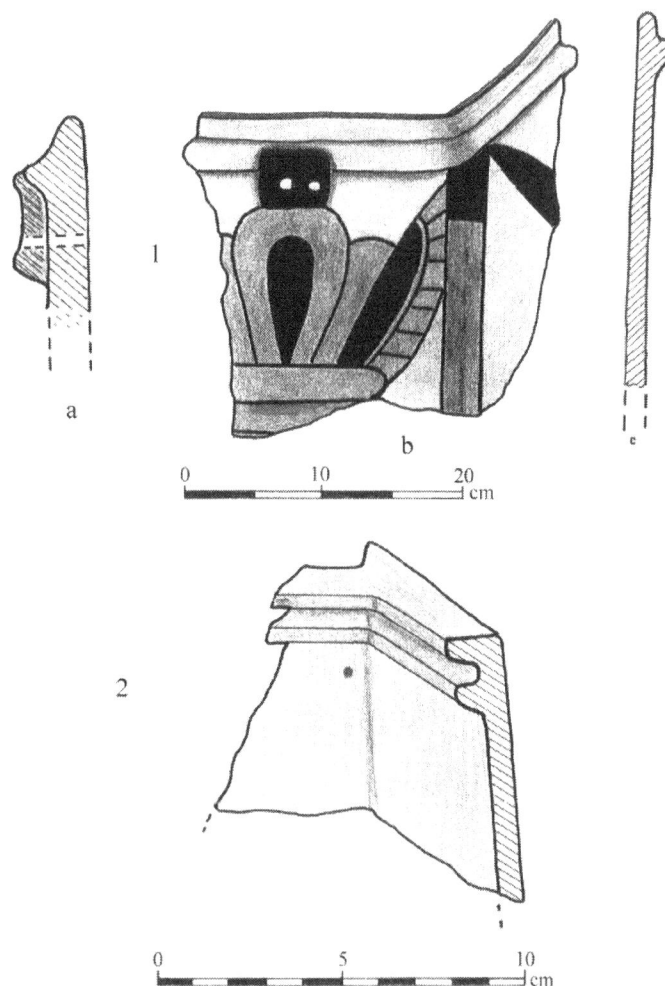

Figure 13. Meroitic ceramic basins. 1, Large terra cotta basin with painted *sa* decoration in black and red (1444), from Level 17. a, Enlarged cross-section through the projecting boss below the rim; b, end view; c, cross-section. 2, Smaller, undecorated basin of Meroitic fine ware (1482), from Level 17. The drawing shows a cross-section as well as an interior view of the one surviving corner.

in the next chapter. However, one small fragment (1110), shown in Plate 20d, no. 3, was found at Level 16 (Subphase 1c).[74]

Ba figurine. The object shown in Plate 20e and Figure 32 (846) is probably of Meroitic origin, although it was found at Level 15a (Subphase 2b). It appears to be the head from a very small *ba* statuette, made from pottery rather than the usual stone. The height of the preserved piece is only 6.4cm, which means that the full original height, if it was indeed a *ba* figure, would have been somewhere between 20 and 30cm. It is made from rather coarse earthenware, and covered by a slip which shades in color from buff to light orange. The hair is painted in dark brown, and there are three vertical red marks, evidently meant to represent facial scars, on the left cheek. This latter feature appears to be very unusual in *ba* statuary, but another example is found on a specimen from Argin (Almagro 1965, pl. VIII). A small square hole in the top of the figure's head was presumably for the insertion of a headdress.

Model of testicles? Figure 15 shows a pair of joined spheres of ceramic, covered by a dark red slip (1093). They may

be intended as models of testicles, since a broken surface above and between the two suggests the place where a phallus might have been attached.

Objects of stone
A wide variety of lithic materials was used to make the various stone artifacts found at Meinarti. Except for black granite and quartzite, all were exotic to the island. Petrographic identifications for most objects were provided by Professor David Whiteman of Khartoum University.

Offering tables. Plate 10a shows one nearly complete and three fragmentary offering tables of Meroitic type (493, 5, 907, and 297), all relatively small and simple in design. Two of the specimens retain traces of Meroitic inscriptions on the rims, but none appears to have had any decorative design within the libation area.[75] None of the specimens was found in the Phase 1 levels; all were recovered from much later deposits, where three of the four had been used as door pivot stones.

The finding of these objects raises the possibility that there may once have been Meroitic graves at Meinarti, although no graves earlier than the Classic Christian pe-

[74] Nearly identical fragments are illustrated in Woolley 1911, pl. 13, upper right.

[75] For other simple Meroitic offering tables see especially Randall-MacIver and Woolley 1909, pls. 34-37.

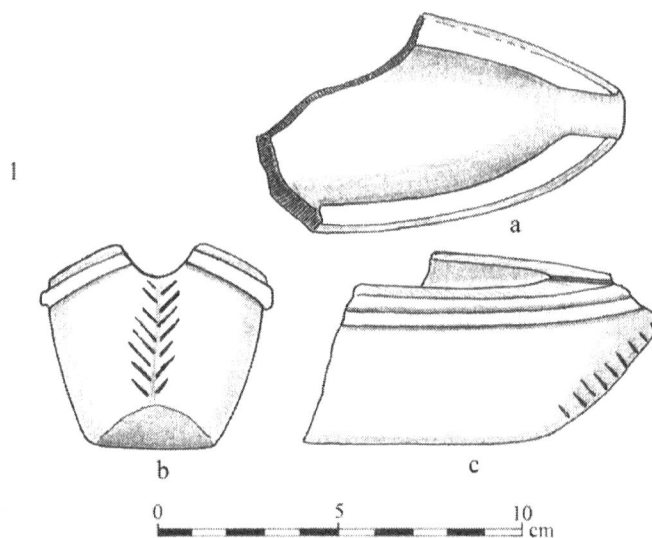

Figure 14. Fragments of boat-shaped ceramic lamps. 1, From Level 17 (1436). a, Top view; b, end view; c, side view. 2, From Level 15b (1079). a, Top view; b, cross-section; c, side view.

riod were located by us. The possibility also exists, however, that the offering tables were brought in from a cem-

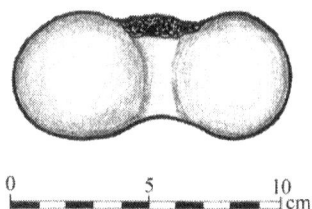

Figure 15. Ceramic model, apparently of testicles (1093), from Level 17.

etery site on the West Bank, specifically for use as pivot stones, since all sandstone for use at Meinarti had in any case to be imported.

Lion-head spout. The lion-head spout (1220), which formed part of the wine-pressing apparatus at Subphase 1a, has already been described, and is shown in Plates 5c-e.

Statue base. The object (487) shown in Plate 10b is evidently the base of a small statue, made of fine hornblende gabbro. Nothing survives except the two bare feet of what was presumably a standing figure. After breakage this frag-

ment was subjected to some secondary usage which resulted in a smoothing off of the broken edges around the base, and also of the breakage surface at the top of the ankles. This object, though found at Level 8 (Subphase 4b) is clearly of either Pharaonic or Meroitic origin, and is described here for that reason.[76]

Oil presses? Of the two granite objects shown in Plate 10c, no. 1 (S9) was found on the floor of a Late Christian building at Level 5 (Subphase 5b), while no. 2 (1221) had been set into the floor of Meroitic House L, at Level 17 (Subphase 1b). Except for the slight difference in size, however, the two specimens are so closely similar in design as to raise a strong probability that they are of contemporaneous origin. Since the smaller specimen came from a secure Meroitic context, the only possibly inference is that the other was salvaged by the medieval Christians from an earlier deposit. Both are made from large, square blocks of Aswan granite, smoothly finished on the top and bottom surfaces but somewhat more roughly finished around the sides. The upper surfaces, shown in Plate 10c, have a kind of small recess in the center, sloping down to a line of neatly drilled holes in the bottom—three in

[76] For a similar fragment from a Meroitic grave at Faras see Griffith 1924, pl. LXVIII, 2-3.

58

one case and four in the other. On the undersides, of which one (no. 2) is shown in Plate 10d, the holes open into a small, deeply carved slot. Curiously, the lower surfaces are even more smoothly finished than are the upper ones. I have not been able to find any parallels to these objects in the published literature. Their use as oil presses has been suggested, but no. 2 could not have been used as such in the location where it was found, since it was set into a house floor, with its upper surface just flush with the floor.

Bowl. Four small pieces (1172) were found, which are probably parts of a single, finely made vessel of white alabaster. Two of the pieces are perfectly flat, and are evidently parts of the vessel bottom; one shows an angle where the side began to curve up from the bottom, and one is a rim sherd, having a projecting ledge at the outer side. The inner surfaces in all the fragments are highly polished, while the exteriors have a matte finish. If these are pieces of single vessel, we estimate the original diameter to have been about 25cm.

Jar stamps. The two objects shown in Plate 11a, nos. 1 and 2, are sandstone jar stamps, both found at Level 17 (Subphase 1b). Both have an elongate pyramidal shape, when seen from the side or top. The smaller stamp (1100) carries a very simple, tree-like design, whose impression is shown in Plate 11b. The larger specimen (1175) exhibits a much more elaborate design, with an elongate fish and several figures above it, two of which appear to be birds while three might be stylized human figures. The actual stamp is shown in Plate 11c, and the seal impression in Plate 11d. I have not found any description or illustration of similar objects in other Meroitic site reports.

Quern. The object shown in Plate 12a is the upper element of a rotary quern (1121), nicely made from grey porphyritic lava. The projecting flange at the right, perforated with a small hole, is for the insertion of a stick with which the device would have been rotated. Similar querns have been in common use throughout the Near East from early times to the present, but no other specimen has been reported from a Meroitic site.

Pestles. The object (1153) shown in Plate 12b, no. 7, looks at first glance like the broken elbow section from a statue. In fact however it is broken only at the smaller, upper end; the larger end is ground off to a very smooth surface. Apparently this was some kind of L-shaped pestle. It is made from purple slate. A second, small pestle of quartzite (1141—not illustrated) has a conical shape, with slightly rounded ends.

Other grinding and abrading apparatus. Plate 12c shows a number of small stone implements that were used in one way or another for grinding and/or abrading. Number 1 is a flat pebble of hard, ferricrete sandstone (1174) which has been ground off smooth on the top and bottom surfaces, and has a shallow groove running all around the edges. Number 5 is a small rectangular block of sandstone (1173), rather roughly finished except on its top surface, which is smooth. In the center of the upper surface is a shallow groove, discolored with hematite, which suggests that the object was used for grinding pigment.

Number 6 is a small piece of fine white limestone (1154) which has been ground down to an elongate rectangular form. The four long surfaces are very smoothly finished, while the ends are only roughly finished. One end looks somewhat battered, while the opposite end has a neatly drilled round hole, 2cm deep, in its center, perhaps for the insertion of a haft.

Numbers 11 and 14 are fragments of two small, finely made palettes of greywacke (1113 and 1114 respectively), such as are commonly found in sites of the Ballaña period.[77] Both have the beveled edges that are characteristic of these implements, and number 11 also has a small perforation at one end. Number 13 is a thin rectangular slab of fine, light grey granite (1120), ground off very smooth on the lower surface. The upper surface is also smoothed but exhibits a longitudinal groove near one edge, as shown in the photo. The edges are battered all the way around, as through the implement had been used for pounding as well as for grinding. Number 16 is a long, thin slab of grey slate or greywacke (1119), all of whose edges are apparently natural fractures. However, one of the large flat surfaces has been artificially smoothed for use as an abrading tool.

Weight? A small piece of sandstone (1115) has been ground down to the shape of a slightly flattened sphere, having a diameter of 8cm. The flattened face has an incised design as shown in Plate 21b, no. 5, and in Figure 16, and at one side of the upper portion there is a pair of incised vertical lines. These markings suggest the probability that the object was used as a weight on a balance scale.

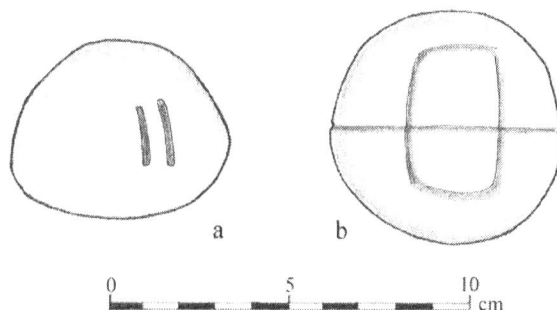

Figure 16. Sandstone weight (1115) from Level 16 , showing incised designs. a, Side view; b, bottom view.

Ornaments of all kinds were extremely rare in the Meroitic levels at Meinarti. However, Plate 12d shows a large, very nicely made carnelian bead (1171), in the form of a flattened sphere.[78] The perforation hole has a groove running across it on one face, as shown in the photo. Another ornament, not shown, is a rectangular pendant bead of fine white alabaster (1145).

Anchors? Plate 12e shows a collection of five large, perforated sandstone weights (S41, S42, S43, S44, and S45)

[77] For another Meroitic find see Griffith 1924, pl. LVIII, 14. For examples from Ballaña sites see Emery and Kirwan 1938, pl. 85, F-H; and Kirwan 1939, pl. XVI, top right.
[78] For parallels see Emery and Kirwan 1938, pl. 38, A; and Griffith 1924, pl. LIX, 12.

that are believed to be boat anchors. Although they are all complete and usable, all had been thrown into the rubbish fill in the wine press, after the time of its abandonment (Subphase 1b).

Architectural elements. Plate 12f shows a group of three sandstone lintel fragments (S1, S30, and S47 from top to bottom) that are illustrated here because they are clearly of Pharaonic or Kushite type, although none was found in a Pharaonic or Meroitic context. Number S1 was found on the surface, no. S30 had been re-used as a door lintel in an Early Christian house (Subphase 3b), and no. S47 was used as a foundation stone under a wall at Subphase 1c. If these elements were ever installed in a structure at Meinarti, it would almost certainly have been in the Administration Building (Building XLVIII). However the possibility also exists, as in the case of the offering tables, that they were salvaged from the nearby site of Kor on the West Bank.

Objects of iron
All of the iron objects from the Meroitic levels were in extremely rusty condition. Because of our lack of laboratory facilities, they could not be treated prior to photography, and they can only be shown in Plate 13 appearing more or less as they were found. Figures 17 and 18 however show the objects as they are presumed to have looked if the rust had been removed. Because of their fragmentary and rusty condition, the function of many of the finds

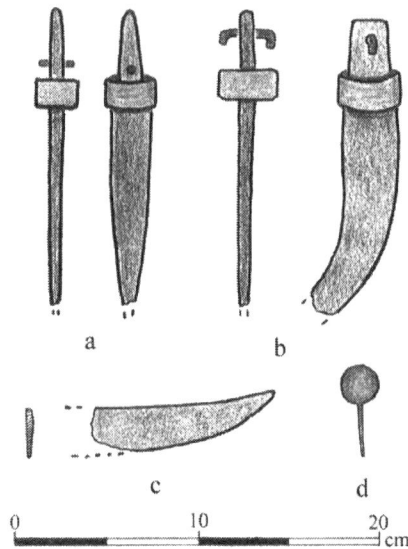

Figure 17. Iron implements and/or weapons. a, Knife (1142) from Level 16; b, curved knife, sickle, or dagger (1162) from Level 15b; c, tip of curved knife or dagger (1143) from Level 16; d, punch (1169) from Level 17.

is uncertain.

<u>Knives or daggers.</u> Plate 13a, no. 2, and Figure 17, a, show the blade of a short, straight-bladed knife or dagger (1142), which is broken off at the tip. The instrument retains the ferrule that would have surrounded the distal end of a wooden handle, and also a single rivet that would have fastened the blade to the handle. The presence of

this kind of hafting makes it much more probable that the object is a knife than that it is a dagger.[79] A second fragment (1164), not shown, is probably the upper end of a similar blade; it also has a perforation and a rivet that would have served to fasten a handle. It is possible that these were arm-knives of the type favored by Nubians in the Christian and post-Christian periods.[80]

<u>Knives or sickles.</u> The section of curving blade (1143) shown in Figure 17, c is one of two specimens that might be parts either of knives, or of curving sickles of the type used in Nubia in the Christian period. However, they lack the serrations on the concave edge that were usually present on Christian sickles.[81]

<u>Punch?</u> The object shown in Figure 17, d (1169) is an iron ball, 2cm in diameter, which is attached to a round, sharp-pointed shaft 5cm long. The instrument is assumed to be some kind of punch, perhaps for working leather.[82]

<u>Pointed instrument.</u> An object (1166) which is not illustrated is a section of iron rod, 1cm in diameter at the center, which tapers to a point at both ends. It appears to be very nearly complete as found, but its function is uncertain.

<u>Problematical instrument.</u> The object (1167) shown in Figure 18 is the basal end of what was apparently a rather complex instrument. As preserved it is a section of round rod which at one end has been hammered into a spatulate shape, although most of the spatulate portion is not preserved. Two very small iron rings are inserted through the flattened portion, just above where the base joins. The

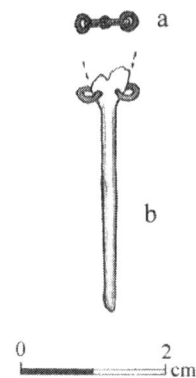

Figure 18. Spatulate implement of unknown use (1167), from Level 17. a, End view from the broken end; b, side view.

bottom end of the shaft is rounded off, and appears to be intact as preserved. The object bears some resemblance to kohl sticks, having one spatulate end, that are illustrated from Karanòg, from the Ballaña tombs, and from Roman Egypt,[83] but none of the others have the inserted rings found in our specimen.

<u>Large ring.</u> Not illustrated is a segment of a large ring

[79] For comparable objects from Roman Egypt see Petrie 1927, pl. XXVIII, 207 and 211.
[80] See Shinnie and Shinnie 1978, pl. XLI, 2.
[81] See Adams 1996, pl. 11b; and Mills 1982, pl. LXXXVI, no. 5.
[82] For parallels from Roman Egypt see Petrie 1927, pl. LXV, 37, 54.
[83] Woolley and Randall-MacIver 1910, pl. 36, upper; Emery and Kirwan 1938, pl. 85, A-B; Petrie 1927, pl. XXIII, 36-40.

(1201) which is half-round in cross-section. The item is too large to be a finger-ring, and is most probably part of a harness or some other fastening apparatus.

Spikes. Plate 13b shows several iron spikes that were found in the Meroitic levels. At the left in the plate are three spikes (1101) rusted together, of which one is straight, one is bent into a sharp curve, and one survives only in a fragment of the head. These are the kind of heavy spikes normally employed in Nubian boat-building.[84] Number 2 in the plate is a somewhat smaller spike (1165), possibly used either in a boat or in a house door. Number 4 (1170) is a section of long, square shaft which tapers to a point at one end, but may possibly be broken off at the other.

Sections of rod. Two fragmentary sections of iron rod were found, both of which are broken off at both ends. One (1163) is a section of rod 14mm in diameter, which is bent at a right angle near one end; the other (1112) is a short, straight section of rod 17mm in diameter.

Objects of copper and bronze[85]
Objects of copper and bronze are the most numerous, and certainly the most interesting, of the non-pottery finds from the Meroitic levels. Although corroded, they are very much better preserved than are the iron objects.

Steelyard scale. The object shown in Figure 19 and in Plate 13c, no. 2 is a steelyard scale (1130), a weighing device still widely used in the Orient today. When in use, the scale is suspended from an overhead beam by the ful-

give the weight, being read at the point where the counterweight is positioned. Our specimen appears to have one large hook attached directly to the end of the weighing beam, and two others at the end of short sections of chain; in these respects the device is identical to a Roman or Byzantine steelyard found at Aphrodisias.[86] There are different calibrations along each of the four faces of the weighing beam, as shown in Figure 19. The calibrations on two sides are marked by stylized Roman numerals, leaving no doubt that the object is of Roman or Roman Egyptian manufacture.[87]

The principle of the steelyard is identical to that in a modern physician's scale, where a heavy weight is slid along a balance beam until the weight of the patient's body is exactly offset. The great advantage of this device is that it permits the weighing of heavy and bulky objects, without the use of very large and cumbersome weights. The steelyard is especially suitable for weighing grain or other loose matter that can be contained in a bag or basket, and the presence of multiple hooks makes it possible to weight more than one bag at a time.

Balance-beam scales. The object shown in Figure 20, in Plate 13c, no. 1, and in Plate 13d, no. 1 is the balance beam for a scale (1131), which would originally have had a pan suspended from the small ring at each end.[88] When found, the suspension fulcrum and hook were folded down into a horizontal position, because of the loss of one rivet, but Figure 20 shows the device as it would have appeared

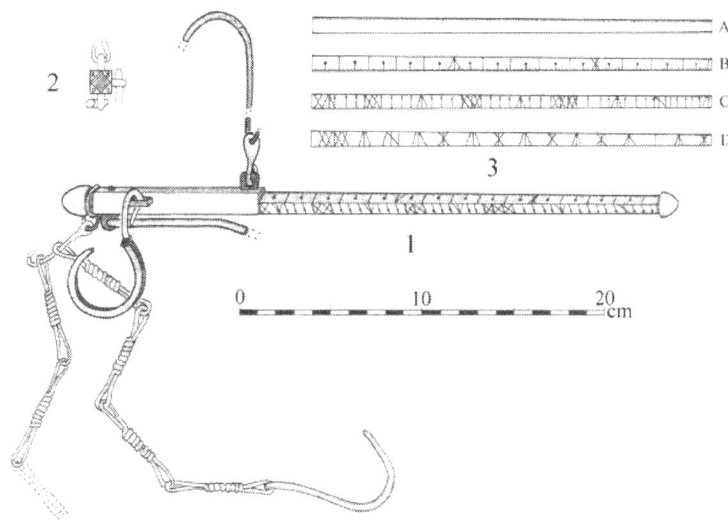

Figure 19. Bronze steelyard scale (1130) from Level 17. 1, Side view of the scale. 2, End-on view of the weighing beam, to show positioning of the four calibrated faces. 3, Calibrations on the four faces of the weighing beam.

crum hook on its upper side. The object to be weighed is then hung from one or more of the hooks at the shorter and stouter end of the weighing beam, and a heavy counterweight is positioned along the other end of the weighing beam at a point where it offsets the weighed object, leaving the beam in a level position. Calibrations along the four sides of the weighing beam, shown in Figure 19,

when in use. Plate 13d also shows fragments of two other balance beams, both made of copper. The fragments at left, nos. 2 and 3, were found together, and are perhaps parts of a single instrument (1160). The fragment at right, no. 4, was found elsewhere, and is most probably part of another scale (1111).

---

[84] For parallel examples from the medieval site of Kulubnarti see Adams and Adams 1998, 50 and pl. 6.2D.

[85] The term "bronze" will here be used to designate any alloy of copper, other than brass.

[86] See *Illustrated London News*, 28 December 1963, p. 1066

[87] For discussion and illustration of other steelyards from Egypt see especially Petrie 1926, 29-33 and pl. XVI.

[88] For virtually identical scales with their pans intact see Emery and Kirwan 1938, pl. 105.

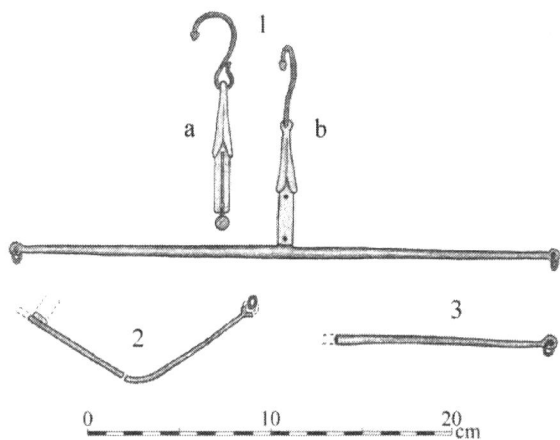

Figure 20. Bronze balance beam scales. 1, Complete scale (1131), from Level 17. a, End view; b, side view. 2, Bent and twisted fragments of beam arm (1160), from Level 17. 3, Fragment of beam arm (1111), from Level 16.

Needle. Not illustrated is a long, narrow strip of copper, pointed at one end and having a slight but uniform curvature, which is believed to be a large needle (1139). The length as preserved is 118mm, but the proximal end, where there was presumably an eyelet, is broken off. The implement has a uniform width of 4mm, except where it tapers toward the tip. The sides are rounded off.

Tripod censer. The small vessel of hammered bronze (1133) shown in Plate 14a represents a type that has often been found in both Meroitic and Ballaña sites, and is believed to be of West Asian origin or derivation.[89] Like nearly all such vessels it is encircled by three pairs of finely scored lines, respectively around the neck, the waist, and the lower body. These vessels are thought to have been censers.

Miniature beaker. The small breaker shown in Plate 14b (1158) is similar in size to the censer, and it too is paralleled by finds from other Meroitic and Ballaña sites.[90] Like the censer it has small tripod feet, but it is made from cast rather than from hammered bronze, and it has a long, sharp projecting spout at one side. Liquid from the vessel interior did not pass directly over the rim and into the spout; rather it passed through a very small hole just below the rim. The size of the hole would suggest that the vessel was meant to dispense some thin liquid, in very small doses.

Miniature vessels. Plate 14c shows three miniature vessels, each no more than 5cm high, of which those at the right and left are clearly models of the qadus (saqia pot). Each has the gentle ribbing from top to bottom of the body, which is characteristic of the Meroitic and X-Group pottery qadus that these toys imitate. The vessel at right (1134) came from Level 17 (Subphase 1b), while the other two miniature vessels in the photo came from Phase 2 levels. These objects are not paralleled by finds from other Meroitic or Ballaña sites. Another bronze object (1507), not shown, appears to be the rim and neck of a miniature jar, also made in imitation of a common Meroitic form.

Vessel handles. Plate 14d and Figure 21 show three ornate bronze handles, each of which has evidently been detached from the rim of a pan, bowl, or jar. The elongate handle at the left in the photo and in Fig. 21, no. 2 (1156) has almost certainly been detached from the neck and shoulder of a jug or flagon, as suggested in the drawing.[91] The large handle in the center and in Fig. 21, no. 1(1155) is more probably from the rim of a large serving bowl.[92] The small specimen at right (1157) is more problematical; the most likely suggestion is that it was a flange projecting from the rim of a small jug or amphora, which had a handle attached on its underside.

Votive lamp. The object shown in Plates 14e and 14f is a kind of votive lamp (1132) that was clearly made in Chris-

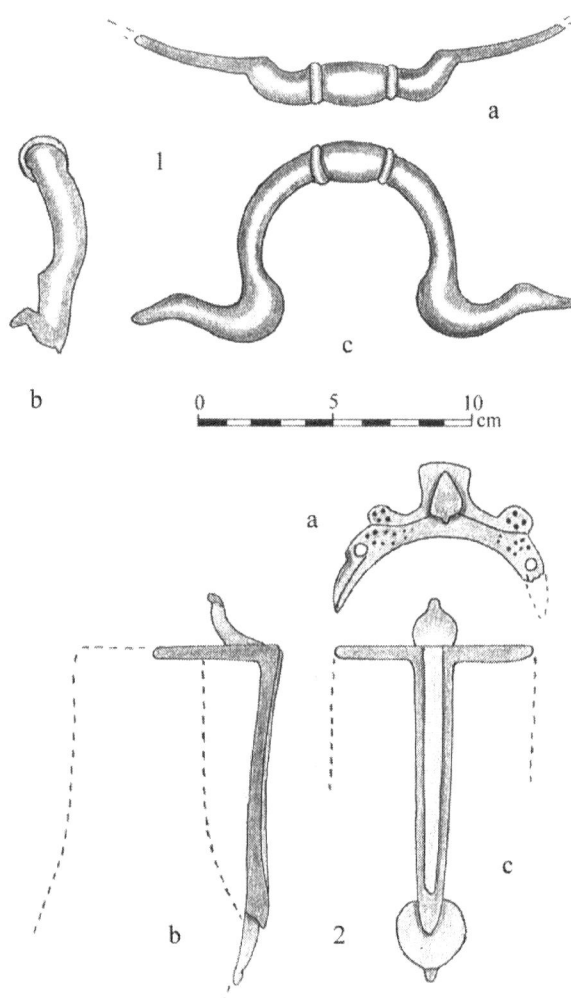

Figure 21. Bronze vessel handles. 1, Bowl handle (1155) from Level 17. a, End view; b, side view; c, top view. 2, Tankard handle (1156) from Level 17. a, Top view; b, end view; c, side view.

[89] For other Meroitic examples see Griffith 1924, pl. LIII, 4; Woolley and Randall-MacIver 1910, pl. 25, 7137 and pl. 31, 7145. For Ballaña examples see Emery and Kirwan 1938, pl. 74, A-D; Kirwan 1939, pl. 8, 3; pl. 12, 5; Bates and Dunham 1927, pl. XXXII, 3, C and pl. XXXII, 5, B.

[90] Griffith 1924, pl. LIV, 12-16; Woolley and Randall-MacIver 1910, pl. 32, 7144; Emery and Kirwan 1938, pl. 74, E.

[91] For comparable handles from the Meroe royal tombs see Dunham 1957, pl. LVII, I and N. For comparable handles from the Ballaña royal tombs see Emery and Kirwan 1938, pl. 69, B, and pls. 77-80

[92] For comparable handles from the Ballaña tombs see Emery and Kirwan 1938, pl. 70, A; for a specimen from Gemai see Bates and Dunham 1927, pl. XXXI, 5.

tian Egypt, but that found its way as an import into pagan Nubia more than once in Ballaña times.[93] Our specimen came from the floor of House XLIV, a house that was newly built at the very beginning of the Ballaña period, at Subphase 1c.

Rings. Bronze and copper rings were popular in Nubia at all periods. Among the specimens shown in Plate 15a, nos. 1-4 are from the Meroitic levels. Numbers 1 (1137) and 4 (1138) are of twisted wire, while nos. 2 (1135) and 3 (1161) are thin, flat strips bent into a ring but not fully closed.

Coins. The four Ptolemaic and Roman coins shown in Plate 15b are illustrated here because of the probability that they came to Meinarti in Meroitic times, although they were all found in much later archaeological contexts. Identification of the coins was provided in all cases by the Department of Coins and Medals at the British Museum, whose help is gratefully acknowledged. Number 1 (1031) is a coin issued in the name of Flaccilla, wife of Theodosius I, around A.D. 383.[94] Number 2 (675) is a coin of Ptolemy I or Ptolemy II, struck between 305 and 246 BC. The obverse (not shown) bears the head of Alexander the Great wearing an elephant scalp headdress; the reverse (shown in detail in Plate 15c) shows the familiar Ptolemaic eagle standing on a thunderbolt. The word ΒΑΣΙΛΕΟΣ can also be read, although the king's name cannot.[95] Number 3 (559) is again an issue of Ptolemy I or Ptolemy II. The obverse shows the head of Zeus-Amon, while the reverse has the same eagle device found on no. 2. Number 4 (1048) is an Alexandrian drachma, probably of Hadrian (r. A.D. 117-138), although identification is difficult because of the extremely worn condition.

Binding bands. A couple of small bronze finds (1136 and 1140) that are not illustrated are strips of thin sheet metal that have been doubled back into a U-shape, and that have perforations at each corner for the insertion of rivets. In one case a small rivet actually survives. Probably these were binding bands used on implement handles.

Decorative element. The item shown in Plate 15d (729) is a small piece of thin sheet bronze, having an elaborate lotus-flower design in repoussé. The piece appears to be complete at the top, where there are two small perforations at the corners, but it may be broken off at the bottom. Probably it was meant to be nailed as a decorative element to a wooden chest.[96] The piece was part of a horde of about 30 copper and bronze scraps found in the Early Christian Level 12 (Subphase 3b), but the Meroitic origin of the design in this specimen is unmistakable.

Bronze scraps. The rubbish fill in the Meroitic wine press (Building LIV) yielded an extraordinary assortment of small bronze scraps (1505). Among them could be recognized the rim fragments of a large bowl and several smaller

bowls, a rim fragment of a miniature *qadus* similar to the ones shown in Plate 14c, two round, pointed rods, two sections of square rod, parts of at least three finger rings, and numerous sheet metal scraps.

Object of ivory
Plate 15e, no. 9 shows a piece of what is evidently hippopotamus ivory (1102) that has been worked for some purpose. One of the larger surfaces retains the original, natural curvature, while the other as well as the sides have been ground off flat. Both ends are broken off, and the purpose of the object cannot be determined.

Ostracon
Plate 15f shows a Meroitic ostracon (1146)—the only such object found at Meinarti. The fragment is from a small bowl of Ware R32, and has three lines of Meroitic cursive writing just below the rim. The inscription is evidently incomplete, as it runs off both at the left and at the right side.[97]

Glass
There were no registered objects of glass from the Phase 1 levels. However, a substantial collection of sherds was recovered. Along with the other glass collections from Meinarti, they were submitted for study to the late Ray Winfield Smith, then Director of the American Research Center in Egypt.[98] The following is quoted from his preliminary report:[99]

Late Meroitic from Meinarti — The material is not sufficient to permit any firm conclusions as to the number or relative frequency of matrices or types of vessels represented. However, the following distinct types do definitely occur:

a. A nearly colorless material which occurs in rather thick specimens which show slight greenish tinge as a result of the thickness, but which is a markedly limpid material.

b. An uncolored material with slight greenish tinge that typically takes on a solid white layer in decay. It is conceivable that this and (a) are identical.

c. A marked dark greenish glass which might be described as blue-greenish which occurs in two specimens that are almost completely flat, conceivably window panes.

d. A very deep, dark blue-green used in a vessel, characterized by a dense cracquelee pattern of decay on both sides.

e. A thin, clear ware that seems to decay into very strongly pitted surfaces.

f. A brownish-yellow transparent material that takes on a solid black decay layer. On careful examination this material reveals itself as quite clear, the yellowish color being produced by the layer of decay.

g. A manganese red material that varies from the purple side to the red side, but is almost certainly produced with

[93] For an identical specimen from one of the Ballaña tombs see Emery and Kirwan 1938, pl. 101, B.

[94] British Museum, Late Roman Bronze Coinage collection, no. 2737.

[95] Comparable issues are listed in *Suoronos Tanumismata Ptolemaium,* in the British Museum Catalogue of Greek Coins.

[96] For somewhat comparable pieces from Jebel Barkal and Meroe see Dunham 1957, pls. LXIII-LXIV

[97] This object was loaned for study to the late Professor Bryan Haycock of Khartoum University, but was not found among his effects after his death. Its whereabouts are unknown.

[98] The glass collections from Meinarti were later loaned for study to Mr. Ralph Pinder-Wilson of the British Museum, and they remain in the British Museum collections today.

[99] Unpublished MS in the author's possession.

manganese. At present, it looks almost black, or at least very deep purple in reflected light.

h. A deep blue material represented in a single specimen that might be the remnants of a stemmed lamp or goblet.

i. A yellow-greenish material represented by a fragment of a hollow-cut bowl with large and very well executed oval cuts. This material has taken on a very thick layer of tight [?light] buff decay. On the basis of material known from other areas, the specimen may well be dated to the 3rd-4th century A.D.

Comparisons and discussion

The architectural remains

Subphase 1a (Level 18)

The surviving remains at Level 18 were so limited in extent that comparisons with other sites must be taken with a certain measure of caution. Taken as a whole, however, the original ensemble of buildings at Meinarti does not bear a close resemblance to any other known Meroitic site. Each of the major surviving structures has parallels elsewhere, but nowhere else were they found in the same close and apparently preconceived conjunction.

The Administration Building (Building XLVIII) although it was almost certainly not a temple, seems clearly to reflect the canons of Kushite and Egyptian monumental architecture. Its closest parallels are to so-called Meroitic palaces at Meroe (cf. especially Garstang 1914, 1-8 and pls. II-III), at Wad ben Naqa (Vercoutter 1962), and especially to a recently excavated structure at Jebel Barkal (Donadoni 1993)—all major centers of Kushite political authority. The Jebel Barkal structure shares with that at Meinarti the peculiarity of having the main entrance, approached by a flight of stone steps, at one side of the building. On the other hand, no Meroitic building of comparable size and complexity has been found elsewhere in Lower Nubia.

The Market Compound (Building XLIII), with its vaulted cellars, seems much more clearly to reflect the canons of Lower Nubian and of Roman Egyptian vernacular architecture. Its closest parallel was to the so-called Western Palace at Faras, which, despite the name, was most probably also a commercial center and not a palace (see Griffith 1926, 21-2 and pls. XIII-XIV). It was however considerably larger than the Meinarti establishment. Unlike the Meinarti market, it was apparently not built in close proximity to other buildings.

The third of the surviving Subphase 1a installations, the Wine Press (Building LIV), is a strictly Lower Nubian phenomenon, represented by 12 examples between Ikhmindi and Meinarti but by nothing further south (see Adams 1966). Yet the Administration Building, the Market Compound, and the Wine Press, despite representing different architectural traditions and different functions, seem to have been built from the beginning as an integrated complex, along with the largely destroyed Building XLVI.

What strikes the eye about Phase 1, then, is the suggestion of town planning, and hence of a central authority.

By contrast, the communities of Wadi el-Arab (Emery and Kirwan 1935, pl. 17), of Karanog (Woolley 1911, pls. 26-29), and of Arminna (Trigger 1967, fig. 23), as well as the smaller settlements dug by us at Gaminarti (Adams and Nordström 1963, 26-8), Kasanarti (Adams 1964c, 220), and Meili Island (Adams and Nordström 1963, 28), all seem to have grown by accretion, and in a somewhat disorderly fashion. Evidence of state planning, or at least of a high level of state involvement, can be seen in a great many of the Meroitic settlements in the Central Sudan, but Meinarti stands alone among Lower Nubian sites in this respect.

It seems probable, then, that the original settlement at Meinarti was undertaken as an enterprise of the Kushite state. It perhaps represents an effort by the rulers to establish a measure of control over, and perhaps also involvement in, the increasingly flourishing trade with Roman Egypt. At the same time, the wine presses here and elsewhere may reflect an effort to lessen the Nubians' heavy dependence on wine imports from Egypt—a dependence that must have created a serious trade imbalance. That the effort was not ultimately successful is indicated by the fact that all the presses were abandoned before the end of the Meroitic period (Adams 1966b, 278), while the volume of wine importation, as attested by sherds of Aswan amphorae, was hardly affected (see Adams 1986, 630).

If my interpretation is correct, then the first settlement at Meinarti need not be dated to a time coeval with the earliest Meroitic reoccupation of Lower Nubia. Presumably, it would not have been deemed as necessary until a considerable volume of trade had already developed within the area.

Subphase 1b (Level 17)

The evidence, through not conclusive, suggests rather strongly that Kushite sovereignty had come to an end by the time of Subphase 1b. This is indicated most obviously by the destruction of the Administration Building—an act that might have been the work of Blemmye marauders, but was just as probably a repudiation of an unwelcome authority by the Nubians themselves. By this time the wine press had already been abandoned, and the Market Compound, after major damage by a flood, was not restored. If the Kushite state did indeed still remain sovereign in Lower Nubia at this time, it clearly had no further interest in maintaining a major installation at Meinarti.

At Subphase 1b we have, for the first time, evidence of rather haphazardly built domestic structures, clustering up against the walls of the older and more monumental buildings. In this respect Meinarti begins much more to resemble the townsites of Wadi el-Arab, Karanòg, and Arminna, each of which is characterized by a rather erratic conjunction of regular, stout-walled houses and more flimsy buildings.

Subphase 1c (Level 16)

The restorations that took place at Subphase 1c bespeak a certain renewal both of commercial activity and of some kind of resident authority, as evidenced by the two newly built, stout-walled residences that were added to the community. These buildings are of a type found both in other

Meroitic settlements[100] and in the Ballaña levels at Qasr Ibrim (Plumley and Adams 1974, 214-25), so their presence is not definite evidence either for or against a continuation of Meroitic sovereignty. What they do prove is that someone at Meinarti was again planning for a long future, and now had wealth enough to command the services of professional architects. Taken in conjunction with the evidence from earlier levels, I think this most probably happened under the umbrella of stability provided by the newly emerged Nobatian (Qustul-Ballaña) monarchy.

Summary of the architectural evidence
While it can hardly be more than conjecture, I am inclined to see in Subphase 1a the last evidences of Kushite state authority at Meinarti; in Subphase 1b the evidence of a period of poverty and instability following the collapse of Kushite authority, and before the emergence of an effective Nobatian successor-state; and in Subphase 1c the return of a measure of stability under the Nobatian successor-state.

The artifactual remains

Pottery
Unlike the architectural remains, the pottery collections from Phase 1 present no surprises. They exhibit the same combination of Meroitic fine wares, Meroitic household wares, and early X-Group wares already encountered in the habitation sites at Gaminarti (Adams and Nordström 1963, 26-8), Kasanarti (Adams 1964c, 220-21), and Meili Island (Adams and Nordström 1963, 28). We can observe, in the finds from Subphases 1a, 1b, and 1c, the successive displacement of the traditional Meroitic wares by the earliest X-Group wares. The very few registered vessels from Subphase 1a are all of late Meroitic types (Index Cluster M2), while at Subphase 1b (where most finds were made) there is about an equal mixture of Meroitic and X-Group wares (Index Cluster MX), and at Subphase 1c only X-Group wares are found (Index Cluster X1).[101]

In and of itself, this evidence cannot be taken as *prima facie* evidence for the end of Meroitic sovereignty at any particular point in time. At Qasr Ibrim, we have found purely X-Group pottery in association with Meroitic textual material so consistently as to suggest either that the ceramic transformation was complete long before the end of Kushite sovereignty, or that the use of Meroitic writing continued long after it; neither possibility will be ruled out until further excavations are conducted at Qasr Ibrim (See Adams 1982b, 211-16). But in any case, as I have demonstrated elsewhere (Adams 1979, 727-44), pottery styles "march to their own drummer;" they do not always reflect concurrent developments in the political, economic, or even the religious spheres.

The non-pottery finds
The non-pottery finds from Meinarti, like the pottery finds, are nearly all of previously familiar Meroitic types. They

are also in many cases of familiar Ballaña types, for, outside the domain of pottery, there was not much change in the material inventory of the Nubians from Kushite to post-Kushite times. The most novel items found were the large granite objects which have been interpreted as oil presses, the two jar stamps, and the single steelyard scale. The latter however is of a familiar Roman type, and its presence in a site that was clearly involved in trade with Roman Egypt should occasion no surprise.

It is worth noting nevertheless that a great many of the object types, other than pottery, have been previously familiar from finds in Meroitic graves rather than from habitation sites. This is true in particular of the various kinds of bronze vessels. Their presence at Meinarti may indicate that the inhabitants here enjoyed a higher standard of living than did those in other Meroitic communities in Lower Nubia, or at least those that have been excavated.

Implications and issues
The findings from Phase 1 at Meinarti bear in one way or another on several unresolved issues concerning the timing, the extent, and the nature of Meroitic occupation in Lower Nubia.

The Napatan and early Meroitic hiatus
It was C. M. Firth who first suggested, three-quarters of a century ago, that Lower Nubia had been almost wholly depopulated following the time of the New Kingdom occupation (Firth 1927, 28). In the ensuing decades nothing has been found, archaeologically, to disconfirm that suggestion. The exhaustive, kilometer-by-kilometer exploration of both banks of the Nile from Faras to Dal, by the Unesco Archaeological Survey and by the Scandinavian Joint Expedition, failed to disclose a single site or grave that could be assigned unambiguously to the Napatan period. It is possible, as some have suggested, that certain graves assigned to the late New Kingdom belong instead to the early Napatan period, but the graves so identified conspicuously lack the large component of hand-made pottery that is present in the Napatan graves at Sanam (Griffith 1923, 73-90) and at Meroe (Dunham 1963, 357-449).

It could be suggested too that Napatan remains were not found by us, or by more than half a dozen previous expeditions,[102] because they were built on low ground and had been either swept away by floods or buried under silt. This is a plausible suggestion with reference to habitation sites, as will be seen presently when Meroitic habitations are discussed. On the other hand, all of the successive peoples of Nubia were concerned to locate their cemeteries above the level reached by floodwaters, and the idea that Napatan cemeteries would have been entirely on or near the floodplain is inconceivable.

With the single exception of Qasr Ibrim, to be discussed in a moment, the evidence that has been adduced in favor of a Napatan occupation in Lower Nubia is all textual.[103] This evidence confirms something that was never in doubt: that the Kushites throughout the Napatan and early Meroitic periods continued to claim sovereignty over

---

[100] At Wadi el-Arab, Karanòg, Arminna, and ash-Shaukan; see Emery and Kirwan 1935, pl. 17, Trigger 1967, fig. 23; and Woolley 1911, pls. 26-29.

[101] For discussion of the clusters and their significance see Adams 1986, 627-9.

[102] For references and discussion see Adams 1964b, 106.

[103] cf., among other sources, Priese 1973; 1975; and 1976.

Lower Nubia, and that trading expeditions regularly passed through it. Certainly, too, a way-station was maintained at Qasr Ibrim,[104] and there may well have been others at other points. So far as a popular occupation is concerned, however, the evidence is simply not there. For parallel situations it is only necessary to point out that today many nations, both north and south of the Sahara, continue to assert sovereignty over huge tracts of uninhabited desert, for the sake of control over resources and trade routes.

The Meroitic reoccupation
The eventual reoccupation of Lower Nubia in Meroitic times is of course attested by scores of sites, but the actual date and the circumstances of resettlement remain matters of controversy. There is no reason to suppose that the reoccupation took place at or near the beginning of what is conventionally designated as the Meroitic era, or indeed very long before its end. My reasons for believing in a relatively short and late Meroitic reoccupation are twofold: first, the lack of any recognizable change in the pottery from beginning to end of the Meroitic occupation, and second, the lack of any appreciable stratigraphic depth in any of the Meroitic habitation sites dug by me.[105]

It is however the site of Qasr Ibrim that provides the proverbial "exception that proves the rule" in regard to both the early Meroitic hiatus and the late Meroitic reoccupation. The Roman deposits at Qasr Ibrim, which in places were over 3 m deep (see Adams 1985, 10-11), have yielded a series of more than two dozen pottery wares that are totally unlike anything found in Meroitic sites in Lower Nubia.[106] Particularly conspicuous are several amphora types that occur in enormous quantities, but that are unknown from Meroitic sites.[107] Since the Roman deposits (identifiable by both coins and Latin papyri) cannot date before 30 B.C., and since their depth suggests an occupation of at least a century, I take it that the Meroitic sites that lack the distinctive Qasr Ibrim pottery wares must date at least after about A.D. 100.

With regard to Meinarti itself, I have suggested already that the first settlement here need not have been contemporaneous with the bulk of Meroitic reoccupation; it could have taken place at a time when settlement and trade had already reached a point where some degree of control was considered desirable.

A single radiocarbon date of A.D. 80 ± 130 years, was obtained in 1965 from one of the charred timbers in the foundation of the Administration Building.[108] If reliable, this would establish the date for the original settlement on the island, assuming that the Administration Building was one of the first buildings constructed. The date is certainly within the realm of historical possibility, yet it must be treated with extreme caution, deriving as it does from a single sample. Radiocarbon dating was still relatively in its infancy in 1965, and we did not yet fully understand that "one date is no date," and that a fully acceptable radiocarbon determination must be based on at least half a dozen samples.[109]

The low Niles
It was C. M. Firth who suggested also that the depopulation of Nubia in Napatan and early Meroitic times was due to declining levels of the Nile, which made effective irrigation impossible (Firth 1915, 21). Some *post hoc* support for this thesis is provided by Meinarti and other Meroitic habitation sites of Lower Nubia, which were built on, or so close to, the floodplain that they were repeatedly damaged by floods, and many may have been destroyed altogether (see Adams n.d.1). I take it for granted that the settlers would not have chosen such exposed localities had they been able to anticipate the kind of floods that regularly occurred in later years, but that were apparently not known to them from previous experience.

It is probably the same circumstance that accounts for the scarcity of known Meroitic settlements in Lower Nubia. The evidence for Meroitic resettlement is in fact overwhelmingly mortuary: cemeteries outnumber habitation sites by a factor of more than 10 to 1 (cf. the map in Adams 1977, 339). The Meroites, it seems, took pains to locate their cemeteries, but not their homes, on safely elevated ground.

The role of the saqia
While Firth is responsible for the theory of Napatan depopulation, I believe it was I who first suggested that the Meroitic reoccupation was made possible by the introduction of *saqia* irrigation (Adams 1964b, 119-20). This thesis has recently been challenged on a number of grounds by David Edwards, who asserts that "The presence of the *saqia* within unequivocally Meroitic contexts is far from certain" (Edwards 1996, 80). While I agree with Edwards that I may have overstated the importance of the *saqia,* particularly as a factor in the initial Meroitic reoccupation, he is in error in supposing that my evidence was derived entirely from Meinarti (ibid.). Before I began excavating at Meinarti, *qadus* knobs had already been found by us in Meroitic sites at Faras, Gaminarti, Kasanarti, and Meili Island, and I had already illustrated the *qadus* as a typical Meroitic vessel form in the *Introductory Classification of Meroitic Pottery* (Adams 1964a, 139, no. 8) [110] a monograph written before the excavations at Meinarti began. From Meinarti itself it is true that both the real *qadus* (1152) and the miniature bronze *qadus* (1134) came from Level 17 (Subphase 1b), which may post-date the end of Kushite sovereignty. There is on the other hand the indisputable evidence of the *saqia* well that had been dug at Level 18, but had already been filled over at Level 17.

I think, in sum, that the presence of the *saqia* at least in the last century of Meroitic occupation is sufficiently attested, although its economic significance may still be a

---

[104] As attested by the finding of a Taharqa temple there; see especially Anderson and Adams 1979, 31-3.

[105] Specifically at Gaminarti (Adams and Nordström 1963, 26-8), Kasanarti (Adams 1964c, 220-21), Meili Island (Adams and Nordström 1963, 28), and Meinarti.

[106] The only comparable finds so far known have come from Kerma and from the cemetery of Emir Abdallah, in the Abri district. See Fernandez 1980 and 1984.

[107] The wares are described in detail in Adams n.d.2.

[108] University of Arizona Radiocarbon Lab, # A-606.

[109] The Sudan Antiquities Service had no funds to pay for radiocarbon dates. The single date from Meinarti was provided as a personal favor by a colleague at the University of Arizona.

[110] For another illustration of a Meroitic *qadus* see Griffith 1924, pl. XXI, no. XXVa.

matter for dispute. Edwards himself acknowledges that "Prior to the introduction of the *saqia,* there can be little doubt that the economic potential of the region, especially in terms of its basic subsistence resources, was minimal" (Edwards 1996, 81). He goes on to argue that "...we may suggest that the real significance of Lower Nubia in the Meroitic period continued to lie in its role as the primary line of communication between the savannahs of the central Sudan and Egypt. The string of Meroitic settlements established along the length of the valley maintained and protected this line of communication...." (ibid.). Without discounting the strategic factor, which may indeed account for the colonization of Meinarti itself, it must nevertheless be observed that the "string of settlements" was far too extensive to be explained simply by the need to keep open a trade route. Edwards' own generally excellent monograph enumerates no fewer than 120 Meroitic cemeteries between Maharraqa and Dal (ibid., 103-5). If we divide that figure into the total distance involved (about 300 km), we come up with an average of one site every 2.5 km. I think we can be confident therefore that the Meroitic population was far larger and, especially, far more dispersed than was required by political and strategic considerations alone, nor can we assume that it was sustained largely by trade with Egypt. Some considerable role must still be allowed to agriculture, and therefore to the *saqia,* in the economy of Meroitic Nubia.

Edwards and I agree, it is clear, that the *saqia* must have been essential to any large-scale resettlement of Lower Nubia, but disagree as to the date of its introduction. He argues that the Meroitic population must have been small because the *saqia* was absent, while I approach the matter from the opposite direction, arguing that the *saqia* must have been present because the Meroitic population was large.

The end of Kushite sovereignty

The date when the Kushite Empire came finally to an end—usually referred to as the "fall of Meroe"—has been and remains a matter of dispute. I would suggest however that the end of Kushite sovereignty in Lower Nubia was not necessarily coeval with the fall of Meroe itself. It could have occurred either earlier or, conceivably, even a little later, if a splinter-state had survived in the same way that, a thousand years later, the splinter-state of Dotawo outlived the parent kingdom of Makouria (see Adams 1977, 532-6). In the Meroitic case, however, I think the evidence points strongly toward an earlier demise in Lower Nubia.

I have always believed that a majority of the resettlers in Lower Nubia were not Meroitic-speaking Kushites but Nubian-speaking Nobatae, migrating either from the upriver districts of Kush or from the steppelands of Kordofan, or both. Arrived in the north, they settled under Kushite rule and absorbed most of the indigenous Meroitic culture, while retaining a separate linguistic and ethnic identity. This is, in my view, the most likely explanation for the establishment of the Nubian language in Lower Nubia (see Adams 1982a, 11-38). Despite their cultural assimilation, the newcomers might well have been restive under the control of an elite Kushite minority, and

have seized the opportunity to throw off Kushite control before the final disintegration of the empire in the Central Sudan.

On this point the testimony of Procopius, though given long after the fact, deserves consideration. He asserts that in A.D. 297 the Emperor Diocletian withdrew the Roman frontier from Maharraqa to Philae, under an agreement made with the Blemmyes and the Nobatae.[111] The text seems clearly to imply that the Nobatae were in *de facto* control of Lower Nubia at the time, and there is conspicuously no mention of Meroitic sovereignty. If this interpretation is correct, then Kushite authority had already ended by 297. This in turn would imply, if my reading of the archaeological evidence is correct, that Subphase 1b at Meinarti would have begun before A.D. 297. Ceramic evidence nevertheless suggests a somewhat later dating, to which I have adhered in the present volume.

The end of Phase 1 at Meinarti

None of the findings from Meinarti provide a satisfactory answer as to when or why the Phase 1 occupation came to an end. On this subject, architecture, stratigraphy, and ceramics seem to give rather differing testimony. Architecturally, virtually all of the buildings of Subphase 1c were still standing, and were incorporated into the village plan, at Subphase 2a, suggesting little or no hiatus between the two episodes of occupation. On the other hand there was, in most parts of the site, an accumulation of 70 to 80cm of drifted sand between the Level 16 (Subphase 1c) and Level 15b (Subphase 2a) floor levels. Moreover the pottery found at Subphase 1c is all of very early X-Group types, and many typical Ballaña artifact types such as female figurines and lugged mortars are missing. On the other hand the pottery of Subphase 2a is of distinctively late X-Group types, with some Early Christian wares already beginning to appear. I have reconciled the various lines of evidence as best I can by estimating the terminal date for Phase 1 at A.D. 425, and the beginning date for Phase 2 at A.D. 475, allowing a 50-year hiatus in between.

The reasons for this abandonment, as for many other, later abandonments at Meinarti, are far from clear. It may be suggested however that Subphase 1c represents the last gasp of Meinarti's importance as a commercial entrepot, with abandonment taking place when trade with the upriver districts came virtually to an end. This would be a reflection not of impoverishment in Lower Nubia itself, but of the very conspicuous impoverishment that took place in the more southerly regions of Kush, in post-Meroitic times. When no more traders came from the south, there was no further reason to maintain an entrepot at the foot of the Second Cataract.

[111] *De Bello Persico* I: xix. For a translation of the text see Emery 1965, 234-5.

PHASE 2:
THE LATE BALLAÑA AND TRANSITIONAL OCCUPATION

It requires no more than a glance at Plate 16 to show that, at Phase 2, we are in what Americans would call "a whole new ballgame." The surviving architectural remains, particularly at Subphases 2a and 2b, were among the best preserved of all the Meinarti levels, and they covered an area more than twice that of the preceding Subphase 1c (Level 16). In addition, the harvest of registered artifacts was enormous; it was exceeded in quantity only by the total of artifacts from Late Christian Subphase 5b.

Phase 2 was inaugurated by a wholesale program of new building, involving almost entirely thin-walled and irregular residential structures,[1] tightly clustered along narrow and winding streets. Subsequent to the initial rebuilding, however, there was relatively little change in the plan of the community during its three subphases. The depth of sand and refuse deposition that accumulated was nevertheless substantial, amounting to almost two meters in the central part of the site (see Figs. 5 and 6). This points to a considerable length of occupation, in spite of the relative lack of architectural change.

Phase 2 is comprised of the three Subphases 2a, 2b, and 2c, represented by stratigraphic Levels 15b, 15a, and 14 (see Fig. 22). The finds leave no doubt that Subphases 2a and 2b belong to the later Ballaña period, beginning perhaps around A.D. 475. By the time of Subphase 2c we have almost certainly entered what is, historically, the earliest phase of the Christian period. However, no church had as yet been built at Meinarti, and the great bulk of the pottery and other artifacts were still of X-Group types. For this reason I have, in keeping with earlier terminology, referred to Subphase 2c as Transitional rather than as Early Christian (see Adams 1964c, 243). The terminal date for the Phase 2 occupation was probably around the middle of the 7th century A.D., after which there was another wholesale program of rebuilding, signaling the beginning of Phase 3. This development will be discussed in a later volume, *Meinarti II*.

Because of the generally good preservation of buildings, including their floors, the stratigraphic controls for artifacts found in the Phase 2 levels are a good deal more reliable than they are in the Phase 1 levels. Nevertheless, the allocation of particular artifacts to Subphase 2a or to Subphase 2b is sometimes arbitrary, since in many parts of the site there was no architectural change, and little buildup of deposit, between the two levels. A further complication arises from the fact that some, but certainly not all, of the intact objects had probably been deliberately

buried under house floors. In such cases their dating should of course be associated with the overlying rather than the underlying floor, but there was often no way of confirming this.

Subphase 2a (Level 15b)

The nucleus of the newly enlarged community consisted of four buildings, Houses XXXIV, XLII, XLIII, and XLIV, which survived with relatively little modification from Subphase 1c. However, they were now surrounded on all sides by a warren of newly built, thin-walled rooms, comprising Houses XXXV, XXXIX, XL, XLI, XLV, LVIII, LIX, and LX, as shown in Figure 23. These house designations are somewhat arbitrary, since the numbers were assigned before the buildings had been fully cleared.[2] Houses XXXV, XLIII, and LVIII in fact formed a single contiguous cluster, and House XLI abutted directly against House XLII.

Except for the surviving Houses XXXIV and XLII, and the small new House LX, each of the "houses" actually comprised an irregular aggregation of two or more suites of rooms, having no direct communication with each other. Each suite was entered through a single doorway from the outside, and each contained from two to eight interconnected rooms within, but there was no access from one suite to the next. Many exterior as well as interior doorways were flanked by buttresses, indicating that they had been equipped with closing wooden doors, but this was by no means universally true. Here and there throughout the houses there were individual, mostly small rooms that seem to have been entered through overhead hatchways, since no ground-level entrances were present.

The very irregular plans convey the impression that each of the larger "houses" had grown by accretion, with new suites built against the outer walls of previously existing ones. If this is so, then of course the plan of Level 15b (Figure 23) does not show the village as it appeared at the beginning of Subphase 2a, but only as it appeared when the process of accretion was largely complete. The size and layout of the suites suggests the probability that most were single family dwellings, though a few were large enough to have accommodated larger kin groups. On the plan, suites within each "house" are designated by the letters A, B, C, etc., and the boundaries separating contiguous suites are indicated by dotted lines.

The remains at Subphase 2a, although much more extensive than those at Subphase 1c, still do not represent the full original extent of the community, for the outer limits on all sides had, as before, been eaten away by

---

[1] Brick sizes throughout Phases 2 and 3 were typically 36cm long, 18cm wide, and 9cm thick. For convenience, walls built of stretcher bricks only are here described as 20-cm walls (allowing for the thickness of plaster), and walls having a thickness of two stretcher bricks or one header brick are described as 40-cm walls.

[2] For discussion see *Introduction*

floodwaters. Moreover, as in all phases, the northern half of the site remained unexcavated.

Surviving remains from Subphase 1c

House XXXIV

This was the more westerly of the two stoutly built, square houses that were first added to the community at Subphase 1c. Apart from a slight raising of the floor levels in Rooms 1 and 3, and the addition of a small mastaba in one corner of Room 3, there was no interior modification. Floor levels in this house could not of course be raised very much, without seriously reducing the headroom under the brick-vaulted ceilings. Outside the house, a stout projecting wing wall was added to its southeast corner, but its purpose seems to have been to provide a protected entryway to the neighboring House XLII, rather than to effect any change in House XXXIV. Curiously, this house continued to stand free from all neighboring structures, as it had in Subphase 1c, although it was now separated only by the narrowest of alleys from other buildings on all four sides. This physical separation, along with the architectural quality of the building itself, seems to argue that the occupant was a person of special, elevated status.

House XLII (Pl. 16d)

This house, nearly identical in plan to House XXXIV and also built at Subphase 1c, nevertheless underwent considerably more modification than did its neighbor. Within the house proper (designated as <u>Suite A</u>) the floor level in the large outer Room 1 was raised by almost a meter, and in the inner rooms it was raised by more than 50cm. This exceptionally deep fill was apparently considered necessary as a reinforcement because the eastern wall of the house had begun to buckle dangerously inward. After the floor was raised, an additional reinforcing thickness of masonry was built against the inner face of the east wall. The central pilaster that had formerly provided partial support for the roof in Room 1 was now dismantled, and its stump buried under the newly raised floor, so that there was no longer any interior support for the roof. A small brick-lined bin was built adjoining the west wall of Room 2, and two hand-made globular pots were buried under the floor in Room 3.

However, by far the most conspicuous change was external: a very stout staircase of brick, over 1m wide, was built against the south outside wall, and undoubtedly provided access to a second storey. This addition was probably necessary because the roof levels had been raised, concurrently with the raising of the interior floor levels. As a result, the upper storey could no longer be reached via the original, interior stairs, which were now largely buried under the floor of Room 3. Only the lower six steps of the outside stairway were preserved, since the upper part of the structure had been destroyed along with the adjoining wall. The width of the six surviving treads was 30cm.

House XLII continued as before to be adjoined on the east by a walled courtyard (<u>Suite B</u>), from which it was entered. The floor level here was raised by about 40cm above that of Subphase 1c, but there was otherwise little

modification of the interior arrangements. However, the original doorway from the outside, at the southwest corner of the courtyard, was now adjoined on its outer side by a small antechamber which may have been intended to restrict access, since other structures had now been built alongside. The courtyard was adjoined as before by House XLIV on its northern side, and it was now adjoined also by House XLI on its southern side. The most easterly extremity of the courtyard was not preserved at this level.

House XLIII

This was the surviving remnant of the old Meroitic Market Compound, already extensively rebuilt and modified at Subphase 1c. It was the last remaining trace of the original Meroitic architecture at Meinarti. At Subphase 2a it underwent further modifications, as interior partitions were rearranged, and new, thin-walled rooms were added at the eastern side. Essentially, the remnants of the old house were now swallowed up within the large residential cluster comprised of itself along with the adjoining House LVIII to the north and House XXXV to the west.

House XLIV

This was the structure built at Subphase 1c, on top of the ruins of the Eastern Range of the Market Compound. The rooms built at Subphase 1c survived, without a great deal of modification, as Suite C at Subphase 2a, but they were now adjoined on the north by newly added Suites A and B. Both of these had the typical features of other Subphase 2a houses: irregularly shaped rooms and thin, sometimes curving walls.

Newly built structures at Subphase 2a

The eight "houses" newly built at Subphase 2a were in reality aggregations of residential suites, tightly clustered together and highly irregular in plan. Walls were exclusively 20cm thick, and were often curving. No single suite had a completely regular, square or rectangular plan, as did the older Houses XXXIV and XLII. Exterior walls exhibited odd angles, and the arrangement of interior partitions can only be described as chaotic. Every suite shared a party wall with at least one neighbor, and each of the residential complexes gave very much the impression of a house of cards, with each suite leaning for support partially on its neighbors.

House XXXV

This was the largest and the most irregular of the Phase 2 "houses," directly adjoining the west side of the old House XLIII. On its other three sides it was separated by narrow streets and/or small plazas from the neighboring houses: from House LVIII on the north, from Houses XXXIX, XXXIV, and XLII on the south, and from House LIX at the southwest corner. The western extremity of the cluster was not preserved (see Fig. 23 and Plate 16c).

House XXXV as preserved at Subphase 2a (Level 15b) consisted of 34 rooms in seven suites. Individual suites varied in size from two to eight rooms, the average size being five rooms. Suite A, at the northwest corner of the complex, was the largest of the suites and the most regular in plan, and it may very well have been the first one built. Its main room (Room 5) was large enough to require a central pilaster to support the master roof beam. The adjoining, four-room Suite B was also fairly regular in plan, at least in that all its walls were straight. Suite C, D, and E were very much more irregular in plan, and almost certainly represent accretions to the original complex. Their rooms were considerably smaller than those in Suites A and B, and several had irregularly curving walls. Suites F and G, directly adjoining the west side of old House XLIII, were the most erratic of all in plan. It seems virtually certain that these were the last components of the "house" to be added, encroaching on what had formerly been open streets.

Interior features of House XXXV included a sunken basin and a *quseba* in Suite A, two mastabas in Suite E, two ceramic ovens in Suite F, and several pots buried in room floors.

House LVIII
This cluster of rooms, adjoining House XLIII on the north, was the most regular in plan of the newly built Phase 2 "houses." The complex was well preserved except at its northwest corner, where some rooms were evidently lost through flood destruction (see especially Plates 16a and 16b, foregrounds). The surviving remains consisted of 18 rooms in seven suites. Although the cluster had certainly grown by accretion over time, at least some of the suites were apparently built concurrently.

House LVIII differed from all the other Subphase 2a buildings in that four of its seven suites consisted of two rooms only: a relatively long outer room and a smaller inner room, an arrangement recalling that of the late Meroitic houses at Gaminarti (Adams and Nordström 1963, 26-8). The individual suites seem too small to have been anything but individual family dwellings, and most were not interconnected in such a way that larger kinship groupings could be recognized. However, Suites E and G, at the southeastern corner of the complex, were both entered through Suite A of the adjoining House XLIII, suggesting a family connection among the inhabitants of the three suites.

Floor features were relatively few in House LVIII, but one room had a small corner bin, one had the remains of a *quseba,* one had a very small mastaba, and several had hand-made vessels buried in the floor. Without exception, these features were in room corners.

House XLV
This "house," at the northeast corner of the village, was not fully investigated, as it extended beyond the limits of the excavation area to the east, and possibly also to the north. The portion excavated consisted of 10 rooms, in three suites that were rather arbitrarily differentiated. Suite A, at the western end, was a fairly typical five-room suite. It was adjoined to the east by large rooms, designated as Suites B and C, whose function is uncertain.

House LIX
This was one of the smallest of the Subphase 2a "houses," consisting only of six rooms in two suites, which together formed a nearly regular square. It seems very probable that the whole complex was built at one time. The house was separated by narrow, angled streets from House XXXV to the north and east, and House XXXIX to the south. Preservation of the walls was generally rather poor, as the building stood at the western edge of the village. There were a few suggestions that the house originally extended westward beyond the portion that was preserved.

House LIX was comprised of a smaller Suite A at the north and a much larger Suite B at the south. Suite A was entered from the west by a wide doorway with three descending steps, which therefore was almost certainly an outside doorway. Suite B was unusual in that it had two entryways from the outside, one at the south and one at the west. Its very large Room 6 had two *qusebas* standing side by side in the northeast corner, and the smaller neighboring Room 5 had a stone grinding slab set into the floor.

House XXXIX
This formerly large "house" stood at the southwestern side of the community, and was separated by very narrow streets from Houses LIX and XXXV to the north, and from Houses XXXIV and XL to the east. Because the whole western side of the complex had been destroyed by flooding, the surviving portion presented the appearance of a long and narrow building, but this may not be a true indication of its original shape. Preservation was generally poor, except in the case of the most easterly walls.

The plan of House XXXIX resolves itself quite readily into two sections that were probably built at different times. The northern section comprised Suites A, B, and C, while the southern section comprised Suite D and the remnants of one or more additional suites that were not numbered. The complex included altogether 20 rooms that were numbered. Both Suite A and Suite C were exceptionally large, and Room 5 in Suite A had a narrow mastaba running along the full length of its south wall. Just beside it, at the west end, were three ceramic cones to support a pot.

The wall between Suites C and B was unusual in that it was one of the very few in any of the newly built houses that was 40cm rather than 20cm thick; that is, it was built of alternating header and stretcher bricks instead of stretchers only. The same however was true of the interior wall separating Rooms 16 and 17 in Suite D. Apart from the mastaba in Suite A, previously mentioned, there were no surviving interior features in House XXXIX.

House XL
This small house stood immediately to the south of the old House XXXIV, from which it was separated by a gap less than 40cm wide. The surviving remains at Subphase 2a were very poorly preserved for, unlike any of the neighboring structures, this house had subsequently been rebuilt, on different foundations, at Subphase 2b. The remains at Subphase 2a were those of two suites, Suite A and Suite C, both of which were incompletely preserved.

House XLI
This very oddly shaped "house" stood at the southeast edge of the village, and directly adjoined the south side of the House XLIII courtyard. It consisted of three suites

and 14 rooms, which were almost fully preserved at ground level, though the upper walls were much denuded. The house was enclosed, all along its eastern side, by a long section of curving wall, whose curvature was also paralleled by the neighboring interior walls. In fact, the only straight walls in the house were some of those running east and west.

The most southerly of the three suites, Suite C, was the most regular in outline of the three, and looks as if it may have been the first constructed. It consisted of a very large southern room, which opened onto three smaller rooms on the north. The large but very irregular Suite A was probably added later, filling up the formerly open space between Suite C and House XLII. Finally, the two or three rooms of Suite B were built along the eastern side of Suite A. House XLI had no interior features except for a ceramic oven in Suite A.

House LX

This was the surviving remnant of an apparently small house, at the southern extremity of the community. As preserved it contained only four rooms, in a single suite. A long section of curving wing wall connected the northeast corner of the house to the south wall of House XLI, Suite B, but the wall does not appear to have been adjoined by any rooms.

Summary and interpretation of Subphase 2a

At this phase the four main buildings of Subphase 1c still survived, with relatively little modification. The stout-walled Houses XXXIV and XLII were perhaps still the residences of persons having a measure of authority, either political or economic or both. However, these buildings were now surrounded, and virtually engulfed, within a warren of more than 150 mostly small rooms, irregularly clustered along narrow and winding streets. The various houses included at least 40 residential suites, each comprised of from two to eight interconnected rooms. The smaller suites can only have been the residences of nuclear families, while the larger ones could have housed more extended kin groups.

Meinarti at Subphase 2a presents for the first time the aspect of a typical Nubian farming community, similar to many others, especially of the Christian period. Some commercial activity may have continued in House XLII and its adjoining courtyard, but this was clearly no longer a mainstay of the community's economy. Except for House XLII, all of the Subphase 2a houses had the earmarks of ordinary family residences. Presumably the community was now sustained chiefly by farming, either on the neighboring island of Majarab or on the East Bank, or both.

The combination of a few stoutly walled "deluxe" houses, adjoined and surrounded by flimsier structures, may already have been present at Subphase 1c, but it is not clearly attested until Subphase 2a. It seems to have been characteristic of many late Meroitic as well as Ballaña communities in Lower Nubia,[3] and is probably evidence of some degree of social stratification (cf. Adams 1977,

356-8, and Edwards 1996, 83-4). At Meinarti however the "deluxe" houses were fewer, and the ordinary houses far more numerous, than at any other community that has been reported in the literature.

The apparently deliberate physical isolation of House XXXIV seems to represent a unique case, not paralleled in other communities. This building stood cheek-by-jowl with others on all four sides, but it was not directly adjoined by any of them before Subphase 2b. There is a suggestion of something special either about the occupant or about the building itself, although the plan differs in no way from that of the neighboring House XLII. In later times it was only churches that were thus isolated from neighboring structures, but nothing was found in House XXXIV to suggest a sacred function.

In terms of the size of rooms, and the number of rooms per living suite, the quality of ordinary family housing at Meinarti seems comparable to that at other communities of the same period,[4] but considerably poorer than at either earlier or later periods. There was substantial variation in the size of suites, from a minimum of two to a maximum of eight rooms, but this is probably an indication of the variable size of families rather than of differences in wealth or status. Floor areas for individual living suites varied from about 15 m^2 to about 60 m^2, the average being 33 m^2. This may be compared to an average figure of 54 m^2 for residential suites at Phase 4, and 49 m^2 for suites and unit houses at Phase 5. (The size of living units at Phase 3 could not be estimated because of poor preservation.)

As a whole, the village of Meinarti at Phase 2 was considerably more congested than others that have been reported in the literature, which may reflect the lack of available space on which to expand. Anything on the island of Meinarti that was not built on the mound was certain to be repeatedly flooded, and the inhabitants must by now have been well aware of this.

The extensive pottery finds from Level 15b (Subphase 2a) seem to belong clearly to Index Cluster X2,[5] which falls at the end of Rose's Middle phase of X-Group ceramic development (Rose n.d., 135-40). The beginning date for Cluster X2, at Qasr Ibrim, was originally placed at A.D. 600, but this must certainly be revised backward by as much as a century, in light of data both from Qasr Ibrim and from Meinarti. Rose now estimates a beginning date for her Middle phase in the early fifth century (ibid., 131), but I do not think that the beginning of the Phase 2 occupation at Meinarti can be dated back that far. For reasons that will be further explored at the end of the chapter, I am inclined to place the beginning of the Phase 2 occupation at about A.D. 475. The pottery finds will be much more fully discussed in a later section.

The relatively minor architectural changes that took place between Subphase 2a and Subphase 2b, and the generally shallow accumulation of refuse, suggest a duration of not much more than a generation for Subphase 2a. I therefor date its conclusion at around A.D. 500.

---

[3] e.g. Wadi el-Arab, Karanòg, and Arminna. See Emery and Kirwan 1936, pl. 17; Woolley 1911, pls. 26-9; and Trigger 1967, fig. 23.

[4] See references cited in n. 3; also Adams and Nordström 1963, 26-8.

[5] For explanation of the system of index clusters see Adams

Figure 23. Plan of the remains at Level 15b (Subphase 2a), c. A.D. 550.
Heavy lines indicate the outlines of separately numbered buildings; dotted lines indicate the boundaries between suites.

Subphase 2b (Level 15a)

The interval between Subphases 2a and 2b was probably not much more than a generation, and changes that took place were correspondingly minor, as a comparison of Figures 24 and 23 will show. Floor levels in nearly all the houses were raised by 10 to 25cm (cf. Fig. 22), and there was a considerable rearrangement of interior partitions and doors, while the overall shape of the houses was hardly altered. Preservation was not quite as good as at Subphase 2a, especially along the western side of the site.

Survivals from Subphase 1c

Houses XXXIV and XLII

Apart from a further raising of the floor levels, there was almost no change in these two stout buildings, which still survived from Subphase 1c. However, some of the walls of House XLII did not survive at this level, and the eastern wall of the house had evidently collapsed, and been replaced by a thin wall of 20-cm masonry. The interior partitions within the courtyard of House XLII were partially dismantled and sanded over, leaving only a single large open plaza, of which only the western half was preserved. House XXXIV, which formerly had stood apart from all its neighbors, was now for the first time adjoined on the south side by House XL.

Houses XLIII and XLIV

These two further relics of Subphase 1c also survived with little modification, except that there was a considerable rearrangement of interior partitions and doors in House XLIII. A cluster of rooms along the south side, which had formerly been Suite G of House XXXV, now became Suite C of House XLIII through the opening of a new doorway and the closing of an old one. A few small remnants of wall, in House XLIII, still preserved the original alignments of the old Meroitic Market Compound, built four centuries earlier. The wall masonry at Subphase 2b was not of course the original Meroitic brickwork; it had been built up over the centuries from the tops of the original walls, which were now buried.

Continued occupation in houses of Subphase 2a

House LVIII

In this house there were no surviving traces of the westernmost Suite A at Level 15a, since only the lowermost parts of the walls had been preserved, and these were now below ground level. Suites B, C, D, and G underwent no significant modification, while Suites E and F were combined into a single, much larger suite by the complete rearrangement of the interior partitions. At the south side of the complex a new two-room Suite H was added, encroaching on an area that had formerly been a small plaza.

House XLV

There seems to have been no change in the western Suite A. All of the former walls of Suites B and C were dismantled, and replaced with flimsier walls having somewhat different alignments. A large ceramic oven was now installed in Suite C.

House XXXV

In this large house Suite A remained basically unchanged, while former Suites B and C were combined into a much larger Suite C. Suite D was little changed except for the installation of a mastaba in each of its two rooms; both mastabas had hand-made pots buried to the rim within them. Suite E was enlarged by the addition of a long room along its south side. Suite G lost a room at the south, which was partially dismantled and sanded over, but it gained a room at the north which had formerly belonged to Suite F.

House LIX

Only the eastern half of this house survived at Subphase 2b. The main changes were the dismantling of the original room at the northeast corner (former Room 3), in order to allow a street to pass at this point, and the opening of a new outside doorway into the large Room 6, at its east side.

House XXXIX

There was a very considerable rearrangement of partitions in the northern portion of this house, and two outside rooms at the northeast corner were removed, so as to widen the street between House XXXIX and House XXXIV. Suite B seems to have been unmodified, and the only change in Suite D was the installation of an area of stone-flagged flooring in one of the rooms.

House XL

This was the only house at Meinarti that was extensively rebuilt at Subphase 2b, with only the two rooms at the southern end (Suite C) retaining the alignment of the earlier walls. Suites A and B were rebuilt almost entirely with new walls, and now for the first time they directly adjoined the south side of the previously isolated House XXXIV. In Suite A, the fairly large Room 2 was remarkable in that it had two brick-walled bins adjoining the west wall, but even more so because it had no fewer than six hand-made pottery vessels buried within the floor at various points. Four were close together at the southeast corner, while one was close to the northeast and one close to the northwest corner. There were also two sub-floor vessels in Suite C and one in Suite B, while elsewhere such vessels were uncommon at Subphase 2b. It may be that House XL served as a kind of "bank" in which several families stored their valuables in the sub-floor repositories—something that seems even more clearly attested in one of the Early Christian houses of Phase 3.

House XLI

In this house, the northern Suite A had some interior partitions removed, and some new ones built. Suite B, at the eastern side of the house, was dismantled, and much of the space it had occupied was converted into an open terrace with a stone retaining wall along its eastern side. Suite C, at the south end of the house, seems to have been unmodified.

House LX

There was no evidence of change in this small house.

Summary and interpretation of Subphase 2b

The changes that took place at this subphase were confined almost entirely to the rearrangement of interior partitions and doorways. They probably reflect nothing more than the dynamics of ongoing family life—the continual need for housing to adapt itself to the changing needs for space resulting from the cycle of births, marriages, and deaths that take place in every community (cf. Goody 1958). Similar architectural adaptations can be observed in peasant communities in many parts of the world today.[6]

The pottery found in the Subphase 2b (Level 15a) deposits was not greatly different from that at Subphase 2a, except for the presence of a certain number of vessels of Transitional and Early Christian types. The ceramic complex as a whole seems to represent a period of transition from Index Cluster X2 to Cluster XC1. On the basis of combined stratigraphic, architectural, and ceramic evidence, I now estimate the duration of Subphase 2b from A.D. 500 to 575. The pottery finds will be discussed more fully in a later section.

Subphase 2c (Level 14)

Preservation at this subphase was substantially poorer than at Subphase 2b, as a comparison of Figures 25 and 24 will show. The surviving remains covered no more than 2000 m[2], as against 2300 m[2] at Subphase 2b, and 2500 m[2] at Subphase 2a. It should not be supposed however that this circumstance reflects an actual shrinkage of the community before or during the Subphase 2c occupation. More probably it was the result of flood damage and destruction at later times, and particularly during Phase 3. In addition to attrition at the edges, there was also a sizable, partially denuded area in the central part of the village, where walls were very incompletely preserved. The fact that this was at the highest part of the mound suggests that the major destructive force here was not flooding, but the wholesale "urban renewal" that took place at Subphase 3a.

Throughout the site, the Subphase 2c floor levels were raised by at least 50cm, and in some places by as much as a meter, above those of Subphase 2b, indicating that the interval of elapsed time between the two was considerable (cf. Figure 22). There was no surviving trace of three of the Subphase 2b houses, and changes within nearly all of the other houses were substantial. Here and there, we can recognize the beginnings of a transformation that became general at Subphase 3a: the replacement of flimsy older walls by stouter and generally straighter new ones.

Survival from Subphase 1c

House XXXIV

This onetime "deluxe" structure was the last surviving remnant from Phase 1. However it had long since lost its vaulted roof, and was now deeply filled with refuse. On top of this midden deposit a compacted occupation surface was established, at a level about one meter above the Subphase 2b floor. It is unlikely however that the walls

were built up concurrently; probably the house had become, temporarily, some kind of open-air activity area. The structure was still entered through a doorway at its southeast corner, opening into Room 1. However, there was no longer any connection to the interior Rooms 2 and 3, as the original, arched doorway leading into these rooms was now buried below floor level. The original wall that separated Rooms 2 and 3 was also buried below floor level, but a new, thin partition, without a doorway, was built in its place. The lack of any lateral doorway to Rooms 2 and 3 suggests the probability that the surviving walls were not very high, so that the rooms could be entered by stepping over the walls. There were no surviving finds to indicate what kind of activity had been carried out in the remnant of House XXXIV, but the presence of a compacted floor as well as the newly built partition between Rooms 2 and 3 indicates that the building still had some kind of function. Before the end of Subphase 2c, however, it had once again become a refuse dump.

House XLII

This close neighbor and architectural twin on House XXXIV, already seriously damaged by the time of Subphase 1b, had entirely disappeared at Subphase 1c. Its remains were partly overbuilt by the new House LVI, which did not retain any of the earlier wall alignments.

Continued occupation in Subphase 2a houses

House XLIII

In this house, whose origins traced back to the Western Range of the old Meroitic Market Compound, nothing now survived of the original wall alignments. Indeed, not very much survived even of the Subphase 2b house, for nearly all the interior walls, and the western outer wall, had been dismantled and overbuilt with new walls of 40-cm masonry, whose alignment did not reproduce that of their predecessors. In addition, the house had been extended northward to incorporate a part of what was formerly House LVIII, Suites E and G, while at the same time its most southerly rooms were dismantled to make way for a newly relocated street. In the process of rebuilding, all the former interior doorways were eliminated. As a result, the house now comprised a very irregular clustering of three two-room suites and one three-room suite, each of which had some 20-cm and some 40-cm walls, and each of which was entered from a different direction. There were no surviving interior features in the house.

House XLIV

Only a very small remnant of this house survived, constituting a single suite of four rooms in what had formerly been Suite C, in the middle of the house. The east wall, a part of the north wall, and one interior partition were survivals from Subphase 2b, while the other walls had been newly built, in each case with 20-cm masonry. A very large ceramic oven was installed in the corner of one room.

House LVIII

Of this formerly large house, at the north end of the village, only Suite C and one room of Suite B, in the central

[6] See, for example, Ammar 1966, 42-4.

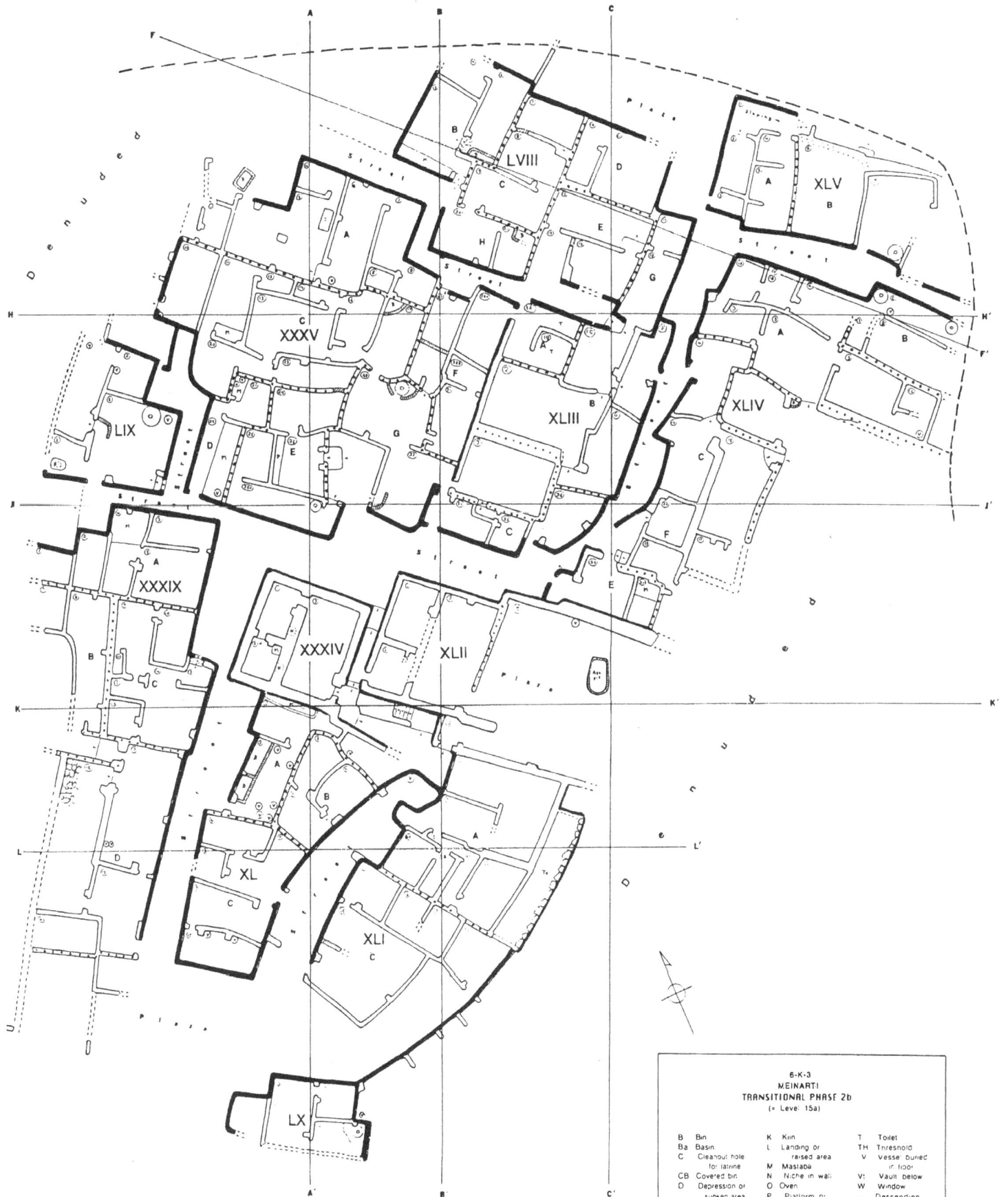

Figure 24. Plan of the remains at Level 15a (Subphase 2b), c, A.D. 575.
Heavy lines indicate the outlines of separately numbered buildings; dotted lines indicate the boundaries between suites.

6-K-3
MEINARTI
TRANSITIONAL PHASE 2b
(= Level 15a)

B	Bin	K	Kiln	T	Toilet
Ba	Basin	L	Landing or	TH	Threshold
C	Cleanout hole		raised area	V	Vessel buried
	for latrine	M	Mastaba		in floor
CB	Covered bin	N	Niche in wall	Vt	Vault below
D	Depression or	O	Oven	W	Window
	sunken area	P	Platform or		Descending
F	Fireplace		raised area		step
G	Grindstone	Q	Quseba		

XL House or building number   15 Room number
B15 Burial number   T15 Tomb number
F1 Foetal burial in pot

House wall
Blockage of door or window
Low partition or retaining wall
Limit of excavation
A ──── A' Line of cross section

Meters

part of the house, survived. These underwent little modification, except for the installation of one new interior partition. In the former eastern portion of the house, a part of Suites E and G was now incorporated in House XLIII, but the larger part had become an outdoor refuse dump. This was one of the very few areas at Meinarti where there was a relatively dense midden accumulation instead of simply drifted sand. Of the former western Suites A and B no trace survived, and it is possible that this area had already become an open plaza, as it clearly was at Subphase 3a.

House XXXV
Most of this large house survived at Subphase 2c, except for the western extremity which was evidently destroyed by flooding. Although six of the original seven residential suites could still be recognized, the interior partitioning in all except Suite A had been significantly rearranged. Near the southeast corner of the house, a large, nearly square room with 40-cm walls was built, over what had formerly been parts of Suites F and G. This room uncharacteristically had three doorways, in the east, west, and south walls, opening into different parts of Suites F, G, and H. It may therefore have been a kind of "common room" or antechamber shared by the three suites.

House XXXIX
This long structure, at the southwest side of the village, was the least modified of the Subphase 2b houses. However, the formerly contiguous northern and southern sections, comprising Suites A, B, and C on the north and Suite D on the south, were now separated by the creation of a narrow street between them. The space that it occupied was carved out of the former northern end of Suite D. The surface of the street was laid out in a set of five irregularly spaced steps, descending from east to west. To the north of the street, the interiors of Suites A and B had undergone little modification, while the partitions within Suite C were considerably rearranged. South of the street, only the most northerly rooms of Suite D had survived at this level, but they exhibited very little modification.

House XL
In this structure, much of the eastern Suite B did not survive. In Suite A there was little modification, but all of the former interior features—the wall bins, the mastaba, and the six subfloor pots—were buried beneath the newly raised floor level, and the rooms were now entirely featureless. In Suite C, at the south end of the house, there was no change except for the removal of one interior partition.

Houses XLI and LX
In House XLI, the only wall that retained its original alignment was the long, straight wall that separated the southern Suite C from the northern Suite A. This wall however was now doubled in thickness, from 20 to 40cm. The area to the north of it, formerly occupied by Suite A, was now incorporated into newly built Houses LVI and LVII, to be described below. To the south, all the interior partitions of the old Suite C were rearranged, to create four large but irregularly shaped rooms. One of the new rooms had

in one corner a raised platform, with two ceramic ovens built into the top of it. House XLI was also extended southward so that it adjoined the surviving remnant of House LX. In this latter, the main interior partition was widened from 20 to 40cm, while an adjoining thin-walled partition was eliminated.

Newly built houses at Subphase 2c

House LVI
This was a collective designation of convenience given to several disconnected and fragmentary aggregations of rooms that were preserved in a large space at the top of the mound, formerly occupied by parts of Houses XLI and XLIII, and the whole of House XLII. The remains were very denuded and incomplete, as this area had been subjected to a complete overbuilding at Phase 3. There is no way of knowing if the separate segments, designated as Suites A, B, C, and D, were ever really connected into one contiguous structure.

Suite A is the designation given to a group of four rooms in an east-west line at the north end of the House LVI area. None of the four were actually interconnected. They were built directly over what had once been a street, at the south side of House XLIII. Suite B was the designation given to a north-south line of three rooms, at the west side of the House LVI area. The most northerly room adjoined the west end of Suite A, and the most southerly room adjoined the east side of House XXXIV. Suite C was the designation given to a compact group of four rooms in the central part of the House LVI area, directly over what had formerly been the courtyard of House XLII. The location of doorways suggests that these were actually parts of two different suites, of which one had a large corner mastaba and two sub-floor pots. Suite D was an apparently complete two-room suite at the southern edge of the House LVI area, directly adjoining the north wall of House LVI. This suite had two pots buried in the floor.

House LVII
Adjoining the east wall of House LVI, Suite D, and the north wall of House XLI was the remnant of a very stout-walled house, of which only one small, square room and the remnant of another survived. This kind of heavy masonry became general at the time of Subphase 3a, but House LVII was definitely built originally at the time of Subphase 2c.

House XXXIII
Adjoining the north wall of House LVIII, at the northern extremity of the village, a single very large and very stout-walled room, designated as House XXXIII, was constructed. It was entered from the outside through a doorway, with recessed jambs on the inner side, at the northeast corner. At Subphase 3a this was to become part of a much larger complex of stout-walled rooms, but when first built at Subphase 2c it seems to have stood alone, except for the adjoining, older House LVIII. It contained no interior features that could provide any clue to its function.

Summary and interpretation of Subphase 2c
At Subphase 2c Meinarti remained, as before, a congested

farming village, albeit a somewhat dilapidated one. There was no major change in the overall layout of the community, or in the prevailing canons of architecture, that had been established at Subphase 2a. Families still lived in irregularly shaped houses of much the same size and design as before, although no house retained its complete original form. It seems clear however that the one surviving "deluxe" house, House XXXIV, was no longer a residence, and for the first time there is no suggestion of social stratification in the architectural remains of Subphase 2c.

Although most of the houses at Subphase 2c were recognizably survivors from the two preceding subphases, they had evidently become considerably dilapidated during the passage of more than a century, as is hardly surprising considering their rather flimsy original construction. A fair amount of interior rebuilding was undertaken, above and beyond the normal rearrangement of partitions and doorways that went on at all times. In many of the repairs we can recognize the first stage of the general community renewal that took place at Phase 3, when nearly all of the thin-walled houses of Phase 2 were replaced by much more substantial structures.

The pottery finds from Level 14 (Subphase 2c) seem to represent a transition from Index Cluster XC2 to Index Cluster EC1—the first clusters in which Early Christian wares are present in significant numbers (see Adams 1986, 631). This corresponds to the Late phase in X-Group ceramic development, according to the classification of Rose (n.d., 161-7). The beginning date calculated for Cluster EC1 at Qasr Ibrim was A.D. 650, but this should almost certainly be revised downward in light of the Meinarti data. On the basis of stratigraphic, architectural, and ceramic evidence I now estimate the duration of Subphase 2c from about A.D. 575 to 650. The pottery finds will be more fully discussed below.

The finds

Registered finds from Phase 2 were especially numerous, thanks to the extraordinary propensity of people in Ballaña times to bury things under their floors, and then to forget about them.[7] They can not, of course, be compared either in quantity or in quality to the enormous haul of finds that has come from some of the Ballaña tombs (cf. Emery and Kirwan 1938; Mills 1982; Bates and Dunham 1927; and Kirwan 1939). On the other hand, the stratigraphy of the Meinarti deposits makes possible a more precise dating of certain artifact types than is possible in the case of tomb finds.

The pottery
The system of classification into Families, Ware Groups, and Wares was explained in the previous chapter. Table 11 lists the families, ware groups, and wares found, either as whole vessels or as sherds, at Levels 15b, 15a, and 14. In the sherd counts, however, Levels 15b and 15a are combined.

The registered pottery finds from Phase 2 are listed in-

dividually in Table 12. Note that, in this table, finds are grouped in the first instance by family and ware, and secondly according to form class (cups, goblets, bowls, etc.). Within each form class, the finds are grouped according to level: first, all the finds from Level 15b (Subphase 2a), then all the finds from Level 15s (Subphase 2b), then all the finds from Level 14 (Subphase 2c), finally the finds of unknown provenience. This schema makes it possible to document the chronological changes that took place in prevailing vessel forms from subphase to subphase. It is necessary to remind readers again, however, that the level and phase attributions for Meinarti artifacts are not totally reliable, for reasons discussed in the Introduction.

In the discussion that follows, the term "X-Group" will be used in its typological sense, to refer to pottery types and to grave types, while "Ballaña" will be used to refer to the cultural horizon to which they belong. Comparison will be made frequently to the pottery finds from the Ballaña levels at Qasr Ibrim. These observations are based on my personal familiarity with the Qasr Ibrim material, and on the unpublished doctoral dissertation of Pamela Rose (n.d.), which has been of very considerable help.

Family M: the Meroitic fine wares
The fine-paste "eggshell wares" of Family M were described in the last chapter. Although they are widely regarded as the "signature wares" of the Meroitic period, their manufacture did not altogether cease at the end of the it. One fine ware, W30, actually made its first appearance in the Ballaña period. Instead of the elaborately painted cups and bowls of the Meroitic period, however, it was given over very largely to goblets imitative of the X-Group red wares, and almost its only decoration consisted of rim stripes and plain body stripes.[8] Two specimens of this ware were found at Phase 2 levels: an *aryballos* (896) and a lamp (1184), illustrated in Plate 7a, nos. 1 and 3.

Family N, Group N.II: X-Group wares
These were the overwhelmingly predominant wares of Phase 2, accounting for over 85% of all the pottery registered. Stylistically, they represent the apogee of Roman influence in Nubian pottery. The conspicuous preference for red wares, rather than white wares, mirrors the general development of ceramics in the late Roman and early Byzantine world, and most of the individual Nubian vessel forms are copies of Roman Egyptian forms. The most common decorative style, N.IIA, is also derivative from contemporary decoration in the Aswan Wares (specifically, Style A.IB).

Ware W11: Early X-Group white ware.[9] This ware, probably a descendant of Meroitic Ware W25, was rare at all times. In view of its scarcity, and the fact that its decorative style (N.IIB) is not closely similar to that of other X-

[7] The same was true also in the Ballaña levels at Qasr Ibrim; see Plumley and Adams 1974, 217, 225-6.

[8] For the full ware description and illustrations see Adams 1986, 438, 440.

[9] For the full ware description and illustrations see Adams 1986, 472-3.

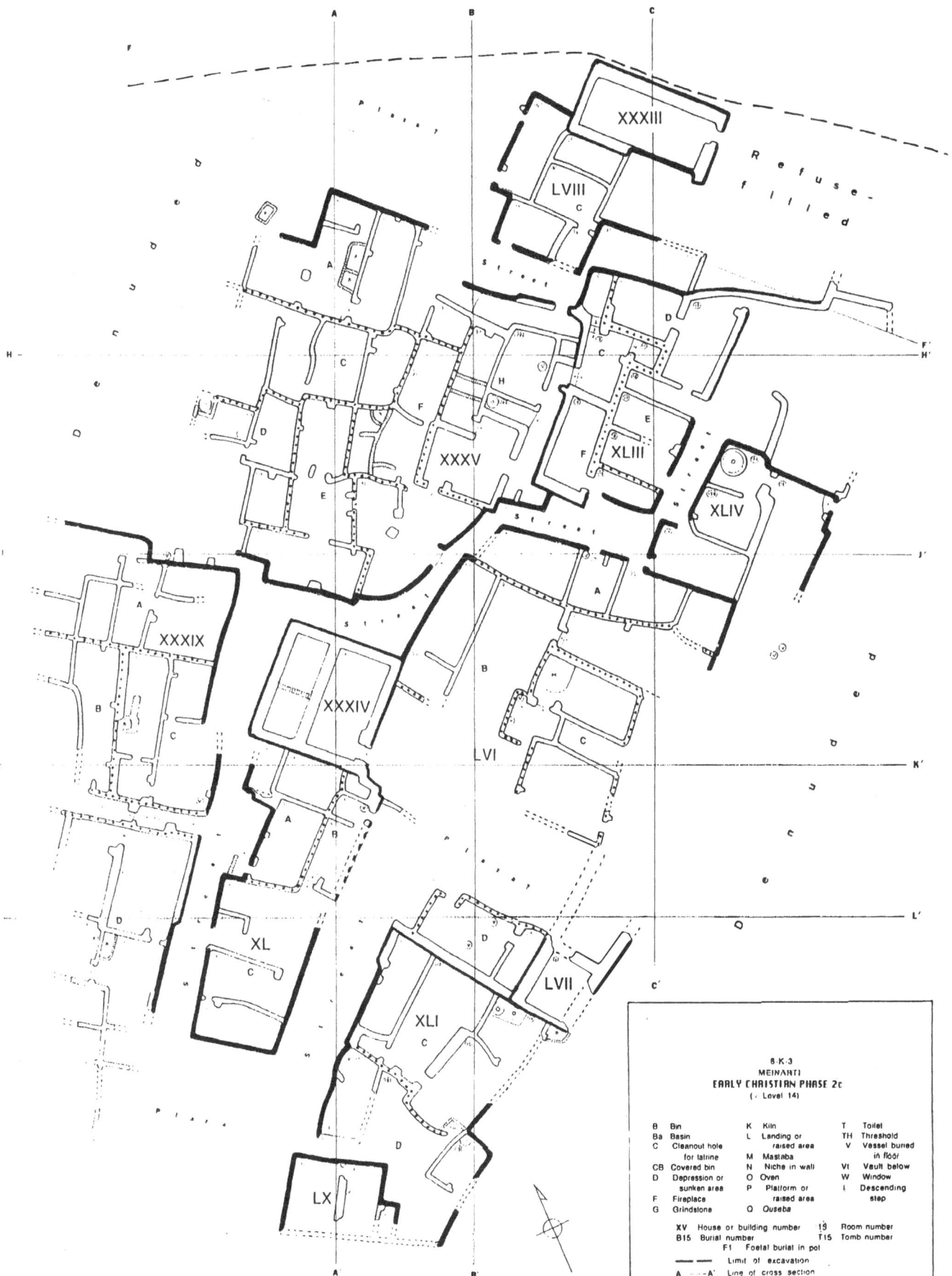

Figure 25. Plan of the remains at Level 14 (Subphase 2c), c. A.D. 625.
Heavy lines indicate the outlines of separately numbered buildings; dotted lines indicate the boundaries between suites.

TABLE 11. LIST OF FAMILIES, WARE GROUPS, AND WARES FOUND AT PHASE 2[1]

| | Numbers | | | | | | | |
| | Registered vessels | | | | | Sherds | | |
	15b	15a	14	?	Total	15	14	Total
Family M. Meroitic fine wares								
Ware W26. Meroitic fine white ware (IA)		1	1		2			
Family N. Nubian ordinary wares								
Group N. II. "X-Group" wares								
Ware W11. X-Group decorated white ware (*10*)			2	1	3	36	44	80
Ware R25. Early X-Group brown ware (IIH)	4	4	2	3	13			
Ware R1. Classic X-Group red ware (*1*)	49	61	38	5	153	Ab*	48	
Ware R2. Transitional red ware (*2*)	2	3	17		22	28	39	57
Group N.III. Early Christian wares								
Ware W1. Early Christian peach ware (*11*)		1	1		2	19	117	136
Ware W2. Early Christian matte white ware (*12, 18*)	1	4	8		13	23	141	164
Ware R5. Early Christian polished red ware (*5, 8, 9*)			6		6	73	312	385
Group NU. Nubian coarse utility wares								
Ware U1. Pre-Christian brown utility ware (IIH; *21*)	2				2	47	29	76
Ware U5. Christian red utility ware (*25*)		1	1		2		14	14
Family D. Nubian hand-made domestic wares								
Group D.II. X-Group and earlier Christian domestic wares								
Ware H1. Early domestic plain utility ware (VA)	4	2	2		8			
Ware H13. Transitional white-on-red domestic ware	1		1		2			
Family A. Aswan wares								
Group A.I. Graeco-Roman Aswan wares								
Ware W24. Aswan Graeco-Roman cream ware (IVA, IVD)		1			1	4	9	13
Ware R31. Aswan Graeco-Roman flaky pink ware (IVC)	1	2	1		4			
Group A.II. Byzantine Aswan wares								
Ware R4. Aswan Byzantine polished red ware (*4*)		3	4		7	37	78	115
Ware R14. Aswan Byzantine decorated pink ware		1			1			
Ware U2. Aswan Byzantine pink utility ware (*22*)	1	2	1		4	35	30	65
Miscellaneous Egyptian trade wares								
Ware U3. 'Saqqara' buff amphora ware (*23*)						Ab*	1	
Ware U4. Middle Egyptian brown utility ware (IIH; *24*)						8	17	25
Ware U12. Ballas drab utility ware						2	7	9
Ware U13. Fostat ordinary utility ware						2	7	9
Totals	**65**	**86**	**85**	**9**	**244**			

[1] Entries in parentheses, following the group and ware names, are the original designations appearing in *Kush*, vol. 10 (1962), pp. 272-276, and vol. 12 (1964), pp. 157-161. Roman numeral entries in roman type are Meroitic wares described in *Kush* 12; Arabic numeral entries in italics are X-Group and Christian types described in *Kush* 10.

* Abundant

Group wares, there is a considerable probability that the ware was made in Egypt rather than in Nubia. In the Phase 2 collections it is represented only by a fragmentary footed bowl (1374), a table amphora (987), and a footed storage jar (925). The latter two are illustrated in Plate 17a, nos. 1 and 3.

Ware R25: Early X-Group brown ware.[10] This archetypal X-Group ware, described in the last chapter, was probably no longer being made by the time of Phase 2, when it was vastly outnumbered by the successor Ware R1. The 13 specimens registered from Levels 15b, 15a, and 14 were most probably survivals from an earlier time. They are, variously, goblets, bowls, small bottles, ointment jars, a lamp and a pot. Most are illustrated in Plates 7d (nos. 1, 2, 4, 5, and 7-9), 7e (n. 4), and 7f (n. 2).

Ware R1: Classic X-Group red ware.[11] This is the "signature ware" of the Ballaña period, well known from the excavation of literally hundreds of X-Group graves. It was an outgrowth of Ware R25, distinguished by better finish, a polished red slip, and a distinctive style of decoration (Style N.IIA). Both Ware R25 and Ware R1 were, ultimately, local manifestations of the late Roman redware tradition. At Meinarti, almost two-thirds of all the registered pottery finds from Phase 2 levels were vessels of Ware R1. They were almost equally numerous at Subphases 2a and 2b, but were slightly less so at Subphase 2c, when they had begun to be displaced by the successor Wares R2 and R5.

More than half of all the registered Ware R1 vessels were cups and goblets, of a few distinctive forms. A representative selection of cups is shown in Plate 17b, nos.

[10] For the full ware description and illustrations see Adams 1986, 468-9.

[11] For the full ware description and illustrations see Adams 1986, 469-70.

TABLE 12. REGISTERED POTTERY FINDS FROM PHASE 2

Reg. no.	Ware	Form desig.	Form	Portion[1]	Colors[2]	Style	Level (Phase)	Plate
				Family M: Meroitic fine wares				
896	W30	N10	Aryballos	Portion	Cream	II	14 (2c)	7a, 3
1184	W30	P15	Lamp	Almost whole	Cream	II	15a (2b)	7a, 1
				Family N: Nubian ordinary wheel-made wares				
				Group N.II: X-Group wares				
1374	W11	D61	Footed bowl	Fragment	Br/W	N.IIB	?	
987	W11	J4	Table amphora	Almost whole	Cream	II	14 (2c)	17a, 1
925	W11	X14	Footed jar	Almost whole	R/W	N.IIB	14 (2c)	17a, 3
971	R25	B1	Goblet	Portion (R)	Red	I	15b (2a)	17d, 3
1424	R25	B9	Goblet	Portion	Brown	X	15a (2b)	7d, 7
1427	R25	B17	Goblet	Portion	Red	I	?	7d, 8
1015	R25?	C57	Bowl	Portion (R)	Red	I	15a (2b)	
878	R25	C46	Bowl	Portion (R)	Brown	X	14 (2c)	7e, 4
1073	R25	C72	Bowl	Almost whole	Red	I	?	7d, 5
1426	R1	D11	Footed bowl	Portion (R)	B+W/R	N.IIA	?	7d, 9
1078	R25	G29	Small bottle	Almost whole	Red	I	15b (2a)	7d, 2
760	R25	G10	Small bottle	Portion	Brown	X	15a (2b)	
1004	R25	P21	Lamp	Whole	Brown	X	14 (2c)	7d, 4
979	R25	O3	Ointment jar	Whole	Brown	X	15b (2a)	7d, 1
886	R25	O3	Ointment jar	Whole	Brown	X	15a (2b)	
1067	R25	U19	Pot	Whole (R)	Brown	X	15b (2a)	7f, 2
972	R1	A8	Cup	Almost whole	Red	I	15b (2a)	7e, 1
973	R1	A8	Cup	Whole	W/R	N.IIA	15b (2a)	17b, 5
974	R1	A7	Cup	Whole (R)	Red	I	15b (2a)	17b, 12
975	R1	A8	Cup	Portion	Red	I	15b (2a)	
978	R1	A8	Cup	Whole	W/R	N.IIA	15b (2a)	17b, 6
992	R1	A7	Cup	Whole	Red	I	15b (2a)	17b, 11
996	R1	A8	Cup	Whole	W/R	N.IIA	15b (2a)	
997	R1	A8	Cup	Almost whole	Red	I	15b (2a)	
1021	R1	A8	Cup	Whole (R)	Red	I	15b (2a)	
1022	R1	A8	Cup	Whole	W/R	N.IIA	15b (2a)	17b, 2
1023	R1	A8	Cup	Whole (R)	Red	I	15b (2a)	
1052	R1	A8	Cup	Portion	W/R	N.IIA	15b (2a)	
1053	R1	A8	Cup	Whole	Red	I	15b (2a)	
1054	R1	A8	Cup	Whole	Red	I	15b (2a)	
1077	R1	A8	Cup	Almost whole	Red	I	15b (2a)	17b, 8
1083	R1	A8	Cup	Almost whole (R)	Red	I	15b (2a)	
1084	R1	A8	Cup	Whole	Red	I	15b (2a)	
1085	R1	A8	Cup	Almost whole	Red	I	15b (2a)	
1091	R1	A8	Cup	Whole	B+W/R	N.IIA	15b (2a)	
744	R1	A8	Cup	Whole	W/R	N.IIA	15a (2b)	
747	R1	A8	Cup	Whole	Red	I	15a (2b)	17b, 7
748	R1	A8	Cup	Portion	Red	I	15a (2b)	
842	R1	A7	Cup	Whole	Red	I	15a (2b)	17b, 10
900	R1	A8	Cup	Portion (R)	B+W/R	N.IIA	15a (2b)	
901	R1	A8	Cup	Whole	Red	I	15a (2b)	17b, 4
994	R1	A7	Cup	Almost whole	Red	I	15a (2b)	
1005	R1	A8	Cup	Whole	W/R	N.IIA	15a (2b)	17b, 3
1010	R1	A7	Cup	Almost whole (R)	Red	I	15a (2b)	17b, 15
1034	R1	A8	Cup	Whole	W/R	N.IIA	15a (2b)	
1037	R1	A8	Cup	Almost whole	B+W/R	N.IIA	15a (2b)	
820	R1	A7	Cup	Almost whole	Red	I	14 (2c)	
852	R1	A7	Cup	Whole	Red	I	14 (2c)	17b, 9
861	R1	A7	Cup	Whole	Red	I	14 (2c)	17b, 16

[1] (R) = restored

[2] B=Black; Br = Brown; R = Red; W = White or cream; B/W = Black on white; B+R/W = Black and red on white; B+W/R = Black and white on red; W/R = White on Red; R-W = Red exterior, white interior; R-X = Red exterior, unslipped interior; W+R = White upper body, red lower body; X = Unslipped

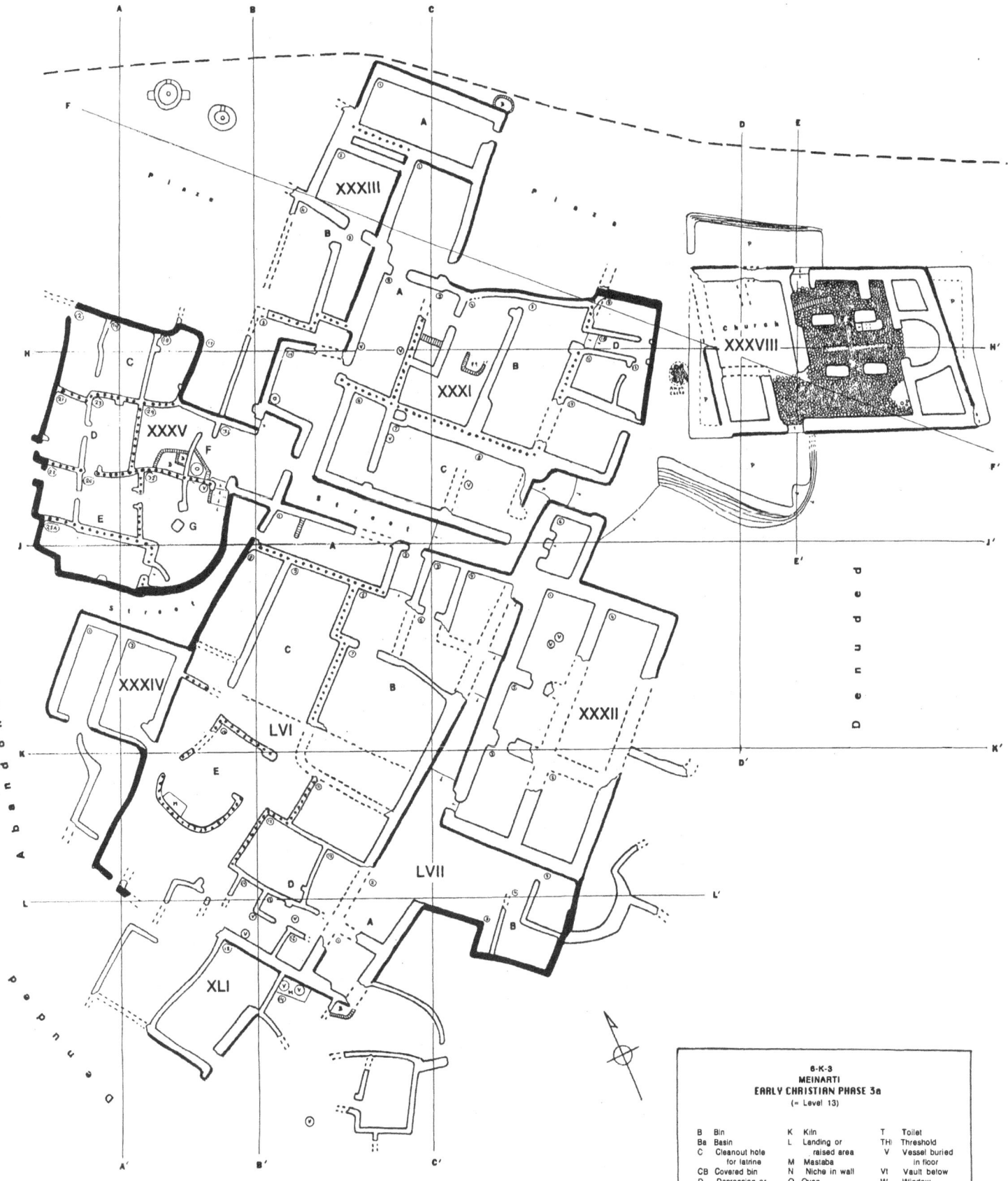

Figure 26. Plan of the remains at Level 13 (Subphase 3a), c. A.D. 675.
Heavy lines indicate the outlines of separately numbered buildings; dotted lines indicate the boundaries between suites.

6-K-3
MEINARTI
EARLY CHRISTIAN PHASE 3a
(= Level 13)

B	Bin	K	Kiln	T	Toilet
Ba	Basin	L	Landing or	TH	Threshold
C	Cleanout hole		raised area	V	Vessel buried
	for latrine	M	Mastaba		in floor
CB	Covered bin	N	Niche in wall	Vt	Vault below
D	Depression or	O	Oven	W	Window
	sunken area	P	Platform or	↓	Descending
F	Fireplace		raised area		step
G	Grindstone	Q	Quseba		

LIII House or building number ⑮ Room number
B15 Burial number T15 Tomb number
F1 Foetal burial in pot

House wall
Blockage of door or window
Low partition or retaining wall
Limit of excavation
A———A' Line of cross section

0 1 2 3 4 5 6 7 8 9 10 Meters

TABLE 12. REGISTERED POTTERY FINDS FROM PHASE 2 (CONT.)

Reg. no.	Ware	Form desig.	Form	Portion[1]	Colors[2]	Style	Level (Phase)	Plate
885	R1	A7	Cup	Whole	Red	I	14 (2c)	17b, 13
893	R1	A7	Cup	Portion	Red	I	14 (2c)	
849	R1	A8	Cup	Whole	B/R	N.IIA	14 (2c)	
917	R1	A7	Cup	Almost whole	Red	I	14 (2c)	17b, 14
938	R1	A8	Cup	Whole (R)	Red	I	14 (2c)	
1430	R1	A2	Cup	Fragment	B+W/R	N.IIA	?	
969	R1	B14	Goblet	Almost whole	B+W/R	N.IIA	15b (2a)	
970	R1	B14	Goblet	Whole	B+W/R	N.IIA	15b (2a)	
998	R1	B14	Goblet	Whole (R)	B+W/R	N.IIA	15b (2a)	
1002	R1	B14	Goblet	Almost whole	W/R	N.IIA	15b (2a)	17c, 8
1017	R1	B14	Goblet	Almost whole	B+W/R	N.IIA	15b (2a)	17c, 17
1018	R1	B17	Goblet	Almost whole	B+W/R	N.IIA	15b (2a)	17c, 5
1019	R1	B17	Goblet	Whole (R)	B+W/R	N.IIA	15b (2a)	
1058	R1	B17	Goblet	Almost whole	B+W/R	N.IIA	15b (2a)	17c, 1
1068	R1	B9	Goblet	Portion (R)	Red	I	15b (2a)	
1086	R1	B14	Goblet	Whole	B+W/R	N.IIA	15b (2a)	17c, 4
1090	R1	B14	Goblet	Whole	B+W/R	N.IIA	15b (2a)	
1177	R1	B14	Goblet	Whole	W/R	N.IIA	15b (2a)	17c, 9
1178	R1	B14	Goblet	Almost whole (R)	B+W/R	N.IIA	15b (2a)	17c, 16
1182	R1	B14	Goblet	Portion (R)	?	?	15b (2a)	
741	R1	B14	Goblet	Whole	W/R	N.IIA	15a (2b)	17c, 10
								17d, 11
742	R1	B14	Goblet	Almost whole	W/R	N.IIA	15a (2b)	
743	R1	B14	Goblet	Whole	B+W/R	N.IIA	15a (2b)	
746	R1	B14	Goblet	Almost whole	Red	I	15a (2b)	17d, 7
808	R1	B18	Goblet	Portion (R)	Red	I	15a (2b)	17d, 8
836	R1	B14	Goblet	Almost whole	B+W/R	N.IIA	15a (2b)	17c, 12
840	R1	B26	Goblet	Portion	W/R	N.IIA	15a (2b)	17d, 1
841	R1	B9	Goblet	Portion	Red	I	15a (2b)	
848	R1	B18	Goblet	Whole	W/R	N.IIA	15a (2b)	
855	R1	?	Goblet	Portion	Red	I	15a (2b)	
873	R1	B14	Goblet	Almost whole	B+W/R	N.IIA	15a (2b)	
875	R1	B9	Goblet	Portion (R)	Red	I	15a (2b)	
879	R1	B9	Goblet	Whole	Red	I	15a (2b)	
930	R1	B17	Goblet	Whole	B+W/R	N.IIA	15a (2b)	17c, 2
								17d, 13
931	R1	B14	Goblet	Almost whole	B+W/R	N.IIA	15a (2b)	17c, 13
								17d, 10
958	R1	B14	Goblet	Almost whole (R)	B+W/R	N.IIA	15a (2b)	17c, 11
993	R1	B9	Goblet	Whole	Red	I	15a (2b)	17d, 5
1008	R1	B14	Goblet	Portion (R)	B+W/R	N.IIA	15a (2b)	17c, 14
1009	R1	B17	Goblet	Almost whole	B+W/R	N.IIA	15a (2b)	
1011	R1	B9	Goblet	Whole	Red	I	15a (2b)	17d, 4
1016	R1	B14	Goblet	Almost whole	B+W/R	N.IIA	15a (2b)	17c, 15
1035	R1	B14	Goblet	Almost whole	B+W/R	N.IIA	15a (2b)	17d, 12
1036	R1	B14	Goblet	Whole	B+W/R	N.IIA	15a (2b)	17c, 6
1065	R1	B14	Goblet	Almost whole	B+W/R	N.IIA	15a (2b)	
920	R1	B14	Goblet	Whole	W/R	N.IIA	14 (2c)	17c, 7
								17d, 9
922	R1	B18	Goblet	Almost whole (R)	Red	I	14 (2c)	
957	R1	B19	Goblet	Portion (R)	Red	I	14 (2c)	17d, 2
1425	R1	B9	Goblet	Fragment	B+W/R	N.IIA	?	
965	R1	C54	Bowl	Whole	Red	I	15b (2a)	7e, 9
1059	R1	C10	Bowl	Portion	W/R	V	15b (2a)	7e, 2
1080	R1	C10	Bowl	Almost whole (R)	W/R	V	15b (2a)	7e, 3
833	R1	C87	Bowl	Almost whole (R)	B+W/R	N.IIA	15a (2b)	7e, 5
872	R1	C79	Bowl	Almost whole (R)	W/R	N.IIA	15a (2b)	
874	R1	C87	Bowl	Portion (R)	W/R	V	15a (2b)	
782	R1	C66	Bowl	Whole	Red	I	14 (2c)	7e, 8

[1] (R) = restored

[2] B=Black; Br = Brown; R = Red; W = White or cream; B/W = Black on white; B+R/W = Black and red on white; B+W/R = Black and white on red; W/R = White on Red; R-W = Red exterior, white interior; R-X = Red exterior, unslipped interior; W+R = White upper body, red lower body; X = Unslipped

TABLE 12. REGISTERED POTTERY FINDS FROM PHASE 2 (CONT.)

Reg. no.	Ware	Form desig.	Form	Portion[1]	Colors[2]	Style	Level (Phase)	Plate
792	R1	C55	Bowl	Portion	W/R	V	14 (2c)	
794	R1	C16	Bowl	Portion	Red	I	14 (2c)	
834	R1	C59	Bowl	Whole (R)	Red	I	14 (2c)	7e, 10
844	R1	C55	Bowl	Almost whole	Red	I	14 (2c)	7e, 6
903	R1	C28	Bowl	Almost whole	Red	I	14 (2c)	17e, 4
924	R1	C89	Bowl	Whole (R)	Red	I	14 (2c)	7e, 12
962	R1	C28	Bowl	Whole	Red	I	14 (2c)	17e, 1
1020	R1	D11	Footed bowl	Whole	B+W/R	N.IIA	15b (2a)	
1061	R1	D27	Footed bowl	Almost whole	Red	I	15b (2a)	
1076	R1	D11	Footed bowl	Whole	B+W/R	N.IIA	15b (2a)	17d, 14
790	R1	D24	Footed bowl	Whole	Red	I	14 (2c)	
967	R1	G40	Spouted goblet	Almost whole	B+W/R	N.IIA	15b (2a)	
1089	R1	G40	Spouted goblet	Almost whole	B+W/R	N.IIA	15b (2a)	17d, 16
835	R1	G40	Spouted goblet	Whole	B+W/R	N.IIA	15a (2b)	17d, 17
952	R1	G40	Spouted goblet	Whole	B+W/R	N.IIA	15a (2b)	17d, 15
791	R1	G30	Small bottle	Portion	Red	I	14 (2c)	
1424	R1	G7	Small pot	Fragment	W/R	V	?	
1088	R1	M8	Lekythos	Almost whole	Red	I	15b (2a)	17e, 16
947	R1	M9	Lekythos	Almost whole	Red	I	15a (2b)	17e, 17
1055	R1	M9	Lekythos	Whole	Red	I	15a (2b)	17e, 18
977	R1	N10	Aryballos	Almost whole	Red	I	15b (2a)	17e, 14
1087	R1	N10	Aryballos	Almost whole	Red	I	15b (2a)	17e, 15
863	R1	N10	Aryballos	Whole	Red	I	15a (2b)	17e, 13
910	R1	N10	Aryballos	Portion	Red	I	15a (2b)	17e, 12
1056	R1	N10	Aryballos	Whole	Red	I	15a (2b)	
935	R1	N10	Aryballos	Whole	Red	I	14 (2c)	
980	R1	P14	Lamp	Almost whole	Red	I	15b (2a)	
1001	R1	P15	Lamp	Almost whole	Red	I	15b (2a)	
1060	R1	P9	Lamp	Whole	Red	I	15b (2a)	7f, 9
1076	R1	P1	Lamp	Whole	Red	I	15b (2a)	7f, 6
839	R1	P1	Lamp	Almost whole	Red	I	15a (2b)	7f, 1
865	R1	P15	Lamp	Whole	Red	I	15a (2b)	
882	R1	P15	Lamp	Whole	Red	I	15a (2b)	17e, 8
883	R1	P15	Lamp	Almost whole	Red	I	15a (2b)	
884	R1	P16	Lamp	Almost whole	Red	I	15a (2b)	
897	R1	P15	Lamp	Almost whole	Red	I	15a (2b)	
898	R1	P14	Lamp	Almost whole	Red	I	15a (2b)	
946	R1	P16	Lamp	Whole	Red	I	15a (2b)	17e, 9
959	R1	P16	Lamp	Almost whole	Red	I	15a (2b)	
960	R1	P15	Lamp	Almost whole	Red	I	15a (2b)	
749	R1	P15	Lamp	Almost whole	Red	I	14 (2c)	
751	R1	P16	Lamp	Almost whole	Red	I	14 (2c)	
759	R1	P15	Lamp	Portion	Red	I	14 (2c)	
773	R1	P15	Lamp	Portion	Red	I	14 (2c)	
774	R1	P15	Lamp	Almost whole	Red	I	14 (2c)	
786	R1	P16	Lamp	Almost whole	Red	I	14 (2c)	
838	R1	P16	Lamp	Almost whole	Red	I	14 (2c)	
853	R1	P1	Lamp	Whole	Red	I	14 (2c)	17f, 3
894	R1	P15	Lamp	Whole	Red	I	14 (2c)	
895	R1	P15	Lamp	Whole	Red	I	14 (2c)	17f, 7
913	R1	P1	Lamp	Almost whole	Red	I	14 (2c)	17f, 2
914	R1	P16	Lamp	Almost whole	Red	I	14 (2c)	
915	R1	P16	Lamp	Almost whole	Red	I	14 (2c)	
916	R1	P13	Lamp	Almost whole	Red	I	14 (2c)	17f, 8
939	R1	P15	Lamp	Almost whole	Red	I	14 (2c)	
1432	R1	Q6	Lid	Portion	B+W/R	N.IIA	15a (2b)	
807	R1	Q6	Lid	Whole	B+W/R	N.IIA	14 (2c)	
966	R1	U21	Pot	Almost whole	W/R	V	15b (2a)	7e, 11
1075	R1	W25	Jar	Almost whole	Red	I	15b (2a)	18e

[1] (R) = restored
[2] B=Black; Br = Brown; R = Red; W = White or cream; B/W = Black on white; B+R/W = Black and red on white; B+W/R = Black and white on red; W/R = White on Red; R-W = Red exterior, white interior; R-X = Red exterior, unslipped interior; W+R = White upper body, red lower body; X = Unslipped

TABLE 12. REGISTERED POTTERY FINDS FROM PHASE 2 (CONT.)

Reg. no.	Ware	Form desig.	Form	Portion[1]	Colors[2]	Style	Level (Phase)	Plate
1071	R1	W23	Jar	Whole	Red	I	15a (2b)	18a, 2
								18d, 1
1180	R1	W23	Jar	Portion (R)	Red	I	15a (2b)	18d, 3
955	R1	W23	Jar	Whole (R)	Red	I	14 (2c)	18d, 2
1428	R1	?	Bottle	Fragment	Red	I	?	
880	R1	ZZ3	Keg	Whole	Red	I	15a (2b)	
976	R2	A26	Cup	Portion	W/R	N.IIC	15b (2a)	17b, 21
877	R2	A26	Cup	Portion	B/R	V	15a (2b)	17b, 19
1033	R2	A26	Cup	Portion (R)	B+W/R	N.IIC	15a (2b)	17b, 17
776	R2	A31	Cup	Portion	Red	I	14 (2c)	17b, 23
890	R2	A31	Cup	Almost whole	B/R	V	14 (2c)	17b, 20
891	R2	A31	Cup	Portion	Red	I	14 (2c)	17b, 24
892	R2	A31	Cup	Portion (R)	B/R	V	14 (2c)	17b, 22
937	R2	A26	Cup	Portion (R)	B/R	V	14 (2c)	
1047	R2	A31	Cup	Portion (R)	Red	I	14 (2c)	
780	R2	B18	Goblet	Almost whole	B/R	V	14 (2c)	
921	R2	B18	Goblet	Whole	B/R	V	14 (2c)	17d, 6
754	R2	C66	Bowl	Portion (R)	B/R	V	14 (2c)	
777	R2	C28	Bowl	Almost whole (R)	B/R	V	14 (2c)	17e, 2
778	R2	C28	Bowl	Portion (R)	B/R	V	14 (2c)	17e, 3
933	R2	C29	Bowl	Portion	B/R	V	14 (2c)	
934	R2	C66	Bowl	Portion	Red	I	14 (2c)	17e, 5
956	R2	C66	Bowl	Portion (R)	B/R	V	14 (2c)	17e, 7
940	R2	D39	Footed bowl	Portion (R)	B/R	V	14 (2c)	
1012	R2	G14	Small bottle	Almost whole	B/R	V	15a (2b)	17e, 19
1118	R2	G42	Spouted pot	Almost whole	B+W/R	N.IIC	15b (2a)	
779	R2	G42	Spouted pot	Portion	Red	I	14 (2c)	
889	R2	G42	Spouted pot	Portion	B+W/R	N.IIC	14 (2c)	

Group N.III: Early Christian wares

Reg. no.	Ware	Form desig.	Form	Portion[1]	Colors[2]	Style	Level (Phase)	Plate
1271	W1	C74	Bowl	Portion (R)	Cream	II	14 (2c)	
1040	W1	D17	Footed bowl	Whole (R)	B/W	N.III	15a (2b)	18a, 8
850	W2	C74	Bowl	Almost whole	Cream	II	14 (2c)	
1006	W2	C57	Bowl	Almost whole	Cream	II	14 (2c)	18a, 4
1007	W2	C74	Bowl	Portion	R/W	V	14 (2c)	
1269	W2	C66	Bowl	Fragment	B/W	V	14 (2c)	
1261	W2	D68	Footed bowl	Fragment	Cream	II	14 (2c)	
876	W2	G11	Small bottle	Almost whole	R/W	?	15a (2b)	
941	W2	G10	Small bottle	Whole	R/W	?	15a (2b)	
981	W2	P17	Lamp	Whole	Cream	II	15b (2a)	17f, 5
847	W2	P3	Lamp	Whole	Cream	II	15a (2b)	17f, 4
758	W2	P14	Lamp	Almost whole	Cream	II	14 (2c)	18a, 2
1038	W2	Q20	Lid	Whole	Cream	II	15a (2b)	
756	W2	Q6	Lid	Almost whole	B+W/R	N.III	14 (2c)	18a, 1
862	W2	?	Lid	Whole	Cream	II	14 (2c)	
1274	R5	C23	Bowl	Fragment	Red	I	14 (2c)	
755	R5	D47	Footed bowl	Portion (R)	Red	I	14 (2c)	18b, 12
								18c, 2
793	R5	D68	Footed bowl	Portion	Red	I	14 (2c)	18b, 14
1248	R5	E2	Plate	Portion (R)	Red	I	14 (2c)	18b, 18
781	R5	Q9	Lid	Whole	Red	I	14 (2c)	
943	R5	X3	Footed jar	Whole (R)	Red	I	14 (2c)	

Group NU: Nubian undecorated utility wares

Reg. no.	Ware	Form desig.	Form	Portion[1]	Colors[2]	Style	Level (Phase)	Plate
964	U1	V2	Qadus	Whole	Brown	X	15b (2a)	7f, 3
								8b, 3
1069	U1	V2	Qadus	Whole	Brown	X	15b (2a)	8b, 1
1070	U5	W21	Jar	Almost whole	Red	I	15a (2b)	
944	U5	W21	Jar	Almost whole	Red	I	14 (2c)	18f, 1

[1] (R) = restored

[2] B=Black; Br = Brown; R = Red; W = White or cream; B/W = Black on white; B+R/W = Black and red on white; B+W/R = Black and white on red; W/R = White on Red; R-W = Red exterior, white interior; R-X = Red exterior, unslipped interior; W+R = White upper body, red lower body; X = Unslipped

TABLE 12. REGISTERED POTTERY FINDS FROM PHASE 2 (CONT.)

Reg. no.	Ware	Form desig.	Form	Portion[1]	Colors[2]	Style	Level (Phase)	Plate

Family D: Nubian hand-made wares

<u>Group D.II: X-Group and earlier Christian domestic wares</u>

Reg. no.	Ware	Form desig.	Form	Portion	Colors	Style	Level (Phase)	Plate
783	H1	B34	Goblet	Whole	Brown	X	14 (2c)	
1063	H1	P22	Lamp	Whole	Brown	X	15b (2a)	
982	H1	Q17	Lid	Whole	Brown	X	15b (2a)	8c, 6
1062	H1	Q17	Lid	Whole	Brown	X	15b (2a)	8c, 1
837	H1	Q17	Lid	Whole	Brown	X	15a (2b)	8c, 5
1014	H1	Q17	Lid	Portion	Brown	X	15a (2b)	
1092	H1	U3	Pot	Almost whole	Brown	X	15b (2a)	
923	H1	U3	Pot	Whole	Brown	X	14 (2c)	
1074	H13	U1	Pot	Almost whole (R)	W/R	H13	15b (2a)	19b, 2
851	H13	U1	Pot	Whole	W/R	H13	14 (2c)	8d, 2
								19b, 3

Family A: Aswan wares

<u>Group A.I: Graeco-Roman wares</u>

Reg. no.	Ware	Form desig.	Form	Portion	Colors	Style	Level (Phase)	Plate
1003	W24	I18	Jug	Almost whole	Br/W	W24	15a (2b)	19d, 1
750	R31	G32	Small bottle	Almost whole	B+W/R	R31	15a (2b)	19c, 10
								19d, 8
								19e, 2
1072	R31	M9	Lekythos	Whole	Red	I	15b (2a)	9a, 8
								19c, 4
1013	R31	M5	Lekythos	Whole	Red	I	15a (2b)	9a, 7
								19c, 3
919	R31	M5	Lekythos	Almost whole	Red	I	14 (2c)	9a, 5

<u>Group A.II: Byzantine wares</u>

Reg. no.	Ware	Form desig.	Form	Portion	Colors	Style	Level (Phase)	Plate
789	R4	D74	Footed bowl	Whole (R)	Red	I	14 (2c)	
810	R4	D74	Footed bowl	Portion (R)	Red	I	14 (2c)	
1400	R4	D35	Footed bowl	Portion (R)	Red	I	14 (2c)	8f, 8
1410	R4	D55	Footed bowl	Fragment	Red	I	?	
881	R4	N10	Aryballos	Almost whole	Red	I	15a (2b)	9a, 2
								19c, 1
899	R4	N10	Aryballos	Almost whole	Red	I	15a (2b)	9a, 4
918	R4	N10	Aryballos	Almost whole	Red	I	14 (2c)	9a, 3
961	R4	P2	Lamp	Whole	Red	I	15a (2b)	
1408	R14	E12	Plate	Fragment	B+W/R	VI	15a (2b)	
968	U2	I1	Jug	Whole	Red	I	15b (2a)	19e, 3
757	U2	N3	Oil bottle	Whole	W/R	V	15a (2b)	9a, 1
								19c, 2
745	U2	Z6	Amphora	Almost whole (R)	Red	I	15a (2b)	9b, 2
								19f, 3
929	U2	Z16	Amphora	Whole	Red	I	14 (2c)	

[1] (R) = restored

[2] B=Black; Br = Brown; R = Red; W = White or cream; B/W = Black on white; B+R/W = Black and red on white; B+W/R = Black and white on red; W/R = White on Red; R-W = Red exterior, white interior; R-X = Red exterior, unslipped interior; W+R = White upper body, red lower body; X = Unslipped

1-16, and a selection of goblets is shown in Plate 17c. The vessel forms and decoration will be discussed separately a little later. Apart from cups and goblets, the most common vessels of Ware R1 were lamps, of which a selection is shown in Plate 7f. Other, less common forms are bowls (Plates 7e and 17e), footed bowls (Plate 7d, no. 9), spouted goblets (Plate 17d), *lekythoi* and *aryballoi* (Plate 17e), lids (not illustrated), pots (Plate 7e, no. 11),

jars (Plate 8a, no. 2; Plate 18d; Plate 18e), and a keg (not illustrated).

<u>Ware R2: Transitional red ware.</u>[12] This was a rather short-lived successor to Ware R1, occurring in a somewhat different range of vessel forms and having a slightly different

[12] Designated in Adams 1962b, 272, as Ware 2. For the full ware description and illustrations see Adams 1986, 470.

decorative style (N.IIC), which often included a rim stripe. The ware when found is an extremely useful horizon marker, because its manufacture seems to have been confined entirely to the first century or century and a half of the Christian Nubian era. Although it was clearly derived from the X-Group Ware R1, and in at least one case was made at the same factory (see Adams 1962c, 68-70), fewer than a half dozen specimens of Ware R2 have ever been found in X-Group graves (Adams 1986, 634, n. 2). At Meinarti, two vessels of the ware were found at Subphase 2a and three at Subphase 2b, while 17 specimens were registered from Subphase 2c.

The various vessel form classes in Ware R2 are much the same as in Ware R1, though many individual forms are different. There is once again a heavy preponderance of cups, of which a representative selection is shown in Plate 17b, nos. 17-24. Goblets on the other hand were rare, with only two registered specimens, one of which (921) is shown in Plate 17d, no. 6. Bowls were fairly common, and are shown in Plate 17e. A vessel form which is not illustrated is the spouted pot (Form G42), represented by three finds.

Family N, Group N.III: Early Christian Wares[13]
These are the "signature wares" of the Early Christian period. They are distinguished from their forebears by a markedly distinct group of vessel forms, in which cups and goblets have been very largely replaced by an enormous diversity of bowl forms, both plain and footed. There is also a somewhat more formal decorative style (N.III), consisting largely of arches and festoons executed in fine lines. Although the production of these wares belongs chiefly to the period represented by Phase 3, three of the wares (W1, W2, and R5) had already made their appearance in considerable numbers at the time of Subphase 2c, and a few specimens were found earlier still.

Ware W1: Early Christian peach ware.[14] The antecedents of this unusual and rather uncommon ware are uncertain, since it is not obviously derived from an X-Group predecessor. The ware occurs mostly in the form of bowls having a highly polished, lustrous surface. The vessels were fired in such a way that the interiors are most commonly white to cream colored, while exteriors shade from lemon yellow to a golden pink or light orange (hence the name "peach ware"). Sherds of this ware were quite numerous at Level 14 (Subphase 2c), but registered finds were confined to two bowls, one (1040) found at Level 15a, and one (1271) found at Level 14. The former is illustrated in Plate 18a, no. 8.

Ware W2: Early Christian matte white ware.[15] This ware, a direct outgrowth of X-Group Ware W11, was to become in time the most common of the Early Christian wares. At Meinarti it was already becoming fairly common at Subphase 2c, and had largely displaced its pred-

ecessor. It is represented by large numbers of sherds and also by 13 registered vessels, mostly from Subphase 2c. The finds include five small bowls, of which one (1006) is shown in Plate 18a, no. 4; two small bottles (not illustrated); three lamps (Plates 17f, nos. 4 and 5; Plate 18a, no. 2); and three lids, of which one (862) is illustrated in Plate 18a, no. 1.

Ware R5: Early Christian polished red ware.[16] This ware, highly abundant in Early Christian times, was in one sense an outgrowth of Ware R2, in that it was made at the same factories (see Adams 1962c, 68-70). However, the vessel forms were nearly all copied from the contemporary Aswan Ware R4, which had already begun to appear in Nubia somewhat earlier. At Meinarti the ware was abundantly represented by sherds at Subphase 2c, but only six registered vessels were found—all at Subphase 2c. The finds include a plain bowl (not illustrated), two footed bowls (Plate 18b, nos. 12 and 14; Plate 18c, no. 2); a plate (Plate 18b, no. 17); a lid (not illustrated), and a footed jar (not illustrated).

Family N, Group NU: Nubian coarse utility wares
In this family, the rather thin-walled brown utility Ware U1, discussed in the last chapter, was predominant throughout the Meroitic and the first half of the Ballaña period. In the later Ballaña period it began to give way to the heavier walled, brick-red Ware U5, which persisted through the whole of the Christian period. This evolutionary development is reflected both in the sherd data and in the registered vessels from Meinarti, at Phase 2.

Ware U1: Pre-Christian brown utility ware.[17] Sherds of this ware were abundant at all three Phase 2 levels, though less so in Subphase 2c than in its predecessors. Only two vessels were registered: both *qadus* (964, 1069) from Subphase 2a. They are identical in form to the *qadus* found at Subphase 1c, and are illustrated along with it in Plate 85, nos. 1 and 3.

Ware U5: Christian red utility ware.[18] This ware is distinguished from its Ware U1 predecessor by its heavier walls, by its brick-red color, by the absence of ribbing on vessel bodies, and by the occasional use of a thin red wash. It was used throughout the Christian period for a wide variety of large, coarse pots and jars, but occasionally also for smaller forms. Vessels very occasionally have narrow bands of painted decoration, in broad white lines, but incised decoration in the form of fine scored lines is considerably more common. However, the great majority of vessels have no decoration.

At Meinarti, sherds of Ware U5 were uncommon in Phase 2, and were confined entirely to Subphase 2c. Registered vessels were limited to two bag-shaped jars, one found at Level 15a (Subphase 2b) and one at Level 14 (Subphase 2c). The latter (944) is shown in Plate 18f, no. 1.

[13] For the full ware group description and discussion see Adams 1986, 473-81.
[14] Designated in Adams 1962b, 273, as Ware 11. For the full ware description and illustrations see Adams 1986, 483.
[15] Designated in Adams 1962b, 273-4, as Wares 12 and 18. For the full ware description and illustrations see Adams 1986, 483-4.

[16] Designated in Adams 1962b, 272-3, as Wares 5, 8, and 9. For the full ware description and illustrations see Adams 1986, 481-92.
[17] Designated in Adams 1962b, 275, as Ware 21. For the full ware description and illustrations see Adams 1986, 515-22.
[18] Designated in Adams 1962b, 275, as Ware 25. For the full ware description and illustrations see Adams 1986, 516-22.

Family D, Group D.II: X-Group and earlier Christian domestic wares.[19]
The two members of this group that were present in Phase 2, Wares H1 and H13, are the same two found at Phase 1, and previously described.

Ware H1: Early domestic plain utility ware.[20] This ware, made first in Meroitic times if not earlier, continued with little change throughout the whole of the Ballaña period and the first half of the Christian period. Registered finds at Meinarti came from all three of the Phase 2 levels. They consist of a goblet, a lamp, four lids, and two globular pots. Three of the lids, identical to other lids found at Phase 1, are shown in Plate 8c. The two registered globular pots are not illustrated, but many other examples, which were not registered, are shown in Plate 19a.[21] These vessels were found, almost without exception, buried in house floors; they came about equally from Phase 2 and Phase 3 contexts.

Ware H13: Transitional white-on-red domestic ware.[22] This unusual ware was found almost exclusively in the form of globular pots and jars, of which four were found at Phase 1, and two at Phase 2. The latter two are shown in Plate 19b, nos. 2 and 3.

Family A, Group A.I: Graeco-Roman Aswan wares.[23]
By the time of Phase 2, this ware group had largely given way to the successor Group A.II. The only registered survivals were a jug of Ware W24, and four vessels of Ware R31.

Ware W24: Aswan Graeco-Roman ordinary cream ware.[24] This uncommon ware was a variant of the much more common Aswan Ware R30, distinguished from it by the presence of a thin cream slip and sometimes painted decoration in black. Decoration is usually confined to simple body stripes. Although Ware W24, like other wares of Group A.I, has usually been found in Meroitic contexts, the only registered example from Meinarti is a small jug (1003) found at Level 15a (Subphase 2b). It is shown in Plate 19d, no. 1.

Ware R31: Aswan Graeco-Roman flaky pink ware.[25] As noted in the previous chapter, this ware is found almost

exclusively in the form of *lekythoi, aryballoi,* and other small bottles, which occurred in about equal numbers in Phase 1 and Phase 2. The finds from Phase 2 include a small pot (750), shown in Plate 19c, no. 10 and Plate 19d, no. 8, and three *lekythoi,* shown in Plate 9a, nos. 5, 7, and 8, and in Plate 19c, nos. 3 and 4.

Family A, Group A.II: Byzantine Aswan wares.[26]
These wares, already present at Phase 1, continued to be imported in considerable numbers throughout Phase 2.

Ware R4: Aswan Byzantine polished red ware.[27] In this ware, the goblets, *aryballoi,* lamps, and other small forms of Ballaña times gave way almost completely to wide bowls and plates in the Early Christian period. The transition can be observed clearly in the finds from Phase 2, where the vessels from Subphase 2b are three *aryballoi* (shown in Plate 9a, nos. 2-4) and a lamp, while the vessels from Subphase 2c are four footed bowls, of which one (1400) is shown in Plate 8f.

Ware R14: Aswan Byzantine decorated pink ware.[28] This very uncommon ware, found mainly in the Early Christian period, has the odd peculiarity that the vessels lack a slip, but have designs in black painted directly on the natural pink surfaces. The single find from Meinarti is a fragment of a large plate (1408—not illustrated), from Subphase 2b.

Ware U2: Aswan Byzantine pink utility ware.[29] This was the standard Aswan utility ware of the Ballaña period, when it wholly displaced its predecessor, Ware R30. It is found occasionally in the form of bottles, jugs, and jars, but the overwhelming majority of finds are amphorae. They are distinguished from their Meroitic predecessors by having short loop handles, rather than strap handles, and a "button" base rather than a small ring base, as shown in Plate 19f. In Ballaña times all amphorae of Ware U2 were in Form Z6; in Early Christian times these gave way to the more tapered Form Z4 (see Adams 1986, 541).

Sherds of Ware U2 were fairly numerous at all three of the Phase 2 levels, but registered finds were confined to a jug (968), shown in Plate 19e, no. 3; an oil bottle (757), shown in Plate 9a, no. 1 and Plate 19c, no. 2; and two amphorae, of which one (745) is shown in Plate 9b, no. 2 and Plate 19f, no. 2. Both the amphorae have ribbed rather than flat surfaces, a feature characteristic of Ware U2 amphorae only in the latter half of the Ballaña period.

Other Egyptian utility wares
As in Phase 1, several utility wares, in addition to Ware U2, were present in the form of sherds. Wares U3, U4, and U12 were already present at Phase 1, and were discussed in the last chapter. The Fostat Ware U13 however

[19] For the full ware group description and discussion see Adams 1986, 421-2.
[20] Designated in Adams 1962b, 276, as Ware 27. For the full ware description and illustrations see Adams 1986, 418.
[21] These vessels were not collected because of their extreme fragility, and the near impossibility of mending them once broken. We had not the facilities to pack them adequately to withstand the rough-and-tumble of the rail trip to Khartoum.
[22] For the ware description see Adams 1986, 424-5.
[23] For the full ware group description and discussion see Adams 1986, 526-34.
[24] Designated in Adams 1964a, 160, as Wares IVA and IVD. For the full ware description see Adams 1986, 537-8.
[25] Designated in Adams 1964a, 160, as Ware IVC. For the full ware description and illustrations see Adams 1986, 536-7. The suggestion of Pamela Rose (n.d.), that this ware was made in Nubia and does not belong among the Aswan wares, was noted in the last chapter.

[26] For the ware description see Adams 1986, 542-3.
[27] Designated in Adams 1962b, 272, as Ware 4. For the full ware description and illustrations see Adams 1986, 543-4.
[28] For the ware description see Adams 1986, 544.
[29] Designated in Adams 1962b, 275, as Ware 22. For the full ware description and illustrations see Adams 1986, 543-4.

made its first appearance at Phase 2. Conspicuously missing was the micaceous brown utility Ware U18, although this ware has been found in other late Ballaña sites.

Sub-family LB, Ware U12: Ballas drab utility ware.[30] This distinctive ware was represented by a few sherds at Phase 2, as it was also at Phase 1. The vessel forms could not be determined.

Sub-family LF, Ware U13: Fostat ordinary utility ware.[31] This ware, whose manufacture has continued down to modern times, is distinguished by its porous, greenish-grey paste. It has been used throughout history primarily for water vessels, which are designed to keep cool by "sweating." A few very small sherds were found in the Phase 2 levels at Meinarti; the vessel forms could not be determined.

Sub-family LS: Saqqara buff amphora ware.[32] This ware, probably of Lower Egyptian origin, is found so abundantly in Ballaña graves as almost to constitute one of the "signatures" of the period. At Meinarti it was represented by no registered vessels, but by an abundance of sherds, virtually all from Subphases 2a and 2b. Only a single sherd was found at Subphase 2c.

Family T, Ware U4: Middle Egyptian brown utility ware.[33] This ware is found mostly in the form of thick-walled amphorae having a tapered profile and very heavy surface ribbing (Forms Z3 and Z3a). These vessels were imported throughout both the Ballaña and the Early Christian periods. They have been found only occasionally in X-Group graves, but were highly abundant in the Tavern refuse at Qasr Ibrim (Plumley and Adams 1974, 217-19). In Phase 2 at Meinarti they were represented only by sherds, a few of which were found in each of the three levels.

The principal vessel forms
Vessels of 17 form classes were found at Phase 2. With only one or two exceptions, they are the same form classes that were prevalent at Phase 1. However, the much more abundant material from Phase 2 provides an opportunity to follow the evolutionary development of some forms from earlier to later variants.

A: Cups.[34] These vessels, common in late Meroitic times, became even more so during the Ballaña period. The prevailing forms however were quite different. In Ware R1 of the earlier Ballaña period, the usual form was the rather squat Form A8, illustrated in Plate 17b, nos. 1-8. At Meinarti, most of these vessels were found at Subphase 2a. Later, at Subphases 2b and 2c, Form A8 gave way to the slightly taller and more straight-sided Form A7, illustrated in Plate 17b, nos. 9-16. This form persisted in the Transitional period, but was then accompanied by the sloping-sided Forms A26 and A31, made in Ware R2. Examples of the latter forms are shown in Plate 17b, nos. 17-24. In the Early Christian period they gave way in their turn to a whole series of new cup forms, to be discussed in *Meinarti II*.

B: Goblets.[35] As we saw in the last chapter, these vessels made their first appearance as imports from Egypt, in Wares R30 and R25. They were soon copied by the Nubian potters, and in the indigenous Ware R1 they became perhaps the single most popular vessel form. The earliest versions, shown in Plate 17c, nos. 1-6, were relatively squat and angular in profile (Form B17), like their Egyptian prototypes. Later the vessels became both larger and more rounded in profile (Form B14), as shown in Plate 17c, nos. 7-17.[36] The two exceptionally slender vessels shown in Plate 17d, nos. 7 and 8, represent the latest variants of this form. Vessels of Form B17 were predominant at Subphase 2a, while those of Form B14 were predominant at Subphase 2b. Goblets of both forms were usually decorated; the evolution of decorative designs will be discussed in a later paragraph.

Curiously rare at Meinarti was the small, rounded goblet Form B9, of which a single specimen is illustrated in Plate 17d, no. 4. Unlike the goblets of Forms B17 and B14, these vessels were never decorated. They were highly abundant in the Ballaña levels at Qasr Ibrim, but only six examples were registered from Meinarti.

Goblets of all kinds were scarce at Phase 2c, and disappeared altogether in the Christian period. The reason for this development is far from clear, since the importation and consumption of wine did not by any means cease in Early Christian times. Indeed, the continuation of wine trade was one of the specific provisions of the *baqt* treaty of A.D. 652 (see Adams 1977, 451-2).

C: Bowls.[37] In Ballaña as in Meroitic times, these vessels were fairly common, but there was no one prevailing form. Indeed, the 14 registered specimens in Ware R1 exhibit 10 different forms, several of which are illustrated in Plate 7e. The main common characteristic of these vessels is their relative simplicity of design and their lack of decoration. Conspicuously missing at Phase 2 is the "flowerpot" Form C46, of which a single example (from Phase 1) is shown in Plate 7e, no. 4. These vessels were highly abundant at Qasr Ibrim, and are considered one of the best horizon markers for the earlier Ballaña period.

In the Transitional period, in Ware R2, a group of distinctive bowl forms (C64, C66, and C67) emerged, which are characterized by slightly inset rims. Examples are shown in Plate 7e, no. 8, and in Plate 17e, nos. 5 and 7. These vessels are useful as horizon markers because they had only a brief popularity, at the very beginning of the Christian period. Before long they gave way to a truly extraordinary variety of new bowl forms, which were the most common vessels of the Early Christian period.

---

[30] For the ware description see Adams 1986, 574-5.

[31] For the ware description see Adams 1986, 576-8.

[32] Designated in Adams 1962b, 225, as Ware 23. For the ware description see Adams 1986, 580.

[33] Designated in Adams 1964a, 160, as Ware IIH. For the full ware description and illustrations see Adams 1986, 567-8.

[34] For discussion of the class see Adams 1986, 101; for illustrations see ibid., 108-11.

[35] For discussion of the class see Adams 1986, 101; for illustrations see ibid., 112-15.

[36] This development has previously been noted by N. B. Millet (1963, 159), and by Bruce Trigger (1967, 61-2) and has been further discussed by Pamela Rose, (n.d., 188).

[37] For discussion of the class see Adams 1986, 101-2; for illustrations see ibid., 116-22.

D: Footed bowls.[38] These remained uncommon in the Ballaña period, as they were also in Meroitic times. The first locally made examples, in Wares R25 and R1, were all copied after prototypes in the contemporary Aswan Ware R4. The most prevalent form, D11, is actually a slightly wider variant of the common goblet form B17. An example, in Ware R25, is shown in Plate 7d, no. 9, and a footed bowl in Aswan Ware R4 is shown in Plate 8f, no. 8. In the Transitional period (Subphase 2c), in Ware R2, a new and much more diverse range of footed bowl forms appeared, presaging the further proliferation of these vessels in the Early Christian period. However, only one example (not illustrated) is present in the Meinarti collections.

E. Plates.[39] These vessels were never common in Nubia at any time, and were all either Aswan products or direct Nubian copies of them. They occur mainly in the Early Christian period, but a single fragmentary specimen, in Aswan Ware R4, was found at Level 15a (Subphase 2b) at Meinarti.

G: Small pots and bottles.[40] These vessels were considerably more common in Ballaña than in Meroitic times. Of the ten registered specimens, in Wares R1 and R2, seven are spouted goblets (Form G40) or spouted pots (Form G42)—both forms unique to the X-Group wares. They differ from each other only in that the spouted pots lack a ring base. Three examples of spouted goblets are shown in Plate 17d, nos. 15-17. A small pot of a quite different form, in Ware R2, is shown in Plate 17e, no. 19.

I: Jugs.[41] Vessels in this class were fairly prevalent in the Meroitic period, but extremely rare thereafter. They are nearly all in the Aswan wares, or in direct Nubian copies of them, and were inspired by common Hellenistic or Byzantine forms. At Meinarti, as it happens, no jugs were found in the Meroitic levels, but two specimens, both of Aswan ware, were found in the Phase 2 levels. One (1003) in Ware W24, Form I18, is shown in Plate 19d, no. 1; the other (968), in Ware U2, Form I1, is shown in Plate 19e, no. 3.

J. Table amphorae.[42] These vessels differ from jugs only in the possession of two handles instead of one, and in the lack of a pouring lip. They too were common in Meroitic times, but less so thereafter. As in the case of jugs, however, the only specimen from Meinarti came from the late Ballaña Subphase 2c. It is an undecorated vessel in the white Ware W11, and is shown in Plate 17a, no. 1.

M: Lekythoi.[43] These miniature jugs, already imported on a small scale in Meroitic times, continued to be imported but were now also locally made in Ballaña times. Of the six registered examples from the Phase 2 levels, three are in Aswan Ware R31, already present at Phase 1, and three are local copies in Ware R1. The Aswan vessels are shown in Plate 9a, nos. 5, 7, and 8, and the Nubian vessels in Plate 17e, nos. 16-18. The use of lekythoi ceased altogether at the beginning of the Christian period.

N: Aryballoi.[44] These small, round-bodied bottles, already present in Meroitic times, were rather common in the Phase 2 levels at Meinarti. The nine registered specimens are all of a single form, N10, but six are in the local Ware R1, and three in the Aswan Ware R4. The Aswan aryballoi are shown in Plate 9a, nos. 2-4, and four of the local specimens are shown in Plate 17e, nos. 12-15. Aryballoi, like lekythoi, disappeared very early in the Christian period.

P: Lamps.[45] These objects, rare in Meroitic times, became abundant in the Ballaña period; they are one of the three most common vessel forms found in the Phase 2 levels at Meinarti. Of the 34 registered specimens, 29 are in the Classic X-Group Ware R1, three in the Early Christian Ware W2, one in the hand-made Ware H1, and one in Aswan Ware R4. Among the local products, the overwhelming majority are in Forms P15 and P16—the quintessential X-Group lamp forms. Examples of Form P15 are shown in Plate 17e, no. 8, and Plate 17f, no. 7, and an example of Form P16 is shown in Plate 17e, no. 9.

Plate 17f shows a number of less common lamp forms found at Phase 2. The first five specimens, having a slightly elongate outline, were mold-made. Numbers 2 and 3 (913 and 852) are lamps of Aswan Ware R4, Forms P1 and P2; they have embossed designs which include floral motifs, crosses, and sometimes the names of saints. These vessels were widely traded throughout both Egypt and Nubia, and were closely associated with Christian votive ritual. In Early Christian Nubia, they were the preferred form of votive lamp that was left burning alongside grave superstructures (see Griffith 1927, 79-80 and pl. LVIII). Number 1 (839), in Plate 7f, is a Nubian imitation of the Aswan lamps.

The two mold-made lamps numbers 4 and 5 (847 and 981), in Plate 17f, have the figure of a frog embossed on the upper side (Form P3). These vessels are in the Early Christian white Ware W2, but they are probably copied after Egyptian vessels.[46] The frog figure, which appears often on Meroitic painted pottery, is believed to be a survival of pagan eschatological belief (See Woolley and Randall-MacIver 1910, 57).

The Nubian-made lamp shown in Plate 17f, no. 6 and in Figure 27 (1176), is unique in that it appears to have been hand-modeled rather than mold-made. It has decoration in low relief around the edges, but also an embossed cross on the rear side, behind the filler hole. The cross is not positioned exactly along the centerline, but is slightly off to one side. Number 7 in Plate 17f (895) is a typical lamp

---

[38] For discussion of the class see Adams 1986, 102; for illustrations see ibid., 129-32.

[39] For discussion of the class see Adams 1986, 102; for illustrations see ibid., 130.

[40] For discussion of the class see Adams 1986, 103; for illustrations see ibid., 135-8.

[41] For discussion of the class see Adams 1986, 103; for illustrations see ibid., 140-43.

[42] For discussion of the class see Adams 1986, 103; for illustrations see ibid., 143-4.

[43] For discussion of the class see Adams 1986, 103; for illustrations see ibid., 147.

[44] For discussion of the class (under the name "Oil bottles") see Adams 1986, 103; for illustrations see ibid., 148.

[45] For discussion of the class see Adams 1986, 103-4; for illustrations see ibid., 150-54.

[46] For examples see Roeder 1959, 321 and pls. 40, m and n, and 77, m and n.

of Form P15, while Number 8 (916) is a unique variant of this form, having three wick-holes instead of the usual one. Number 9 (1060) is a lamp of Form P9, an early form that differs from the more common X-Group lamps in having a hollow handle and a small pedestal base.

There can be little doubt that the prevalence of lamps at Phase 2 is attributable to the increasing adoption of Christian votive practice. Thus, lamps were rare at Subphase 2a, more common at Subphase 2b, and still more common at Subphase 2c. It is noteworthy too that two of the vessels have incised owner's graffiti in the form of crosses. However, the presence of lamps at Subphases 2a and 2b does not necessarily indicate that the "official" conversion of Nobatia had already taken place, but only that there were individual votaries among the Nubian population (see Adams 1977, 417-18). On the other hand there is substantial evidence to suggest that the official conversion had taken place by the time of Subphase 2c; this will be further discussed at the end of the chapter.

Q: Lids.[47] These were rare in Meroitic times, and were found only in the hand-made Ware H1. Identical hand-made lids continued to be made in Ballaña times, but they were now joined also by small lids, usually with painted decoration, in the wheel-made Wares R1 an W2. Three examples of the hand-made lids are shown in Plate 8c, nos. 1, 5, and 6, and a wheel-made lid in Ware W2 is shown in Plate 18a, no. 1.

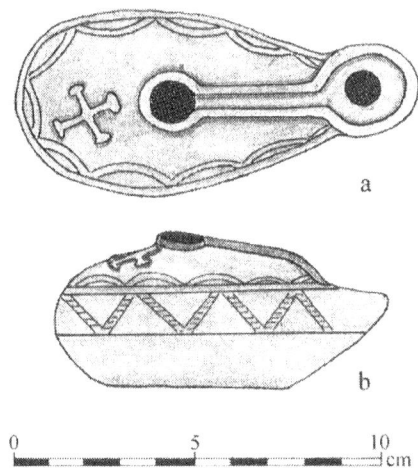

Figure 27. Lamp of Ware R1, with incised and embossed decoration (1176), from Level 15b. a, Top view; b, side view.

U: Pots.[48] The overwhelming majority of pots in the Ballaña period were globular, hand-made vessels of Ware H1, most of which have been found buried under house floors. A group of 48 of these vessels, which were not entered in the register, is shown in Plate 19a. About half those shown were found in Phase 2 levels, and the remainder in Early and Classic Christian levels. However, the single registered pot from Phase 2 (1074) is in the decorated hand-made Ware H13; it is virtually identical to pots found at Phase 1. It is shown in Plate 19b, no. 2.

V: *Qadus*.[49] The same typical form of *qadus* (Form V2) was used in Meroitic and in Ballaña times. Plate 8b shows two examples from the Phase 2 levels (nos. 1 and 3), alongside one from Phase 1 (no. 2). Number 1 is obviously a kiln waster which could never have been attached to a *saqia* rope, and must have been put to some secondary use. The presence of this specimen seems to indicate that *qawadis* were made locally at Meinarti, since it is unlikely that such a misshapen vessel would have been traded over any distance.

W: Jars.[50] Jars with a short, narrow neck, usually described as bottles (Form W38), have been found in great abundance in Ballaña graves, and are often thought to be one of the most characteristic X-Group pottery forms. However, these vessels are much less common in habitation sites, and none were found at Meinarti. The only jars of any kind registered from the Phase 2 levels are two bag-shaped vessels (Form W21) in the undecorated utility Ware U5, one of which is shown in Plate 18f, no. 1.

X: Footed jars.[51] These vessels were somewhat less common in Ballaña than in Meroitic times. The only two examples found in Phase 2 levels were a large jar of white Ware W11 (Form X14), shown in Plate 17a, no. 3, and a jar of red Ware R5 (943), not illustrated. The illustrated vessel has a simple painted design in broad red lines.

Z; Amphorae.[52] Wine amphorae, mostly from Aswan, continued to be imported in very large quantities throughout the Ballaña period, and indeed in the Early Christian period as well. However, there was a change in the prevailing form, from the rather slender vessel with strap handles (Form Z5) of Meroitic times to the somewhat larger vessel with loop handles (Form Z6) of Ballaña times. In Early Christian times there was a further evolutionary development, toward a much more slender and elongate vessel (Form Z4). The evolutionary sequence is shown in Plate 19f, with the Meroitic amphora form on the left, the Ballaña form in the middle, and the Early Christian form on the right.

Another evolutionary change that occurred independently was the introduction of ribbed rather than flat vessel surfaces, which happened more or less in the middle of the Ballaña period. Thus, earlier vessels in Form Z6 have flat surfaces, while later ones have ribbed surfaces. The two registered vessels from Phase 2 at Meinarti (745 and 929) both have ribbed surfaces—another of several indications that the whole of the Phase 2 occupation belongs to the latter half of the Ballaña period. One of the two registered amphorae (745) is the middle vessel shown in Plate 19f.

---

[47] For discussion of the class see Adams 1986, 104; for illustrations see ibid., 155-6. For another frog lamp from Nubia see Mills 1982, pl. XLVIII, no. 17.

[48] For discussion of the class see Adams 1986, 104-5; for illustrations see ibid., 161-4.

[49] For discussion of the class see Adams 1986, 105; for illustrations see ibid., 165.

[50] For discussion of the class see Adams 1986, 105; for illustrations see ibid., 166-71.

[51] For discussion of the class see Adams 1986, 105; for illustrations see ibid., 172-4.

[52] For discussion of the class see Adams 1986, 107; for illustrations see ibid., 177-82.

Numerous sherd finds attest to the fact that many amphorae of "Saqqara" Ware U3 (Form Z14) and of "Theban" Ware U4 (Form Z3) also continued to be imported, although there are no registered vessels in either ware.

ZZ: Kegs.[53] These are more or less cylindrical vessels whose only aperture is a short neck and mouth in the middle of one side—essentially the same form found in wooden kegs, though on a much smaller scale. Evidently, like amphorae, they were designed for liquid transport and storage, but the practical advantages of the keg over the amphora form are difficult to discern. Unless they were tightly stoppered, the vessels could obviously rest only on their sides. Kegs first made their appearance in the Roman Egyptian wares, and were copied very occasionally by the Nubians, but they were never numerous except in the imported Ware U12 in the Late Christian period. In Phase 2 at Meinarti, a single keg (880—not illustrated) of Ware R1 was found. It is, so far as I know, the only example of a keg in this indigenous Nubian ware.

Decorative colors
Although red-slipped wares were already common in Meroitic times, they became overwhelmingly predominant in the X-Group wares. Indeed the X-Group White Ware W11 is so rare as to suggest the possibility that it was an import.[54] A holdover from Meroitic tradition was the prevalence of three-color decoration: either black and white on a red slip (Styles N.IIA and N.IIC), in Wares R1 and R2, or black and red on a white slip (Style N.IIB), in the case of Ware W11. This usage became much less common in the Early Christian period.

Decoration
The X-Group pottery wares of the Ballaña period are the most infrequently and the most simply decorated of all Nubian pottery in the post-pharaonic period. In this as in other respects, they followed the general lead of the late Roman redwares, and more specifically of their Aswan variant. The prevailing Nubian Style N.IIA was clearly derivative from the Aswan Style A.IB, although in time it developed nuances of its own.

It is conspicuous, in the Nubian wares, that some vessel forms were much more often decorated than were others. For example, goblets of Forms B14 and B17 usually had painted decoration from the rim to the waist, as can be seen in Plate 17c. On the other hand goblets of Form B9 were never decorated. Cups were usually not decorated, but there were a few exceptions, as can be seen in Plate 17b. Among larger vessels the bottle Form W38 (not found at Meinarti) usually had painted designs, while most other forms did not.

Style N.IIA: Classic X-Group style.[55] This is the familiar X-Group style, characterized by the sparing use of a few recurring design elements. Its most immediately conspicuous feature, in contrast to all earlier and later Nubian styles, is the absence of framing lines above and below the designs. Frequent and distinctive elements are groups of disconnected "blobs" and vertical slashes (Motifs 8 and 2).

All decorated vessels in Ware R1 are decorated in Style N.IIA. The finds from Meinarti exhibit only a few of the recorded variants of the style, but they are interesting in that an evolutionary development can be recognized, at least in the case of goblets. The most common decoration on the earlier goblets consists of "swags" or festoons, dependent from the rim and forming a continuous frieze (Motif G12). Usually, but not always, there are two or three vertical stripes descending between each pair of swags (Motif H12/2). These designs are illustrated in Plate 17c, nos. 1-6 and 11-12. In later goblets the swags have largely disappeared, to be replaced either by widely spaced groups of "blobs" (Motif H8), alternately in black and white, or by widely spaced sets of vertical slashes (Motif H2), in which black and white may again alternate. These designs can be seen in Plate 17c, nos. 7-10 and 13-17. It is noteworthy however that cups never exhibit the swag designs of the earlier goblets, but only the blobs or slashes found on the later goblets. Examples are shown in Plate 17b, nos. 1-3. Occasionally cups, but not goblets, may exhibit white ticking, or disconnected spots (Motif A8) around the rim.

In addition to their painted decoration, many X-Group vessels exhibit fine scored lines, either singly or in groups, around the circumference of the vessel. In the case of both cups and goblets there is usually a single scored line around the widest portion of the vessel, as can be seen on several specimens in Plates 17b and 17c. Pairs of lines, though less common, can be seen in Plate 17b, nos. 11 and 15, and in Plate 17c, nos. 9 and 16. Larger vessels (not included among the illustrated vessels from Meinarti) usually exhibit a "bundle" of three or more scored lines.

Style N.IIB: X-Group white ware style.[56] This rather elaborate style is found only on the white Ware W11. Its most common and most distinctive feature is the use of boldly executed arch designs, in either black or red or both, embellished along the edges with large tangent dots. As it happens there are no examples of this kind of decoration among the registered vessels from Meinarti, although numerous fragmentary examples were observed among the sherds. Of the three vessels of Ware W11 illustrated in Plate 17a, no. 1 is undecorated, no. 2 has a swag design (Motif B12) which is faintly visible, and no. 3 has a very simple zigzag frieze (Motif G5).

Style N.IIC: Transitional style.[57] This short-lived style, found only on Ware R2, was transitional between the norms of Classic X-Group (Style N.IIA) and Early Christian (Style N.III) decoration. From the parent Style N.IIA it retains the black-and-white on red tradition and the use of detached spots (usually no longer "blob"-shaped) and vertical slashes, although both spots and slashes now usually occur in continuously repeating series rather than in widely separated clusters. Style N.IIC anticipates the Early

---

[53] For discussion of the class see Adams 1986, 107; for illustrations see ibid., 183.

[54] For discussion see Adams 1986, 470-72.

[55] For discussion of the style see Adams 1986, 542; for illustrations see ibid., 291-4.

[56] For discussion of the style see Adams 1986, 542-3; for illustrations see ibid., 296-7.

[57] For discussion of the style see Adams 1986, 243; for illustrations see ibid., 298-9.

Christian style in its frequent use of a rim stripe, and of frieze designs pendant from a horizontal line. A unique feature of the style is the occasional use of designs in bold black lines, on which fine white dots or criss-cross lines are superimposed. In addition to their painted decoration, some vessels in Style N.IIC are encircled by fine incised lines, like their predecessors in Style N.IIA. However, the incised lines are now usually a short distance below the vessel rim, rather than at the waist.

Finds of Ware R2 were rather rare at Meinarti, and vessels with Style N.IIC decoration were even rarer. The only illustrated examples are two cups, nos. 17 and 21 in Plate 17b, both of which have decoration in fine lines around the rim. Number 17 has a design of fine white festoons superimposed on a black rim stripe, while no. 21 has white cross-crossed lines around the rim. In addition to the painted designs, nos. 19, 20, and 21 all have fine scored lines about 1cm. below the rim.

Style N.III: Early Christian style.[58] Vessels in the Early Christian Wares R5 and W2 were often decorated in a simple style (Style N.III), consisting mostly of either arch or festoon friezes framed by single lines, and executed in one color only. However, this decoration was not present on any of the Early Christian vessels found in the Phase 2 levels. They were decorated, if at all, only with plain rim or body stripes. It is possible that the arch and festoon motifs had not yet developed in the Transitional period.

Incised graffiti

Seven of the registered vessels from Phase 2 bore scratched or incised graffiti, which are illustrated in Figure 28. As can be seen, most are rather carelessly and irregularly scratched marks, having no obvious meaning. Three however are clearly crosses, and one is a kind of monogram combining the letters lambda, chi, and possibly alpha.

The non-pottery finds

Table 13 lists the 79 registered non-pottery objects that were either found in the Phase 2 levels, or are of presumed Ballaña origin. As in Table 12, objects of the same material and type are listed in chronological order, from Subphase 2a to Subphase 2c.

Ceramic objects

Incense burner or lamp stand. The object (854) shown in Plates 20a and 20b and in Figure 29 is the upper portion of what was most probably either an incense burner or a lamp stand. It is wheel-made from a rather coarse red pottery, similar in fabric to the Nubian utility Ware U5. The top, in the form of a shallow dish with a slightly everted rim, rests on a cylindrical column, perforated at regular intervals by triangular and rectangular cutouts whose purpose can only have been decorative. A further decorative feature is a protruding collar with scalloped indentations, all around the top of the column. The preserved portion of the column has a very slightly conical profile, meaning that the base must have been somewhat wider than the preserved upper portion.

[58] For discussion of the style see Adams 1986, 243-5; for illustrations see ibid., 301-8.

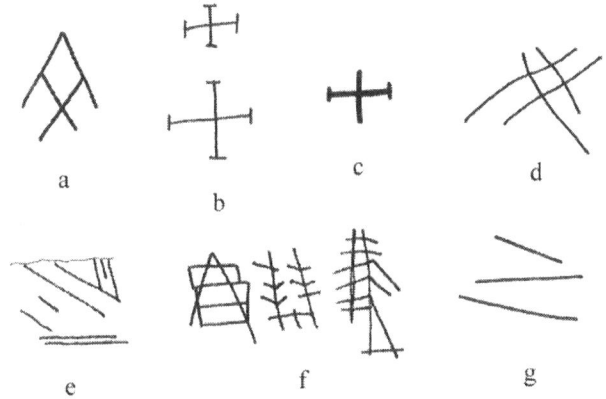

Figure 28. Owner's graffiti on pottery from Phase 2. Registration numbers of vessels are as follows: a, 1248; b, 865; c, 895; d, 1083; e, 1034; f, 1055; g, 1180. *Not to scale.*

Although the object is not smoothly finished, it has a brick-red slip, with painted decoration in black and white. The everted rim is painted white, on which a fine zigzag line is overpainted in black. At the top of the column, just above the collar, there is a second broad white band, with a fine black stripe overpainted. Between the rectangular cutouts are additional, rectangular areas painted in white and bordered on each side by black lines. The various features of decoration are generally reminiscent of the Transitional Nubian pottery Style N.IIC, which was developed at the same period (Subphase 2c).

I have not been able to identify close parallels to this

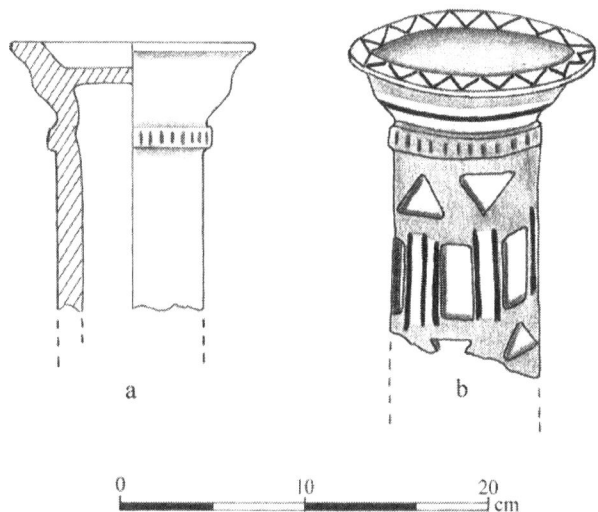

Figure 29. Ceramic incense stand (854) from Level 14. a, Profile and cross-section; b, side view.

object in other Nubian archaeological collections, although it has a generalized resemblance to bronze incense burners and lamp stands found in the Ballaña and Qustul tombs (Emery and Kirwan 1938, pls. 97, 101). The nearest ceramic equivalents have been found in early Byzantine sites in Egypt (cf. Quibell 1912, pl. XLIX, 4; and Mond and Myers 1934, pls. CXXVII-CXXXII), and in particular in the Monastery of Epiphanius at Thebes (Winlock and Crum 1926, pl. XXX, B and C). However, none of the Egyptian stands have the cutout areas exhibited by our specimen.

TABLE 13. REGISTERED NON-POTTERY FINDS FROM PHASE 2 *

Reg. no.	Object	Material	Condition	Level (Phase)	Plate
		Ceramic			
854	Incense stand	Ceramic	Portion	14 (2c)	20a-b
951	Female figurine	Ceramic	Mostly complete	15b (2a)	20c, 6
999	Female figurine	Ceramic	Head fragment	15c (2a)	20c, 1
775	Female figurine	Ceramic	Mostly complete	14 (2c)	20c, 5
785	Female figurine	Ceramic	Body portion	14 (2c)	20c, 7
845	Female figurine	Ceramic	Head fragment	14 (2c)	20c, 1
902	Female figurine	Ceramic	Body portion	14 (2c)	20c, 4
1466	Female figurine	Ceramic	Portion	?	
795	Horse figurine	Ceramic	Complete	15a (2b)	20d, 8
1081	Horse figurine	Ceramic	Body portion	15a (2b)	20d, 7
1082	Horse figurine	Ceramic	Head fragment	15a (2b)	20d, 1
816	Horse figurine	Ceramic	Body portion	14 (2c)	20d, 9
817	Horse figurine	Ceramic	Body fragment	14 (2c)	20d, 5
1042	Horse figurine	Ceramic	Body fragment	?	
1413	Horse figurine	Ceramic	Body fragment	?	20d, 2
1414	Horse figurine	Ceramic	Head fragment	?	20d, 4
846	Ba statuette?	Ceramic	Head fragment	15a (2b)	20e
1459	Bell	Ceramic	Portion	?	20f, 3
1460	Bell	Ceramic	Mostly complete	?	20f, 2
1461	Bell	Ceramic	Portion	?	20f, 1
1462	Bell	Ceramic	Portion	?	20f, 4
1079	Lamp	Ceramic	Complete	15b (2a)	
1064	Disc	Potsherd	Complete	15b (2a)	
806	Perforated square	Potsherd	Complete	14 (2c)	
1108	Beads	Faience	c. 55 beads	15b (2a)	
857	Beads	Faience	14 beads	15a (2b)	
		Glass			
911	Glass	Goblet	Portion	14 (2c)	
		Stone			
1066	Small capital	Sandstone	Complete	15a (2b)	21a, 1
950	Perforated object	Sandstone	Large portion	15a (2b)	21b, 1
1028	Jar stamp	Sandstone	Complete	15a (2b)	11a, 3 21d
1029	Jar stamp	Sandstone	Complete	15a (2b)	11a, 4 21c
864	Archer's loose	Quartzite	Nearly complete	15a (2b)	21e, 2 21f, 2
738	Archer's loose?	Granite	Half	13 (3a)*	21e, 3 21f, 3
761	Archer's loose	Felsite?	Half	?	21e, 1 21f, 1
871	Mortar	Hornblende	Nearly complete	15a (2b)	22a, 3
988	Mortar	Hornblende	Complete	15a (2b)	22a, 2
S39	Mortar	Hornblende	Fragment	14 (2c)	
S40	Mortar	Hornblende	Fragment	14 (2c)	
469	Mortar	Granodiorite	Nearly complete	7 (4c)*	22a, 4
411	Mortar	Hornblende	Complete	6 (5a)*	22a, 1
562	Mortar	Hornblende	Mostly complete	5 (5b)*	22a, 5
869	Pestle	Sandstone	Complete	15a (2b)	12b, 8
989	Pestle	Hornblende	Complete	15a (2b)	12b, 5
762	Pestle?	Granite	Complete	14 (2c)	12b, 4
870	Grinding stone	Granite	Complete	15a (2b)	12b, 6
985	Palette	Greywacke	Portion	15b (2a)	12c, 9 22b, 5
906	Palette	Greywacke	Mostly complete	15a (2b)	12c, 13 22b, 6

* The asterisk identifies finds from later phases that are obviously of Ballaña origin.

TABLE 13. REGISTERED NON-POTTERY FINDS FROM PHASE 2 (CONT.) [*]

Reg. no.	Object	Material	Condition	Level (Phase)	Plate
942	Palette	Greywacke	Portion	15a (2b)	12c, 11 22b, 8
1109	Palette	Greywacke	Portion	15a (2b)	12c, 4 22b, 2
831	Palette	Greywacke	Mostly complete	14 (2c)	12c, 10 22b, 3
410	Palette	Greywacke	Portion	6 (5a)*	12c, 16 22b, 7
1057	Whetstone?	Greywacke?	Complete	15a (2b)	12c, 2
1043	Perforated disc	Hornblende	Complete	15a (2b)	
887	Natural ring	Chert	Complete	15a (2b)	
945	Egg-shaped pebble	Talc?	Complete	14 (2c)	
1051	Pendant	(Unidentified)	Complete	15b (2a)	
908	Bead	Jade?	Complete?	14 (2c)	

Iron

1162	Dagger or knife	Iron	Mostly complete	15b (2a)	13a, 1
859	Knife?	Iron	Portion	14 (2c)	22d, 1
912	Spear point	Iron	Complete	15a (2b)	13a, 3
1168	Arrowhead	Iron	Nearly complete	15a (2b)	13a, 4
1045	Pointed implements	Iron	7 fragments	15a (2b)	13a, 5 22d, 3-7
1032	Bent rod	Iron	3 fragments	15a (2b)	22d, 10
948	Nail	Iron	Mostly complete	15a (2b)	13b, 3
954	Unidentified object	Iron	Fragment	15a (2b)	

Bronze and copper

983	Miniature qadus	Bronze	Mostly complete	15b (2a)	14c, 1
984	Miniature vessel	Bronze	Complete	15b (2a)	14c, 2
1030	Small vessel?	Bronze	Fragment	15a (2b)	
860	Miniature turiya?	Bronze	Mostly complete	15a (2b)	
963	Casket fittings	Bronze + copper	Several pieces	15a (2b)	
888	Archer's loose?	Bronze + wood	Nearly complete	15a (2b)	
1049	Rod	Bronze	Fragment	15b (2a)	
866	Rod	Bronze	2 fragments	14 (2c)	
819	Bracelet	Copper	Portion	14 (2c)	
1044	Earring	Bronze	Complete	15a (2b)	
949	Unidentified object	Bronze	Fragment	15a (2b)	
953	Waster	Copper	Complete	15a (2b)	

Ivory

1050	Bead or button	Ivory	Complete	15b (2a)	

Ostrich eggshell

909	Beads	Ostrich eggshell	5 beads	15a (2b)	

[*] The asterisk identifies finds from later phases that are obviously of Ballaña origin.

Female figurines. Plate 20c and Figure 30 show one nearly complete and several fragmentary examples of small pottery figurines, of a type found both in Ballaña sites in Nubia and in Egyptian sites of the same age.[59] When complete, the figures have several distinctive characteristics. They wear an elaborate, tiara-like headdress or coiffure which comes to a peak over the top of the head; they have a rosette medallion or decoration in the middle of the forehead; the arms are always in upraised position; and they wear some kind of necklace, from which there is often a pendant medallion in the middle of the chest. The sex of the figures is indicated by small, widely separated breast protrusions, but there is no attempt to represent anatomical features on the lower part of the body, which is merely columnar in form.

The specimens found at Meinarti, and illustrated in Plate

[59] For other Nubian finds see Woolley 1911, pl. 13; Woolley and Randall-MacIver 1910, pl. 109; Hewes 1965, 181; and Lister 1967, 50, fig. 19. For Egyptian examples see Petrie 1927, pl. LV; Roeder 1959, pl. 58, m; and Mond and Myers 1940, 98-9 and pl. XXVI. There is a complete specimen of Aswan pink ware, acquired at Damanhur but of unknown archaeological provenience,

20c and Figure 30, are of three types. The most elaborate, represented by numbers 1 (999) and 4 (902) in the photo and by a and d in the drawing, are hollow, mold-made in two pieces, and exhibit the same hard, pink fabric found in the Aswan pottery wares. On these specimens the details of relief modeling, of the hair, the eyes, and the decorative elements, are very clear and sometimes elaborate. The figures have a cream or pale yellow slip, with painted designs in red and dark brown. There seems to be a good

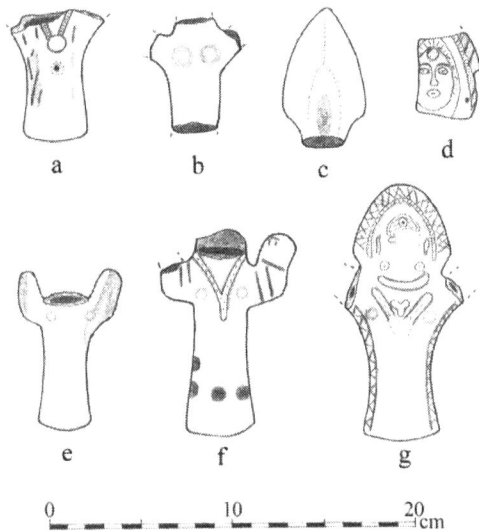

Figure 30. Ceramic female figurine and fragments. a, Torso portion (902) from Level 14. Mold-made in two pieces from pink Aswan ware; decoration in dark brown and red on a cream slip. b, Torso fragment (1466) of uncertain provenience. Molded in one piece from Nile silt; cream slipped with very faint traces of brown decoration at the neck. c, Head portion (845) from Level 14. Apparently molded in one piece from Nile silt; has cream to light yellow-orange slip but no surviving trace of painted decoration. d, Face fragment (999) from Level 15b. Mold-made in two pieces from pink Aswan ware; painted in red and dark brown on a lemon yellow slip. e, Torso and arms (775) from Level 14. Mold-made in two pieces from Nile silt, with painted decoration in red rather carelessly applied on arms only; cream to pale yellow slip. e, Torso and one arm (785) from Level 14. Mold-made in two pieces from Nile silt, with dark brown painted decoration on dark cream slip. g. Mostly complete figurine (951) from Level 15b. Mold-made in two pieces from Nile silt, with dark brown decoration on a cream slip.

deal of variation in the way that painted decoration is applied, but the headdress or hair is always delineated by fine brown lines. In our specimen no. 1, the headdress is painted a solid red, with fine brown lines overpainted, while the eyebrows and eyes are finely outlined in brown. Specimen no. 4, which lacks the head and arms, has rather casually applied, vertical slashes of red and brown, perhaps meant to suggest the folds of a robe, down the sides of the torso. Number 1 has a small perforation at the side of the head, presumably for insertion of an earring—a feature often found on figurines of this type (cf. Lister 1967, 50, fig. 19, a).

A second type of figurine, represented by numbers 5 (775), 6 (951), and 7 (785) in the photo, and by e, f, and g in the drawing, is also mold-made in two pieces, but of Nile silt rather than of fine pink clay. These specimens

may have been Nubian-made, although it is not a certainty. The basic iconography is the same as that in the pink-ware specimens, but the details of modeling are generally less elaborate. All three of our illustrated specimens are painted in one color only. Number 6, the most complete specimen, has fine brown criss-cross lines around the headdress, and an additional, narrow band with criss-cross decoration running down each side of the body, below the arms. Number 7 has fine brown lines on the shoulders and arms, and a series of large brown spots around the lower part of the gown. Painted decoration on no. 5 is confined to large red areas on the undersides of the arms.

The simplest type of figurine, also made from Nile silt, was solidly made in a single piece—probably but not certainly in a mold. It is represented in Plate 20c by numbers 2 (845) and 3 (666) and in Figure 30 by b and c; there is also a fragment (1466) that is not illustrated. Two of these specimens exhibit no trace of embossed decoration, although faint traces of embossed dots can be seen on no. 2. Number 3 retains its painted decoration, in brown, most nearly intact, and exhibits the typical outlining of the eyes and eyebrows, and fine lines on the hair or headpiece, that is characteristic of all the figurines.

The interpretation of these figures raises interesting problems. Everything about them suggests formal iconography, yet they cannot be clearly related to any known sacred figure. They have been found both in Christian Egypt and in pagan Nubia, but they almost certainly do not represent either the Virgin Mary or Isis. The sexual features are very understated, rather than being exaggerated as they commonly are in Hellenistic secular art.[60] They might conceivably be angels, but the upraised arms are not in any way similar to the representations of wings in early Coptic art. According to Dr. Helen Whitehouse they are "...the final and highly stylized development of a type familiar in Roman Egypt, found in graves and domestic contexts and seeming non-specific but intended to fulfill a prayer for the fertility/well-being of the owner...."[61] It is noteworthy however that the Nubian specimens, at least, have always been found in domestic refuse, never in graves.

A further problem of interpretation is raised by the apparent association between the female figurines and horse figurines, to be discussed in the next paragraphs.

Horse figurines. Plate 20d and Figure 31 show one compete and eight fragmentary specimens of horse figurines. These, like the female figurines, were widely distributed in sites of the Ballaña period both in Nubia and in Egypt.[62]

[60] In the treatment of the hair and face, the figurines bear some resemblance to female figurines found by Kaufmann at the Menasstadt, but the latter have the hands clasped at the breast rather than upraised. See Kaufmann 1918, pl. 181.

[61] Personal communication. For a bibliography see Friedman 1989, 225, no. 138.

[62] For other Nubian horse figurines see Lister 1967, 19, fig. 50. For Egyptian examples see Roeder1959, pl. 59, h-l; Mond and Myers 1934, 99 and pl. XXVI; and Petrie 1910, 132. There is a complete specimen of Aswan pink ware, acquired at Armant but of unknown archaeological provenience, in the Ashmolean museum. Petrie dated the Egyptian specimens to the 3rd century A.D. which may be incorrect in view of the consistent occurrence of these figures in Ballaña rather than in Meroitic sites.

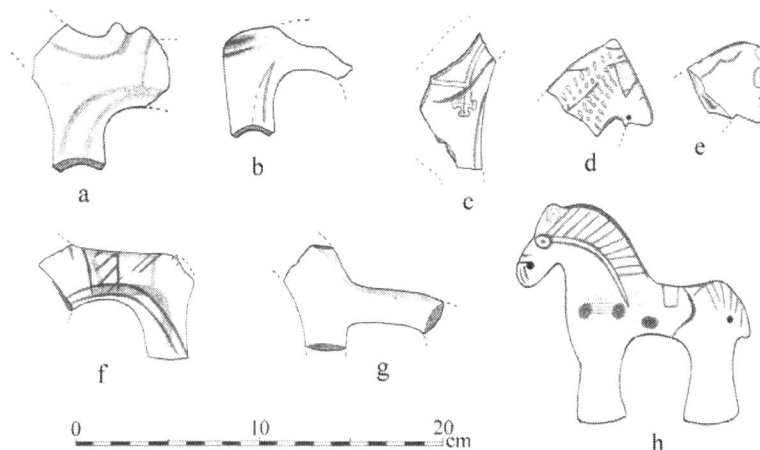

Figure 31. Ceramic horse figurine and fragments. a, Front legs and front of body (817), from Level 14. Mold-made in two pieces from pink Aswan ware, with decoration in pale red on a cream slip. b, Fragment representing hind legs and rump (1413), of uncertain provenience. Mold-made in two pieces from pink Aswan ware; decoration in black and red on a cream slip. c, Fragment representing the throat and part of the forelegs (1110), from Level 16. Mold-made in two pieces from pink Aswan ware; decoration in dark brown on a cream to light orange slip. d, Head fragment (1414) of uncertain provenience. Mold-made in two pieces from pink Aswan ware; decoration in dark brown and red on a yellow-tan slip. e, Head fragment (1082) from Level 15a. Mold-made in two pieces from pink Aswan ware; decoration in black on a cream slip. f, Body, hind quarters, and hind legs (1081), from Level 15a. Mold-made in two pieces from pink Aswan ware; decoration in black and very dark red on dark tan slip (overfired). g, Body portion (816), from Level 14. Molded in one piece from Nile silt; decoration in dark red on buff slip. h, Complete figurine, restored from two fragments (795), from Level 15a. Mold-made in two pieces from Nile silt; decoration in dark brown in a pale

Like the females also they occur in three variants: hollow, mold-made specimens of hard pink ware (nos. 1-5 and 7 in Plate 20d; a-f in Figure 31); hollow, mold-made specimens of Nile silt (no. 8 in Plate 20d and h in Figure 31); and solid specimens (nos. 6 and 9 in Plate 20d; g in Figure 31). These objects have the same distribution in time and space, and are found in the same sites, as are the female figures. Given the similarities of fabric and of manufacturing technology, it seems very probable that the two types were made at the same factories.

All the horse figurines have a cream slip, and at least some measure of painted decoration. As in the case of the females, decoration is most elaborated in the pink-ware specimens, which have designs in both black and red. On the other hand the horses of Nile silt have decoration only in one color: brown in the case of nos. 6 and 8, and red in the case of no. 9. The actual designs seem to vary considerably, but always include the delineation of the facial features and the mane. On the complete specimen (no. 8) there are also fine lines at the rump, which are presumably meant to represent the tail, as well as isolated brown spots on the shoulder and belly. Specimens in the pink ware exhibit a great many painted lines, some of which may indicate harnessware. There are no representations of bridles, although we know from the Ballaña tomb finds that their use was common in Ballaña times (see Emery and Kirwan 1938, pls. 58-61).

In addition to the painted lines, embossed decoration is visible on several of the horse figures. Among the illustrated specimens it can be seen most clearly in no. 4, where the mane is indicated by descending rows of dots alongside the neck, and in no. 8 (the complete specimen), which has horizontal rows of dots extending around the breast.

On no. 3, a small embossed Greek cross can be seen at the shoulder. All of the specimens in which the head is preserved have a small hole through the nose, perhaps for

the insertion of a simulated bridle, and the complete specimen has a hole through the tail as well. Another possibility is that the two holes were for the insertion of a suspension cord.

Although the form of the horse figurines appears to be as standardized as that of the female figurines, there is nothing about the horses that is suggestive of ritual iconography. This must raise questions about the ritual significance of the females as well, given that the two types were apparently made at the same time and by the same makers. Petrie believed that they were merely children's toys, the females being essentially dolls for girls while the horses were, for boys, the ancient equivalent of our modern toy cars (Petrie 1927, pl. LV). Dr. Helen Whitehouse (personal communication) agrees in regard to the horses; she observes that "The little horses look just like the wooden toys on wheels of the same period [made in Egypt]." These specimens also represent the stylized continuation of an earlier, more naturalistic Roman type.

Ba figurine. The ceramic head shown in Plate 20e and Figure 32 (846) was found at Level 15a (Subphase 2b), but is almost certainly of Meroitic origin. Accordingly it has been described in the previous chapter.

Bells? Plate 20f shows four fragmentary objects which are presumed to have been bells, although they could also have been covers to be placed over a narrow-mouth jar or amphora.[63] They are wheel-made from a rather coarse brown ware, essentially that of utility Ware U1, and are without either painted or relief decoration. Each has a small aperture in the top, directly underneath the handle, where a clapper could presumably have been suspended. I have

[63] I am not able to account for the unsatisfactory provenience recording for these objects. At the time when my pottery type collection was registered, after the season, they were found in a box with other sherds of Ware U1, from the X-Group period.

93

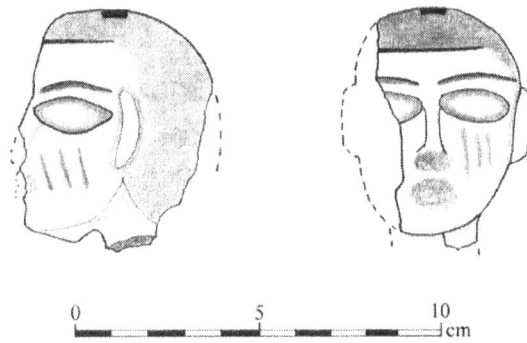

Figure 32. Head of ceramic *ba* figure (846) from Level 15a.

not found any illustrations of similar objects from other Ballaña sites, but the specimens bear a generalized resemblance to bronze bells made in Roman Egypt.[64]

Lamp. Figure 14, no. 2 shows a rather crudely formed, boat-shaped vessel of low-fired pottery (1079), that has been used as a lamp or incense burner. There were evidently upward projections at the "bow" and "stern" ends, that have been broken off.

Beads. The registered finds from Phase 2 include two groups of beads that are mainly of blue-green faience. A group of more than 50 beads (registered collectively as 1108) was found cached in a pot below the floor of House XXXV, at Level 15b (Subphase 2a). The collection includes about 50 beads of pale blue-green faience, Types IB1a and IB4fb, with an average diameter of 4mm. There is also one bead of orange stone (carnelian?), Type IB4fb, with a diameter of 4mm, and one bead of green glass, Type IB1b, with a diameter of 3mm. Very probably all the beads were originally on a single string, although no trace of it survived. Found with them was a ground sherd disc of plain Nubian ware (U5?), which however was not perforated and could not have been strung.

A second collection (857) includes 14 tubular beads of blue-green faience, Type IC2b. They have an average length of 8mm and a diameter of 5mm. They were found in a cluster in the refuse fill at Level 15a (Subphase 2b).

Objects of glass

Goblet. The only registered object of glass from Phase 2 is the base portion of a goblet of fine, thin-walled pale green glass (911), shown in Figure 33. It evidently had a widely out-flared pedestal base, most of which is broken away.

Sherd collection. In his preliminary report, Ray Winfield Smith reported only that "In this material there appears to be glass of several late Meroitic types, notably (b) and possibly (c)."[65] The two types to which he refers were described in the last chapter.

Objects of stone

Capital. The object shown at left in Plate 21a is a small, unsculptured capital of fine white sandstone. It had been reused as a door pivot stone in House XXXV at Level 15a, and in fact had been repositioned three times, as evi-

denced by two round depressions in its top surface, and one in the bottom. As in the case of other sandstone finds, such as the Meroitic offering tables, it cannot be assumed *a priori* that this specimen was salvaged from an earlier context at Meinarti itself. Since all sandstone had in any case to be imported to the island, it is possible that the capital was brought in from the nearly site of Kor on the West Bank.

Perforated object. The curiously shaped object (950) shown at left in Plate 21b is made of fine, reddish-grey sandstone. The upper portion, comprising about one-third of the total length, is smoothly finished to a round cross-section, and is adorned at the top with a carved rosette design. There is a large round hole through this portion of the object, but it shows no signs of wear that might have resulted from a rope passing through it. The lower two-thirds of the specimen is much more roughly finished and has a rectangular rather than a round cross-section. The rough finish suggests the possibility that this portion was meant to be embedded in a wall, or in the ground, with only the more finished portion protruding.

The lower end is rounded, as can be seen in the photo, and there is a half-round niche at one side. This would appear at first glance to be the remaining half of what was once a complete perforation, yet the surfaces adjoining the hole, above and below, show signs of having been worked to their present profile. The most likely explanation, I think, is that this object has been refashioned from a broken anchor stone, of the type described and illustrated in the last chapter (Plate 12e). The niche near the bottom would be the surviving portion of the original perforation in the anchor stone. While it can be no more than

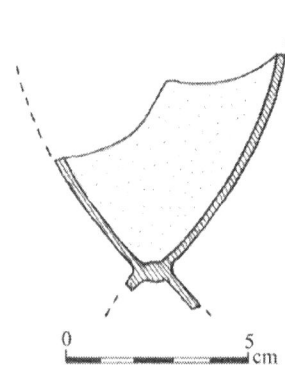

Figure 33. Glass goblet base (911) from Level 14.

speculation, I think one possible interpretation for the object is that it was meant to be set into a wall, and to serve as a kind of sconce for an upright staff that passed through the hole in the projecting end. A number of rather similar objects, though without the perforation, were found at the Classic Christian Level 9 (Subphase 4a).

Jar stamps. The Phase 2 levels yielded two small jar stamps of fine white sandstone. Both were found at Level 15a (Subphase 2b). One (1029), shown in Plate 11a, no. 4, is rectangular in form, and has stamp designs on two opposite sides. Impressions from the two sides are shown in Plate 21c. The second stamp (1028) is a small, rather roughly shaped cone, perforated near the top, shown in

---

[64] See Petrie 1927, pl. L, top. For similar bronze bells from Nubia see especially Bates and Dunham 1927, pl. XXXIV, 4.

[65] Unpublished MS in the author's possession.

Plate 11a, no. 3. An impression of the design is shown in Plate 21d.

Archer's looses. The stone objects shown in Plates 21e and 21f (top row) belong to the class of polished stone rings, common in both Meroitic and Ballaña sites, that have been called archer's looses, although this interpretation is somewhat problematic.[66] Of the three illustrated specimens, only no. 2 (864) actually came from a Ballaña context (Level 15a). Number 3 (738) came from an Early Christian house (Level 13), while the provenience of no. 1 (761) is unrecorded. All three are included for discussion here because of the probability that they came originally from Ballaña contexts, and most probably from Phase 2. The possibility exists however that no. 3 is an Early Christian specimen, and also that it is not an archer's loose, since it is not typologically similar to the others.

All three of the illustrated specimens are highly polished. Those at left (761) and at center (864) have the tapered profile that is usual in these objects. Number 1 is made of a dark pink granite, apparently felsite, and no. 2 is of light pink quartzite. In the latter specimen, the interior of the perforation still shows fine concentric scoring marks, left by the boring apparatus. The specimen at right (738) is not as tall as the others, and has a rectangular rather than a triangular cross-section. Like many archer's looses it is made of black and white mottled stone, identified as pegmatite soda-granite.

Lugged mortars. Heavy granite mortars, having four projecting lugs at the rim, are among the distinctive artifacts of the Ballaña period, though they may have been made in Christian times as well. Of the specimens shown in Plate 22a, only nos. 2 (988) and 3 (871) were found in Ballaña contexts (Subphase 2b), while the other three were all found in Late Christian houses (Subphases 4c, 5a, and 5b). There is a considerable probability however that these latter specimens were salvaged from the Ballaña levels, since mortars of this type have not been found in other Christian sites. The largest illustrated specimen (469) is made from porphyritic granodiorite, while all of the others are of hornblende diorite. The interiors of all the vessels are smoothly polished, while the exteriors, although well shaped, have a rough texture. These items were probably though not certainly made in Egypt, where similar mortars have also been found.[67]

Pestles and grinding stones. Four of the eight stone items shown in Plate 12b are from the Phase 2 levels. Number 4 (762) is a truncated cone of a fine, brecchiated rock, very smoothly polished on all its surfaces. Both the top and the bottom are very slightly convex. There is actually nothing to indicate the use of this specimen as a pestle except a small amount of battering around the lower edges. It could conceivably be a weight, since it bears some resemblance

to stone weights from Egypt illustrated by Petrie.[68] Number 5 (989), a more conventional pestle of hornblende diorite, has a very smooth lower surface, while the other surfaces are slightly rough.[69] Number 6 (870), of reddish granite, is probably a stone designed for back-and-forth grinding rather than for pounding. The flat upper and lower surfaces are very smooth, while the sides are uniformly roughened to provide a better grip. Number 8 (869) is a water-worn pebble of ferruginous sandstone whose shape appears to be largely natural. However, both ends have been ground off to a round contour, for use as a pestle.

Palettes. Rectangular palettes of fine grey stone, with beveled edges, are among the artifact types distinctive of the Ballaña period. Three examples were found at the early Ballaña Subphase 1c, and were described in the last chapter. Six others were found in the Phase 2 levels, and are shown in Plate 22b, nos. 2, 3, and 5-8. (They are also shown in Plate 12c, nos. 4, 9, 10, 11, 13, and 16.) All but two of the palettes are fragmentary, as the thinness of the material evidently rendered them very liable to breakage. The specimens are all closely similar in design, though varying substantially in size. The largest (903) had a length of over 16cm when complete, while the smallest (1109) probably had a length of no more than 8cm. All but two of the palettes show evidence of considerable battering around the edges, as though the sharp edges had been used for chopping some fine material. Two specimens (nos. 1 and 8) have perforations through the middle, but these were not necessarily original features.

Whetstone? The object (1057) shown in Plate 12c, no. 2 is a piece of very thin grey schist or slate, whose oval shape seems to be the result of natural water-wear. However, part of one end is darkened in color and has an exceptionally high polish, suggesting that the stone was used for some special grinding or sharpening purpose.

Carved bead. The object (908) shown in Plate 22c and in Figure 34 is a thin, finely carved bead of some translucent dark green stone, which may be jade. The measurements are 12 x 10 x 5mm. The carving of lines on the flat sides vaguely suggests the head of Horus.

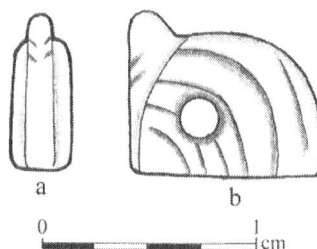

Figure 34. Carved stone bead (908) from Level 14.

Objects of iron

As usual at Meinarti, all items of iron were very corroded, and most were fragmentary.

Blades and weapons. Among the objects shown in Plate

[66] For other Meroitic examples see, among other sources, Bates and Dunham 1927, pl. LVIII, 15-16; Garstang, Sayce and Griffith 1911, pl. XXXVI, 2; and Säve-Söderbergh 1981, pl. 95, a. For Ballaña examples see Emery and Kirwan 1938, pl. 53.

[67] For other mortars from Nubia see Griffith 1927, pl. LVII, nos. 20-23; Emery and Kirwan 1938, pl. 104, D-E; Mills 1982, pl. XXIII; and Kirwan 1939, pl. XV. For Egyptian examples see Jacquet-Gordon 1972, pl. CCXXIX, nos. 9-10.

[68] Petrie 1926, pls. III-VIII. The closest resemblance is to no. 924 in pl. VIII.

[69] For similar pestles from Faras see Griffith 1927, pl. LVII, nos. 19, 21.

13a, the curved blade at left (1162) might be a dagger (also shown in Figure 17, b). However, it is just as probably a sickle, since a very similar blade from Qasr Ibrim exhibits clearly marked serrations along its concave edge (Mills 1982, pl. LXXXVI, no. 5). Our specimen retains, at the top of the blade, a ferrule that would have surrounded the end of a wooden haft, as well as a single rivet for affixing the haft. Number 2 in the plate is the straight blade (1142) from Level 16 (Subphase 1c), described in the previous chapter. Number 3 (912) is a spear point, and no. 4 an arrow point (1168), both of common Ballaña types.[70] The two are shown also in Plate 22e, nos. 2 and 8. Another blade (859) is the long narrow specimen, curved at one end, that is shown in Plate 22e, no. 1. The sharp edge was the convex side.

Rods and pointed instruments. Plate 22d and Figure 35 show several members of a group of iron objects (1045) that were found together on the floor of House XXXV, at Level 15a (Subphase 2b). In the photo, Number 3 is the slightly spatulate end of a round rod; no. 4 is a section of

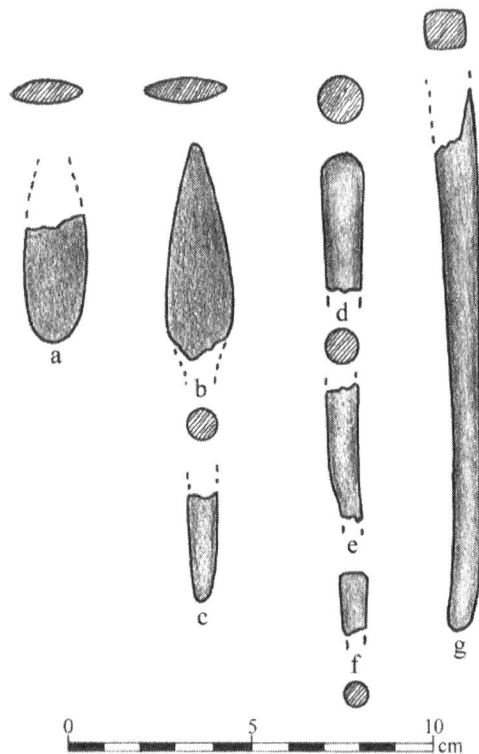

Figure 35. A group of fragmentary iron implements and/or weapons (1045) found together at Level 15a. b and c are probably parts of the same object, as are d and e.

rod that is square in cross-section; no. 5 is a very small spear point (also shown in Plate 13a, no. 5); no. 6 is the rounded end of a stout rod; and no. 7 is a section of thin, tapered rod, round in cross-section. Also shown in the plate (no. 10) is a separate find (1032), comprising three sections of a stout iron rod that was bent at a right angle

at both ends. Since both ends are broken off, it is impossible to say how much further the rod might have extended beyond the points where it is bent.

Nail. Plate 13b, no. 3 shows a stout nail having a square, tapered shaft. The head is very much splayed, as though it had been hot-hammered.

Objects of copper and bronze[71]

Miniature vessels. Of the three tiny bronze vessels shown in Plate 14c, the miniature *qadus* at right (1134) is from Level 16 (Subphase 1c), and was described in the previous chapter. The nearly identical *qadus* at left (983) is from Level 15b (Subphase 2a), as is the pot (984) in the center. Both *qawadis* clearly exhibit the body ribbing that was characteristic of the pottery vessels from which they are modeled. The pot is not ribbed, but exhibits four pairs of fine scored lines, surrounding the vessel at regular intervals.

Miniature *turiya* ? Figure 36 shows a small item of very thin sheet bronze (860), no more than 54mm long, which looks like a miniature *turiya* blade. The round depression near the top end may indicate where a handle was attached. The piece has a very slight but consistent curvature in profile.

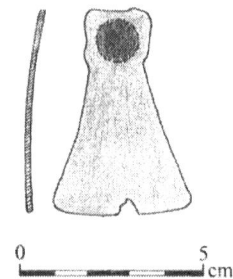

Figure 36. Miniature bronze implement, possibly a *turiya* (860), from Level 15a.

Casket fittings. The various items of bronze and copper (963) shown in Plate 22e and in Figure 37 were found together on the floor of House XXXV, at Level 15a (Subphase 2b). Almost certainly, they are the fittings from a casket, or jewel box, similar to some of those found in the Ballaña royal tombs (Emery and Kirwan 1938, 278-82; see especially n. B.47-3) and at Gemai (Bates and Dunham 1927, 77-8 and pls. XXXIII, XXXIIIA, and XXXIIIB). The original arrangement on the casket is suggested in Figure 38.

Among the illustrated pieces, no. 1 is an anchor plate for the handle and hasps; it would have been attached to one side of the casket lid. It is a curving piece of sheet bronze, decorated along each edge with a row of raised dots in repoussé. The lower end (in the photo) is complete, and has near the end a single perforation where a bronze nail is preserved. The upper end is broken off, and was not found. Number 2 is a curved handle of heavy copper wire, bent into loops at the ends and attached to the anchor plate by means of bronze split pins (or cotter

---

[70] For other spears see Mills 1982, pl. LXXXVI, no. 7; Griffith 1927, pl. LVII, nos. 10-13; Emery and Kirwan 1938, pl. 50, no. 42; and Säve-Söderbergh 1981, pl. 91, no. 3. For other arrowheads see Säve-Söderbergh 1981, pl. 91, no. 1; Griffith 1927, pl. LVII, nos. 6-9; and Williams 1991, pls. 64-5.

[71] The term "bronze" will here be used to designate any alloy of copper, other than brass.

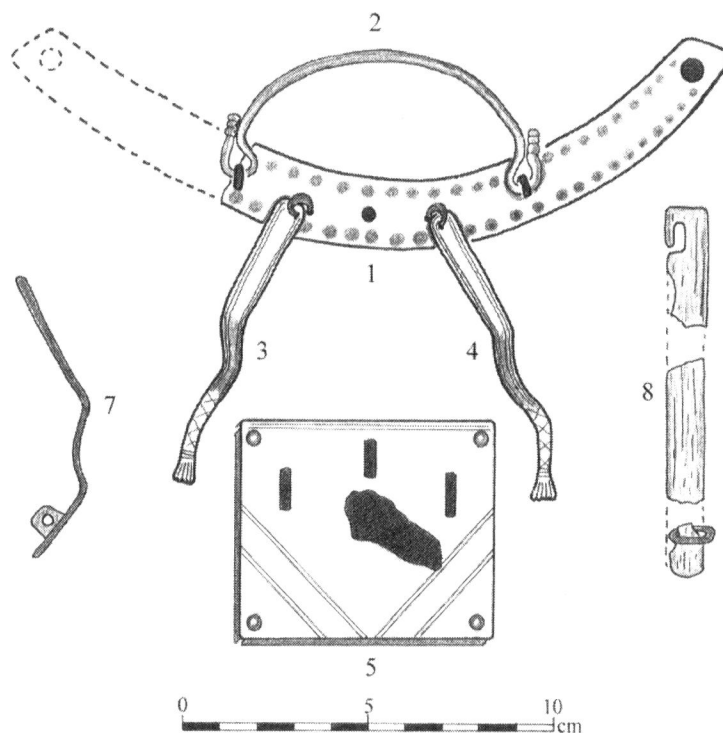

Figure 37. Bronze and copper casket fittings (963), found together at Level 15a. 1, Bronze anchor plate; 2, copper handle with decorative finials, attached to the anchor plate with split pins; 3 and 4, copper hasps attached to the anchor plate with split pins; 5, bronze lock housing; 7, detached copper hasp, show in profile; 8, fragments of iron key. Numbers correspond to those appearing in Plate 22e.

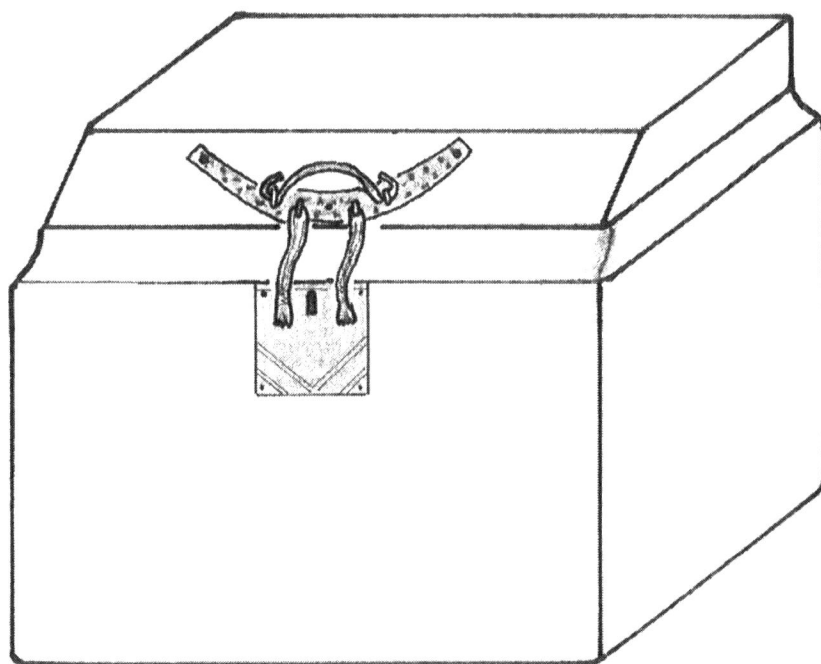

Figure 38. Hypothetical reconstruction of wooden casket, to show how bronze and copper fittings (963) were attached.

pins, in American parlance). The ends of the handle wire have finial decoration as shown in the drawing.[72] Numbers 3 and 4 are two copper strips, also attached to the anchor plate by means of split pins. They served as hasps to fasten the lid to the body of the casket. Carried down-

ward from the lid, their flanged lower ends would have been inserted into the lock housing (no. 5) attached to the body of the casket, and locked into place. Each hasp is bent into a complex curvature, which evidently reproduces the contours of the casket itself. Each of the strips has a decorative finial with four digits, presumably meant to represent either a human hand or an animal's paw. Above the finial "hand" is a short section of stamped, criss-cross decoration, and above that the sides of the strip are deco-

[72] For very similar handles from Karanòg and from the Ballaña tombs see Woolley and Randall-MacIver 1910, pl. 21; and Emery and Kirwan 1938, pl. 109.

rated with border-lines of stamped decoration, running the full length of the piece. On the undersides of each strip, just above the lower end, is a small projecting, perforated flange, which was meant to be inserted into a hole in the lock housing.

Number 5 is evidently the lock housing, which would have been attached to the body of the casket. It is a rectangle of sheet bronze, bent down at a right angle on the top and bottom sides. In each of the corners there is a perforation where a round-headed iron nail is preserved. The housing would probably have been inset into the wood of the casket so that its surface was flush with that of the surrounding wood, as is suggested by caskets found at Karanòg and Ballaña (Woolley and Randall-MacIver 1910, pl. 21; Emery and Kirwan 1938, pl. 108). Of the three rectangular holes near the top of the piece, the central hole is undoubtedly a keyhole, while those at either side of it would receive the perforated flanges on the hasps. When the key was turned, tongues would extend and would engage the holes in the hasps. However, no trace of an actual lock mechanism was preserved. The face of the housing is decorated with fine scored lines, as shown in the drawing. The jagged hole represents the place where a very rusty iron key rested when the object was found.

Number 6 (not shown in the line drawing) is a second curving strip of sheet bronze, generally similar to no. 1 but lacking its repoussé decoration, and lacking also perforations where the two copper hasps might have been attached. The piece appears to be complete, apart from a chip out of one edge, but the curvature is not quite uniform. The distance between the two uppermost holes is identical to the distance between the attachment holes for the handle in piece no. 1. It is possible that this piece was another anchor plate, possibly from a second casket, but it might also have been a backing plate placed on the inner side of the casket, opposite the anchor plate on the outer side.

Number 7 (shown only in profile in Figure 37) is another copper hasp with complex bending, identical to numbers 3 and 4 except that it lacks the criss-cross stamped decoration above the finial "hand." The lower end appears to have attached to it a hooked flange rather than a perforated one, but this may be due to earlier breakage.

Number 8, shown only in the line drawing (Figure 37) comprises three very rusty segments of round iron rod which were found resting on top of the lock housing, where the jagged hole appears in the photo. One of the pieces has a rounded end with a bronze ring inserted through it; another piece has a squared end, with a notch as shown in the drawing. The three are undoubtedly pieces of an iron key.

The two small items in Plate 22e that are not numbered are two bronze split pins, one of which retains an iron washer just below the head.

Most of the caskets found at Ballaña and Gemai were of beaten silver or bronze, although two of the Ballaña finds were of wood.[73] The caskets were of various sizes

and shapes: round, oval, octagonal, and rectangular. Most, but not all, were taller than they were wide, the heights ranging from 10 to 20cm, and the widths (or diameters) from 12 to 31cm. The largest specimens, as might be expected, were those of wood.

The various bent nails and split pins that were preserved along with the Meinarti fittings leave no doubt that these items were affixed to a wooden casket, with side walls approximately 1cm thick. The original size and shape of the casket cannot of course be determined, but both the size of the anchor plate and the length of the hasps (9cm) suggest that it must have been fairly large. (In the case of the Ballaña caskets, the length of the hasps was less than half the full height of the box.) The peculiar bending of the hasps suggests also that the Meinarti casket had a stepped or carinated shoulder, and that the lid was somewhat smaller than the body of the vessel, as suggested in the reconstructed drawing (Figure 38).

At first glance, the curved form of our anchor plate might suggest that this was attached to the top of a round lid. However, there are two arguments against such an interpretation. First, the hasps, fastened as they were to holes in the middle of the anchor plate, could not have functioned properly if the anchor plate was affixed to the top rather than to the side of the vessel. Second, the arc of the anchor plate is such that any lid to which it was attached must have been at least 40cm in diameter—far larger than that of any of the known caskets from other sites.

The finding of the iron key, alongside the bronze and copper fittings, would seem to indicate clearly that the casket was intact when buried. That is, the fittings were not simply part of a bronze founder's salvage. The position of the key, resting directly on the lock housing, would further suggest that the box was buried on its side, with the lock upward.

There is very little likelihood that such a treasure would have been carelessly abandoned. Much more probably it was deliberately buried, for safekeeping, under the floor of House XXXV. If this is so, then the casket should obviously be associated, for dating purposes, not with the underlying Level 15a floor but with the overlying Level 14 (Subphase 2c) floor. It might have been buried with the lock upward so that the owners could access the contents without having to take the box completely out of its hole. However, nothing that might have been contained in the casket was found in the vicinity of the fittings.

Ring of unknown use. The object shown in Figure 39 (888) is a ring of hard, dark wood, clad all over the outside (but not on the inside) in sheet bronze. The outside and inside dimensions (respectively 43 and 22mm) are similar to those

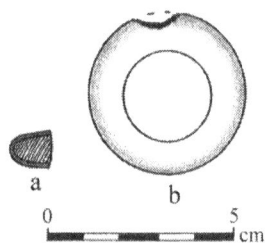

Figure 39. Large wooden ring, clad in bronze (888), from Level 15a. a, Cross-section; b, top view.

of archer's looses, but the contours of the piece otherwise bear no similarity to those of looses.

Bracelet. Plate 22f and Figure 40 show the remnant of a small bracelet (819) of soft copper wire. One end has been worked into a finial vaguely reminiscent of snake head; the other end is broken off.[74] Since the maximum diameter is only 48mm, the bracelet could only have been worn by a child.

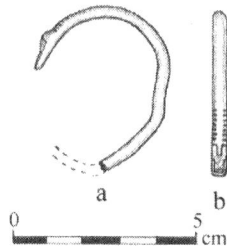

Figure 40. Copper bracelet (819) from Level 14. a, Side view; b, end view.

Miscellaneous objects

Ivory gaming piece? Figure 41 shows a small hemisphere of ivory (1050), perforated through the center and encircled by fine incised grooves as shown. It bears a considerable resemblance to ivory gaming pieces found in the Ballaña royal tombs (Emery and Kirwan 1938, pl. 87, C).

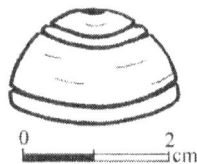

Figure 41. Ivory gaming piece (1050) from Level 15b.

Ostrich eggshell beads. A group of six small beads (909) was found in the fill of House XXXV at Level 15a (Subphase 2b). There are five beads of ostrich eggshell, Type IA2b, with a diameter of 8mm, and one bead of alabaster, Type ID4fb, with a diameter of 7mm.

Comparisons and discussion

The architectural remains
The new buildings of Phase 2 clearly signify a major architectural departure at Meinarti, but they do not of course represent a new tradition in Nubian building more generally. A few thin-walled and irregular structures were already present at Subphases 1b and 1c, as noted in the last chapter. Moreover, there were other Meroitic sites in Lower Nubia that were made up largely or entirely of irregular room clusters, involving mostly thin brick walls. Particularly noteworthy in this regard is the site of Gaminarti, which had two clusters respectively of 11 and of 21 rooms. Within them it was possible to recognize suites of various sizes, but the largest number of suites were comprised only of one large and one small room (Adams and Nordström 1963, 24-8 and pl. III, a). Other

Meroitic sites having large numbers of thin-walled and irregular buildings were those at Tila Island and Kedurma (Edwards 1996, 106-17).

At Meinarti itself, however, Phase 2 represents a complete and, for all practical purposes, a closed chapter of architectural history. The village was almost wholly rebuilt both at the beginning and at the end of this phase, and there was little resemblance between the houses of Phase 2 and those of either the preceding or the following phases.

There are, unfortunately, not many sites of comparable age to which the Phase 2 remains can be compared. The Meroitic villages of Wadi el-Arab, Karanòg, and Arminna all continued to be occupied in post-Meroitic times, but the published plans are mostly those of the Meroitic houses, and there seems to have been no general overbuilding in Ballaña times as there was at Meinarti.[75] There is no resemblance at all between the flimsy and crowded domiciles at Meinarti and the stoutly built, two-storey houses of Ballaña age that have so far been excavated at Qasr Ibrim (Plumley and Adams 1974, 214-27; Plumley 1975, 10-19; Plumley, Adams and Crowfoot 1977, 31-7). These latter exhibit no domestic features, and the ground-floor areas that are preserved were probably commercial shops.

The closest analogs to the Phase 2 remains at Meinarti are represented by a few sites excavated by us in the survey of the West Bank between Faras and Gemai, in the seasons immediately preceding the Meinarti dig. Of the five sites excavated during the 1960-61 season, we noted that "The X-Group settlements which have been encountered were of considerable size, consisting of small rectangular chambers of mud brick with occasional courses of rude stone masonry" (Adams 1962a, 15). Of the sites encountered in the following season we wrote that "Remains of X-Group dwellings were found at three sites.... By comparison to Meroitic houses they are decidedly small and crude, comprising random clusters of from three to eight small rooms. Walls are either of mud brick or coarse stone masonry, or very commonly both..., and rarely exceed 30cm in thickness" (Adams and Nordström 1963, 30; fig. 4, b; and pl. 4, a).

The houses having from three to eight rooms evidently correspond to the individual suites at Meinarti, but at other sites they were detached rather than contiguous.

Comparison can be made also to Site 6-G-6 at Gezira Dabarosa, a village first investigated by us (Verwers 1962, 30-31) and then more thoroughly excavated by the University of Colorado Expedition (Hewes 1964, 180-83). The architectural history of this site paralleled that of Meinarti at Phases 2 and 3, in that it was first built in late Ballaña times, mostly with thin-walled structures, and was then overbuilt with more substantial houses in the Early Christian period. The remains of Ballaña age consisted of

---

[74] For an Egyptian bracelet with a similar finial see Petrie 1927, pl. VI, no. 70.

[75] Emery and Kirwan 1935, pl. 17; Woolley 1911, pl. 27; Trigger 1967, fig. 23. A further problem of comparison arises from the propensity of many early cartographers to "regularize" architectural features by showing every room with straight walls and right-angle corners—conditions which I have very rarely encountered in my own excavations, especially in the case of 20-cm walls. I suspect that the villages of Wadi el-Arab and Karanòg may have looked more like Meinarti on the ground than they do in the plans.

two fairly sizable room clusters, plus remnants of at least three others that were not fully investigated (ibid., 181, fig. 3). The two larger clusters were separated by a street or plaza, and each clearly comprised several residential suites. The more easterly cluster was of special interest, vis-à-vis Meinarti, because it had grown by accretion, beginning with a stout-walled, three-room house identical in plan to Meinarti Houses XXXIV and XLII. Around this there had gradually grown up, on all four sides, a tight cluster of irregular, thin-walled rooms, exactly as happened at Meinarti in Subphase 2a. However, many of the rooms at Gezira Dabarosa were considerably larger than were most of those at Meinarti.

None of the other known Ballaña settlements exhibit quite the same degree of congestion as does Meinarti. Almost certainly, this was due to the lack of available building space, since anything not constructed on the mound would be subject to regular and severe flooding. Yet the fact that so many people were willing to crowd into this one settlement, when there was plenty of open living space available on the nearby east and west banks, suggests that Meinarti in Ballaña times had some special attraction as a place to live. The reasons for this will be considered later.

Summary of the architectural evidence
Meinarti throughout Phase 2 was a congested farming village, not unlike many Nubian villages of later times. There was no surviving evidence of the public functions or state-supported activity so conspicuous at Phase 1. The inhabitants were presumably living under the political hegemony of the Nobatian monarchy, but this supposition can be based only on the contemporaneity of artifactual finds from Meinarti and from the Ballaña royal tombs. There is nothing at Meinarti suggestive of any royal interest in the island or its inhabitants—nothing to indicate that the place had the same strategic and economic role that it had during Phase 1.

Standards of housing, as measured by the size of rooms and of suites, were lower than they were at most other periods—a condition that seems to have been general in the Ballaña period. The average floor space of Phase 2 residential suites at Meinarti was 33 m² as against 54 m² at Phase 4.[76] It seems clear that Lower Nubia had ceased to enjoy the same level of prosperity as it had in Meroitic times, a prosperity that was based largely on trade with Roman Egypt. The trade certainly kept up, as evidenced by the volume of imported luxury goods in the royal tombs, and also by the existence of an apparent commercial center at Qasr Ibrim.[77] However, its benefits seem now to have flowed more exclusively than in earlier times to a very small class of rulers and nobility.

The artifactual remains

Pottery
The pottery found at Levels 15b and 15a (Subphases 2a and 2b) exhibits the typical ceramic complex of later Ballaña times, already well known through the excava-

---

[76] Average floor areas could not be calculated for Phase 3 because of poor preservation.

[77] As suggested by the architecture of the houses, and also by abundant finds of trade goods.

tion of hundreds of X-Group graves. The finds fall within the Middle phase of X-Group ceramic development, in the chronological scheme of Rose (n.d., 129-31), and more specifically within Index Clusters X2 and XC1, in the seriational scheme devised by me initially at Qasr Ibrim (Adams 1986, 629). The percentage figures for wares present and absent are closely similar to those at Qasr Ibrim, except for the considerably lower percentage of imported wares at Meinarti. Presumably, this is a reflection of the greater prosperity enjoyed by the citadel-dwellers at Qasr Ibrim, in contrast to the peasantry at Meinarti.

The pottery from Level 14 (Subphase 2c) is again typical of other Nubian sites of the same age; it corresponds to Rose's Late phase of X-Group ceramic development (Rose n.d., 135-40), and to my Index Clusters XC2 and EC1 (Adams 1986, 629). Although this ceramic complex was still heavily dominated by X-Group wares, it included also certain wares (specifically those of Group N.III) that have never been found in X-Group graves, presumably because their introduction post-dated the time of Nubia's conversion to Christianity. For this reason it is assumed that Subphase 2c belongs, in a strictly historical sense, to the Christian period, although there had as yet been no major change either in architectural standards or in the artifact complex at Meinarti.

The non-pottery finds
The non-pottery finds at Meinarti, like the pottery, are paralleled by finds from many other sites of the Ballaña period. The female figurines, the horse figurines, the lugged mortars, the greywacke palettes, and the archer's looses are among the familiar artifactual signatures of this period. The one real—and major—surprise among the Meinarti finds is the set of casket fittings (963) found in House XXXV, at Subphase 2b. The probability that the casket was deliberately buried, intact, has previously been noted. Elsewhere, such objects have been found only in the Qustul and Ballaña royal tombs (Emery and Kirwan 1938, 276-82 and pl. 69), and in an almost equally rich tomb at Gemai (Bates and Dunham 1927, 77-8 and pls. XXXIII, XXXIIIA, and XXXIIIB). Among all the artifacts recovered from Phase 2 at Meinarti, this alone seems clearly to fit the category of "elite goods." How it came into the hands of an ordinary peasant at Meinarti, living in the crowded and distinctly proletarian House XXXV, can only be a matter of speculation. It might conceivably have been given as a reward for services to one of the nobility at Ballaña or Gemai, but it could also have been plundered from a grave.

Implications and issues

The reoccupation of Phase 2
The evidence for a hiatus between Phases 1 and 2 was discussed at the end of the last chapter. By the time Meinarti was reoccupied, at the beginning of Phase 2, about 75cm of sand had drifted over most of the surviving floors of Subphase 1c. Of the four surviving buildings from Phase 1, Houses XLII, XLIII, and XLIV had all suffered considerable structural damage, suggesting the probability that their wooden roofs had been removed during the interval of abandonment. House XXXIV on

the other hand had suffered no appreciable damage, and had received only a shallow fill of sand. This circumstance is possibly explained by the fact that House XXXIV, alone among the structures of Subphase 1c, had a vaulted brick roof which remained intact, and had also a doorway facing away from the prevailing wind direction.

The evidence for dating the reoccupation to the later Ballaña period, beginning around A.D. 475, is purely ceramic, but it is nevertheless convincing. There is, on the one hand, a scarcity or absence of many early X-Group ceramic features, notably including the "flower-pot" bowl form (Form C46) which at Qasr Ibrim is one of the hallmarks of the early Ballaña levels (see Rose n.d., 152,161). On the positive side, the later Ballaña ware R1 has very largely displaced its earlier predecessor, Ware R25, which survives only in a few "legacy" vessels, and the Byzantine Aswan wares have largely displaced their Graeco-Roman predecessors. Very significantly too, the Aswan amphorae of Ware U2 have ribbed rather than level walls (see Adams 1986, 545).

The date of reoccupation at Meinarti is actually easier to adduce than is the reason. Neither architecture nor artifacts suggest that commercial or strategic considerations were involved, as they were at Phase 1. With the single exception of the casket find (963), discussed earlier, there is nothing to suggest that the inhabitants at Meinarti were anything but peasant farmers. Most probably, therefore, it was the attraction of low-lying arable land on the Meinarti and Majarab islands that brought the settlers back. The reoccupation may perhaps be seen as part of a general, gradual process of population expansion that took place in the later Ballaña period, aided perhaps by the increasingly widespread use of the *saqia* (Rose n.d., 121; Edwards 1996, 80-81).

Living conditions in later Ballaña times
The evidence of Ballaña period tombs points to a very wide economic gap between a small handful of rulers and nobles, and a somewhat impoverished peasantry. Society was certainly not more formally stratified than in Meroitic times—indeed it might have been somewhat less so—but the economic gap between the classes was wider than before. In this respect it might be suggested, in keeping with currently fashionable anthropological theory, that Nubia had reverted from a state-level society to a chiefdom (cf. Service 1963).

The remains at Meinarti and many other sites nevertheless bespeak, if not high prosperity, at least a period of stability in later Ballaña times. The sites do not give evidence of any serious disruptions, caused either by flooding or by enemy action, nor is there any suggestion of defensive arrangements.[78] Housing standards for the peasantry were not very good, by comparison with later times, but people had a sufficient quantity of everyday goods so that they could afford to bury large numbers of them in their graves, as well as under house floors. Imported goods however, for all but the privileged few, were nearly all

utilitarian in character, and were largely confined to pottery.

In sum, it might be suggested that, except along the northern frontier, the extraordinary *pax nubica* of medieval times began, not with the *Baqt* treaty of 652 (cf. Adams 1977, 452-3), but about two hundred years earlier, when the Nobatian rulers first consolidated their hegemony in Lower Nubia. From that time forward there were no serious internal disruptions in the country for the better part of eight centuries. The peace was undoubtedly disturbed briefly by the Arab invasions of 642 and 652, but the historical records do not speak of any serious destruction on either of these occasions, and the outcome of the two incursions was to finalize the peace itself (ibid., 450-51).

The contrast with Qasr Ibrim
Apart from Meinarti, the one other site of Ballaña age that has been subjected to systematic, stratigraphically controlled excavation is Qasr Ibrim. The contrast between it and Meinarti, and indeed between it and all other habitation sites of Ballaña age, could hardly be more extreme.[79] The rather limited Ballaña remains that have so far been excavated at Qasr Ibrim are those of very substantial, stone-built houses, many of which were two storeys high. The conspicuous lack of domestic features like fireplaces, bins, and sub-floor pots in the ground-floor rooms suggests that these areas may have been devoted mainly to commercial activity, though there could have been residences on the floors above (see (Plumley and Adams 1974, 214-27; Plumley 1975, 10-19; Plumley, Adams and Crowfoot 1977, 31-7). Not only the houses but many of the artifactual finds convey the impression that Qasr Ibrim in Ballaña times served as a trade entrepot, much as did Meinarti at an earlier period. It was also however a place of pilgrimage.

Two factors may be adduced to account for the special conditions at Qasr Ibrim, and more specifically for the contrast with Meinarti. First, all of the substantially built houses appear, on the basis of their ceramic content, to have been constructed in early Ballaña times; that is, before the resettlement at Meinarti. Nearly all of them continued in use in later Ballaña times, but they were allowed to become very dilapidated and refuse-encumbered. Moreover, the few new houses that were built in later Ballaña times were much more insubstantial.[80] In short, then, the substantial houses at Qasr Ibrim and the insubstantial houses at Meinarti were not chronologically contemporaneous.

Second, Qasr Ibrim in early Ballaña times stood close to the frontier of the Dodecaschoinos, a region of Lower Nubia which at the time was distinct, culturally and ethnically, from the remainder of Lower Nubia, and was closer in most respects to Upper Egypt. Qasr Ibrim, in other words, was for all practical purposes on the cultural frontier between Nubia and Egypt, and it could serve as an entrepot between the two regions in the same way that

---

[78] At Qasr Ibrim, the fortification walls of Roman and Meroitic times began to fall into disrepair in the Ballaña period; see Plumley, Adams and Crowfoot 1977, 37-9.

[79] With the partial exception of Gebel Adda, which has been so incompletely reported that comparisons are difficult.

[80] These observations are based largely on my unpublished excavation notes.

Aswan has more usually done. But the Dodecaschoinos lost its separate identity in later Ballaña times, when Lower Nubia became culturally and ethnically homogenized under its Nobatian rulers, and this may have triggered the decline of Ibrim's commercial importance and prosperity. This theme has been much more thoroughly explored in the recent dissertation of Pamela Rose (n.d.).

The spread of Christianity

The missionary efforts that resulted in the Christianization of Nobatia (Lower Nubia) began, according to historical annals, around A.D. 543 (Adams 1977, 443). However, the finds from Meinarti leave no doubt that there were Christian votaries among the Nubian population well before that date. There is for example a Nubian-made lamp (1176) with an embossed cross design, found at Level 15b (Subphase 2a). The spread of Christianity among the population can thereafter be measured, after a fashion, by the increasing numbers of votive lamps. At Meinarti they were virtually absent in Phase 1, while their numbers increased steadily during Phase 2, from four at Subphase 2a to 10 at Subphase 2c, and to 15 at Subphase 2c. The official conversion took place, if historical records can be believed, around the middle of Subphase 2b, although no church was built at Meinarti until a century afterward.

The end of Phase 2

At first glance, a comparison of the site plans at Subphase 2c (Fig. 25) and at Subphase 3a (Fig. 26) would suggest an almost complete lack of architectural continuity. By the middle of the seventh century the village had been almost wholly rebuilt, largely with heavy-walled construction. There was in addition a considerable accumulation of sand overlying the Level 14 floors. Taken together, these circumstances would seem indicative of a hiatus between Phases 2 and 3. However, a closer study of the plans will show that a considerable number of the stout walls of Subphase 3a rest directly on the denuded tops of older and thinner walls of Subphase 2c, retaining their somewhat erratic alignments. This suggests that property lines remained unchanged, pointing to continuity rather than interruption in the occupation of the village.

The most likely explanation, I think, is that the farmers at Meinarti had simply decided to rebuild their rather dilapidated houses with stouter construction. In so doing they might have taken advantage of the presence of professional builders, who had come to erect the first Meinarti church at Subphase 3a. Such a rebuilding endeavor need not, obviously, have taken place all at once. More probably it was drawn out over a decade or two. Indeed, we noted in this chapter that the first examples of stout walls could already be seen at Subphase 2c, in Houses XXXIII and LVII.

If this interpretation is correct, then the dividing line between Phases 2 and 3 cannot be fixed precisely in any one year. I have chosen the year A.D. 653 partly because it accords well enough with the ceramic and depositional evidence, but also because it coincides with the second Arab invasion, which resulted in the *Baqt* treaty. The invaders did not necessarily attack Meinarti, which was not in their direct path of advance; still, we know that advancing Arab armies supported themselves by plundering the country as they went. The news of their coming might at least have frightened the inhabitants out of their homes for a short time, and afterward persuaded them to strengthen their walls. At all events, the year 653 may serve as a convenient historical milestone, to mark the transition to a fully practicing Christian community at Meinarti.

It will be the subject of the next volume, *Meinarti II*.

APPENDIX
COMPREHENSIVE REGISTER OF FINDS FROM PHASES 1 AND 2

With Sudan Museum accession numbers

Reg. no.	Item	Sudan number
741	Goblet	15028
742	Goblet	15223
744	Cup	15174
745	Amphora	15374
747	Cup	15220
749	Lamp	15155
751	Lamp	15142
754	Bowl	15230
755	Footed bowl	15423
756	Lid	15407
757	Oil bottle	15365
758	Lamp	15406
759	Lamp	15163
760	Small bottle	15214
761	Archer's loose	17525
762	Pestle	17430
773	Lamp	15158
774	Lamp	15145
775	Female figurine	15594
776	Cup	15216
777	Bowl	15182
778	Bowl	15209
779	Spouted pot	15259
780	Goblet	15226
781	Lid	15391
782	Bowl	15129
783	Goblet	15118
785	Female figurine	15585
786	Lamp	15164
789	Footed bowl	15360
790	Footed bowl	15113
791	Small bottle	15102
792	Bowl	15125
793	Footed bowl	15424
794	Bowl	15253
795	Horse figurine	15586
806	Perforated sherd	17512
807	Lid	15083
808	Goblet	15092
810	Footed bowl	15367
816	Horse figurine	15582
817	Horse figurine	15590
819	Bracelet	17669
820	Cup	15218
831	Palette	17457
833	Bowl	15134
834	Bowl	15112
835	Spouted goblet	15041
836	Goblet	15048
837	Lid	17381
838	Lamp	15139
839	Lamp	15152
840	Goblet	15177
841	Goblet	15175
842	Cup	15065
844	Bowl	15116

Reg. no.	Item	Sudan number
845	Female figurine	15580
846	Miniature Ba head	15583
847	Lamp	15159
848	Goblet	15042
849	Cup	15108
850	Bowl	15447
851	Pot	17375
852	Cup	15037
853	Lamp	15150
854	Incense stand	15417
855	Goblet	15076
857	Beads	17496
859	Knife blade?	17782
860	Model turiya?	17728
861	Cup	15180
862	Lid	(Lost)
863	Aryballos	15173
864	Archer's loose	17489
865	Lamp	15141
866	Bronze rod	17729
869	Pestle	17412
870	Grinding stone	17435
871	Mortar	17387
872	Bowl	15130
873	Goblet	15044
874	Bowl	15225
875	Goblet	15225
876	Small bottle	15043
877	Cup	15077
878	Bowl	15114
879	Goblet	15170
880	Keg	15234
881	Aryballos	15348
882	Lamp	15157
883	Lamp	15136
884	Lamp	15144
885	Cup	15107
886	Ointment jar	15190
887	Stone ring	17502
888	Wood ring	17687
889	Spouted pot	15049
890	Cup	15094
891	Cup	15095
892	Cup	15120
893	Cup	15058
894	Lamp	15165
895	Lamp	15140
896	Aryballos	15524
897	Lamp	15122
898	Lamp	15138
899	Aryballos	15363
900	Cup	15115
901	Cup	15055
902	Female figurine	15593
903	Bowl	15064
906	Palette	17440

Reg. no.	Item	Sudan number
907	Offering table	(Lost)
908	Effigy bead	17487
909	Beads	17503
910	Aryballos	15186
911	Glass goblet	17622
912	Spear point	17786
913	Lamp	15154
914	Lamp	15148
915	Lamp	15147
916	Lamp	15137
917	Cup	15026
918	Aryballos	15392
919	Lekythos	15358
920	Goblet	15169
921	Goblet	15188
922	Goblet	15132
923	Pot	17374
924	Bowl	15106
925	Footed jar	15523
929	Amphora	15370
930	Goblet	15054
931	Goblet	15070
933	Bowl	15171
934	Bowl	15175
935	Aryballos	15089
937	Cup	15091
938	Cup	15074
939	Lamp	15156
940	Footed bowl	15131
941	Small bottle	15063
942	Palette	17420
943	Footed jar	15445
944	Jar	15755
945	Shaped pebble	17449
946	Lamp	15151
947	Lekythos	15103
948	Nail	17789
949	Bronze object	17739
950	Perforated stone	17397
951	Female figurine	15595
952	Spouted goblet	15096
953	Copper waster	17657
954	Iron object	17787
955	Bottle	15540
956	Bowl	15075
957	Goblet	15069
958	Goblet	15099
959	Lamp	15143
960	Lamp	15046
961	Lamp	15153
962	Bowl	15187
963	Casket fittings	15598
964	Qadus	15542
965	Bowl	15098
966	Pot	15061
967	Spouted goblet	15097
968	Jug	15369
969	Goblet	15071
970	Goblet	15068
971	Goblet	15025
972	Cup	15232
973	Cup	15213
974	Cup	15082
975	Cup	15208

* University of Kentucky Museum of Anthropology

Reg. no.	Item	Sudan number
976	Cup	15118
977	Aryballos	15053
978	Cup	15176
979	Ointment jar	15184
980	Lamp	15160
981	Lamp	15162
982	Lid	17377
983	Toy qadus	17663
984	Toy pot	17660
985	Palette	17442
987	Table amphora	15545
988	Mortar	17456
989	Pestle	17443
992	Cup	15221
993	Goblet	15039
994	Cup	15088
996	Cup	15101
997	Cup	15206
998	Goblet	15211
999	Female figurine	15589
1001	Lamp	15135
1002	Goblet	15168
1003	Jug	15362
1004	Lamp?	15110
1005	Cup	15212
1006	Bowl	15401
1007	Bowl	15439
1008	Goblet	15123
1009	Goblet	15073
1010	Cup	15191
1011	Goblet	15085
1012	Small bottle	15121
1013	Lekythos	15350
1014	Lid	17364
1015	Bowl	15037
1016	Goblet	15084
1017	Goblet	15109
1018	Goblet	15117
1019	Goblet	15258
1020	Footed bowl	15126
1021	Cup	15050
1022	Cup	15124
1023	Cup	15254
1028	Jar stamp	17500
1029	Jar stamp	17466
1030	Bronze vessel?	17724
1031	Coin	UKMA*
1032	Iron rod	17785
1033	Cup	15133
1034	Lamp	15111
1035	Goblet	15217
1036	Goblet	15185
1037	Cup	15027
1038	Lid	15405
1040	Footed bowl	15426
1042	Horse figurine	15592
1043	Stone disc	17430
1044	Earring	17794
1045	Iron implements	17790
1047	Cup	15215
1048	Coin	UKMA*
1049	Bronze rod	17735
1050	Ivory counter	17629
1051	Pendant	17515
1052	Cup	15192
1053	Cup	15056

Reg. no.	Item	Sudan number
1054	Cup	15051
1055	Lekythos	15062
1056	Aryballos	15052
1057	Whetstone	17454
1058	Goblet	15219
1059	Bowl	15128
1060	Lamp	15146
1061	Footed bowl	15047
1062	Lid	17372
1063	Lamp	17368
1064	Sherd disc	17476
1065	Goblet	15087
1066	Capital	17395
1067	Pot	15541
1068	Goblet	15034
1069	Qadus	15539
1070	Jar	15770
1071	Bottle	15546
1072	Lekythos	15354
1073	Bowl	15090
1074	Pot	15513
1075	Jar	15033
1076	Footed bowl	15045
1077	Cup	15227
1078	Small bottle	15193
1079	Lamp	17498
1080	Bowl	15060
1081	Horse figurine	15588
1082	Horse figurine	15581
1083	Cup	15072
1084	Cup	15067
1085	Cup	15040
1086	Goblet	15166
1087	Aryballos	15183
1088	Lekythos	15127
1089	Spouted goblet	15104
1090	Goblet	15235
1091	Cup	15035
1092	Pot	17378
1093	Model of testicles?	17493
1094	Cup	15517
1095	Cup	17370
1096	Bowl	15518
1097	2 Bowls	15526
1098	Bowl	15224
1099	Bowl	15093
1100	Jar stamp	17494
1101	Spikes	17775
1102	Ivory object	17597
1104	Lid	17379
1105	Footed bowl	15257
1106	Footed bowl	15520
1108	Beads	17497
1109	Palette	17432
1110	Horse figurine	15587
1111	Balance scale	18083
1112	Iron rod	17773
1113	Palette	17419
1114	Palette	17423
1115	Stone weight?	17411
1116	Grinding pebble	17425
1117	Aryballos	15515
1118	Spouted pot	15105
1119	Whetstone?	17414
1120	Palette	17416
1121	Quern	17390

Reg. no.	Item	Sudan number
1122	Bowl	15522
1123	Footed bowl	15521
1124	Jar	15544
1125	Lekythos	15351
1126	Small pot	17367
1127	Lid	17380
1130	Steelyard scale	18084
1131	Balance scale	18088
1132	Lamp	17766
1133	Tripod censer	17760
1134	Toy qadus	17765
1135	Ring	17798
1136	Binding band	17733
1137	Ring	17802
1138	Ring	17801
1139	Needle	17682
1140	Binding band	17721
1141	Pestle	17452
1142	Dagger blade?	17783
1143	Sickle blade?	17768
1144	Knife blade?	17778
1145	Pendant	17488
1146	Ostrakon	(Lost)
1147	Cup	15210
1148	Goblet	15349
1149	Pot	15228
1150	Cup	15207
1151	Footed bowl	15253
1152	Qadus	15543
1153	Pestle	17427
1154	Whetstone	17413
1155	Handle	17712
1156	Handle	17707
1157	Handle	17711
1158	Tripod beaker	17767
1159	Awl?	17738
1160	Balance scales	18085
1161	Ring	17793
1162	Dagger blade?	17775
1163	Iron rod	17780
1164	Knife	17772
1165	Spike	17769
1166	Iron point?	17774
1167	Bronze object	17777
1168	Arrow point	17781
1169	Punch?	17779
1170	Spike?	17770
1171	Bead	17492
1172	Stone bowl	17422
1173	Grinding block	17415
1174	Sharpening pebble	17417
1175	Jar stamp	17579
1176	Lamp	15149
1177	Goblet	15029
1178	Goblet	15078
1179	Goblet	15119
1180	Bottle	15547
1181	Jar	15509
1182	Goblet	15039
1183	Lekythos	15353
1184	Lamp	15516
1185	Bowl	15435
1186	Bowl	15514
1187	Bottle?	15229
1188	Bowl	15086
1189	Aryballos	15525

Reg. no.	Item	Sudan number
1190	Amphora	15481
1191	Amphora	16019
1192	Spouted goblet	15100
1193	Goblet	15167
1194	Goblet	15036
1195	Goblet	15031
1196	Ointment jar	15189
1197	Cup	15519
1198	Bowl	15513
1201	Iron ring	17807
1202	Sharpening stone?	17447
1203	Jar	15538
1204	Pot	15510
1212	Quseba	17383
1219	Jar	16004
1220	Lion spout	18101
1221	Oil press?	17407
1234	Lamp	17510
1247	Bowl	16079
1248	Plate	16074
1261	Footed bowl	16108
1269	Bowl	16091
1271	Bowl	16111
1374	Footed bowl	16214
1397	Footed bowl	16298
1398	Bottle?	16309
1399	Bowl	16301
1400	Footed bowl	16302
1403	Miniature bowl	16305
1407	Miniature bowl	16294
1408	Plate	16303
1409	Amphora	16308
1410	Miniature bowl	16291
1413	Horse figurine	17527
1414	Horse figurine	17529
1424	Goblet	16322
1425	Goblet	16336
1426	Footed bowl	16318
1427	Goblet	16317
1428	Bottle	16324
1429	Small pot	16321
1430	Cup	16320
1432	Lid	16338
1433	Bowl	16330
1434	Aryballos	16326
1435	Bottle	16335
1436	Lamp?	17470
1437	Cup	16328
1438	Cup	16327
1439	Cup	16326
1440	Bowl	16334
1441	Lamp?	16333
1442	Lamp	16337
1443	Stopper	16325
1444	Basin	16322
1445	Pot	16331
1446	Jar?	16332
1454	Pot	17373
1459	Bell	15511
1460	Bell	17469
1461	Bell	17468
1462	Bell	17528
1466	Female figurine	15579
1482	Basin	17838
1505	Bronze scraps	17730
1507	Miniature vessel	17764

BIBLIOGRAPHY

Adams, N. K. 1996. 'Textile Materials and Weaves,' in W. Y. Adams 1996, 160-70.

Adams, W. Y. 1961a. 'Archaeological Survey of Sudanese Nubia: Introduction,' *Kush* 9, 7-10.

Adams, W. Y. 1961b. 'The Christian Potteries at Faras,' *Kush* 9, 30-43.

Adams, W. Y. 1962a. 'The Archaeological Survey on the West Bank of the Nile: Introduction,' *Kush* 10, 10-18.

Adams, W. Y. 1962b. 'An Introductory Classification of Christian Nubian Pottery,' *Kush* 10. 245-88.

Adams, W. Y. 1962c. 'Pottery Kiln Excavations,' *Kush* 10, 62-75.

Adams, W. Y. 1964a. 'An Introductory Classification of Meroitic Pottery,' *Kush* 12, 126-73.

Adams, W. Y. 1964b. 'Post-Pharaonic Nubia in the Light of Archaeology, I' *Journal of Egyptian Archaeology* 50, 102-120.

Adams, W. Y. 1964c. 'Sudan Antiquities Service Excavations in Nubia: Fourth Season, 1962-63,' *Kush* 12, 216-50.

Adams, W. Y. 1965a. 'Architectural Evolution of the Nubian Church, 500-1400 A.D.' *Journal of the American Research Center in Egypt* 4, 87-139.

Adams, W. Y. 1965b. 'Post-Pharaonic Nubia in the Light of Archaeology, II,' *Journal of Egyptian Archaeology* 51, 160-78.

Adams, W. Y. 1965c. 'Sudan Antiquities Service Excavations at Meinarti, 1963-64,' *Kush* 13, 148-76.

Adams, W. Y. 1966a. 'Post-Pharaonic Nubia in the Light of Archaeology, III,' *Journal of Egyptian Archaeology* 52, 147-62.

Adams, W. Y. 1966b. 'The Vintage of Nubia' *Kush* 14, 262-83.

Adams, W. Y. 1967. 'Continuity and Change in Nubian Cultural History,' *Sudan Notes and Records* 48, 1-32.

Adams, W. Y. 1968. 'Settlement Pattern in Microcosm: the Changing Aspect of a Nubian Village during Twelve Centuries,' in Chang 1968, 174-207.

Adams, W. Y. 1973. "Progress Report on Nubian Pottery, I. The Native Wares,' *Kush* 15, 1-50.

Adams, W. Y. 1977. *Nubia: Corridor to Africa*. Princeton and London.

Adams, W. Y. 1979. 'On the Argument From Ceramics to History: a Challenge Based on Evidence from Medieval Nubia,' *Current Anthropology* 20, 727-44.

Adams, W. Y. 1982a. 'The Coming of Nubian Speakers to the Nile Valley,' in Ehret and Posnansky 1982, 11-38.

Adams, W. Y. 1982b. 'Meroitic Textual Material from Qasr Ibrim,' *Meroitica* 6, 211-17.

Adams, W. Y. 1985. 'Ptolemaic and Roman Occupation at Qasr Ibrim,' in Geus and Thil 1985, 9-17.

Adams, W. Y. 1986. *Ceramic Industries of Medieval Nubia*, 2 vols. Memoirs of the UNESCO Archaeological Survey of Sudanese Nubia, no. 1. Lexington.

Adams, W. Y. 1992. 'The Nubian Archaeological Campaigns of 1959-1969: Myths and Realities, Successes and Failures,' in Bonnet 1992, vol. 1, 3-27.

Adams, W. Y. 1994a. 'Castle-Houses of Late Medieval Nubia,' *Archéologie du Nil Moyen* 6, 11-46.

Adams, W. Y. 1994b. *Kulubnarti I: the Architectural Remains*. Lexington.

Adams, W. Y. 1996. *Qasr Ibrim: the Late Medieval Period*. Egypt Exploration Society, Excavation Memoir 59. London.

Adams, W. Y. 1999 {n.d.1}. 'The Late Meroitic Occupation at Meinarti,' in D. A. Welsby (ed.). *Recent Research in Kushite History and Archaeology. Proceedings of the 8th International Conference for Meroitic Studies*. London, 111-131.

Adams, W. Y. n.d.2. *Ptolemaic and Roman Pottery from Qasr Ibrim*. MS available from the author.

Adams, W. Y. and E. W. Adams 1991. *Archaeological Typology and Practical Reality*. Cambridge.

Adams, W. Y. and N. K. Adams 1959. *An Inventory of Prehistoric Sites on the Lower San Juan River, Utah*. Museum of Northern Arizona Bulletin 31. Flagstaff.

Adams, W. Y. and N. K. Adams 1998. *Kulubnarti II: the Artifactual Remains*. Sudan Archaeological Research Society Publication no. 2. London.

Adams, W. Y, N. K. Adams, D. Van Gerven and D. L. Greene 1999. *Kulubnarti III: the Cemeteries*. Sudan Archaeological Research Society Publication no. 4, London.

Adams, W. Y, A. J. Lindsay and C. G. Turner 1961. *Survey and Excavations in Lower Glen Canyon, 1952-1958*. Museum of Northern Arizona Bulletin 36. Flagstaff.

Adams, W. Y. and H-Å Nordström 1963. 'The Archaeological Survey on the West Bank of the Nile: Third Season, 1961-62,' *Kush* 11, 10-46.

Aebi, E. 1997. 'Beneath the Shifting Sands,' *Archaeology* 50, no. 2, 84.

Almagro, M. 1965. *La Necropolis Meroítica de Nag Gamus*. Comité Español de la UNESCO para Nubia, Memórias de la Misión Arqueológica 8, Madrid.

Ammar, H. 1966. *Growing Up in an Egyptian Village*. New York.

Anderson, R. D. and W. Y. Adams 1979. 'Qasr Ibrim 1978,' *Journal of Egyptian Archaeology* 65, 30-41.

Bates, O. and D. Dunham 1927. 'Excavations at Gammai,' *Harvard African Studies* vol. 8, 1-121.

Bonnet, C. (ed.) 1992. *VIIe Congrès International d'Études Nubiennes,* vol. 1. Geneva.

Chang, K-C. (ed.) 1968. *Settlement Archaeology.* Palo Alto.

Daremberg, C. and E. Saglio 1919. *Dictionnaire des Antiquités Grecques et Romaines* vol. 3. Paris.

Donadoni, S. 1993. 'Excavations of University of Rome at Natakamani Palace (Jebel Barkel)', *Kush* 16, 101-115.

Driskell, B. N., N. K. Adams and P. French 1989. 'A Newly Discovered Temple at Qasr Ibrim. Preliminary Report,' *Archéologie du Nil Moyen* 3, 11-34.

Dunham, D. 1957. *Royal Tombs at Meroë and Barkal.* Royal Cemeteries of Kush, vol. 4., Boston.

Dunham, D. 1963. *The West and South Cemeteries at Meroë.* Royal Cemeteries of Kush, vol. 5, Boston.

Edwards, D. N. 1996. *The Archaeology of the Meroitic State.* Cambridge Monographs in African Archaeology 38; BAR International Series 640.

Ehret, C. and M. Posnansky (eds.) 1982. *The Archaeological and Linguistic Reconstruction of African History.* Berkeley.

Emery, W. B. 1965. *Egypt in Nubia.* London.

Emery, W. B. and L. P. Kirwan 1935. *The Excavations and Survey between Wadi es-Sebua and Adindan 1929-1931.* Cairo.

Emery, W. B. and L. P. Kirwan 1938. *The Royal Tombs of Ballana and Qustul.* Cairo.

Fernandez, V. M. 1980. 'Excavations at the Meroitic Cemetery of Emir Abdallah (Abri, Northern Province, the Sudan). Some Aspects of the Pottery and its Distribution (1),' *Meroitic Newsletter* 20, 13-22.

Fernandez, V. M. 1984. 'The Meroitic Cemetery of Emir Abdallah (Abri, Northern Province, the Sudan). A Preliminary Outline of its Funerary Patterns,' *Meroitica* 7, 427-32.

Firth, C. M. 1915. *The Archaeological Survey of Nubia, Report for 1909-1910.* Cairo.

Firth, C. M. 1927. *The Archaeological Survey of Nubia, Report for 1910-1911.* Cairo.

Flannery, K. V. 1967. 'Culture History v. Cultural Process: a Debate in American Archaeology,' *Scientific American* 217, no. 2, 119-22.

Friedman, F. *et al.* 1989. *Beyond the Pharaohs.* Newark.

Garstang, J. 1914. 'Fifth Interim Report on the Excavations at Meroë in Ethiopia. Part I—General Results,' *University of Liverpool Annals of Archaeology and Anthropology* 7, 1-10.

Garstang, J, A. H. Sayce and F. Ll. Griffith 1911. *Meroë, the City of the Ethiopians.* Oxford.

Geus, F. and F. Thil (eds) 1985. *Mélanges Offerts à Jean Vercoutter.* Paris.

Goody, J. (ed.) 1958. *The Developmental Cycle in Domestic Groups.* Cambridge Papers in Social Anthropology 1.

Greene, D. L. 1966. 'Dentition and the Biological Relationships of Some Meroitic, X-Group, and Christian Populations from Wadi Halfa, Sudan,' *Kush* 14, 284-8.

Greene, D. L. 1967. *Dentition of Meroitic, X-Group, and Christian Populations from Wadi Halfa, Sudan.* University of Utah Anthropological Papers, no. 85. Salt Lake City.

Greene, D. L. 1972. 'Dental Anthropology of Early Egypt and Nubia,' *Journal of Human Evolution* 11, 315-24.

Greene, D. L. 1982. 'Discrete Dental Variations and Biological Distances in Nubian Populations,' *American Journal of Physical Anthropology* 58, 75-9.

Greene, D. L. 1984. 'Fluctuations in Dental Asymmetry and Measurement Error,' *American Journal of Physical Anthropology* 65, 283-9.

Griffith, F. Ll. 1923. 'Oxford Excavations in Nubia XVIII-XXVI,' *University of Liverpool Annals of Archaeology and Anthropology* 10, 73-171.

Griffith, F. Ll. 1924. 'Oxford Excavations in Nubia XXVII-XXIX,' *University of Liverpool Annals of Archaeology and Anthropology* 11, 115-125.

Griffith, F. Ll. 1926. 'Oxford Excavations in Nubia XL-XLII,' *University of Liverpool Annals of Archaeology and Anthropology* 13, 17-37.

Griffith, F. Ll. 1927. 'Oxford Excavations in Nubia XLIX-LV,' *University of Liverpool Annals of Archaeology and Anthropology* 14, 57-113,

Hewes, G. W. 1965. 'Gezira Dabarosa: Report of the University of Colorado Nubian Expedition, 1962-63 Season,' *Kush* 12, 174-87.

Jacquet, J. 1971. 'Remarques sur l'Architecture Domestique à l'Époque Méroitique,' *Beiträge zur Ägyptischen Bauforschung und Altertumskunde* 12, 121-31.

Jacquet-Gordon, H. 1972. *Les Ermitages Chrétiens du Désert d'Esna.* Fouilles de l'Institut Français d'Archéologie Orientale du Caire, tome 29/3.

Kaufmann, E. M. 1918. *Die Heilige Stadt der Wüste.* Munich.

Kirwan, L. P. 1939. *The Oxford University Excavations at Firka.* Oxford.

Lipe, B. 1997. 'Why Did We Do It That Way? The U. of Utah Glen Canyon Project in Retrospect,' Paper read at the annual meeting of the Society for American Archaeology, Nashville, Tennessee.

Lister, F. 1967. *Ceramic Studies of the Historic Periods in Ancient Nubia.* University of Utah Anthropological Papers, no. 86. Salt Lake City.

Lloyd, S. 1963. *Mounds of the Near East.* Edinburgh.

Michalowski, K. (ed.) 1975. *Nubia, Récentes Recherches.* Warsaw.

Millet, N. B. 1963. 'Gebel Adda, Preliminary Report for 1963,' *Journal of the American Research Center in Egypt* 2, 147-65.

Mills, A. J. 1965. 'The Reconnaissance Survey from Gemai to Dal—a Preliminary Report for 1963-64.' *Kush* 13, 1-12.

Mills, A. J. 1968. 'The Archaeological Survey from Gemai to Dal—Report for the 1965-1966 Season,' *Kush* 15, 200-210.

Mills, A. J. 1982. *The Cemeteries of Qasr Ibrim.* Egypt Exploration Society, Excavation Memoir 51. London.

Mills, A. J. and H-Å. Nordström 1966. 'The Archaeological Survey from Gemai to Dal. Preliminary Report for the Season 1964-65,' *Kush* 14, 1-15.

Mond, R. and O. H. Myers 1934. *The Bucheum,* vol. 3. Egypt Exploration Society, Memoir 41, London.

Mond, R. and O. H. Myers 1940. *Temples of Armant.* Egypt Exploration Society, Memoir 43, London.

Monneret de Villard, U. 1938. *Storia della Nubia Cristiana.* Pontificium Institutum Orientalium Studiorum, Orientalia Christiana Analecta 118. Rome.

Petrie, W. M. F. 1910. *The Arts and Crafts of Ancient Egypt.* London.

Petrie, W. M. F. 1926. *Ancient Weights and Measures.* London.

Petrie, W. M. F. 1927. *Objects of Daily Use.* London.

Plumley, J. M. 1975. 'Qasr Ibrim, 1974,' *Journal of Egyptian Archaeology* 61, 5-27.

Plumley, J. M. and W. Y. Adams 1974. 'Qasr Ibrim 1972,' *Journal of Egyptian Archaeology* 60, 212-38.

Plumley, J. M, W. Y. Adams and E. Crowfoot 1977. 'Qasr Ibrim, 1976,' *Journal of Egyptian Archaeology* 63, 29-47.

Priese, K-H 1973. 'Zur Ortsliste des Römischen Meroe-Expedition unter Nero,' *Meroitica* 1, 123-6.

Priese, K-H 1975. 'Das "Äthiopische" Niltal bei Bion und Juba (Arbeitsbericht),' in Michalowski 1975, 108-10.

Priese, K-H 1976. 'Studien zur Topographie des "Äthiopischen Niltals im Altertum und zur Meroitischen Sprache,' *Humboldt-Universität Ethnographisch-Archäologische Zeitschrift* 11, Berlin, 315-29.

Quibell, J. E. 1912. *Excavations at Saqqara (1908-9, 1909-10).* Cairo.

Randall-MacIver, D. and C. L. Woolley 1909. *Areika.* University of Pennsylvania Museum, Eckley B. Coxe Junior Expedition to Nubia, vol. 1. Philadelphia.

Roeder, G. 1959. *Hermopolis 1929-1939.* Pelizaeus-Museum zu Hildesheim, Wissenschaftliche Veröffentlichung 4. Hildesheim.

Rose, P. n.d. *The Aftermath of the Roman Frontier in Lower Nubia.* Doctoral Dissertation in the Department of Archaeology and Anthropology, Cambridge University, 1994.

Rowe, J. H. 1961. Review of C. W. Meighan, *The Archaeologist's Note Book, American Anthropologist* 63, 1379-80.

Säve-Söderbergh, T. (ed.) 1981. *Late Nubian Cemeteries.* Scandinavian Joint Expedition to Nubia, vol. 6. Stockholm.

Service, E. 1963. *Profiles in Ethnology.* New York.

Sherif, N. M. 1964. 'The Arabic Inscriptions from Meinarti,' *Kush* 12, 249-50.

Shinnie, P. L. and M. Shinnie 1978. *Debeira West.* Warminster.

Trigger, B. G. 1967. *The Late Nubian Settlement at Arminna West.* Publications of the Pennsylvania-Yale Expedition to Egypt, no. 2, Philadelphia.

Vantini, G. 1975. *Oriental Sources Concerning Nubia.* Heidelberg and Warsaw.

Vercoutter, J. 1959. 'The Gold of Kush,' *Kush* 7, 120-53.

Vercoutter, J. 1962. 'Un Palais des "Candaces" Contemporain d'Auguste,' *Syria* 39, fasc. 1-2, 263-99.

Verwers, G. J. 1961. 'Trial Excavations in the Faras Region,' *Kush* 9, 15-29.

Verwers, G. J. 1962. 'The Survey from Faras to Gezira Dabarosa,' *Kush* 10, 10-18.

Welsby, D. A. 1996 *The Kingdom of Kush. The Napatan and Meroitic Empires.* London.

Welsby, D. A. 1997. 'The SARS Survey in the Northern Dongola Reach: Preliminary Report on the Third Season 1994-1995,' *Kush* 17, 85-94.

Wenig, S. 1978. *Africa in Antiquity II. The Catalogue.* Brooklyn.

Williams, B. B 1991. *Noubadian X-Group Remains.* University of Chicago Oriental Institute Nubian Expedition, vol. 9. Chicago.

Winlock, H. E. and W. E. Crum 1926. *The Monastery of Epiphanius at Thebes.* Publications of the Metropolitan Museum of Art Expedition.

Woolley, C. L. 1911. *Karanòg, the Town.* University of Pennsylvania Museum, Eckley B. Coxe Junior Expedition to Nubia, vol. 5. Philadelphia.

Woolley, C. L. and D. Randall-MacIver 1910. *Karanòg, the Romano-Nubian Cemetery.* University of Pennsylvania Museum, Eckley B. Coxe Junior Expedition to Nubia, vol. 3. Philadelphia.

هذا المجلد.

و بالطبقات الأثرية بالموقع و التي تنتمي إلى عصر بلانه تم العثور على مجموعة ضخمة من اللقى الأثرية المسجلة، و معظمها من الأواني الفخارية. و قد ضمت أكواب صغيرة و كؤوس للشرب عثر عليها في أغلب الأحيان و هي ملقاة على أرضية المنزل، و قد عثر عليها سليمة بكامل هيئتها.

تم تذييل المجلد مينارتي ١ بملحق احتوى على قائمة ضمت كل اللقى الأثرية المسجلة التي عثر عليها بالطبقات الأثرية لعصري مروي و بلانه مصحوبة بأرقام المقتنيات بمتحف السودان القومي .

و تقدم المجلدات اللاحقة في سلسلة مينارتي تقارير تغطي العصر المسيحي القديم و الكلاسيكي (مينارتي ٢)، و أيضاً العصران المسيحي المتأخر و النهائي (مينارتي ٣)، و يتطرق المجلد الرابع إلى موضوعي الكنيسة و المدافن. و سيتعرض المجلد الأخير في خاتمته إلى تاريخ المجموعات السكانية بجزيرة مينارتي مرفقاً بشرح تفسيري واف.

و قد عثر على مخلفات العصر المروي المتأخر بالمستوى الأدنى للموقع (مستوى رقم ١٨). و مثلت تلك المخلفات بقايا للعديد من المباني الضخمة، و التي من الواضح أنها كانت أي الأبنية لغرض الاستخدام العام، و من الراجح أن السلطة الكوشية قد قامت ببنائها لأغراض الإدارة و التجارة. تم استخدام الطوب اللَّبِن في البناء رغماً عن أن بعض المباني وضع لها أساساً حجرياً. و قد عثر بأحد تلك المباني و الذي يبدو أنه كان أحد مراكز الإدارة على بوابة ضخمة، و لكن يظل الغرض الحقيقي من بنائه مجهولاً و ذلك نسبة للتعرية الشديدة التي أصابت مكونات البناء نفسه. و احتوى مبنىً آخر على مجموعة من الجدران و المخازن و/أو المتاجر، كما عثر بآخر على أحواض كانت تستخدم في معاصر النبيذ. و يظل الغرض من إنشاء المباني الأخرى مجهولاً، غير أن جدرانها تميزت بالسمك و الإستقامة، مما يشير إلى أنها لم تكن، أي المباني، مساكن عادية. و بتعاقب الأزمان أصاب المباني المروية الخراب و الدمار على إثر الحريق و مياه الفيضان الذي يتضح جلياً بالمستويين ١٦، ١٧. و كما يظهر من الطبقات الأثرية الأولى بالمستوى الذي عليه عصر بلانه فأن الموقع السكني قد بدا خالياً و غير مأهول بالسكان لبعض الوقت.

و بعد مضي نصف قرن من الزمان عادت الحياة إلى جزيرة مينارتي و عمرها الناس من جديد و أقيمت بها الدور من جديد على أطلال و خرائب عصر مروي التي قبرت في باطن الأرض. و قد كانت طبقة البناء الجديد ضمن المستوى الأثري ١٥ب. و امتازت طبيعة البناء الجديد باختلاف كبير عن سابقتها. و بذلك فإنها أي المباني الجديدة لم تكن مركزاً إدارياً أو تجارياً كما كان الأمر من قبل و إنما مثلت المساكن و الدور التي كانت تأوي مجتمعاً ريفياً من المزارعين، لم يختلف كثيراً عن مثيلاته في مناطق النوبة الأخرى. و تم الكشف عن أكثر من ٣٥ منزلاً بالموقع السكني تجمعت في غير نظام، كما اتخذت طرقاتها المعدودة الضيقة مسالك متعرجة. و امتاز بناؤها و الذي استخدم فيه الطوب اللبن بجدران رقيقة واهنة، على عكس الجدران السميكة التي امتاز بها بناء عصر مروي ذو الحوائط السميكة القوية.و احتوت كل المنازل على حجرتين أو خمس حجرات صغيرة، خلت من الأثاث المشيد مثل المساطب و صناديق التخزين.

و قد عمر الناس المكان بهذه الطريقة على ما يقرب من قرنين من الزمان في غير ما تغيير يذكر. و مع ذلك و كعادة المجتمعات الريفية فقد حظيت دواخل المنازل بتغييرات في المداخل و الممرات و التقسيمات في البناء الداخلي و ذلك لتواكب الحاجة الأسرية و المستجدات التي طرأت على تكوينها العائلي. و يمكن الإشارة إلى ذلك بالطبقتين الأثريتين ١٥ أ ، ١٤. كما و تجدر الإشارة هنا إلى الدمار الذي أصاب الموقع بفعل مياه الفيضان، الذي صار متكرر الحدوث و في فترات قصيرة. و بنهاية طور عصر بلانه بالموقع، هجر الناس القرية لفترة من الزمن، و ربما تسبب أحد تلك

مينارتي ١

موجز باللغة العربية

كانت مينارتي عبارة عن جزيرة صغيرة غمرتها مياه بحيرة النوبة و هي تقع إلى الشمال من الشلال الثاني لنهر النيل بالقرب من وادي حلفا. و على الجزء الجنوبي من الجزيرة شغل الموقع الأثري و الذي هو عبارة عن ربوة (كوم) ذات طبقات أثرية يزيد ارتفاعها عن اثني عشر متراً ضمت بين طبقاتها سلسلة من المخلفات الأثرية و التي يؤرخ لها بالفترات المروية و بلانه (العصر المروي المتأخر) و مخلفات العصر المسيحي، ما بين ٢٠٠ و ١٦٠٠ من التقويم الميلادي.

و في عامي ١٩٦٣ و ١٩٦٤ قامت مصلحة الآثار بإرسال فريق من خبراء الآثار تحت ادارة وليام ي. أدمز للتنقيب بالموقع الأثري بجزيرة مينارتي و ذلك نسبة إلى أن الموقع صار مهدداً بالغرق الوشيك، و قد شهدت أعمال التنقيب الأثري بالموقع عدداً ضخماً من الخبراء و عمال الحفريات المدربين إذ بلغ العدد الكلي ٢٥٠ في أغلب الأوقات.و قد بدأ العمل بالتنقيب في أحد نصفي الموقع و الذي شغل مساحة تقدر بحوالي الثمانين متراً مربعاً، و تم الكشف عن طبقاته الأثرية الواحدة تلو الأخرى من أعلى قمته إلى القاعدة. و قد نتج عن ذلك الكشف عدد ١٨ طبقة احتوي عليها الموقع (الكوم) و كانت كل طبقة قد تكونت في مدى زمني تراوح بين ٥٠ و ٢٠٠ عاماً. و في غضون تلك الفترة التي شغلتها أعمال التنقيب تم الكشف عن عدد ٦٠ مبنأً على اختلاف اشكالها، كما تم التوثيق لأكثر من ١٥٠٠ من المخلفات و اللقى الأثرية. و بالإضافة إلى ذلك تم التنقيب بالجبانة و التي احتوت على مايقرب من عدد ٤٠٠ قبراً.

يقدم هذا المجلد و هو الأول في سلسلة من أربعة مجلدات تقريراً عن المخلفات و اللقى الأثرية التي تم العثور عليها بالموقع الأثري بجزيرة مينارتي. و يستهل التقرير بوصف تفصيلي لمناهج البحث و التنقيب الأثري التي تم اتباعها، و التي اختلفت في أغلب صورها عن مناهج البحث و التنقيب الأثري المتعارف عليها. و يقدم الفصلان اللذان تليا الفصل الأول من الكتاب وصفاً تفصيلياً للقى و المباني الأثرية التي عثر عليها بالطبقتين الأثريتين الأكثر قدماً (ألا و هما الطبقتان الموجودتان بالمستويات الدنيا من الموقع (الكوم)، و يؤرخ لهما على التوالي بعصري مروي و بلانه. و بالإضافة إلى الوصف التفصيلي قدم فصلا الكتاب أيضاً الخرائط و الرسومات و الصور الفوتوغرافية الخاصة بالعديد من تلك المباني. و أيضاً قدم الكتاب وصفاً مفصلاً آخر للقى الأثرية مصحوبة بالرسومات و الصور الفوتوغرافية و يختتم الكاتب فصول المجلد بملخص تفسيري احتوى على مقارنة النتائج و اللقى و الموجودات الأثرية التي عثر عليها بجزيرة مينارتي و تلك التي جاءت من المواقع الأثرية النوبية الأخرى، وربطها بالتاريخ النوبي المعروف.

b. Distant view of the Meinarti kom from the south, before excavation. The extensive sand flat in the foreground was underwater at the season of the high Niles.

d. The stairway descending to the south Church door, in the Late Christian period. The photo illustrates how much sand had accumulated around the outside of the church since it was first built, when the threshold was at the same level as the ground outside.

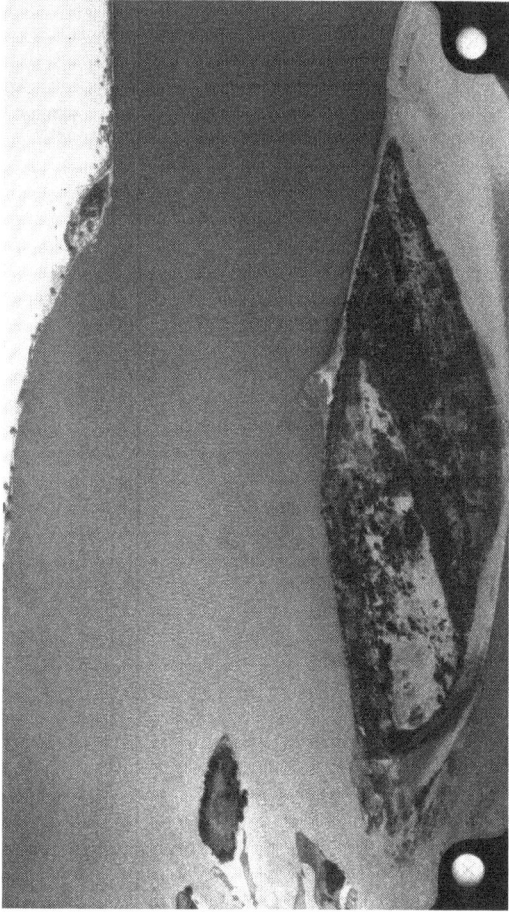

a. Aerial photograph, showing Meinarti Island and part of the neighboring island of Majarab. The site can be seen at the upriver (left) end of Meinarti Island.

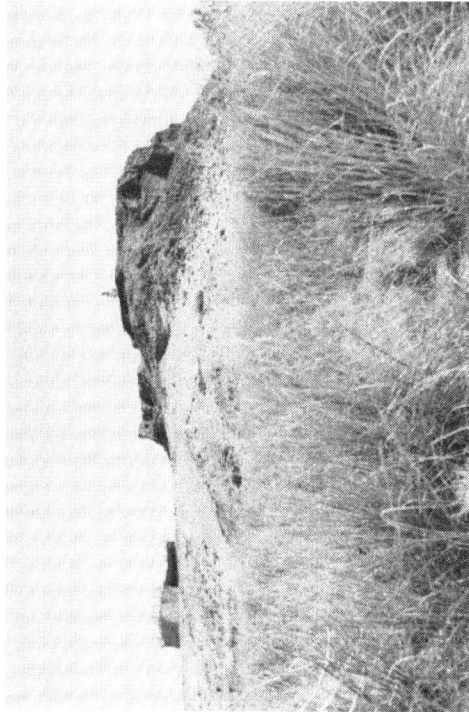

c. Pre-excavation view of the Meinarti kom from the west. The dominant feature is the Late Christian "Castle-house" (House 1), whose top was leveled in the 19th century to make a gun emplacement.

Plate 1. The site.

a. Excavations in progress, in the early days of the dig. The crew at that time numbered 150 men.

b. The excavator's rakuba, *at the north end of the excavation area. Note identification tags nailed to the room walls.*

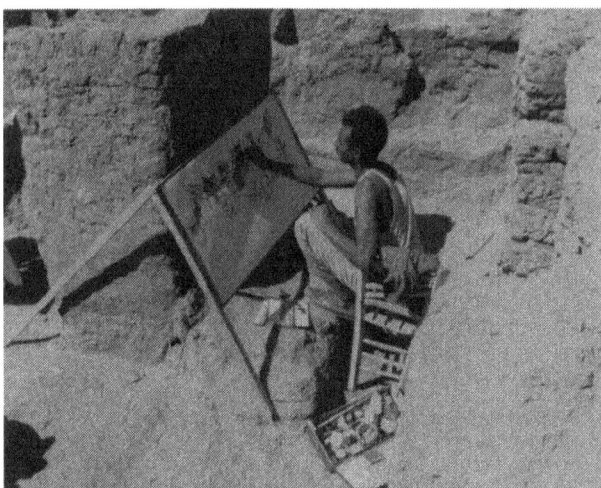

c. The artist Abdel Rahim Hag el Amin at work, copying murals in the Meinarti Church.

d. Restorer Jozef Gazy at work, preparing to remove a mural painting from the church wall.

e. The pile of sorted, tallied, and discarded sherds at the conclusion of the dig.

Plate 2. Excavation procedures.

a. General view over the remains at Level 18, seen from the north. The Administration Building (House XLVIII) is in the center and the Market Compound (House XLIII) directly behind it.

b. The approach stairway to the Administration Building seen from the east. The structure on the left is the Market Compound.

c. Close-up view of the approach stairway and landing, at the east side of the Administration Building. The view is from the east.

d. Remains of the Administration Building, seen from the north. The large building in the background is House XXXIV, which does not belong to this subphase.

e. Close-up view of the sandstone foundation blocks in the Administration Building.

f. Remains of the Administration Building, seen from the south, showing large rooms at the southern end of the building. Note descending stairs in the room at lower left. The large structure in the background is unexcavated House XXII, belonging to Phase 4.

Plate 3. The Administration Building (House XLVIII) at Subphase 1a.

a. Rooms of the Western Range, seen from the southwest, with Room 4 in the foreground. Standing walls in the right background are reconstructions from Subphase 1c, not part of the original structure.

b. Rooms of the Western Range, seen from the north, with Room 2 in the immediate foreground. The thin interior partition seen in this room was an addition at Subphase 1b.

c. Rooms 3 (foreground) and 2 of the Market Compound, showing sub-floor cellars and their openings, after removal of the room floors. The view is from the southeast.

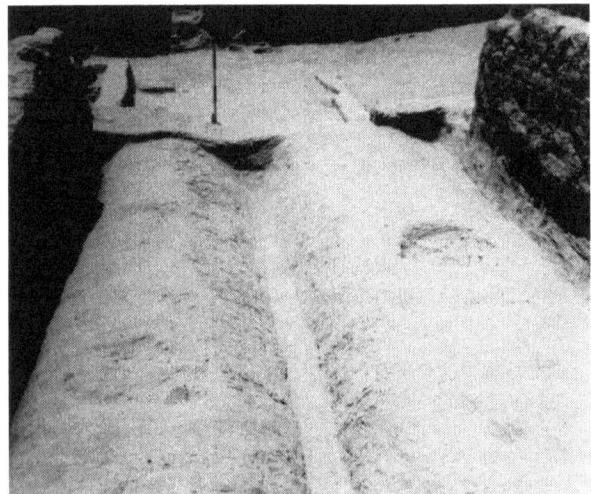

d. Top view of the subfloor cellars in Room 3, after removal of the room floor. Note holes knocked in the tops of the vaults. The view is toward the east.

e The courtyard of the Market Compound, showing dividing partitions inserted at Subphase 1aa. The view is from the south-east, with Room 3 at the far left.

f. Denuded foundations of the Eastern Range rooms, seen from the north.

Plate 4. The Market Compound (House XLIII) at Subphases 1a and 1aa.

a. View over the Wine Press from the south.

b. View over the pressing basins from the north. Note steps in the bottom of the fermentation basin.

c. View of the lion spout and part of the fermentation basin, showing repaired crack in the basin wall.

d. View of the three wine pressing basins from the southwest.

e. Close-up of the lion spout and the middle (settling) basin.

f. View over the pressing basins from the west, showing House XLVII in the background.

Plate 5. The Wine Press (House LIV) at Subphase 1a.

b. Houses XXXIV (right) and XLII (left), seen from the north.

a. General view of remains, with Houses XLIX and L in the foreground. The structure in the center is House XLIV, built on top of the denuded Eastern Range of the Market Compound. The view is from the northwest.

d. View over the wall-tops of House XLII, showing Courtyard XLII in the background. The view is from the east.

c. Interior view of House XLII from the south, showing stairway in Room 3.

f. Interior view of House XXXIV, from the south.

e. Exterior view of House XXXIV, from the southwest.

Plate 6. Remains at Subphases 1b and 1c.

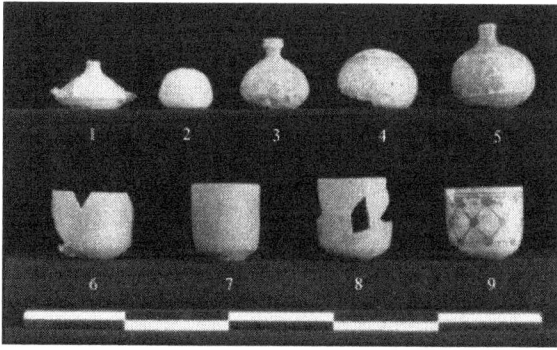

a. *Family M fine Wares W26, W30, and R35.* **1**, *Ware W30 lamp (1184);* **2**, *Ware W26 aryballos (1117);* **3**, *Ware W30 aryballos (896);** **4**, *Ware W26 aryballos (1434);* **5**, *Ware R35 aryballos (1189);* **6**, *Ware R35 cup (1438);* **7**, *Ware R35 cup (1095);* **8**, *Ware R35 cup (1439);* **9**, *Ware W26 cup (1094). Item marked with * is from Phase 2; see Table 12. Scale increments are 10cm.*

b. *Group N.I ordinary wares.* **1**, *Ware W25 footed bowl (1123);* **2**, *Ware R32 footed bowl (1106);* **3**, *Ware R32 cup (1197);* **4**, *Ware R32 bowl (1186);* **5**, *Ware R32 bowl (1188);* **6**, *Ware R32 bowl (1096);* **7**, *Ware R32 bowl (1097);* **8**, *Ware W25 bowl (1198). Scale increments are 10cm.*

c. *Ware W25 painted jar (1219). Scale increments are 5cm.*

d. *Vessels of early Ballaña Ware R25, Ware Group N.II.* **1**, *ointment jar (979);* **2**, *small bottle (1078);** **3**, *ointment jar (1196);* **4**, *lamp (1004)**; **5**, *bowl (1073)**; **6**, *food bowl (1105);* **7**, *goblet (1424)**; **8**, *goblet (1427)**; **9**, *footed bowl (1426)**; **10**, *food bowl (1158);* **11**, *food bowl (1098). Items marked with * are from Phase 2; see Table 12. Scale increments are 10cm.*

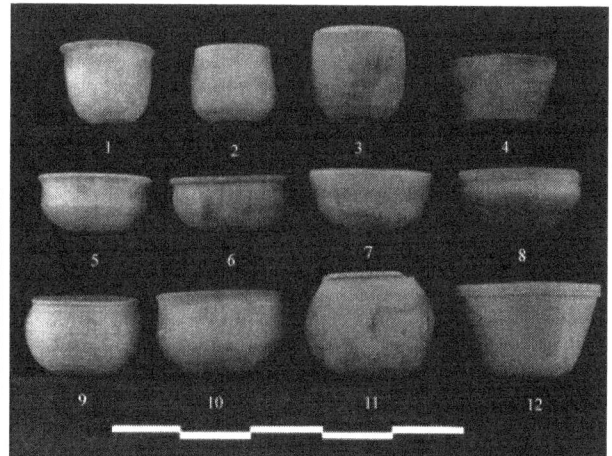

e. *Bowls of Wares R25 and R1.* **1**, *Ware R1 bowl (972);* **2**, *Ware R1 bowl (1059)**; **3**, *Ware R1 bowl (1080)**; **4**, *Ware R25 bowl (878)**; **5**, *Ware R1 bowl (833)**; **6**, *Ware R1 bowl (844)**; **7**, *Ware R25 bowl (1099);* **8** *Ware R1 bowl (782)**; **9**, *Ware R1 bowl (965)**; **10**, *Ware R1 bowl (834)**; **11**, *Ware R1 pot (966)**; **12**, *Ware R1 bowl (924)**. *Items marked with * are from Phase 2; see Table 12. Scale increments are 10cm.*

f. *Large utility vessels of Wares R25 and U1.* **1**, *Ware R25 pot (1124);* **2**, *Ware R25 pot (1067)**; **3**, *Ware U1 qadus (964)**. *Items marked with * are from Phase 2; see Table 12. Scale increments are 10cm.*

Plate 7. Nubian painted pottery wares, Families M and N, from Phases 1 and 2.

a. Large jars of Wares R25. *1*, jar (1203); *2*, jar (1071). Scale increments are 10cm.

b. Qawadis *(saqia pots) of Ware U1.* *1*, qadus (1069)*; *2*, qadus (1152); *3*, qadus (964)*. Items marked with * are from Phase 2; see Table 12. Scale increments are 10cm.

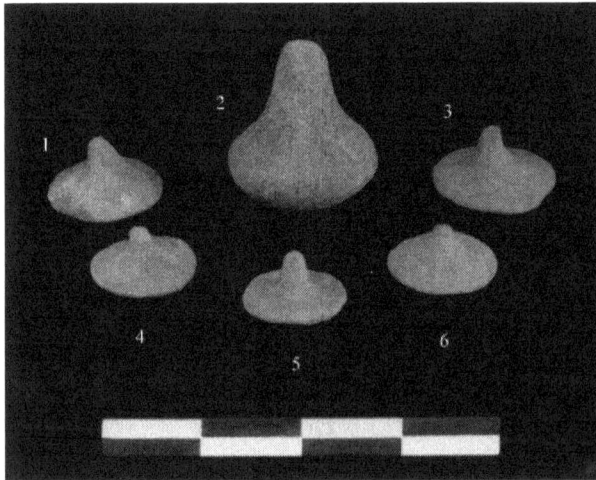

c. Hand-made stopper and lids of Ware H1. *1*, lid (1062)*; *2*, stopper (1443); *3*, lid (1104); *4*, lid (1127); *5*, lid (837)*; *6*, lid (982)*. Items marked with * are from Phase 2; see Table 12. Scale increments are 5cm.

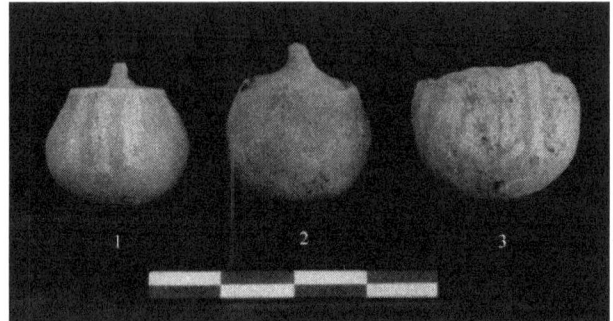

d. Small pots of Ware H13. *1*, Pot (1126); *2*, Pot (851)*; *3*, Pot (1454). Item marked with * is from Phase 2; see Table 12. Scale increments are 5cm.

e. Large pots of Ware H13. *1*, Ware H13 pot (1181); *2*, Ware H13 pot (1204). Scale increments are 10cm.

f. Small vessels of Aswan Wares, Family A. *4*, Ware R4 bowl (1399); *5*, Ware R4 footed bowl (1397); *6*, Ware R30 goblet (1148); *8*, Ware R4 footed bowl (1400)*. Item marked with * is from Phase 2; see Table 12. Items not listed are from Phase 3. Scale increments are 10cm.

Plate 8. Miscellaneous pottery from Phases 1 and 2.

a. Aryballoi *and* lekythoi *of Aswan Wares.* **1**, *Ware U2 oil bottle (757)**; **2**, *Ware R4 aryballos (881)**; **3**, *Ware R4* aryballos *(918)**; **4**, *Ware R4 aryballos (899)**; **5**, *Ware R31 lekythos (919)**; **6**, *Ware R31* lekythos *(1183)*; **7**, *Ware R31 lekythos (1013)**; **8**, *Ware R31 lekythos (1072)**; **9**, *Ware R31 lekythos (1125)*. *Items marked with* * *are from Phase 2; see Table 12. Scale increments are 10cm.*

b. Amphorae of Aswan Ware U2. **1**, amphora (1190); **2**, amphora (745).* Item marked with * is from Phase 2; see Table 12. Scale increments are 10cm.

c. Imported amphorae. **2**, Ware U4 amphora (1191). Other item is from Phase 3. Scale increments are 10cm.

d. Decorated ceramic quseba (1212). Scale increments are 10cm.

e. Detail of painted design on quseba (1212).

Plate 9. Imported pottery; large ceramic objects from Phases 1 and 2.

f. Fragmentary ceramic basin (1444). Scale increments are 5cm.

a. Sandstone offering tables.
***1**, nearly complete specimen (493);* ***2**,*
fragment (5); ***3** fragment (907);*
***4**, fragment (297).*
Scale increments are 10cm.

b. Hornblende statue base (487).
Scale increments are 5cm.

c. Granite oil press (1221), upper side (at right). Item at left is from Phase 4.

d. Granite oil press (1221), underside.
Scale increments are 10cm.

Plate 10. Large stone objects from Phase 1.

a. Jar stamps and seals. **1**, Meroitic sandstone seal (1175); **2**, Meroitic sandstone seal (1100); **3**, Ballaña sandstone seal (1028)*; **4**, Ballaña sandstone seal (1029)*. Items marked with * are from Phase 2; see Table 12. Items not listed are from later phases. Scale increments are 5cm.

b. Impression of seal 1100.

c. Meroitic jar seal 1175, design face. Scale increments are 5cm.

d. Impression of seal 1175.

Plate 11. Smaller objects of stone from Phases 1 and 2.

a. Lava quern (1121).

b. Pestles and grinding stones. **4**, Ballaña pestle of black rock (762)*; **5**, Ballaña pestle of hornblende (989)*; **6**, Ballaña grinding stone of granite (870)*; **7**, Meroitic slate pestle (1153); **8**, Ballaña pestle of ferruginous sandstone (869).* Items marked with * are from Phase 2; see Table 12. Items not listed are from later phases. Scale increments are 5cm.

c. Sharpening, abrading, and smoothing instruments. **1**, grooved ferricrete pebble (1174); **2**, schist or slate whetstone (1057)*; **3**, smoothing pebble (508); **4**, greywacke palette (1109)*; **5**, sandstone grinding block (1173); **6**, limestone ?sharpener (1154); **7**, hone? (594); **8**, greywacke palette (985)*; **9**, greywacke palette (831)*; **10**, greywacke palette (942)*; **11**, greywacke palette (1113); **12**, greywacke palette (906)*;**13**, smoothed granite block (1120); **14**, greywacke palette (410);**15**, greywacke palette (1114); **16**, smoothed slate slab (1119). Items marked with * are from Phase 12. Scale increments are 10cm.

d. Dark red carnelian bead (1171).

e. Sandstone anchor stones.

f. Carved sandstone lintel fragments.

Plate 12. Miscellaneous objects of ground and carved stone from Phases 1 and 2.

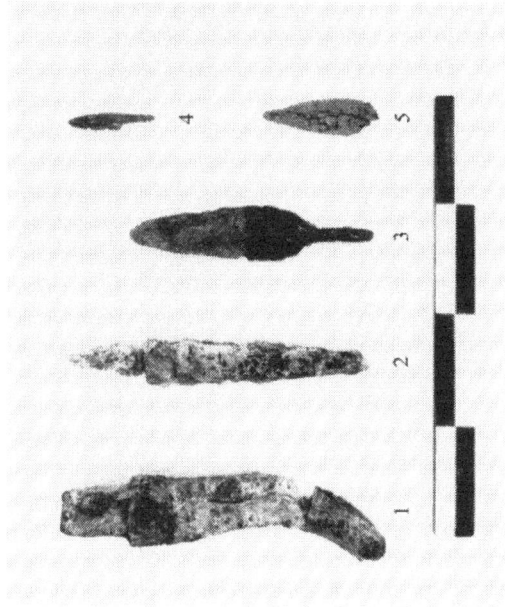

a. Iron knives and weapons. 1, curved knife or sickle (1162)*; 2, knife or dagger blade (1142); 3, spear point (912)*; 4, arrow point (1168)*; 5, small spear point (1045)*. Items marked with * are from Phase 2; see Table 12. Scale increments are 5cm.

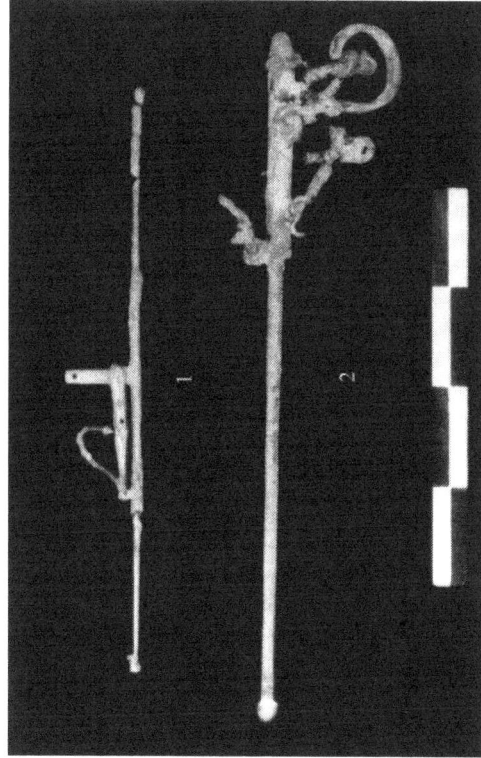

b. Iron spikes. 1, group of three spikes (1101); 2, single spike (1165); 3, nail with square shaft (948);* 4, spike with square shaft (1170). Item marked with * is from Phase 2; see Table 12.

c. Bronze scales. 1, balance-beam scale (1131); 2, steelyard scale (1130). Scale increments are 5cm.

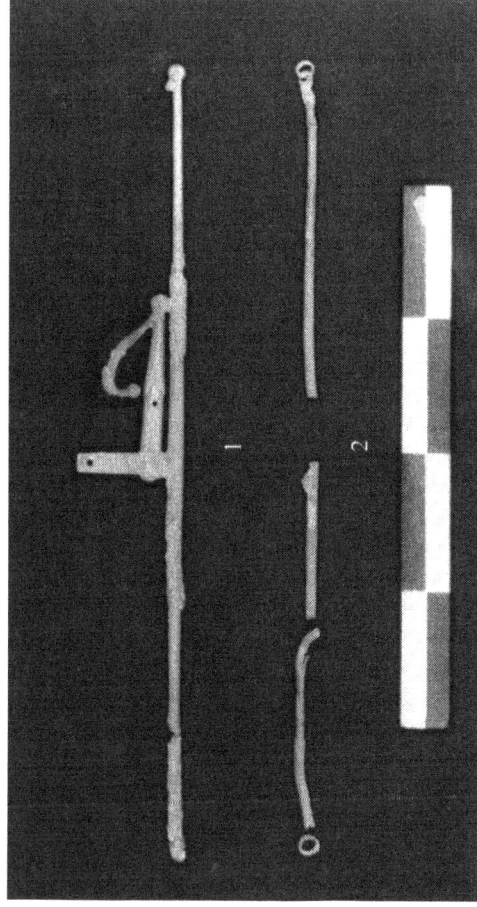

d. Balance-beam scales. 1, complete bronze scale (1131); 2 and 3, fragments of copper scale (1160); 4, fragment of copper scale (1111). Scale increments are 5cm.

Plate 13. Objects of iron, bronze, and copper from Phases 1 and 2.

a. Small tripod censer (1133).
Scale increments are 5cm.

b. Miniature tripod beaker (1158).
Scale increments are 5cm.

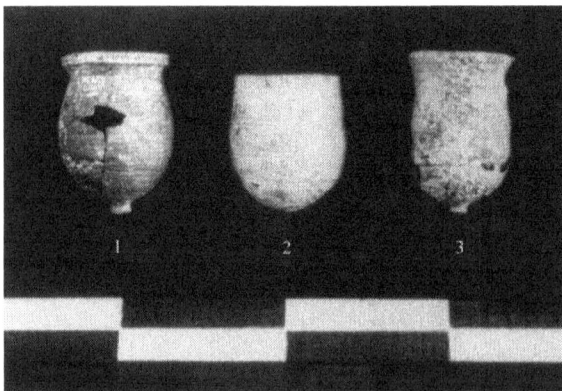

c. Miniature bronze vessels. 1, qadus (983);* 2, pot
(984);* 3, qadus (1134). Items marked with * are from
Phase 2; see Table 12. Scale increments are 5cm.

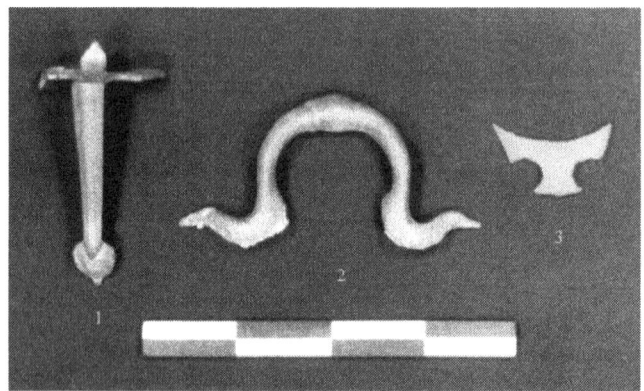

d. Bronze vessel handles. 1, tankard handle (1156); 2, bowl
handle (1155); 3, jug or amphora handle (1157). Scale
increments are 5cm.

e. Votive lamp (1132), front view.
Scale increments are 5cm.

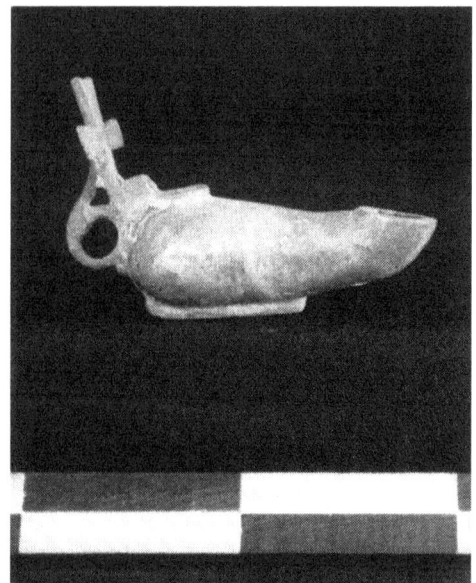

f. Votive lamp (1132), side view.
Scale increments are 5cm.

Plate 14. Bronze vessels and fragments from Phases 1 and 2.

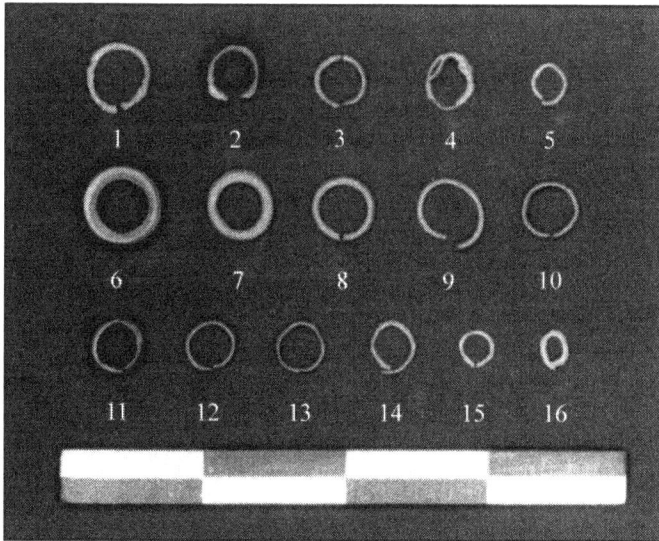

a. Bronze and copper rings. *1*, copper ring of twisted wire (1137); *2*, bronze ring (1135); *3*, bronze ring (1161); *4*, copper ring of twisted wire (1138). Other items are from later phases.
Scale increments are 5cm.

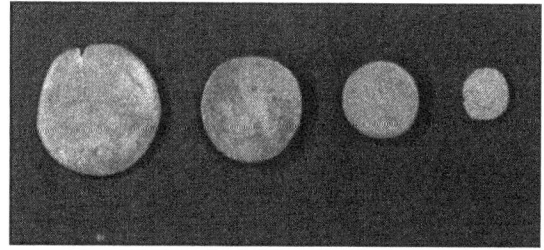

b. Ptolemaic and Roman bronze coins. *1*, coin of Flaccilla (1031); *2*, coin of Ptolemy I or II (675); *3*, coin of Ptolemy I or II (559); *4*, coin of ?Hadrian (1048).

c. Reverse of Ptolemaic coin 675.

d. Sheet bronze with stamped decoration (729).

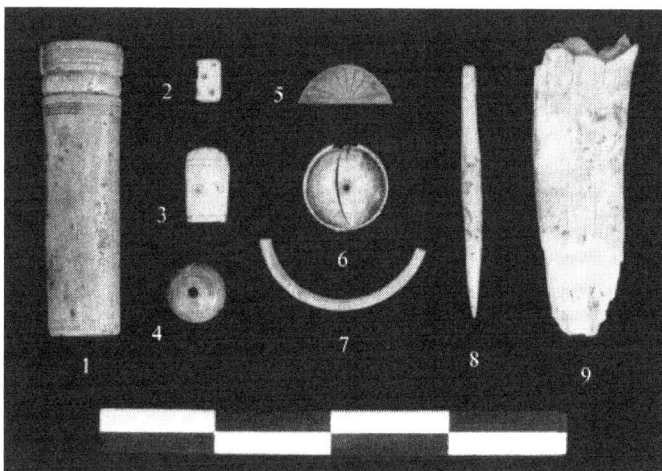

e. Small objects of bone and ivory. *9*, piece of worked hippopotamus ivory (1102). Other items are from later phases.
Scale increments are 5cm.

f. Small Meroitic ostrakon (1146).

Plate 15. Miscellaneous small Meroitic objects from Phase 1.

a. General view over the site at Subphase 2a, from the north.

b. View over the site at Subphase 2a, looking south-east.

c. The southern part of the site at Subphase 2a, looking east. House XXXIX is in the foreground, and House XXXIV in the background.

d. Interior of House XLII at Subphase 2a, from the southwest corner.

e. Pottery objects abandoned on the floor of House XXXV, Subphase 2b.

f. Pottery objects abandoned on the floor of House XLIII, Subphase 2c.

Plate 16. Architectural remains at Phase 2.

a. Ware W11 vessels. *1*, table amphora (987);
2, footed jar (767); *3*, footed jar (925).
Scale increments are 10cm.

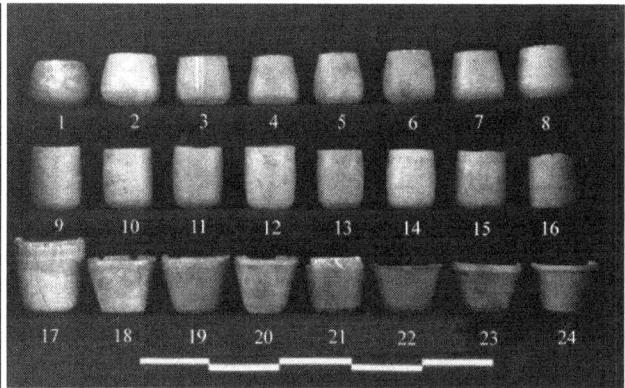

b. Cups of Wares R1 and R2. *1-8*, Ware R1, Form A8: *1*, 1147*;
2, 1022; *3*, 1005; *4*, 901; *5*, 973; *6*, 987; *7*, 747; *8*, 1077. *9-16*:
Ware R1, Form A7. *9*, 852; *10*, 842; *11*, 992; *12*, 974; *13*, 885;
14, 917; *15*, 1010; *16*, 861. *17-21*: Ware R2, Form A26. *17*, 1033; *18*, 717;
19, 877; *20*, 890; *21*, 976. *22-24*: Ware R2, Form A31. *22*, 892; *23*, 776; *24*, 891.
Item marked with * is from Phase 1; see Table 9. Scale increments are 10cm.

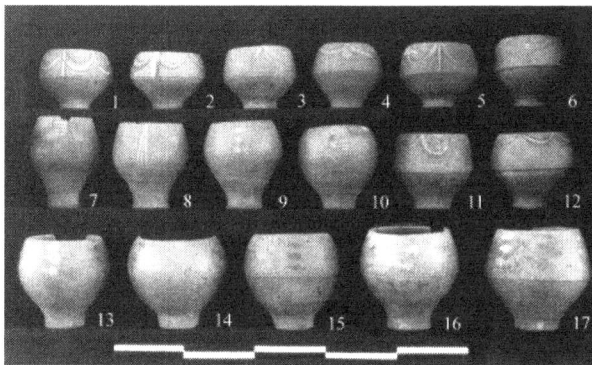

c. Ware R1 goblets. *1-6*, Form B17: *1*, 1058; *2*,
930; *3*, 1193*; *4*, 1086; *5*, 1018; *6*, 1036.
7-12, Form B14: *7*, 920; *8*, 1002; *9*, 1177;
10, 741; *11*, 958; *12*, 836. *13-17*, Form B14:
13, 931; *14*, 1008; *15*, 1016; *16*, 1178;
17, 1017. Item marked with * is from Phase 1;
see Table 9. Scale increments are 10cm.

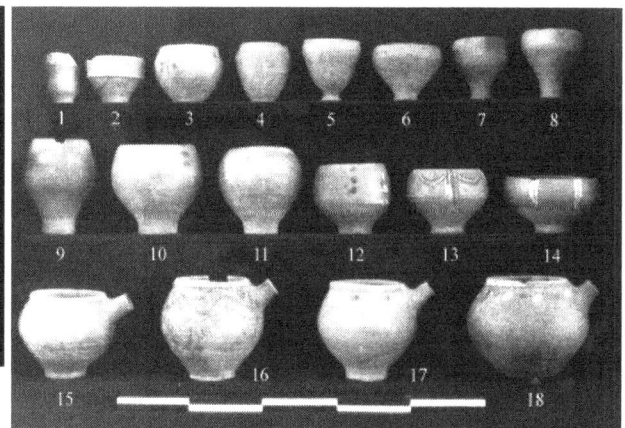

d. Goblets and small pots, Wares R25, R1, and R2. *1-8*, Goblets: *1*, Ware R1
(840); *2*, Ware R1 (957); *3*, Ware R25 (971); *4*, Ware R1 (1011); *5*, Ware R1
(993); *6*, Ware R2 (921); *7*, Ware R1 (746); *8*, Ware R1 (808).
9-14, Goblets: *9*, Ware R1 (920); *10*, Ware R1 (931); *11* Ware R1 (741);
12, Ware R1 (1035); *13*, Ware R1 (930); *14*, Ware R1 (1076). *15-18*, Spouted
goblets; *15*, Ware R2 (952); *16*, Ware R2 (1089);
17, Ware R2 (835); *18*, Ware R2 (1192)*. Item marked with * is
from Phase 1; see Table 9. Scale increments are 10cm.

e. Small bowls, lamps, bottles, and lekythoi, Wares R1 and
R2. *1-7*, Bowls: *1*, Ware R1 (962); *2*, Ware R2 (777);
3, Ware R2 (778); *4*, Ware R1 (903); *5*, Ware R2 (934);
6, Ware R2 (995); *7*, Ware R2 (956). *8*, lamp, Ware R1
(882); *9*, lamp, Ware R1 (946); *10*, lamp, Ware R1 (1176);
11, aryballos, Ware R1 (620) *12*, aryballos, Ware R1 (1056);
13, aryballos, Ware R1 (910); *14*, Aryballos, Ware R1 (977);
15, lekythos, Ware R1 (863); *16*, lekythos, Ware R1 (1088);
17, lekythos, Ware R1 (947); *18*, lekythos, Ware R1 (1055);
19, small pot, Ware R1 (1012). Numbers 6, 10, and 11 are
from Phase 3 levels. Scale increments are 10cm.

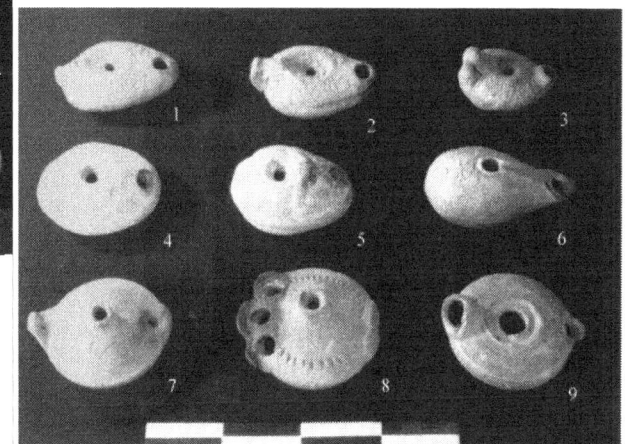

f. Molded and specially formed lamps, Wares R1 and W2. *1*, Ware
R1 (839); *2*, Ware R1 (913); *3*, Ware R1 (853); *4*, Ware W2 (847);
5, frog lamp, Ware W2 (981); *6*, Ware R1 (1176); *7*, Ware R1
(895); *8*, Ware R1 (916); *9*, Ware R1 (1060).
Scale increments are 5cm.

Plate 17. X-Group pottery wares, Group N.II, from Phase
2.

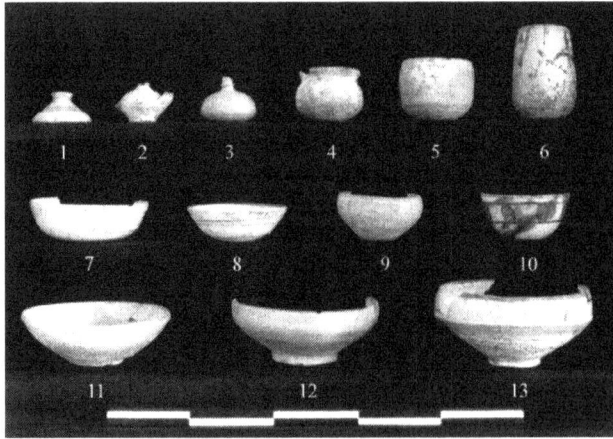

a. Vessels of Early Christian Ware W2. *1*, lid (756); *2*, lamp (758); *4*, small bowl (1006); *8*, footed bowl (1040). Other items are from Phase 3 levels. Scale increments are 10cm.

b. Vessels of Early Christian Ware R5. *12*, footed bowl (755); *14*, footed bowl (739), *17*, footed bowl (1248). Other items are from Phase 3 levels. Scale increments are 10cm.

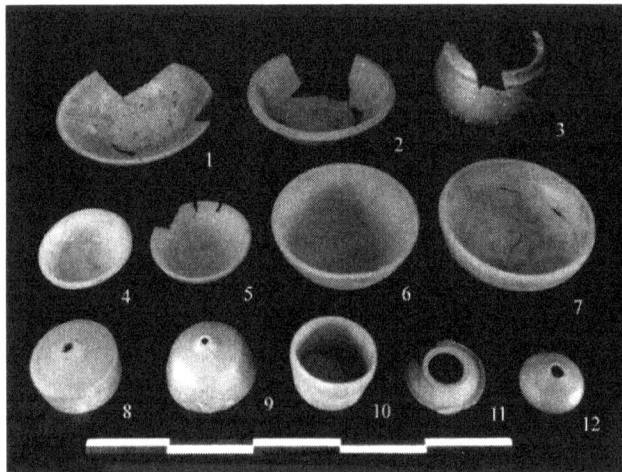

c. Vessels of Early Christian Ware R5. *2*, footed bowl (755). Other items are from Phase 3 levels. Scale increments are 10cm.

d. Jars, Ware R1. *1*, 1071; *2*, 955; *3*, 1180. Scale increments are 10cm.

e. Ware R1 jar (1075). Scale increments are 10cm.

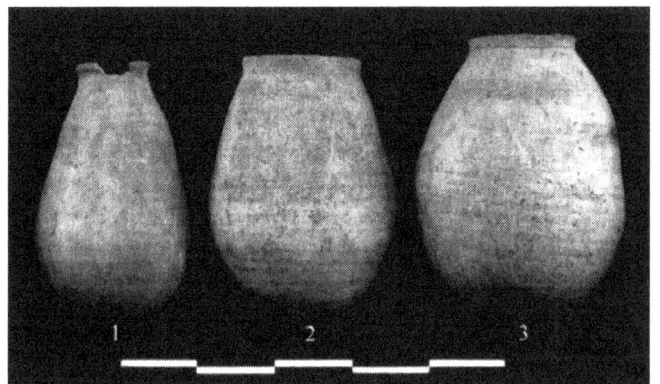

f. Ware U5 pots. *1*, 944. The other items are not from Meinarti. Scale increments are 10cm.

Plate 18. Early Christian wares and utility wares, Groups N.III and NU, from Phase 2.

a. Unregistered pots of Ware H1, Form U12.

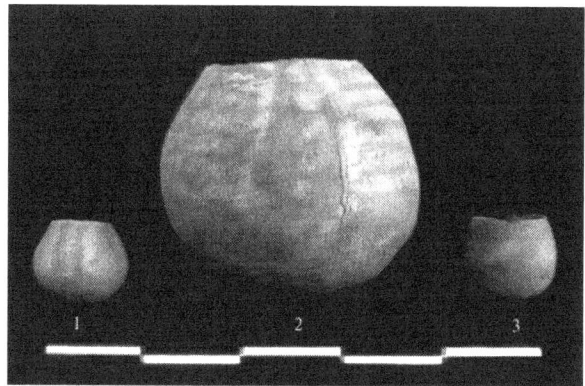

b. Ware H13 pots. 1, 1126*; 2, 1074; 3, 851. Item marked with * is from Phase 1; see Table 9. Scale increments are 10cm.

c. Vessels of Aswan Wares R4, R31, and U2. 1, aryballos, Ware R4 (881); 2, oil bottle, Ware U2 (757); 3, lekythos, Ware R31 (1013); 4, lekythos, Ware R31 (1072); 5, lekythos, Ware R31 (1125)*; 10, small bottle, Ware R31 (750). Item marked with * is from Phase 1; see Table 9. Items not listed are from Phase 3 levels. Scale increments are 10cm.

d. Vessels of Aswan Wares W24, R4, R31, and U2. 1, small jug, Ware W24 (1003); 8, small bottle, Ware R31 (750). Items not listed are from Phase 3 levels. Scale increments are 10cm.

e. Jugs and bottles, Aswan Wares R31 and U2. 1, jug, Ware R4 (573); 2, small bottle, Ware R31 (750); 3, jug, Ware U2 (968); 4, amphora, Ware U2 (929). Numbers 1 and 4 are from Phase 3 levels. Scale increments are 10cm.

f. The evolutionary development of Aswan amphora forms (Wares R30 and U2) in the Meroitic, Ballaña, and Early Christian periods. 1, typical Meroitic Form Z5, Ware R30; 2, typical Ballaña Form Z6, Ware U2 (745); 3, typical Early Christian Form Z4, Ware U2 (927). Number 1 is not from Meinarti, and Number 3 is from Phase 3. Scale increments are 10cm.

Plate 19. Hand-made wares and Aswan wares, Families D and A, from Phase 2.

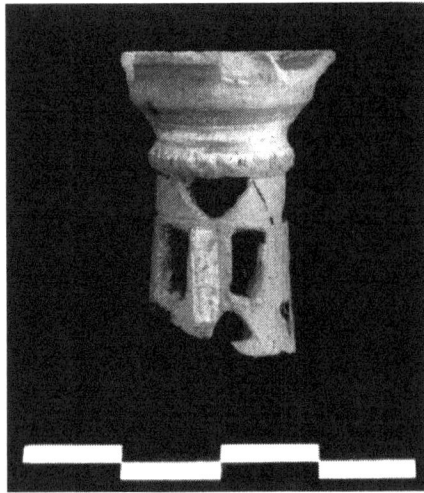

a. Top of incense burner or lamp stand (854). Scale increments are 5cm.

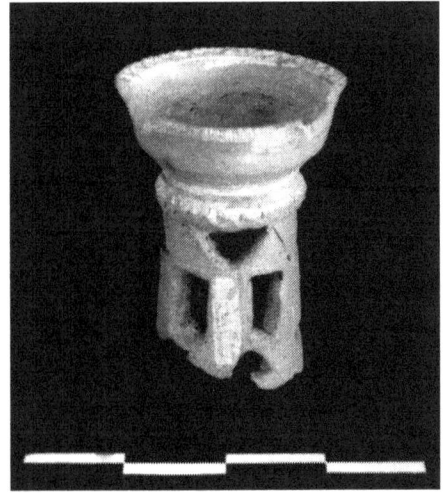

b. Top of incense burner or lamp stand (854). Scale increments are 5cm.

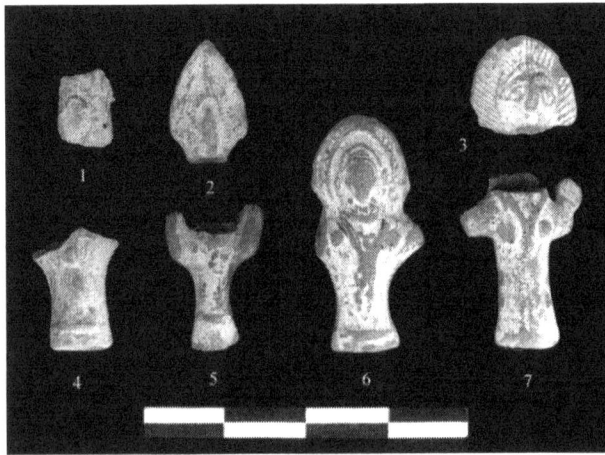

c. Female figurines. *1*, head fragment, Aswan ware (999); *2*, head portion, Nile silt ware (845); *3*, head portion, Nile silt ware (666); *4*, torso portion, Aswan ware (902); *5*, torso and arms, Nile silt ware (775); *6*, torso and head, without arms, Nile silt ware (951); *7*, torso and arms, Nile silt ware (785). Number 3 is from Phase 3. Scale increments are 5cm.

d. Horse figurines. *1*, head fragment, Aswan ware (1082); *2*, body fragment, hind legs and rump, Aswan ware (1413); *3*, body fragment, Aswan ware (1110)*; *4*, head fragment, Aswan ware (1414); *5*, body portion, front legs and part of body, Nile silt ware (817); *6*, portion comprising head, neck, and front part of body, Nile silt ware (696); *7*, portion comprising body and hind legs, Aswan ware (1081); *8*, complete specimen, Nile silt ware (795); *9*, portion comprising body, part of front legs, and part of neck, Nile silt ware (816). Item marked with * is from Phase 1; see Table 10. Number 6 is from Phase 3. Scale increments are 5cm.

f. Pottery bell (?) fragments. *1*, 1461; *2*, 1460; *3*, 1459; *4*, 1462. Scale increments are 5cm.

e. Head of ceramic figurine (846). The height is 64mm.

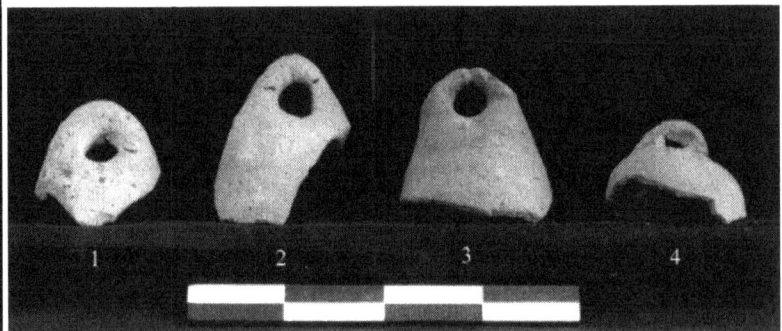

Plate 20. Ceramic objects from Phase 2.

a. *1, small sandstone capital (1066).
Other items are from later phases.
Scale increments are 10cm.*

b. *Miscellaneous perforated stone objects.
1, problematical object having a carved
rosette at the top (950);
5, decorated surface of a sandstone
object, presumed to be a weight (1115),
from Phase 1. Other items are from later
phases. Scale increments are 10cm.*

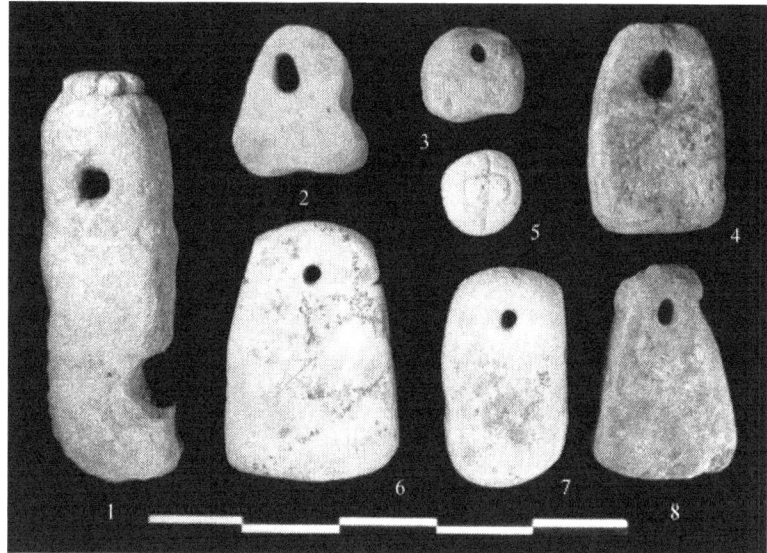

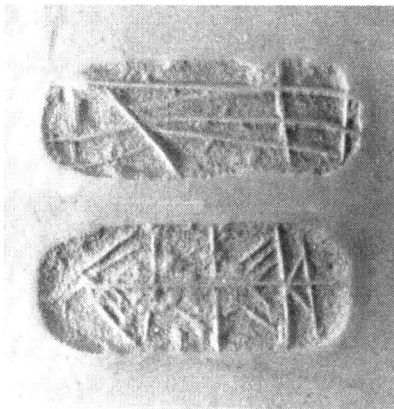

d. *Impression from sandstone
jar seal (1028). The maximum
diameter is 34mm.*

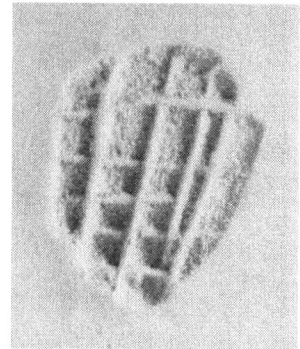

c. *Impressions from the two sides of sandstone jar
seal (1029). The length of the object is 81mm.*

e. *Archer's looses, side view. 1, felsite loose (761)*; 2, quartzite
loose (864); 3, granite loose (738)*. Items marked with * are
from Phase 1; see Table 10. Scale increments are 5cm.*

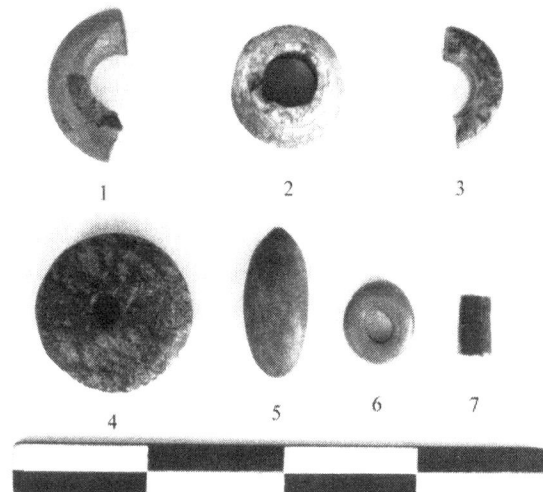

Plate 21. Miscellaneous stone objects from Phase 2.

f. *Archer's looses and other perforated objects, top view.
1, felsite loose (761)*; 2, quartzite loose (864); 3, granite loose
(738)*. Items marked with * are from Phase 1; see Table 10. Items
not listed are from later phases. Scale increments are 5cm.*

a. Granite mortars. *1*, 411; *2*, 988; *3*, 871; *4*, 469; *5*, 562. Numbers 1, 4, and 5 were found in Late Christian levels, but are probably of Ballaña origin. Scale increments are 10cm.

b. Greywacke palettes. *1*, 1113*; *2*, 1109; *3*, 831; *4*, 1114*; *5*, 985; *6*, 906; *7*, 410; *8*, 942. Items marked with * are from Phase 1; see Table 10. Number 7 is from Phase 4. Scale increments are 5cm.

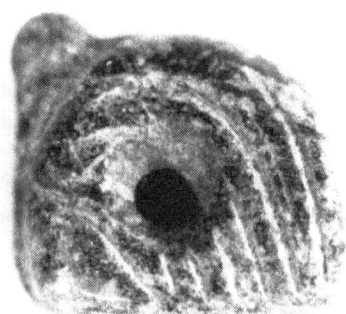

c. Carved bead, possibly of jade (908). The height is 10mm.

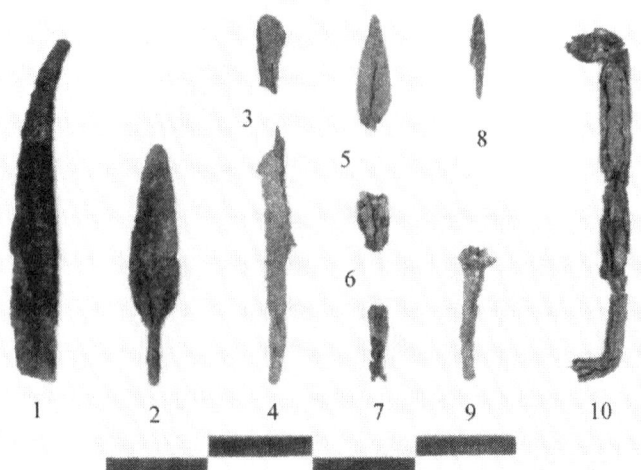

d. Iron objects and weapons. *1*, curved blade (859); *2*, spear point (912); *3*, butt of rounded shaft (1045); *4*, shaft with square cross-section (1045); *5*, small spear point (1045); *6*, butt of rounded shaft (1045); *7*, small section of rounded shaft (1045); *8*, arrow point (1168); *9*, nail (948); *10*, rod with bent ends (1032). Scale increments are 5cm.

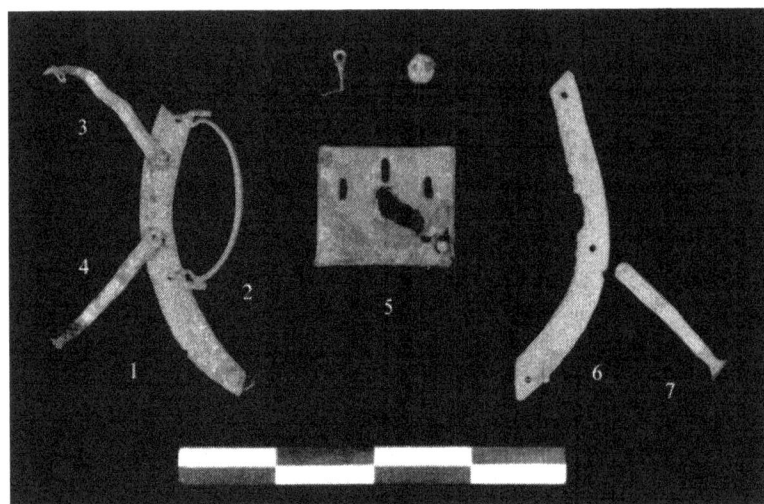

e. Bronze and copper casket fittings (963). *1*, bronze anchor plate; *2*, copper handle; *3* and *4*, copper hasps; *5*, bronze lock housing; *6*, curved bronze plate, possibly a backing plate; *7*, copper hasp. Scale increments are 5cm.

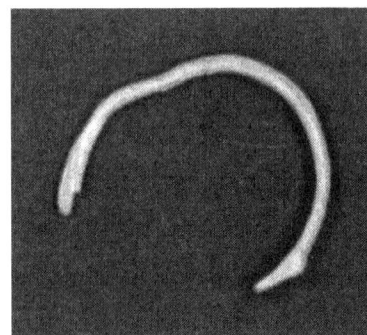

f. Portion of copper bracelet (819). The maximum diameter is 48mm.

Plate 22. Stone and metal objects from Phase 2.

www.ingramcontent.com/pod-product-compliance
Lightning Source LLC
Chambersburg PA
CBHW051301270326
41926CB00030B/4686